Pendulum Swing

Pendulum Swing

Edited by
Larry J. Sabato

Longman

Boston Columbus Indianapolis New York San Francisco Upper Saddle River
Amsterdam Cape Town Dubai London Madrid Milan Munich Paris Montreal Toronto
Delhi Mexico City Sao Paulo Sydney Hong Kong Seoul Singapore Taipei Tokyo

Executive Editor: Reid Hester
Senior Marketing Manager: Lindsey Prudhomme
Development Editor: Elizabeth Alimena
Project Coordination, Text Design, and Page Makeup: Grapevine
    Publishing Services, Inc.
Copyeditor: Leslie Ballard
Senior Cover Design Manager: Nancy Danahy
Cover Designer: Base Art Company
Manufacturing Buyer: Roy Pickering
Printer and Binder: Courier Corporation/Westford
Cover Printer: Demand Production Center

Pendulum Swing, by Larry J. Sabato et al.

2 3 4 5 6 7 8 9 10–V013–13 12 11

Longman
is an imprint of

ISBN 13: 978-0-205-09892-7
ISBN 10:   0-205-09892-4

www.pearsonhighered.com

Table of Contents

Part 2: Money and Media

Part 3: Senate and Gubernatorial Races

Acknowledgments

American voters are full of surprises, and they delivered another one in November 2010. This special midterm election deserves extended analysis and treatment, and that is exactly what we aim to provide our readers in this, the seventh of our biennial election books. The University of Virginia Center for Politics, the sponsor of the book series, exists to encourage civic education and participation (www.centerforpolitics.org). The Center has again assembled a talented mix of some of the nation's top political scholars and journalists. Their mission was to measure the width, depth, and breadth of the 2010 midterm elections, and from our perspective they have done a splendid job. We hope you agree.

The individual authors deserve the lion's share of credit, of course, but the staff of the Center for Politics made the project work, and on a difficult deadline. The irreplaceable and irrepressible Tyler Matuella coordinated the book from start to finish. Remarkably, Tyler is an undergraduate student at U.Va., and one of the Center's most dedicated interns. His maturity and determination to work closely with the authors and the publisher were essential. We thank and salute him, and look forward to his promising career. Senior full-time staffers also turned in extraordinary performances, especially Ken Stroupe, Isaac Wood, Joseph Figueroa, and Mary Daniel Brown. The Center for Politics benefits each semester from the tireless, competent work of student interns, and for this project, we relied on U.Va. undergraduates Michael Alerhand, Emily Bowles, Bethy Hagan, and Neal Modi. Kudos to them. Finally, a good publisher, dedicated to bringing out a book in a timely and professional manner, is a crucial element of success. Pearson/Longman has been our mainstay for all seven volumes, and to Reid Hester and Elizabeth Alimena, I extend our appreciation and resolve to make this the most widely distributed book of the series.

—LARRY SABATO
CHARLOTTESVILLE, VIRGINIA
DECEMBER 2010

PART

1

The Big Picture

Chapter 1

Pendulum Swing

by Dr. Larry J. Sabato

Founder and Director, University of Virginia Center for Politics
Robert Kent Gooch Professor and University Professor
of Politics at the University of Virginia

The title of this book, *Pendulum Swing*, was chosen months before Election Day. By mid to late summer, the approaching GOP tidal wave was apparent to many of us in the world of electoral analysis. It was early, but the political cake was baked, cooled, and iced. 2010 was destined to be a major Republican year.

It is not that we knew precisely how many seats the Republicans would pick up. Yet by late August, before the traditional Labor Day start to the general election campaign, our political website, Sabato's Crystal Ball (www.centerforpolitics.org/crystalball), became the first nonpartisan group to predict flatly and publicly that the GOP would win the U.S. House of Representatives by a comfortable margin.[1] We also handicapped the Senate and governors' contests very close to their final outcomes, forecasting that the Senate would stay Democratic despite Republican gains elsewhere, and that the GOP would make major pickups in the gubernatorial and state legislative races around the nation. This was not a popular prognostication in some quarters. For example, Tim Kaine, the chairman of the Democratic National Committee, denounced us in heated terms and insisted we were utter-ly wrong. Senior Republicans had done much the same when the Crystal Ball projected in July 2008 that Barack Obama would win the presidency the following November by a comfortable margin. Partisans are frequently correct, but only in the years when their party wins. Some years give telltale signs early on about the results to come. In fact, 2010 was a mirror image of another change-oriented midterm election: 2006. The Democrats took control of both the House and Senate in that critical election, which was in essence a repudiation of much of President George W. Bush's agenda—from the Iraq War to disaster relief operations after Hurricane Katrina. Our last midterm book, *The Sixth Year Itch,* covered that earlier transformation.[2]

In *Pendulum Swing,* my coauthors and I will try to bring the 2010 midterms into focus for you. First, we will take a look from the broader perspective, explaining what happened and why, and putting it into the context of American political history. Every election seems important at the time, but only a few elections have long-term significance. Will 2010 be one of these special moments? It is too early to know for sure, but the authors will give you enough information so that you can offer a guess yourself. "The big picture" will define this part of the book, and the initial five chapters will review how Republicans netted 63 seats in the U.S. House of Representatives, six seats in the U.S. Senate, seven state governorships, plus hundreds of additional state legislators.

The political process that produced these results was fed by a massive infusion of money, much of which was devoted to airing TV campaign advertisements hundreds of thousands of times in every nook and cranny of the country. At the same time, the rules of the election game were changing—rules that some said were deteriorating badly. Several chapters tackle these weighty subjects.

Finally, a midterm election is defined by both prevailing national conditions and also individual local contests. Space does not permit an examination of all the fascinating races that played out across the nation, but we have chosen a representative sampling of the battles that defined this election year. In the chapters that follow, local experts have written up superb analyses of the action in 20 key states, providing a taste of the flavors of this past election.

The Midterm Election's Place in American Political Life

The midterm election is a remarkable phenomenon that has become a critical part of democracy's superstructure in the United States.

Coming at the midpoint of each presidential term, the elections for about a third of the U.S. Senate, the entire U.S. House of Representatives, and nearly three-quarters of the state governorships give voters an opportunity to pass preliminary judgment on the person in the White House.

In the strictest sense, a midterm is not a referendum on the president. The president's name is not on the ballot. But increasingly, political scientists have come to realize that campaign outcomes for Congress, governors, and even thousands of state legislative posts around the country have a strong relationship to the voters' level of approval for the White House administration.

It is not a perfect measure since a much lower proportion of Americans turns out to vote in a midterm year than in a presidential year, and the circumstances vary depending on the political climate. One party's activists may be more enthused and thus turn out at a higher rate than the other's, giving them a leg up in producing victories. While 63 percent of adults voted in the 2008 presidential election, about 40 percent voted in November 2010. Republicans were more eager to vote in 2010, in large measure because of their strong opposition to the policies of the Obama administration.

Another reason why a midterm is not a perfect measure of popular opinion is that some states and districts do not have competitive contests in any given year. For example, in 2010, 13 states had no election for governor, another 13 lacked a Senate contest, and dozens of the 435 U.S. House races were either unopposed or lightly opposed. Voter turnout was lower in most of these locales. Ideally, if we wanted to accurately determine national public opinion at the ballot box, there would be highly competitive campaigns everywhere. This would encourage more citizens to register their views.

Yet another basis to question midterm elections can be found by examining the races individually. The skills of the candidates, as well as the campaigns they run, influence the results. Simply put, many election outcomes depend heavily on the abilities and characteristics of the people running for office—their strengths, weaknesses, financial war chests, policies, etc. Some politicians are a better fit for their states or districts than their opponents, and they may raise more money and run smarter campaigns. Also, incumbents running for reelection can skew the results, since they usually have higher name recognition and better contacts with cash contributors. A combination of these factors can produce victory for a candidate even though the national tide is in the other party's direction.

Most analysts start from the national perspective because the conditions existing in the nation set the tone for virtually every campaign across the United States. From the second midterm of Franklin Roosevelt's presidency in 1938 through the first midterm of Bill Clinton's presidency in 1994, the party in charge of the White House lost House seats in the congressional elections, without exception.

Political scientists have laid out logical explanations for this. Some have theorized that midterms serve as natural electoral "reflexes" to counterbalance strong party showings in presidential cycles. The notion of "checks and balances" is deeply rooted in our Constitution and our national psyche. Generally, we recoil from giving one political party too much power for too long. Even though most Americans still have some degree of partisan identification with either the Democrats or the Republicans, they may not trust either party enough to countenance unified control of the White House, the Senate, and the House of Representatives by one party for a long period of time.

In the 70 years since the beginning of World War II, Americans have switched control of the presidency from one party to another eight times, control of the Senate nine times, and control of the House seven times. Unified party control of both the executive and legislative branches is becoming rare. In 33 of the 65 years since 1945, the parties have shared power in one combination or another, and the 2010 election has guaranteed that two more years will be added to the split-control total. In the last 42 years—since President Richard Nixon came to power—there have been just 13 years when one party simultaneously had the White House and majorities of both houses of Congress.

This has considerable implications for governance. It is much easier for a party to enact its platform if its officials are in charge across the board. It was only because of large Democratic majorities in both houses of Congress that President Obama was able to narrowly secure passage of an $800 billion stimulus bill, health care reform, and financial services reform from 2009 to 2010. Divided control usually produces gridlock, and not much is accomplished legislatively.

On the other hand, conservatives would argue, invoking Henry David Thoreau and Thomas Jefferson, "That government is best which governs least." To those who favor smaller and less government, gridlock may be a good thing.

Leading up to Election Day, President Obama faced a stern test in maintaining Democratic majorities for the second half of his term, especially since the economy was not cooperating with the party in power. Democrats won a solid Electoral College presidential majority in 2008, and strengthened their hold on both the Senate and the House at the same moment Barack Obama won the presidency. Beginning in the administration of former President George W. Bush, the economy has been exceptionally weak, leading to low ratings for those in power. Voters in November 2010 experienced a kind of "buyer's remorse" as they remembered the Democratic promises made during the campaign, and compared them to the reality they saw in their lives and the country's fortunes.

This is a common circumstance throughout American history. Even in good times, voters are inclined to trim at least a few seats from the governing White House party, perhaps to remind those in power that the people are the boss. In rocky stretches, when unemployment is up and disposable family income is down, Americans eagerly express their frustrations at the polls. One can think of midterm elections as an opportunity for the voters to send a message to the government. In a very real sense, citizens are suggesting the need for course corrections at the midpoint of a presidency. In 2010, voters applied the brakes to a presidential agenda that most regarded as far-reaching.

Usually, but not always, the president's party loses fewer seats in the first midterm than in the second, which occurs in the sixth year of a two-term presidency. There have been seven of these sixth-year elections in the post–World War II era: 1950, 1958, 1966, 1974, 1986, 1998, and 2006. This tendency is called the "sixth-year itch." But history can play tricks, and there are no iron laws in politics.

For instance, the durability of the sixth-year itch prior to 1998 led most analysts to speculate about how many seats President Clinton's Democrats would lose, especially in the midst of an impeachment effort following the Monica Lewinsky sex scandal. Yet remarkably, the Democrats gained a few House seats and held their own in the Senate, as voters appeared to resent Republican efforts to oust Clinton. If

President Obama is reelected in 2012—a result not to be taken for granted given the 2010 outcome and continuing economic distress—it will be interesting to see whether his second midterm, in 2014, is more or less unhappy for his party than his first midterm. That is, will Obama follow the Clinton model in reversing the usual relationship of mild to moderate losses in the first midterm versus heavy losses in the second? It is far too soon to have any reasonable guess, even if one makes a hasty assumption about a second Obama term.

Another unusual midterm election occurred in 2002—the first of the George W. Bush presidency. In the wake of the terrorist attacks on September 11, 2001, the narrowly elected Bush soared to near-unanimous approval in the opinion polls, and a year later he retained enough of that popularity to add GOP seats in both the House and Senate. This was something that had not occurred in the first midterm election of a presidency since 1934, when Franklin Roosevelt's New Deal program to combat the Great Depression was exceptionally popular.

Both the 1998 and 2002 cycles took place under extraordinary circumstances that enhanced the political positions of the presidents' parties. It is possible that in a couple of decades, we will look back on 1998 and 2002 as the great exceptions to the historic rules that have governed midterm elections. By definition, exceptional elections do not happen often. Sure enough, in 2006 (Bush's sixth-year-itch election), Americans returned to form, and Democrats regained majorities in both the House and the Senate, ending years of unified GOP rule.

As an introduction to the chapters that follow, it would be useful to offer a short history lesson so that you can see for yourself the ebb and flow of public opinion in modern midterm years.

Chronological Countdown to 2010

Just for starters, let us take a glance at the midterm results from 1946 to 2002 (also see tables 1.1 and 1.2, as well as figures 1.1, 1.2, and 1.3 for reference). It is all so easy to analyze after the fact, and every bit of it falls neatly into a sentence or two:

1946: After 14 years of solid Democratic control under Franklin D. Roosevelt (FDR) and Harry S. Truman, voters wanted change.

The end of World War II and postwar economic dislocation encouraged the "time for a change" theme. Truman did not seem up to the job—who would, after Franklin Roosevelt?—and the mantra became "To err is Truman." So Republicans captured both houses of Congress, grabbing 55 House seats and 12 Senate seats, plus two more governorships (for a total of 25 out of 48).

Table 1.1—Gain or Loss for President's Party: Presidential Election Years

Year	President	House	Senate	Governor
1948	Truman (D)	+76	+9	+6
1952	Eisenhower (R)	+24	+2	+5
1956	Eisenhower (R)	−2	0	−2
1960	Kennedy (D)	−20	−2	0
1964	Johnson (D)	+38	+2	−1
1968	Nixon (R)	+7	+5	+4
1972	Nixon (R)	+13	−2	−1
1976	Carter (D)	+2	0	+1
1980	Reagan (R)	+33	+12	+4
1984	Reagan (R)	+15	−2	+1
1988	Bush (R)	−3	−1	−1
1992	Clinton (D)	−10	0	+2
1996	Clinton (D)	+9	−2	−1
2000	Bush (R)	−2	−5	−1
2004	Bush (R)	+3	+4	0
2008	Obama (D)	+21	+8	+1

Source: Compiled by the author.

1950: Truman's come-from-behind presidential victory in 1948 had restored Democratic rule by adding 76 House and nine Senate seats. But 18 straight years of Democratic presidencies and an unpopular war in Korea took their toll again in the midterm, and Democrats gave back 29 House and six Senate seats. Recognize those numbers? They are identical to the Democratic net gains in 2006, when another unpopular foreign war, this time in Iraq, dealt the governing party a severe setback.

1954: Dwight ("Ike") Eisenhower's triumph two years earlier gave the GOP narrow majorities in Congress, even though his coattails were not particularly long. By the time of the midterm, a slight swing away from the Republicans cost 18 of the party's 24 newly gained House seats and one Senate seat.

1958: This is the first dramatic modern example of the so-called "sixth-year itch," when voters decide to give the other party size-able congressional majorities after the first six years of a two-term presidency. While Democrats had already won back control of Congress in 1956, despite Eisenhower's landslide reelection, the additional 48 House and 13 Senate berths for Democrats ensured that Ike's legislative influence would be minimal in his final two years in office.

1962: Like Eisenhower before him, John F. Kennedy (JFK) had almost no coattails in his 1960 presidential squeaker; Democrats actually lost 20 House seats and two Senate seats. JFK feared more losses in his 1962 midterm, but the Cuban Missile Crisis boosted support for his administration just before the balloting. The result was a wash, with Democrats losing four House seats but picking up three Senate seats. Such "October surprises" can affect congressional elections every bit as much as presidential contests.

1966: Lyndon (LBJ) Johnson's historic 61 percent landslide in 1964 appeared to presage a new era of Democratic rule, as he car-ried in 38 House freshmen and two additional senators to an already heavily Democratic Congress. But that was before the Vietnam War began to devour LBJ. Already by 1966, voters were turning against the president's conduct of the war, and it cost the Democrats 47 House seats and two Senate seats—though not overall control of Congress.

Table 1.2—Gain or Loss for President's Party: Midterm Election Years

Year	President	House	Senate	Governor
1946	Truman (D)	−55	−12	+2
1950	Truman (D)	−29	−6	−6
1954	Eisenhower (R)	−18	−1	−9
1958	Eisenhower (R)	−48	−13	−5
1962	Kennedy (D)	−4	+3	0
1966	Johnson (D)	−47	−4	−8
1970	Nixon (R)	−12	+2	−11
1974	Ford (R)	−48	−5	−5
1978	Carter (D)	−15	−3	−5
1982	Reagan (R)	−26	+1	−7
1986	Reagan (R)	−5	−8	+8
1990	Bush (R)	−9	−1	−2
1994	Clinton (D)	−52	−9	−10
1998	Clinton (D)	+5	0	0
2002	Bush (R)	+6	+2	−1
2006	Bush (R)	−30	−6	−6
2010	Obama (D)	−63	−6	−7*

*This total of seven includes Florida, which switched on Election Day from an independent governor, Charlie Crist, to a Republican governor, Rick Scott. Crist was elected as a Republican in 2006 but left the party in spring 2010 to run unsuccessfully for the U.S. Senate. We traditionally count party switches in this fashion, though one could argue that there was no change between the elections of 2006 and 2010, and thus the national gain for the GOP in 2010 was +6 governorships. Take your pick.

Source: Compiled by the author.

1970: Richard Nixon's close 43 percent victory in 1968 did not stop him from dreaming of a "silent majority" of Republicans and conservative Southern Democrats, and he made a major effort to improve the GOP's weak position in Congress. (Nixon had added but seven House members and five senators to the Republican minority in 1968.) His efforts paid off to a certain degree, as the GOP added two Senate seats in 1970, while holding House losses to a relatively small 12 seats. Democrats still ruled the Capitol Hill roost, though.

1974: Oddly, Nixon's 61 percent reelection landslide in 1972 almost precisely returned his party to its paltry 1968 levels in both houses. The Republicans could ill afford a coattail-less election, given what was soon to happen: Nixon's resignation in disgrace, a recession, and an unelected successor GOP president (Gerald Ford) who squandered his initial popularity by pardoning Nixon—all just in time for November 1974. Democrats picked up 48 House seats and five Senate seats; Ford was left mainly with his veto power for his remaining two years in office.

1978: Jimmy Carter's narrow 1976 election left Congress virtually unchanged, though still heavily Democratic. And Carter's fall from grace had barely started in 1978. A quiet midterm before the storm of 1980 nonetheless subtracted 15 House and three Senate seats from the Democratic totals.

1982: Ronald Reagan's 10-point slaughter of Carter in 1980 was a now-rare coattail election, as the GOP also won 33 House seats and 12 Senate seats. That was enough to take over the Senate outright and obtain a working majority on some issues with conservative House Democrats. But this tumultuous period in American politics continued through 1982, when a serious recession deprived the GOP of 26 House seats. The Senate stayed Republican, however, and the GOP actually added a seat.

1986: After yet another coattail-less reelection of a president— Reagan's massive 59 percent win in 1984—the sixth-year itch returned in 1986. Voters turned over eight Senate seats to the

Democrats, and thus control of that body. The GOP lost only five House seats, but the Democrats were solidly in charge of the House in any event.

1990: Vice President Bush had won Reagan's "third term" in 1988 by a solid 54 percent margin, but the Republicans suffered from having no coattails again, losing three House seats and one Senate seat. With partisan politics somewhat at abeyance due to the pre–Persian Gulf War military buildup, a quiet midterm saw Republicans lose nine House seats and one Senate berth. Much like Carter in 1978, Bush did not see the gathering storm clouds in this eerie calm.

Figure 1.1—Political Divisions of the U.S. Senate on Opening Day of Congress

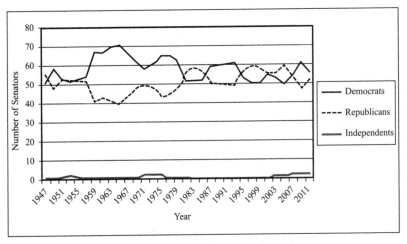

Source: Compiled by University of Virginia Center for Politics.

1994: A recession and a disengaged administration took George H.W. Bush from the all-time height of 90 percent popularity to a humiliating 38 percent finish in the 1992 election. With Ross Perot securing 19 percent, Bill Clinton's 43 percent victory was not impressive, and Democrats lost 10 House seats and stayed even in the Senate. A disastrous overreaching by new President Clinton on health care reform, gays in the military, and other issues, coupled with a slow economy, produced a sixth-year itch in the second year. In 1994 Republicans gained an eye-popping 52 House seats and nine Senate seats to win control of both houses.

Figure 1.2—Political Divisions of the U.S. House on Opening Day of Congress

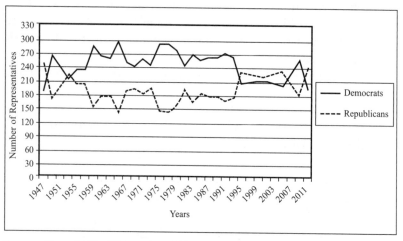

Source: Compiled by University of Virginia Center for Politics.

1998: Proving that every defeat can yield the seeds of victory, Clinton let Republicans overreach just as he had. Running against both ex-Senate majority leader Bob Dole (the GOP nominee) and Speaker Newt Gingrich (the unpopular foil), Clinton won a 49 percent reelection. But Democrats captured only nine House seats and actually lost two more Senate seats, leaving Republicans in charge of Congress. Would Clinton have another catastrophic midterm election? It certainly looked that way as the Monica Lewinsky scandal unfolded. But Republicans again overplayed their hand, beginning unpopular impeachment proceedings that yielded a Democratic gain of five House seats (with the Senate unchanged).

2002: "The George W. Bush Midterm," plain and simple. In an election dominated by terrorism, Iraq, and the president himself, the Republicans defied conventional wisdom by gaining seats in both houses of Congress, making Bush the first president since FDR in

1934 to pick up seats in both houses in his first term. The Democrats were unable to link the poor economy to Bush, and the media's extensive coverage of the impending confrontation with Iraq and the Beltway sniper incidents in Washington, D.C. overshadowed the somewhat fuzzy Democratic election agenda. In the final two weeks of the general election, key White House adviser Karl Rove sent Bush on a whirlwind campaign tour of the battleground states, which ended up reaping rich rewards for the GOP. The Republicans gained two seats in the Senate and six House seats. The only positive note for the Democrats was a net gain of three governorships, but the GOP maintained a narrow overall statehouse majority (26 to 24).

Figure 1.3—Number of Governors by Party, 1949–2011

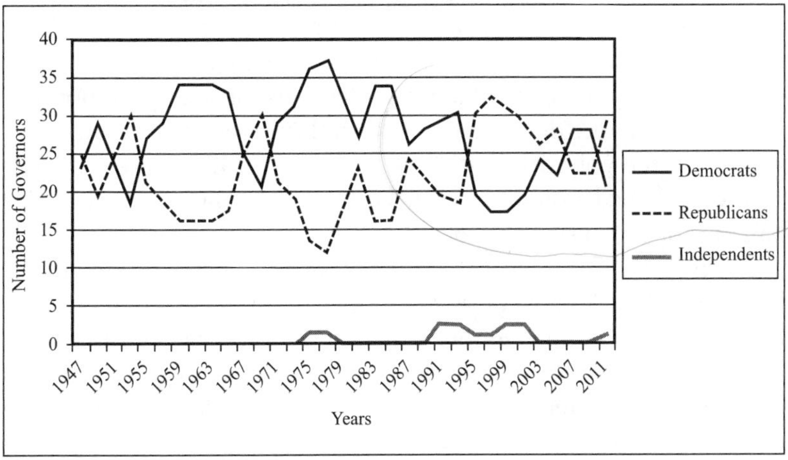

Source: Compiled by University of Virginia Center for Politics.

2006: The unpopularity of the Iraq War, the failure of much of President Bush's second-term legislative agenda, and a series of financial and sex scandals that rocked the Republican congressional caucus combined to produce a major sixth-year itch. On Election Day, Democrats won 29 net additional House seats, six Senate seats, and six governorships. By a narrow 51 to 49 margin, the Senate fell to the Democrats, while the party also won a comfortable majority of 232 in the House. The 2006 election marked the effective end of George W. Bush's domestic presidency. He was unable to influence

Congress, at least until the bank and Wall Street crisis of September 2008, when both parties joined together to prevent what they feared would be a descent into another Great Depression.

Before we move on, take one more look at 1950 and compare those results to the midterm election of 2006. Because of the public's disapproval of the Korean War, in part, President Truman lost 29 House and six Senate seats—precisely the same numbers President Bush lost because of the Iraq War. History does not repeat itself, but it does rhyme. The federal elections so far in the 21st century have been among the nation's most significant. The 2008 election of President Barack Obama is certain to be regarded by historians as remarkable, and the 2010 midterm elections offered the first opportunity for voters to judge his performance at the ballot box. November 2, 2010 was a historic night for Republicans and a sobering one for Democrats, who had seen the past two election cycles go so well for them.

By the way, a record number of elections for state governor and the largest number of Senate seats since 1962 were at stake in 2010. Adding to the political drama was the fact that 405 of the 435 U.S. House seats had nominees from both major political parties—the largest proportion since 1996.

Democrats, Republicans, and others may not agree on very much these days, but Americans were virtually unanimous in seeing 2010 as a critical midterm election. This was another "big picture" election, with the issues of a lagging economy, skyrocketing national debt, health care reform, and many other issues factoring into the decisions that voters were asked to make.

Making Sense of the 2010 Midterm Election

When looking back at any election, we first need to examine the basic facts of what happened on Election Day. The one-sided nature of 2010 makes this exercise a simple one.

In the House of Representatives, Republicans had their best election in 72 years. In 1938, Democratic president Franklin Roosevelt suffered his sixth-year itch, and Republicans gained 80 seats. Amazingly, though, the Republicans still failed to take control of the heavily Democratic House in the New Deal era.

In 2010 Republicans had much better luck since they were starting from a higher seat level. The GOP needed to gain 39 House seats to take control of the lower chamber—218 seats is a simple majority—and the party easily surpassed that number by 24 seats. With 242 total seats in the new House, the Republicans secured their largest majority since the 246 seats they won in 1946, the first post–World War II election. Even in the 1994 Republican congressional sweep, the total of GOP seats had been only 232.

2010 was also the worst year for House incumbents in over three decades. (See table 1.3.) With 58 incumbents losing their seats (four in the primary and 54 in the general), just 85 percent of House members who sought another term were reelected. By contrast, 38 incumbents lost in 1994, a year often thought of as a killing field for Democratic House members.

Table 1.3—Defeated House Incumbents, 1980–2010

Year	Primary	General	Year	Primary	General
1980	6	31	1996	2	21
1982	10	29	1998	1	6
1984	3	16	2000	3	6
1986	3	6	2002	8	8
1988	1	6	2004	2	7
1990	1	15	2006	2	22
1992	19	24	2010	4	54
1994	4	34			

Source: Compiled by University of Virginia Center for Politics.

Take a look at the map in figure 1.4. Each dot represents the switch of a House seat from one party to the other in that district. The 66 dark dots represent Republican pickups, while the three lighter dots in Delaware, Hawaii, and Louisiana represent the only seats Democrats were able to switch from the GOP this cycle.

Figure 1.4—U.S. House Seat Pickups in the 2010 Midterm Election

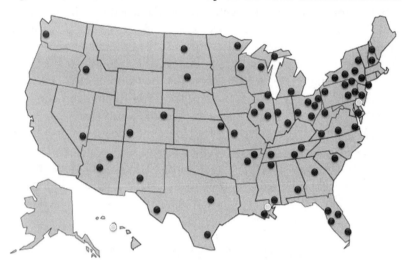

Source: Compiled by University of Virginia Center for Politics.

The Election Day "wave" for the Republicans produced a bumper crop of new seats in the South and southern border states, where the GOP traditionally does well. But the key to the Republican House takeover occurred in the North Central states from Pennsylvania through the industrial Midwest. (Crystal Ball House Race Editor Isaac Wood will discuss this in much more detail in chapter 5.)

Note that even overwhelmingly Democratic New York State added five Republican House seats in 2010, despite Democratic landslides for governor and both U.S. Senate posts in the state. Of course, this is partly explained by the GOP's recent failures in the Empire State; prior to November 2010, the party had fallen to a mere two House seats out of 29, and had nowhere to go but up.

The other side of the coin can be seen in the Pacific Coast states (Alaska, California, Hawaii, Oregon, and Washington). Despite the red wave sweeping America, the net House gain for the GOP in these five states was zero (+1 in Washington and -1 in Hawaii). California, Oregon, and Washington, in particular, have become a blue sandbar that can withstand even a Republican tsunami.

Despite the Republicans' success in the House, the Senate proved a much tougher nut to crack. Democrats had a large 59-seat majority in the 100-member Senate on Election Day. (The total of 59 includes two Independents, Senators Joseph Lieberman of Connecticut and Bernie Sanders of Vermont, who both caucus with the Democrats.) This meant that Republicans needed to gain 10 seats to win control since Democratic vice president Joseph Biden would break a 50–50 tie in his party's favor. While it has been done on occasion, it is difficult to secure that many seat turnovers with only 37 Senate seats on the ballot across the country. (Rhodes Cook will have much more to say about the Senate races in chapter 3.) In the end, Senate incumbents on the ballot had a reasonably good year, with just four of 23 losing reelection (two each in the primary and general). In four recent election years, more incumbent senators have lost their seats. (See table 1.4.)

Table 1.4—Defeated Senate Incumbents, 1980–2010

Year	Primary	General	Year	Primary	General
1980	4	9	1996	1	1
1982	0	2	1998	0	3
1984	0	3	2000	0	6
1986	0	7	2002	1	3
1988	0	4	2004	0	1
1990	0	1	2006	0*	6
1992	1	4	2010	2^	2
1994	0	2			

* Sen. Joseph Lieberman (D) of Connecticut was defeated for renomination in an August 8 primary but won the general election as a petitioning Independent.

^ Sen. Lisa Murkowski (R) was defeated in the Republican primary by Joe Miller, but won the general election as a write-in, so she is not counted in the total.

Source: Compiled by University of Virginia Center for Politics.

While Republicans held all 19 of their Senate seats on the ballot, they were able to gain just six of the 10 seats they needed for control, winning formerly Democratic seats in Arkansas, Illinois, Indiana, North Dakota, Pennsylvania, and Wisconsin. Democrats held onto

12 of the 18 Senate seats they were defending. (See a list of all Senate races in table 1.5 and the corresponding map in figure 1.5)

Table 1.5—Senate Races, 2010

State	Candidate	Percentage	Total
Alaska^	Lisa Murkowski (R–write-in)*	40	102,252
	Joe Miller (R)	35	90,740
	Scott McAdams (D)	23	60,007
Alabama	Richard Shelby (R)*	65	964,329
	William Barnes (D)	35	513,540
Arkansas	John Boozman (R)	58	447,562
	Blanche Lincoln (D)*	37	284,362
Arizona	John McCain (R)*	59	926,372
	Rodney Glassman (D)	35	540,904
California	Barbara Boxer (D)*	52	4,377,730
	Carly Fiorina (R)	42	3,554,066
Colorado	Michael Bennet (D)*	48	799,072
	Ken Buck (R)	47	783,426
Connecticut	Richard Blumenthal (D)	55	627,085
	Linda McMahon (R)	43	493,158
Delaware	Chris Coons (D)	57	173,900
	Christine O'Donnell (R)	40	123,025
Florida	Marco Rubio (R)	49	2,615,262
	Charlie Crist (I)	30	1,588,821
	Kendrick Meek (D)	20	1,076,028
Georgia	Johnny Isakson (R)*	58	1,462,823
	Michael Thurmond (D)	39	986,338
Hawaii	Daniel Inouye (D)*	75	276,928
	Cam Cavasso (R)	22	79,830
Iowa	Chuck Grassley (R)*	65	714,667
	Roxanne Conlin (D)	33	368,202

State	Candidate	Percentage	Total
Idaho	Michael Crapo (R)*	71	318,704
	Tom Sullivan (D)	25	111,924
Illinois	Mark Kirk (R)	48	1,765,594
	Alexi Giannoulias (D)	46	1,694,093
Indiana	Dan Coats (R)	57	950,244
	Brad Ellsworth (D)	42	695,859
Kansas	Jerry Moran (R)	70	578,768
	Lisa Johnston (D)	26	215,270
Kentucky	Rand Paul (R)	56	755,061
	Jack Conway (D)	44	598,885
Louisiana	David Vitter (R)*	57	715,304
	Charles Melancon (D)	38	476,423
Maryland	Barbara Mikulski (D)*	62	1,055,387
	Eric Wargotz (R)	36	619,204
Missouri	Roy Blunt (R)	54	1,051,495
	Robin Carnahan (D)	41	785,719
North Carolina	Richard Burr (R)*	55	1,448,003
	Elaine Marshall (D)	43	1,131,305
North Dakota	John Hoeven (R)	76	181,409
	Tracy Potter (D)	22	52,854
New Hampshire	Kelly Ayotte (R)	60	272,703
	Paul Hodes (D)	37	166,538
Nevada	Harry Reid (D)*	50	361,655
	Sharron Angle (R)	45	320,996
New York (full)	Charles Schumer (D)*	65	2,710,735
	Jay Townsend (R)	33	1,365,439
New York (special)	Kirsten Gillibrand (D)*	62	2,519,806
	Joe DioGuardi (R)	36	1,455,183
Ohio	Rob Portman (R)	57	2,125,555
	Lee Fisher (D)	39	1,447,848

State	Candidate	Percentage	Total
Oklahoma	Tom Coburn (R)*	71	716,347
	Jim Rogers (D)	26	265,519
Oregon	Ron Wyden (D)*	57	775,569
	Jim Huffman (R)	39	564,362
Pennsylvania	Pat Toomey (R)	51	1,995,026
	Joe Sestak (D)	49	1,916,703
South Carolina	Jim DeMint (R)*	62	792,133
	Alvin Greene (D)	28	358,276
South Dakota	John Thune (R)* uncontested		
Utah	Mike Lee (R)	62	360,130
	Sam Granato (D)	33	191,657
Vermont	Patrick Leahy (D)*	64	148,444
	Len Britton (R)	31	71,273
Washington	Patty Murray (D)*	52	1,247,071
	Dino Rossi (R)	48	1,176,017
Wisconsin	Ron Johnson (R)	52	1,125,637
	Russ Feingold (D)*	47	1,020,860
West Virginia	Joe Manchin (D)	54	280,771
	John Raese (R)	44	227,960

Source: Official sources.
* Indicates incumbent.
^ Indicates unofficial results.
Note: Percentages may not total 100 because of rounding.

While delighted with their victories, senior Republicans privately rued the fact that they could have achieved at least a 50–50 Senate tie had stronger candidates been nominated in states such as Colorado, Delaware, and Nevada. In all of those states, the new Tea Party faction of the GOP overwhelmed more mainstream candidates in party primaries to nominate candidates that were too far to the right—and too ill prepared for the rigors of modern campaigning—to win general elections. All three of these contests are dissected later in this volume, so it is enough to say for now that GOP nominees

Ken Buck (CO), Christine O'Donnell (DE), and Sharron Angle (NV) cost the Republicans dearly.

Figure 1.5—Senate Race Results, 2010

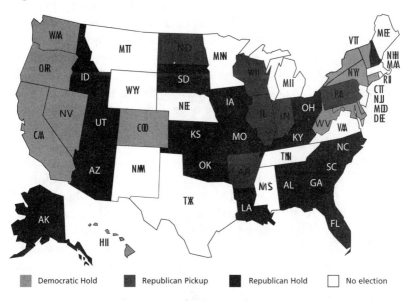

Map credit: Joe Figueroa, U.Va. Center for Politics.

At the same time, it should be noted that Tea Party candidates won several other Senate races (such as those in Kentucky and Utah), as well as several dozen House seats and a few governorships. However, in the vast majority of cases, they won in heavily Republican territory, where almost any GOP nominee was going to be elected in the strongly Republican year of 2010.

The strangest election of the year may well have been in Alaska, where incumbent Lisa Murkowski (R–AK) was upended in a low-turnout GOP primary by Tea Party candidate Joe Miller. Instead of endorsing Miller, Murkowski decided to launch what appeared to be a long-shot write-in candidacy against Miller and a weak Democratic nominee, Scott McAdams. Yet Miller drowned in a sea of gaffes and controversies, and to the amazement of the national political community, Murkowski became the first Senate write-in contender to win since Strom Thurmond (R–SC) did so in 1954. Murkowski will continue to sit in the Republican caucus, though many are watching to see whether she votes more often as a moderate-conservative after her near-fatal brush with the Tea Party.

By the way, the Tea Party is not an official political party, but rather a grassroots movement of conservatives (mainly Republicans) who are concerned about the level of taxation, spending, and national debt. There is no question this group will be a major force in the 2012 Republican presidential process. While these activists bring new energy to GOP efforts, there is also a danger that they could push the party to nominate a candidate unable to win in November, just like the 2010 Senate nominees we have discussed. But it is also possible the movement will mature over the next two years and learn to consider "electability" at the polling places on primary day.

For all the legitimate attention the congressional elections received, the contests at the state level may have more long-term meaning. In adding six net governorships (seven counting Florida, which flipped from Independent-controlled to Republican), the GOP climbed to control of 29 states, including the powerhouses of Pennsylvania, Michigan, and Ohio. This Republican statehouse total was the most in a decade. (See table 1.6 for a listing of the results of all 37 governor's contests and figure 1.6 for the corresponding map.) Moreover, the GOP added some much-needed diversity into their officeholders' ranks with the election of Hispanic governors Susana Martinez of New Mexico and Brian Sandoval of Nevada, as well as Governor Nikki Haley of South Carolina, whose roots are traced to the Indian subcontinent.

Table 1.6—Governors' Races, 2010

State	Candidate	Percentage	Total
Alabama	Robert Bentley (R)	58	857,162
	Ron Sparks (D)	42	623,492
Alaska	Sean Parnell (R)*	59	119,347
	Ethan Berkowitz (D)	38	77,552
Arizona	Jan Brewer (R)*	55	867,323
	Terry Goddard (D)	42	669,793
Arkansas	Mike Beebe (D)*	65	498,755
	Jim Keet (R)	34	260,282

State	Candidate	Percentage	Total
California	Jerry Brown (D)	53	4,552,290
	Meg Whitman (R)	42	3,571,675
Colorado	John Hickenlooper (D)	51	856,569
	Tom Tancredo (C)	37	620,626
	Dan Maes (R)	11	187,998
Connecticut	Dan Malloy (D)	50	564,885
	Tom Foley (R)	49	557,123
Florida	Rick Scott (R)	49	2,589,915
	Alex Sink (D)	48	2,522,857
Georgia	Nathan Deal (R)	53	1,341,589
	Roy Barnes (D)	43	1,094,621
Hawaii	Neil Abercrombie (D)	58	222,510
	Duke Aiona (R)	41	157,098
Idaho	Butch Otter (R)*	59	266,717
	Keith Allred (D)	33	148,223
Iowa	Terry Branstad (R)	53	589,565
	Chet Culver (D)*	43	481,297
Illinois	Pat Quinn (D)*	47	1,721,812
	Bill Brady (R)	46	1,702,399
Kansas	Sam Brownback (R)	63	522,540
	Tom Holland (D)	32	264,214
Maine	Paul LePage (R)	38	215,486
	Eliot Cutler (I)	37	205,601
	Libby Mitchell (D)	19	107,702
Maryland	Martin O'Malley (D)*	56	966,446
	Robert Ehrlich (R)	42	733,491
Massachusetts	Deval Patrick (D)*	48	1,108,404
	Charlie Baker (R)	42	962,848
	Tim Cahill (I)	8	183,933
Michigan	Rick Snyder (R)	58	1,880,438
	Virg Bernero (D)	40	1,289,928

State	Candidate	Percentage	Total
Minnesota	Mark Dayton (D)	44	919,231
	Tom Emmer (R)	43	910,480
	Tom Horner (I)	12	251,491
Nebraska	Dave Heineman (R)*	74	352,267
	Mike Meister (D)	26	121,994
Nevada	Brian Sandoval (R)	53	382,350
	Rory Reid (D)	42	298,170
New Hampshire	John Lynch (D)*	53	239,390
	John Stephen (R)	45	205,433
New Mexico	Susana Martinez (R)	54	317,421
	Diane Denish (D)	47	274,892
New York	Andrew Cuomo (D)	61	2,602,443
	Carl Paladino (R)	34	1,445,779
Ohio	John Kasich (R)	49	1,849,609
	Ted Strickland (D)*	47	1,752,507
Oklahoma	Mary Fallin (R)	60	624,285
	Jari Askins (D)	40	415,150
Oregon	John Kitzhaber (D)	49	680,840
	Chris Dudley (R)	48	665,930
Pennsylvania	Tom Corbett (R)	55	2,137,983
	Dan Onorato (D)	45	1,783,995
Rhode Island	Lincoln Chafee (I)	36	123,398
	John Robitaille (R)	34	114,761
	Frank Caprio (D)	23	78,776
South Carolina	Nikki Haley (R)	51	674,576
	Vincent Sheheen (D)	47	617,733
South Dakota	Dennis Daugaard (R)	62	195,021
	Scott Heidepriem (D)	38	122,010
Tennessee	Bill Haslam (R)	65	1,040,688
	Mike McWherter (D)	33	529,834

State	Candidate	Percentage	Total
Texas	Rick Perry (R)*	55	2,733,784
	Bill White (D)	42	2,102,606
Utah	Gary Herbert (R)*	64	381,244
	Peter Corroon (D)	32	188,832
Vermont	Peter Shumlin (D)	50	116,277
	Brian Dubie (R)	48	111,988
Wisconsin	Scott Walker (R)	52	1,128,159
	Tom Barrett (D)	47	1,005,008
Wyoming	Matt Mead (R)	72	123,764
	Leslie Petersen (D)	25	43,336

Source: Official sources.
* Indicates incumbent.

On the other hand, Democrats kept 20 statehouses and captured the biggest prize of the night, gargantuan California. Retiring GOP governor Arnold Schwarzenegger could not run again—and given his very low popularity, almost certainly could not have won another term. Democrat Jerry Brown, formerly governor from 1975 to 1983, won by a wide margin over Republican Meg Whitman. One state, tiny Rhode Island, was taken by an Independent, former GOP U.S. senator Lincoln Chafee.

The overall GOP trend obscured the sizeable degree of seat-swapping that took place around the nation. Republicans captured 11 governorships formerly in Democratic control, while Democrats managed to wrest three governorships away from the GOP, despite the bad environment for their party. Thad Beyle will delve further into the gubernatorial election environment in chapter 4.

The turnover at the state legislative level was nothing short of astounding, and here the Republicans could do virtually all the crowing. As the map in figure 1.7 shows, the GOP picked up about 720 state legislative seats out of the 6,115 on the ballot in 2010. This enabled the Republicans to grab 20 state legislative chambers (House and/or Senate) in 14 states, including both houses in Alabama, Maine, Minnesota, New Hampshire, North Carolina, and Wisconsin.[3] By comparison, Republicans picked up 472 state legislative seats in their 1994 landslide year, and Democrats won 628 legislative seats in 1974, the year when they benefited enormously from the Nixon Watergate scandal.[4]

Figure 1.6—Governors' Race Results, 2010

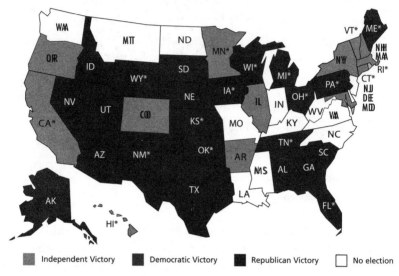

* Denotes the pickup of a new governorship for the victorious party.
Map credit: Joe Figueroa, U.Va. Center for Politics.

Figure 1.7—Republican State Legislature Pickups, 2010

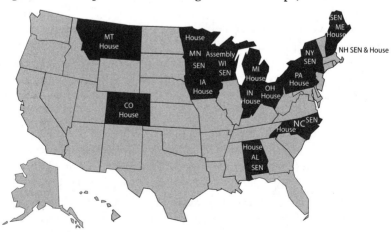

Map credit: Joe Figueroa, U.Va. Center for Politics.

Why is this so noteworthy? Once the decennial census population figures are released in early 2011, the governors and state legislatures in most states will redraw the district lines for U.S. House and state legislative seats. Seven states—Alaska, Montana, North Dakota, South Dakota, Wyoming, Delaware, Vermont—have just one U.S. representative, so the lines cannot be changed there, and seven more states—California, New Jersey, Washington, Arizona, Hawaii, Florida, and Idaho—have nonpartisan redistricting where governors and legislatures have little or no direct influence on redistricting.

As a result of the strongly Republican election results in 2010, the GOP will completely control the redistricting process in 17 states, covering 195 U.S. House seats, while Democrats will have the same power in just six states and 49 House seats. Inevitably, Republicans will be able to protect some of their endangered incumbents and eliminate some Democratic districts during the redistricting process. It is impossible to estimate exactly how many seats will be added to the GOP column via redistricting before the fact, but it will be surprising if Republicans cannot manage at least a dozen-seat gain in the House and many dozens in state legislatures around the country. These new lines, assuming they are confirmed during the inevitable legal challenges that follow, will last until the next redistricting in 2021.[5]

Slicing and Dicing the 2010 Vote

Every election is determined by the people who show up. This truism is amply demonstrated in the 2010 election. Often political observers make the fundamental error of equating all electorates, but in fact, the smaller midterm electorate is *not* a random sampling of the big-turnout presidential group of voters. As mentioned earlier in this chapter, the turnout in 2010 of the voting eligible population (VEP—see definition in table 1.7) was between 40 and 41 percent. This is approximately the same turnout the nation has produced for every midterm election since 1974 (the first one that included the newly enfranchised 18- to 20-year-olds).

Table 1.7—Voter Turnout in Midterm Elections

Year	Turnout of Voting Eligible Population (VEP)
1962	47.7%
1966	48.7
1970	47.3
1974	39.1
1978	39.0
1982	42.1
1986	38.1
1990	38.4
1994	41.1
1998	38.1
2002	39.5
2006	40.4
2010	40.3

Source: United States Elections Project, Michael McDonald (George Mason University) at elections.gmu.edu/voter_turnout.htm.

Voting eligible population (VEP) means the voting-age population (from 1962 to 1970 this was adults age 21 and over, but since 1974 it is age 18 and over) minus those ineligible to vote, such as noncitizens, felons, and mentally incapacitated persons, but adding persons in the military or civilians living overseas who are eligible to cast ballots in U.S. elections.

It is not simply that the 2010 voter turnout is about 22 full percentage points below that of the 2008 presidential election. The citizens who chose to cast a ballot in 2010 were dramatically more Republican, more conservative, and older than in 2008. They were also disproportionately white—a GOP-tilting demographic.

Take a glance at table 1.8. While the 2010 electorate was split evenly between Democrats and Republicans (35 percent each), this profile is far less Democratic than in 2008 (which featured a 7 percent gap in favor of the Democrats). Furthermore, as we shall see, the Independents who cast a ballot (29 percent of the total in both years) were more heavily drawn from the conservative end of the ideological spectrum in 2010 compared with 2008.

Figure 1.8—Voter Turnout in Midterm Elections

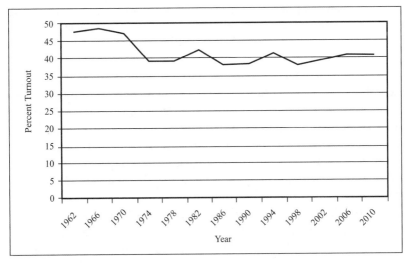

Source: Compiled by University of Virginia Center for Politics.

Table 1.8—Party Identification Among Voters Who Cast a Ballot, 1998–2010

Party Identification	Percent of the Electorate						
	2010	2008	2006	2004	2002	2000	1998
Republican	35	32	36	38	40	32	33
Democratic	35	39	38	38	31	37	34
Independent	29	29	26	25	23	27	30

Sources: 2004, 2006, 2008, and 2010: Exit polls conducted mainly on Election Days by Edison Media Research for the National Election Pool (NEP). For example, in 2010, the NEP surveyed 16,531 voters in selected states as they left the polls and 1,601 early voters who said they had already voted (early voters were contacted via phone). Margin of error is +/- 1% (CNN.com, 11/8/2010). Similar exit polls were conducted by the Voter News Service, a consortium of major national news outlets, for the 1998 and 2000 elections.

2002: Exit poll conducted November 6–7, 2002 and released on November 18, 2002, by Ayres, McHenry & Associates (R) for the American Association of Health Plans. The company surveyed 1,000 voters and had a margin of error +/ – 3 percent. This is the only exit poll available for 2002, since the Voter News Service network consortium had an organizational meltdown on Election Day and was unable to provide verifiable polling data for 2002.

The Republican nature of the 2010 voters is best shown in their actual behavior in marking their ballots (see table 1.9). In the House contests—the best measure since there was an election in each of the 435 districts covering the entire country—Republicans secured 52.2 percent of the votes to the Democrats 44.7 percent. (About 3 percent voted for other candidates.) Thus, Republicans had a lead of 7.5 percent over the Democrats—the largest GOP advantage since the 9 percent gap that occurred in 1946.

Republicans also bested the Democrats for Senate and governor, but by much smaller margins, since the 37 contests in each category left out much U.S. territory. The GOP had a 4.5 percent edge for Senate races and just 1.7 percent for gubernatorial matchups.

The Republican coloration of the 2010 voters—and the sharp distinctions with the 2008 voters who elected President Obama—can best be seen in the exit poll data. The exit poll was conducted by a professional, nonpartisan polling organization and financed by a consortium of news organizations. In total, 18,132 voters were interviewed by telephone or at polling places.[6] Absentee and mail voters (especially in Colorado, Oregon, and Washington state, where three-quarters or more of the ballots come from the mail-in category) were included in the sample, giving us useful comparisons between the demographics of the 2008 and 2010 voters.

And those comparisons are stunning. One of the most Democratic groups in the electorate, young voters aged 18 to 29, saw their turnout plummet from 18 percent of the total in 2008 to 12 percent in 2010. Similarly, heavily Democratic African Americans and Hispanics dropped from 13 percent and 9 percent of the national turnout in 2008, respectively, to 11 percent and 8 percent in 2010. These percentage changes are small but they amount to many tens of thousands of votes subtracted from the Democratic column. Meanwhile, the most Republican-friendly voters were participating in much larger numbers. Those aged 65 and over skyrocketed from 15 percent of the electorate in 2008 to 21 percent in 2010. White voters jumped from 74 percent in 2008 to 77 percent of the 2010 electorate.

Table 1.9—Total Votes by Party, 2010

Party	Number of Votes	Percentage
Governors		
Republicans	32,777,044	48.4
Democrats	31,662,548	46.7
Independents/Others	3,347,676	4.9
Total	77,787,268	
Senate		
Republicans	33,367,194	49.4
Democrats	30,307,407	44.9
Independents/Others	3,811,714	5.6
Total	67,486,315	
House		
Republicans	43,339,838	52.2
Democrats	37,160,314	44.7
Independents/Others	2,562,288	3.1
Total	83,062,440	

Source: Calculations by author. Percentages may not total 100 percent because of rounding.

These marginal changes add up to several million more GOP votes. (Table 1.10, which you will find at the end of this chapter, gives all the key breakdowns, including some not commented upon directly in the text.) Whites voted Republican by 60 percent to 37 percent in 2010, a dramatic increase over their GOP edge of 55 percent to 43 percent in 2008. The same change is visible among older voters, with an 8 percent GOP margin in 2008 swelling to a massive 21 percent landslide in 2010. As usual, men of all races and ages were very Republican, 55 percent to 41 percent—quite a contrast with the near-parity in 2008. The surprise was women, who voted Democratic by 56 percent to 43 percent in 2008, but narrowly backed the GOP by 1 percent in 2010.

As with women, other usually Democratic groups showed some slippage to Republicans. The Democratic edge among Latinos fell from 36 percent in 2008 to 22 percent in 2010. (Some Latino groups dispute the exit poll's findings, suggesting that it over-sampled affluent Latinos who were more GOP-inclined.) Asian Americans went from 27 percent pro-Democratic in 2008 to 18 percent Democratic-tilting in 2010. The most loyal Democratic demographic of all, African Americans, also displayed a slight Republican trend, increasing its backing of GOP candidates from 4 percent in 2008 to 9 percent in 2010. Much the same thing can be observed in every category of voter, as one would expect in a "wave" election like 2010.

While Republican margins grew everywhere, the normal divisions of American politics were still visible, and not just among the races, genders, and age groupings. Democrats handily won voters making less than $50,000 a year, with Republicans carrying those over $50,000 with an even larger majority. Voters making $200,000 or more annually picked the GOP by a two-to-one margin. Democrats were favored by the least well-educated (no high school diploma) and the most well-educated (those with postgraduate training), while Republicans won the in-between categories. Union households were Democratic; those with no union connection were Republican. The GOP won Protestants and Catholics alike (especially white, evangelical Christians), but Democrats were heavily chosen by those belonging to other religions or having no religion. We have seen these patterns repeatedly in recent decades.

As would be expected, Democrats won almost all Democratic Party identifiers in the electorate, and the Republicans swept the GOP voters. It was among Independents that preferences changed from 2008 to 2010. Democrats won the affections of Independents by 8 percent in 2008, but lost them by a much wider margin of 19 percent in 2010. Of course, this was not the same pool of Independents. Those choosing to vote in the midterm election were, on the whole, more conservative and closely aligned with the GOP than those who voted in 2010.

The Republican identity of the 2010 electorate is revealed in the job approval numbers for President Obama. The RealClearPolitics.com preelection polling average for Obama's job approval was 46 percent approve and 49 percent disapprove—not a bad split, considering the condition of the economy.[7] But among voters who actually cast a ballot, Obama's numbers were considerably worse: 44 percent approve, 55 percent disapprove.

Analysts have made the case for any number of influences on the 2010 results, but a fair reading of the complete exit poll points overwhelmingly to one factor: the bad economy. Fully 63 percent of voters named the economy the top issue; nothing else even hit 20 percent. If voters felt their family's personal financial situation had improved recently, they cast a Democratic ballot by 60 percent to 37 percent. But if they judged the family worse off financially, the Republicans won a 61 percent to 35 percent landslide. Just 15 percent said their family was better off, while 41 percent answered worse off. That was the election in a nutshell. (Among the 43 percent who said nothing much had changed financially, the election was essentially a tie.) When the voters say, by close to two to one, that the country is on the wrong track—as they did in 2010—it is almost impossible for the governing party to win an election.

Connecting the Dots—or Not

This last point, about fundamental conditions driving an election, is a wise place to conclude the opening chapter of this book. Elections are nuanced, and in a diverse country, they can be analyzed from a thousand perspectives. Yet they are thematic too, at least in decisive years like 2010. As you read the sections to follow, you will see time and again that the condition of the economy, a president's job approval, and the precariousness of voters' own lives drove the 2010 election as a whole, as well as most of the individual contests that are covered in these pages.

The very same thing will happen in two years during the 2012 presidential and congressional elections. But be careful about connecting the dots too quickly. The Democratic near-landslide of 2008 could never have immediately foretold the thumping Democrats took in 2010. Nor does the Republican near-landslide of 2010 tell us very much about the outcome in 2012. It is only natural to take what we see as true today, and project it forward. But who can say where the economy will go in the next two years—and once again, the economy may prove central to the 2012 election results. Terrorism, Afghanistan, scandal, and social issues, just to name a few, might alter the political landscape.

The past is worth analyzing at length since retrospectives grounded in hard data are revealing. Yet the future is endlessly unknowable, and we should be hesitant to project a reality beyond our knowledge. Events not in anyone's immediate control, and trends that can only be guessed at, will be in the saddle two years hence.

Table 1.10—Exit Polls, 2010

VOTE BY GENDER		
(Percentage of total)	Democrat	Republican
Male (48%)	41% [49%]*	55% [48%]
Female (52%)	48% [56%]	49% [43%]
VOTE BY RACE AND GENDER		
(Percentage of total)	Democrat	Republican
White Men (38%)	34% [41%]	62% [57%]
White Women (40%)	39% [46%]	58% [53%]
Black Men (5%)	86% [95%]	13% [5%]
Black Women (6%)	92% [96%]	6% [3%]
Latino Men (4%)	55% [64%]	44% [33%]
Latino Women (4%)	65% [68%]	33% [30%]
All Other Races (4%)	55% [64%]	42% [32%]
VOTE BY RACE		
(Percentage of total)	Democrat	Republican
White (77%)	37% [43%]	60% [55%]
African American (11%)	89% [95%]	9% [4%]
Latino (8%)	60% [67%]	38% [31%]
Asian (2%)	58% [62%]	40% [35%]
Other (2%)	53% [66%]	44% [31%]

VOTE BY AGE		
(Percentage of total)	Democrat	Republican
18–29 (12%)	55% [66%]	42% [32%]
30–44 (24%)	46% [52%]	50% [46%]
45–64 (43%)	45% [50%]	53% [49%]
65 and Older (21%)	38% [45%]	59% [53%]

VOTE BY INCOME		
(Percentage of total)	Democrat	Republican
Under $30,000 (17%)	57%	40%
$30–50,000 (19%)	51%	46%
$50–75,000 (21%)	45%	51%
$75–100,000 (15%)	42%	56%
$100–200,000 (19%)	43%	56%
$200,000 or More (8%)	34%	64%

VOTE BY INCOME		
(Percentage of total)	Democrat	Republican
Less than $50,000 (36%)	54% [60%]	43% [38%]
More than $50,000 (64%)	42% [49%]	55% [49%]

VOTE BY INCOME		
(Percentage of total)	Democrat	Republican
Less than $100,000 (73%)	49% [55%]	48% [43%]
More than $100,000 (27%)	40% [49%]	58% [49%]

VOTE BY EDUCATION		
(Percentage of total)	Democrat	Republican
No High School (3%)	57% [63%]	36% [35%]
H.S. Graduate (17%)	46% [52%]	52% [46%]
Some College (28%)	43% [51%]	53% [47%]
College Graduate (30%)	40% [50%]	58% [48%]
Postgraduate (21%)	53% [58%]	45% [40%]

VOTE BY EDUCATION		
(Percentage of total)	Democrat	Republican
No College Degree (48%)	45% [53%]	52% [45%]
College Graduate (52%)	45% [53%]	53% [46%]

ANYONE IN HOUSEHOLD IN A UNION?		
(Percentage of total)	Democrat	Republican
Yes (17%)	61% [59%]	37% [39%]
No (83%)	43% [51%]	54% [47%]

VOTE BY PARTY IDENTIFICATION		
(Percentage of total)	Democrat	Republican
Democrat (35%)	91% [89%]	7% [10%]
Republican (35%)	5% [9%]	94% [90%]
Independent (29%)	37% [52%]	56% [44%]

VOTE BY IDEOLOGY		
(Percentage of total)	Democrat	Republican
Liberal (20%)	90% [89%]	8% [10%]
Moderate (38%)	55% [60%]	42% [39%]
Conservative (42%)	13% [20%]	84% [78%]

VOTE BY RELIGION		
(Percentage of total)	Democrat	Republican
Protestant (55%)	38% [45%]	59% [54%]
Catholic (23%)	44% [54%]	54% [45%]
Jewish (2%)	N/A [78%]	N/A [21%]
Other (8%)	74% [73%]	24% [22%]
None (12%)	68% [75%]	30% [23%]

VOTE BY RELIGION AMONG WHITES		
(Percentage of total)	Democrat	Republican
White Protestant (44%)	28% [34%]	69% [65%]
White Catholic (17%)	39% [47%]	59% [52%]
White Jewish (2%)	N/A [83%]	N/A [16%]
White Other Religion (5%)	71% [67%]	28% [28%]
White No Religion (9%)	62% [71%]	37% [26%]
Nonwhites (23%)	75% [79%]	24% [18%]

ARE YOU WHITE EVANGELICAL AND/OR BORN-AGAIN?		
(Percentage of total)	Democrat	Republican
Yes (25%)	19% [24%]	77% [74%]
No (75%)	55% [62%]	42% [36%]

DO YOU HAVE CHILDREN UNDER 18?		
(Percentage of total)	Democrat	Republican
Yes (34%)	46% [53%]	50% [45%]
No (66%)	47% [53%]	51% [45%]

ARE YOU GAY, LESBIAN, OR BISEXUAL?		
(Percentage of total)	Democrat	Republican
Yes (3%)	69% [70%]	29% [27%]
No (97%)	46% [53%]	52% [45%]

HOW OBAMA IS HANDLING HIS JOB		
(Percentage of total)	Democrat	Republican
Approve (44%)	85% [10%]**	14% [89%]
Disapprove (55%)	11% [67%]	84% [31%]

HOW CONGRESS IS HANDLING ITS JOB		
(Percentage of total)	Democrat	Republican
Approve (23%)	79% [62%]	20% [36%]
Disapprove (73%)	33% [51%]	64% [47%]

YOUR VOTE FOR HOUSE MEANT TO SEND A MESSAGE OF		
(Percentage of total)	Democrat	Republican
Support for Obama (23%)	96%	3%
Opposition to Obama (37%)	6%	92%
Obama Not a Factor (38%)	52%	44%

YOUR VOTE FOR HOUSE MEANT TO SEND A MESSAGE		
(Percentage of total)	Democrat	Republican
In Favor of Tea Party (22%)	8%	90%
Against Tea Party (17%)	93%	6%
Tea Party Not a Factor (57%)	44%	53%

OBAMA'S POLICIES WILL		
(Percentage of total)	Democrat	Republican
Help the Country (43%)	86%	12%
Hurt the Country (52%)	8%	89%

OPINION OF DEMOCRATIC PARTY		
(Percentage of total)	Democrat	Republican
Favorable (44%)	91%	8%
Unfavorable (52%)	10%	87%

OPINION OF REPUBLICAN PARTY		
(Percentage of total)	Democrat	Republican
Favorable (41%)	11%	88%
Unfavorable (53%)	73%	23%

OPINION OF GOVERNMENT		
(Percentage of total)	Democrat	Republican
Government Should Do More (38%)	77% [76%]	21% [23%]
Government Doing Too Much (56%)	20% [27%]	76% [71%]

OPINION OF FEDERAL GOVERNMENT		
(Percentage of total)	Democrat	Republican
Satisfied/Enthusiastic (25%)	81%	16%
Angry/Dissatisfied (73%)	32%	65%

OPINION OF TEA PARTY		
(Percentage of total)	Democrat	Republican
Support (41%)	11%	86%
Neutral (24%)	47%	50%
Oppose (30%)	86%	12%

MOST IMPORTANT ISSUE FACING COUNTRY TODAY		
(Percentage of total)	Democrat	Republican
War in Afghanistan (7%)	58%	40%
Health Care (18%)	51%	47%
Economy (63%)	43%	54%
Illegal Immigration (8%)	26%	68%

IS THE ECONOMY THE MOST IMPORTANT ISSUE?		
(Percentage of total)	Democrat	Republican
Yes (63%)	43%	54%
No (33%)	46%	51%

ANYONE IN HOUSEHOLD LOST A JOB IN LAST TWO YEARS?		
(Percentage of total)	Democrat	Republican
Yes (30%)	50%	46%
No (69%)	45%	53%

FAMILY FINANCIAL SITUATION		
(Percentage of total)	Democrat	Republican
Better (15%)	60% [37%]	37% [60%]
Worse (41%)	35% [71%]	61% [28%]
Same (43%)	49% [45%]	48% [53%]

STIMULUS PACKAGE HAS		
(Percentage of total)	Democrat	Republican
Helped Economy (32%)	86%	13%
Hurt Economy (34%)	10%	87%
Made No Difference (31%)	39%	57%

WHO DO YOU BLAME FOR ECONOMIC PROBLEMS?		
(Percentage of total)	Democrat	Republican
Wall Street (35%)	41%	57%
George W. Bush (29%)	83%	15%
Barack Obama (24%)	6%	91%

LIFE FOR THE NEXT GENERATION WILL BE		
(Percentage of total)	Democrat	Republican
Better (32%)	60%	39%
Worse (39%)	33%	64%
About the Same (26%)	52%	45%

WHAT SHOULD CONGRESS DO WITH NEW HEALTH CARE LAW?		
(Percentage of total)	Democrat	Republican
Expand It (31%)	84%	15%
Leave It As Is (16%)	63%	34%
Repeal It (48%)	11%	86%

BUSH-ERA TAX CUTS SHOULD BE CONTINUED FOR		
(Percentage of total)	Democrat	Republican
All Americans (40%)	14%	84%
Families Under $250,000 (36%)	64%	32%
No One (15%)	75%	22%
U.S. WAR IN AFGHANISTAN		
(Percentage of total)	Democrat	Republican
Approve (40%)	24%	75%
Disapprove (54%)	61%	36%
SHOULD SAME-SEX MARRIAGES BE LEGALLY RECOGNIZED?		
(Percentage of total)	Democrat	Republican
Yes (41%)	67%	30%
No (53%)	27%	70%
COUNTRY IS GOING IN		
(Percentage of total)	Democrat	Republican
Right Direction (34%)	82% [27%]	16% [71%]
Wrong Track (61%)	22% [62%]	76% [36%]
VOTE BY SIZE OF COMMUNITY		
(Percentage of total)	Democrat	Republican
Urban (31%)	56% [63%]	41% [35%]
Suburban (49%)	42% [50%]	55% [48%]
Rural (20%)	36% [45%]	61% [53%]
VOTE BY REGION		
(Percentage of total)	Democrat	Republican
Northeast (21%)	54% [59%]	44% [40%]
Midwest (25%)	44% [54%]	53% [44%]
South (31%)	37% [45%]	61% [54%]
West (23%)	49% [57%]	48% [40%]

Source: www.cnn.com/ELECTION/2010/results/polls.main/#.

*Bracketed percentages in "Democrat" column indicate percentages received by President Barack Obama in 2008.

Bracketed percentages in "Republican" column indicate percentages received by Senator John McCain in 2008.

**Bracketed percentages indicate percentages received by each party when question referred to President George W. Bush in 2008.

Endnotes

[1]Larry J. Sabato, "Sixty Days to Go," posted online by Sabato's Crystal Ball at www.centerforpolitics.org/crystalball/articles/ljs2010090201/.

[2]Larry J. Sabato, *The Sixth Year Itch* (New York: Longman, 2007).

[3]National Conference of State Legislatures at www.ncsl.org.

[4]Jeremy P. Jacobs, "Devastation: GOP Picks Up 680 State Leg. Seats," posted online on Hotline On Call at hotlineoncall.nationaljournal.com/archives/2010/11/devastation-gop.php.

[5]In 2011, 10 states are projected to lose U.S. House seats (one or two) as a result of population shifts: New York (–2), Ohio (–2), New Jersey (–1), Illinois (–1), Massachusetts (–1), Louisiana (–1), Iowa (–1), Missouri (–1), Michigan (–1), and Pennsylvania (–1). Eight states are projected to gain U.S. House seats (up to four) at the same time. They are: Texas (4), Florida (2), Georgia (1), South Carolina (1), Utah (1), Nevada (1), Washington (1), and Arizona (1). Keep in mind that with the transfer of House seats also go Electoral College votes. All the changes, for both House seats and the Electoral College, take effect in the 2012 election. It is worth noting, however, that the actual census population figures, once released, may or may not confirm all of these projections.

[6]National Exit Poll at edition.cnn.com/ELECTION/2010/results/polls/#val=USH00p1.

[7]RealClearPolitics at www.realclearpolitics.com/epolls/other/president_obama_job_approval-1044.html.

Chapter 2

Right Turn: The 2010 Midterm Elections

by Dr. Alan I. Abramowitz

*Alben W. Barkley Professor of Political Science at Emory University
and Senior Columnist for* Sabato's Crystal Ball

"**H**ope," "Change." "Yes we can!" Just two years ago the United States reverberated to the uplifting slogans of Barack Obama's presidential campaign. A record 132 million Americans went to the polls and gave Obama and his party a decisive victory. Not only did Democrats take back the presidency with their largest popular vote margin since 1964, but they also made big gains in the House and Senate elections, picking up 21 House seats and eight Senate seats. And that was on top of the dramatic gains Democrats had made in the 2006 midterm elections, when they regained control of the House and Senate for the first time since 1994. With the nation's first African American president in the White House and large Democratic majorities ensconced in the House and Senate, it seemed that a new era in American politics was at hand—an era of Democratic dominance.

That was then. If there is one thing the two years following the 2008 election have taught students of American politics, it is that what comes around, goes around. And sometimes it goes around very quickly. As Americans went to the polls in the 2010 midterm elections, the mood of the country was ugly. While the economy was once again growing and the nation's financial system was no longer on the verge of collapse, job growth was slow and unemployment remained stubbornly high. The federal government appeared sluggish

45

in responding to the enormous environmental and economic disaster created by the oil spill in the Gulf of Mexico. And even as the United States prepared to end its combat role in Iraq, American casualties in Afghanistan continued to mount and public support for that once-popular war continued to erode.

As November approached, President Obama's approval rating appeared stuck in the mid-40s, and, despite an impressive record of legislative accomplishments, the Democratic Congress was even less popular, with an approval rating of less than 20 percent in some polls. Republicans, having opposed almost all of the president's legislative initiatives with near unanimity, smelled blood in the water. Their base was energized while the coalition of young people, minorities, and white liberals that had rallied behind Barack Obama in 2008 appeared rather listless. Democratic strategists, groping for a message to rally their party's supporters, sought to turn the election into a choice between moving forward with the Democratic agenda or going back to the policies of the still enormously unpopular Bush administration. But the best they could hope for was to minimize the damage and hold on to much-reduced majorities in the House and Senate.

The Midterm Phenomenon

As surprising as the Republican Party's rapid recovery from its 2006 and 2008 election debacles might appear to be, much of the story of the 2010 elections was very predictable, based on long-standing patterns of electoral behavior. The tendency of the president's party to lose seats in Congress in midterm elections is one of the best-known regularities in American politics. As the results displayed in table 2.1 demonstrate, the party holding the White House had lost seats in the House of Representatives in 14 of the 16 midterm elections between 1946 and 2006, with an average loss of just over 24 seats. While the pattern in Senate elections was not quite as regular, it was still evident—the president's party had lost seats in the upper chamber in 11 of 16 midterm elections between 1946 and 2006, with an average loss of between three and four seats.

Since World War II, midterm seat losses have been equally prevalent under Republican and Democratic presidents and in first and later midterms, although the average seat losses in second or later midterms have been slightly larger than in the first midterm after a party wins the White House. And, despite the fact that only about a third of Senate seats are up for election every two years, and those seats were last up six years ago (not two years ago, as with all 435 House seats), there is a strong relationship between the results of midterm House and Senate elections. For the 16 postwar midterms, the correlation between the change in Republican House seats and the change in Republican Senate seats is an impressive .82.

Table 2.1—Seats Gained or Lost by President's Party in Midterm Elections, 1946–2006

Year	President's Party	House	Senate
1946	Democratic	– 55	– 12
1950	Democratic	– 29	– 6
1954	Republican	– 18	– 1
1958	Republican	– 48	– 13
1962	Democratic	– 4	+ 3
1966	Democratic	– 47	– 4
1970	Republican	– 12	+ 2
1974	Republican	– 48	– 5
1978	Democratic	– 15	– 3
1982	Republican	– 26	+ 1
1986	Republican	– 5	– 8
1990	Republican	– 9	– 1
1994	Democratic	– 52	– 9
1998	Democratic	+ 5	0
2002	Republican	+ 6	+ 2
2006	Republican	– 30	– 6
Average		**– 24.2**	**– 3.8**

Source: *Congressional Quarterly's Guide to U.S. Elections.*

While there are some exceptions, generally when Republicans do well in the House elections they tend to do well in the Senate elections, and when they do poorly in the House elections they tend to do poorly in the Senate elections. Thus, in 1946, Republicans gained 56 seats in the House and 11 seats in the Senate, while in 1994, Republicans gained 52 seats in the House and eight seats in the Senate. Likewise, in 1958, Republicans lost 47 seats in the House and 13 seats in the Senate, while in 2006 Republicans lost 30 seats in the House and six seats in the Senate. The strong relationship between the House and Senate results suggests that elections to both chambers are affected by the same national political forces.

The question these results raise, of course, is, what explains the midterm phenomenon? First, why does the president's party almost always lose seats in the House and Senate in midterm elections? Second, why does the size of this loss vary so much from one midterm to another?

Political scientists have suggested three major explanations for why the president's party almost always loses seats in midterm elections—*surge and decline*, *negative voting*, and *balancing*. The theory of *surge and decline* explains the results of midterm elections in relation to the results of the preceding presidential election—the president's party generally loses seats in the midterm election because its candidates no longer enjoy the benefits of the short-term forces that propelled the party to victory two years earlier. Thus, in 2010, Democratic candidates had to run without Barack Obama at the top of the ticket, attracting support from African American voters and young people and, just as importantly, without having George W. Bush in the White House to energize the Democratic base, as it had in 2008.

Negative voting refers to the tendency for those who are dissatisfied with the status quo to be more motivated to turn out in midterm elections than those who are satisfied, and to express their discontent by voting against candidates from the president's party. In 2006, it was mainly Democrats, dissatisfied with the Bush administration and congressional Republicans, who were eager to express their displeasure at the ballot box. In 2010, it was Republicans, and especially conservative Republicans. In that sense, the Tea Party movement was just the latest, and perhaps the noisiest, manifestation of a long-standing tradition of discontented voters venting their anger at the president's party in midterm elections.

Finally, *balancing* refers to the tendency of a subset of voters to express their preference for divided party government by voting for congressional candidates from the opposition party. This can happen in presidential as well as midterm elections, but it is easier for voters to express a preference for divided government in midterm elections because of the certainty about which party will control the White House for the next two years. Since voters knew that Barack Obama would be president through 2012, those who wanted Congress to act as a check on the power of the chief executive could vote for Republican House and Senate candidates in 2010. And polls have found that a large proportion of the electorate, which includes many supporters of the president's party, prefers divided party government to unified party control of the executive and legislative branches. For example, an NBC/*Wall Street Journal* poll conducted in May of 2010 found that two-thirds of registered voters preferred divided government to unified party control of Congress and the presidency. Overwhelming majorities of independents and Republicans preferred divided government, as did almost half of Democrats. And opinions on this question seemed to have an influence on voting intentions: 24 percent of registered Democrats who favored divided party control indicated a preference for a Republican Congress compared with only 4 percent of Democrats who favored unified party control.

Explaining Variation in Midterm Results

Negative voting and balancing explain why the president's party almost always loses seats in Congress in midterm elections. But they do not explain why there is so much variation in the results of midterm elections—why some midterms produce massive losses for the president's party while others produce small losses, or even small gains. For example, Republicans lost 13 Senate seats and 47 House seats in 1958 but gained two Senate seats and eight House seats in 2002; Democrats lost eight Senate seats and 52 House seats in 1994 but lost no Senate seats and gained three House seats in 1998.

Two major factors seem to be responsible for much of the variation in the outcomes of midterm elections: the exposure factor and the national political climate. The *exposure factor* refers to the number of vulnerable House and Senate seats that the president's party is defending in a midterm election. When a party has gained a large number of House and Senate seats in the election immediately preceding a midterm—the election that occurred two years earlier in the case of the House seats, and six years earlier in the case of the Senate seats—due to presidential coattails or other national forces, it is likely to lose a large number of seats in the midterm election. That is because many of the new seats will be in districts or states that normally favor the opposition party. The exposure effect is stronger in Senate elections than in House elections because the larger advantage of incumbency in House elections tends to insulate a party from losses when it is defending recently won seats.

The exposure factor in 2010 resulted in Democrats being highly vulnerable to losses in the House of Representatives, but not as vulnerable to losses in the Senate. This is because Democrats were defending a large number of House seats that they had gained not only in the 2008 presidential election but also in the 2006 midterm election. In those two elections, Democrats gained over 50 seats in the House of Representatives. However, the Senate seats up for election in 2010 were last up in 2004—an election in which Republicans gained four seats in the Senate.

We can get an idea of the magnitude of the Democrats' exposure problem in 2010 by examining the results of last two presidential elections in the districts and states Democrats were defending. Of the 256 House seats held by Democrats prior to the 2010 election, 47 were in districts carried by the Republican presidential candidates in both 2004 and 2008. In contrast, of the 179 House seats held by Republicans prior to the 2010 election, only 26 were in districts carried by the Democratic presidential candidates in both 2004 and 2008.

Clearly, Democrats had a much larger exposure problem in the 2010 House elections than Republicans. Based on this factor alone, the day after the 2008 presidential election one could have predicted that Democrats would be likely to lose a large number of House seats in the 2010 midterm election. In the 2010 Senate elections, however, neither party had a clear advantage based on the results of the 2004 and 2008 presidential elections. Of the 19 Democratic seats up for election, five were in states carried once by a Republican presidential candidate and three were in states carried twice by Republican presidential candidates. Likewise, of the 18 Republican seats up for election, five were in states carried once by a Democratic presidential candidate and only one was in a state carried twice by Democratic presidential candidates. The exposure factor is based on the results of past elections. It is, in that sense, a reflection of earlier political events. However, the other major source of variation in the outcomes of midterm elections is the current political climate—the mood of the country at the time of the election. A midterm election is, in part, a referendum on the incumbent president and his party. The more satisfied voters are with the performance of the incumbent president and his party, the fewer seats the president's party tends to lose in the midterm election. It is therefore no coincidence that the two recent midterm elections in which the president's party gained seats in Congress, 1998 and 2002, involved extraordinarily popular presidents—Bill Clinton during the impeachment battle with congressional Republicans and George W. Bush in the aftermath of the 9/11 terrorist attacks. Both enjoyed approval ratings of well over 60 percent. Likewise, midterm elections in which the president's party suffered large losses in Congress have frequently involved unpopular presidents, such as Harry Truman in 1946 and George W. Bush in 2006. Both had approval ratings well below 50 percent. But even when the president is fairly popular, his party can sometimes take a serious hit. In 1958, for example, Dwight Eisenhower was personally popular, with an approval rating of over 50 percent, but voters were unhappy about the state of the economy, therefore, Republicans lost 47 House seats and 13 Senate seats.

The economy is, of course, an important influence on midterm elections. Poor economic conditions almost always result in significant losses for the president's party. Thus, Democrats lost numerous seats in the 1946 recession and Republicans suffered significant losses during economic downturns in 1958 and 1982. However, good economic conditions do not necessarily guarantee a good election result for the president's party. In 1966, the U.S. economy was expanding rapidly, unemployment was low and real disposable income was increasing, but voters were unhappy about domestic political unrest and President Lyndon Johnson's conduct of the war in Vietnam—Democrats suffered big losses in the midterm elections. Likewise, in 2006, the U.S. economy was still in decent shape, but voters were upset over the war in Iraq and Republican congressional scandals, and expressed their dissatisfaction by handing Democrats control of both chambers of Congress for the first time since 1994.

Neither presidential popularity nor economic conditions fully capture the national political climate in every election year. Fortunately, however, there is an indicator that does a better job of measuring the national political climate year in and year out—the generic ballot question. This question simply asks voters whether they would choose the Democratic candidate or the Republican candidate in their own House district without actually naming the candidates who are running. There is a strong relationship between the results of the generic ballot question and the results of midterm elections. For the 16 midterm elections since World War II, the correlation between the Republican margin on the Gallup generic ballot question in early September and the number of seats won by Republicans is .81 for House elections and .63 for Senate elections.

Democrats have enjoyed a lead in the generic ballot question in 14 of the 16 midterm elections since World War II. Over these 16 elections, the average Democratic lead was just over 11 points, although that average has shrunk from over 20 points during the 1970s to only 6 points during the 1990s and 7 points during the 2000s. The only elections in which Republicans led were 1946 and 1994—the two elections in which Republicans achieved their largest gains.

When we look at the results of the Gallup generic ballot question in the weeks leading up to the 2010 midterm election, it is very clear that the national political climate favored the Republican Party. Although Gallup's weekly results ranged from a modest Democratic lead to a modest Republican lead, the average result was about a 5-point Republican lead among registered voters. That was well below the postwar average for Democrats and even below the average for recent elections. It also represented a big change from the double-digit Democratic lead on the generic ballot in the weeks preceding the 2006 midterm election and the 2008 presidential election. Moreover, a number of other national polls during the summer of 2010 showed a Republican lead on the generic ballot question. Such results clearly indicated that substantial Democratic losses were likely in November, especially considering the normal Republican advantage in turnout in midterm elections and the large enthusiasm gap between Democratic and Republican voters. But just how large would those losses be?

Forecasting the Results

Long before Election Day, all three of our key indicators—the presence of a Democratic president in the White House, the number of Democratic seats in marginal or Republican-leaning districts, and the national political climate as measured by the generic ballot—pointed to the likelihood of big Democratic losses in the House of Representatives in the 2010 midterm election. Two of these indicators, all except the exposure factor, pointed to big Democratic losses in the Senate as well. In order to combine these three indicators into a forecast, I conducted regression analyses of the results of all midterm elections since World War II with the change in Republican seats in the House and Senate as the dependent variable and our three indicators—the party of the president, the number of seats held by Republicans going into the election, and the GOP margin on the Gallup generic ballot question in early September, or as close to early September as possible—as independent variables. The results of the regression analyses are displayed in table 2.2.

Table 2.2—Results of Regression Analyses of House and Senate Seat Change in Midterm Elections

Independent Variable	House			Senate		
	B	(S.E.)	t	B	(S.E.)	t
Previous R Seats	−.442	(.139)	−3.18	−.822	(.268)	−3.07
Midterm Party	−14.1	(3.73)	−3.77	−2.28	(0.90)	−2.65
Generic Ballot	1.69	(.298)	5.66	.200	(.080)	2.49
Constant	105.1			15.3		

Note: Dependent variable is change in Republican seats.
Source: Data compiled by author.

This simple three-variable model did an excellent job of forecasting the results of midterm House and Senate elections. Not surprisingly, given the relatively small number of Senate seats at stake in each election and the closeness of so many Senate contests, the

House model was somewhat more accurate. The House model explained over 80 percent of the variation in seat change, while the Senate model explains about two-thirds of the variation in seat change. All three predictors had strong and statistically significant effects in both models. The results indicate that even after controlling for the national political climate and seat exposure, the president's party can expect to take a substantial hit in midterm elections—about 14 seats in the House of Representatives and between two and three seats in the Senate. Seat exposure also matters, especially in Senate elections where the incumbency advantage provides less insulation from national tides. Other things being equal, for every additional Republican seat up for election in the Senate, the GOP can expect to lose about 0.8 seats and for every additional seat held by Republicans in the House, the GOP can expect to lose about 0.4 seats. Finally, the Republican margin on the generic ballot has a substantial impact on seat swing in the House and Senate. A 10-point swing in margin on the generic ballot is associated with a shift of about 17 House seats and two Senate seats.

Table 2.3—Predicted Change in Republican House and Senate Seats

Generic Ballot	House Seats	Senate Seats
D +10	+ 23	+ 1
D +5	+ 32	+ 2
Tie	+ 40	+ 3
R +5	+ 49	+ 4
R +10	+ 57	+ 5

Source: Data compiled by author.

Based on the estimated regression coefficients in table 2.2, I was able to predict the size of the expected Republican gains in the 2010 House and Senate elections depending on the results of the generic ballot question. Those predictions are displayed in table 2.3 and they indicated that Republicans had a very good chance of regaining control of the House of Representatives but much less chance of regaining control of the Senate. Republicans seemed certain to gain a substantial number of House seats and, based on a 5-point lead on the generic ballot, appeared likely to gain about 50 seats, more than enough to take control of the House.

On the Senate side, with a more favorable exposure factor, the outlook for the majority party appeared more positive: Democrats seemed likely to lose several seats, but appeared unlikely to lose the 10 seats that would give Republicans control of the upper chamber. However, the Senate model is considerably less accurate than the House model. With many close contests likely, a swing of a few thousand votes in a handful of states could make the difference between a loss of four or five seats and a loss of nine or ten seats.

Other Factors: The Tea Party Effect

In both chambers, the final results of the 2010 midterm elections were also influenced by factors that are not easily incorporated into a statistical forecasting model—factors such as candidate quality, fundraising, intraparty feuds, media strategies, and voter mobilization efforts. One additional wild card in 2010 was the influence of the Tea Party movement on Republican nomination contests. While the Tea Party movement was seen as helping to energize Republican voters, victories by Tea Party candidates in a number of Republican primaries provided some unexpected opportunities for Democrats to hold seats that had been considered highly vulnerable. In Nevada, for example, Democratic majority leader Harry Reid had long been considered likely to lose his seat with an approval rating mired in the low 40s. However, the victory of controversial Tea Party favorite Sharron Angle in the Republican primary turned what was expected to be an easy Republican victory in a hotly contested race. In the end, thanks to Angle, Reid held onto his seat by a fairly comfortable margin.

Even more clearly, in Delaware, Republicans appeared to miss a golden opportunity to pick up a Democratic Senate seat—the one once held by Vice President Joe Biden. The Republican establishment's choice for the party's nomination was the longtime representative from the state's lone House district, Mike Castle, a candidate with a moderate record well suited to a strongly Democratic state like Delaware. But the state's Republican primary voters apparently did not get the memo from their party's leaders, and instead chose political novice and Tea

Party favorite Christine O'Donnell. O'Donnell's hard-line conservative views and checkered personal history quickly turned what had looked like a nearly certain GOP pickup into a nearly certain Democratic hold. Several polls conducted immediately following the primary showed the Democratic nominee, New Castle county executive Chris Coons, who had been far behind Castle in the polls, with a 15- to 20-point lead over O'Donnell. On Election Day, Coons decisively defeated O'Donnell by a margin of close to 17 points.

The Results

On November 2, 2010, voters swept the Democrats out of power in the House of Representatives and sharply reduced the size of their majority in the U.S. Senate. Republicans made big gains in the midterm elections, picking up six seats in the Senate and 63 seats in the House. In January 2011, the House of Representatives would have more Republicans than at any time since the late 1940s.

The 2010 midterm elections produced a dramatic change in the balance of power in Washington. It was clear from the exit polls that Americans were upset about the condition of the U.S. economy—62 percent of voters in the national exit polls named the economy as the most important issue—and they wanted President Obama and the new Congress to do something to address the problems of slow job growth and high unemployment. Beyond that, however, the message sent by the voters was less clear. Despite the dramatic change in the fortunes of the parties, the election results showed that the American people remained deeply divided over what direction they wanted the country to take. In fact, by some measures, the divisions within the public appeared to be deeper than ever. Given these deep divisions within the public, it is not surprising that the new Congress appeared likely to be even more polarized than the one it was replacing.

Evidence from national exit polls shows that the voters who turned out in 2010 differed in several important respects from the much larger group of voters who turned out in 2008. The midterm electorate was considerably older, whiter, more conservative, and more Republican than the presidential electorate. Nevertheless, evidence from the national exit polls also shows that the voting patterns in 2010 were very similar to those in 2008. Democrats fared best among younger voters, minorities, lower-income voters, union members, and, of course, liberals. Republicans fared best among older voters, whites, upper-income voters, evangelicals, and, of course, conservatives. Regional patterns of support were also similar to those in 2008. Although Republicans made gains in every region of the country, they did best in the South and worst in the Northeast and in the Pacific Coast states, just as they did in 2008.

A careful examination of the exit poll data suggests that the 2010 electorate, in addition to being more conservative and Republican than two years earlier, was even more polarized along racial and ideological lines than the 2008 electorate. According to the national exit polls, Democrats won 90 percent of the African American vote and about two-thirds of the Hispanic vote in 2010, down only slightly from two years earlier, but they lost the white vote by a whopping 22 points, a much larger margin than in the 2008 presidential or congressional elections. It appears that Democrats in 2010 were even more dependent on nonwhite voters than in 2008, while Republicans continue to rely almost exclusively on the support of white voters.

The 2010 electorate was also deeply divided along ideological and policy lines. Both the proportion of liberals voting for Democratic candidates and the proportion of conservatives voting for Republican candidates set all-time records. Likewise, on the issue of health care reform there was a deep chasm between Democratic and Republican voters. Overall, voters divided almost evenly on this issue, with 47 percent favoring either expanding the law or keeping it as is and 48 percent favoring repealing it. Among Democratic voters, 62 percent wanted to see the law expanded, 25 percent wanted it kept as is, and only 13 percent favored repeal. In contrast, among Republican voters, only 8 percent wanted the law expanded and only 10 percent wanted it kept as is, while 82 percent wanted it repealed.

Given the deep divisions between Democratic and Republican voters, it is not surprising that the new Congress seems likely to be the most polarized in the modern era. A disproportionate share of the Democrats who lost their seats in 2010 came from the moderate wing of the party. They were the ones who represented the most vulnerable states and districts—ones that were carried by John McCain in 2008 or barely carried by Barack Obama. As a result, the Democrats serving in the 112th Congress are likely to be considerably more liberal than the Democrats who served in the 111th Congress. But the vast majority of defeated Democrats were replaced not by moderate Republicans, but by very conservative Republicans, many elected with the support of the Tea Party movement. As a result, the ideological center of the Republican Party is likely to shift even further to the right in the new Congress. Thus, the ideological divide between the parties in the new Congress appears to be deeper than ever, making bipartisan cooperation even more difficult than it was in the 111th Congress—while divided control of government makes such cooperation more essential for passing legislation. In short, the most likely result of the midterm elections appears to be legislative gridlock for the next two years, with Republicans focusing on trying to repeal key pieces of legislation passed by the 111th Congress, such as health care reform, and Democrats trying to defend their legislative accomplishments.

Beyond 2010

The implications of the 2010 midterm elections for the 2012 elections are more difficult to evaluate. On the one hand, the results of midterm elections generally do not predict the results of the subsequent presidential or congressional elections. Since the end of World War II, three presidents—Harry Truman, Ronald Reagan, and Bill Clinton—have suffered major defeats in midterm elections and gone on to win reelection two years later. The decisive Republican victory in 2010 does not tell us anything about Barack Obama's chances of winning a second term in 2012, or about the outlook for the 2012 House and Senate elections. In other words, what happens in the midterm election stays in the midterm election.

However, one development seen in the 2010 midterm elections is likely to have an important influence on the future of the Republican Party, including the battle for the 2012 GOP presidential election: the growing influence of the ultraconservative Tea Party movement. In 2010, the loosely organized Tea Party movement succeeded not only in nominating several of its candidates over candidates backed by the Republican establishment, but also in influencing the positions taken by many other Republican candidates and officeholders. The result was to push the ideological center of the Republican Party even further to the right, continuing a trend that has been evident for several decades. In 2012, a number of Republican incumbents could find themselves in danger of being seriously challenged by Tea Party-backed candidates. Republicans such as Olympia Snowe of Maine, Bob Corker of Tennessee, Richard Lugar of Indiana, Scott Brown of Massachusetts, and even Orrin Hatch of Utah could face the wrath of the Tea Party for their moderate voting records, or just for being seen as too willing to cooperate with their Democratic colleagues.

The Tea Party movement will probably have a major influence on the race for the Republican presidential nomination in 2012 as well, since its supporters make up a large share of GOP voters in many primaries and caucuses. This will favor candidates who adopt the hardline conservative positions that appeal to Tea Party supporters, but which could alienate more moderate swing voters in the general election. The contest for the Republican presidential nomination could come down to an establishment conservative versus a Tea Party candidate. No matter who wins the Republican nomination, though, there is little doubt that voters will have a clear ideological choice in the general election, a choice that will undoubtedly produce another exciting and polarizing campaign and high voter turnout in November.

Chapter 3

The Battle for the Senate: The Republicans Fall Short

by Rhodes Cook

Editor of the Rhodes Cook Letter *and*
Senior Columnist for Sabato's Crystal Ball

For Republicans, 2010 was a phenomenal year. The party easily won control of the House of Representatives, a majority of the nation's governorships, and for good measure, picked up a plethora of state legislatures on the eve of the decennial round of congressional redistricting.

But tempering this considerable success was the fact that the GOP did not win the Senate, the one major prize up for grabs in November 2010 that eluded their grasp.

From the start, it was a tall order for the Republicans. They needed to pick up 10 seats to win a Senate majority—a feat that would require them to capture virtually all of the Democratic seats that were considered to be competitive. Ultimately, the GOP ended up with a gain of six, leaving the Democrats with an important beachhead on Capitol Hill.

Republican Senate candidates had many of the same assets that propelled their ticket-mates for other offices. At the top of the list was a struggling economy, which many voters blamed on President Barack Obama and his Democratic congressional allies. In turn, it fueled an environment of voter unease that strongly favored the GOP.

But the Democrats had an asset of their own in their defensive playbook—and that was the element of time. Democrats had been largely blindsided in 1994, when the Republican landslide swept the

GOP into control on both sides of Capitol Hill. In the 2010 election cycle, Democratic candidates had months and months to prepare. And enough of them prepared sufficiently that Republicans were kept from winning a Senate majority.

Arguably, the portion of the electorate most engaged by the volatile conditions was the burgeoning Tea Party movement. In their anger and frustration with what they saw as an overpriced, oversized, liberty-depriving federal government, they generated energy on the Republican side that the Democrats were unable to match.

By providing the primary votes needed to nominate candidates of their own ilk, the Tea Party may have helped to plant the seeds of the Republican Senate failure. At least, that is what critics of the movement have claimed. In Colorado, Delaware, and Nevada, Tea Party favorites captured the GOP nomination but were defeated in the fall—all losing races that other Republican candidates might very well have won.

As it was, Republicans emerged from the election with 47 Senate seats and a consolation prize of sorts. They appear well positioned to win control of the Senate in 2012, when fully two-thirds of the seats at stake are currently held by Democrats. That is, unless the political winds shift again.

Background

The Democrats came out of the 2008 election controlling both ends of Pennsylvania Avenue for the first time since the opening two years of Bill Clinton's administration (1993 to 1994). In actuality, it took two election cycles for the party to gain dominance on Capitol Hill. When George W. Bush won reelection in 2004, the Democrats held just 202 seats in the House and 44 in the Senate. Two years later, they won narrow majorities in both chambers, and expanded them significantly in 2008 when anti-Republican sentiment crested.

Throughout the 111th Congress (2009 to 2010), the Democrats flirted with a "supermajority" of 60 seats—the number needed to cut off filibusters and proceed with action on the Obama administration's legislative agenda.

Democrats came out of the 2008 election with 56 seats, a number that quickly rose to 58 when the Senate's two independents were included. Both Joe Lieberman of Connecticut and Bernie Sanders of

Vermont were elected as independents in 2006, but both caucused with the Democrats on Capitol Hill. The size of the Democratic majority swelled to 59 in April 2009, when veteran Republican, Sen. Arlen Specter of Pennsylvania, switched to the Democratic side. And it reached the "magic" number of 60 that summer, when Democrat Al Franken was finally declared the winner of his long-running, closely contested Senate contest in Minnesota against GOP incumbent Norm Coleman. Franken's final margin: 312 votes out of nearly 3 million cast.[1]

But the Democrats' 60-seat supermajority did not last long. In January 2010, it was gone, as Republican Scott Brown won a special election in Massachusetts for the seat formerly held by liberal Democratic icon Edward M. Kennedy (who had died the previous August). It was a huge upset, the first GOP Senate victory in the Bay State since 1972.

The result had instant ramifications. In the honeymoon months after Obama's inauguration, there had been talk that the Democrats might increase the size of their Senate majority in 2010. After the Massachusetts vote, however, there were rumblings that the Democrats might not be able to keep their majority at all. If they could not win in "dark blue" Massachusetts, political pundits asked, where could they safely count on winning in 2010?

Still, throughout the election cycle it would remain a formidable task for Republicans to win the 10 seats needed to gain a Senate majority. Not since Republican Ronald Reagan swept into the White House in 1980 had there been an election with a double-digit swing in Senate seats from one party to the other. And not since 1958 had it occurred in a midterm election.

Even in 1994, when a huge Republican surge gave the party control of both sides of Capitol Hill, the GOP gains in the Senate fell short of 10. The total stood at eight that election night, and rose to nine the next day when Sen. Richard Shelby of Alabama decided it was a favorable time to make his move to the GOP.

Nor was the partisan breakdown of the Senate seats up in 2010 particularly encouraging to a major Republican advance. Of the 37 seats at stake in the general election, 19 were held by Democrats, 18 by Republicans.

It was not a conspicuously exposed group of Democratic senators who were up for reelection in 2010. They had last run (and won) in

2004, a favorable Republican year. That stood in stark contrast to the large group of Democratic House members first elected in 2006 or 2008, when the wind was at their back.

Normally, 33 or 34 Senate seats are up every two years. However, the 2008 election of Senators Barack Obama (D-IL) and Joe Biden (D-DE) as president and vice president, respectively, followed by subsequent cabinet selections, and the deaths of Senator Ted Kennedy (D-MA) in August 2009 and Senator Robert C. Byrd (D-WV) the following summer, necessitated additional Senate elections in Delaware, Massachusetts, New York, and West Virginia. Obama's Illinois seat did not require a special election since it was due to come up in 2010 anyway, and the Massachusetts seat was decided in January. The other three were added to the November general election ballot.

January 2010: The Tide Turns

The off-year elections of November 2009 had been rough for the Democrats. They lost the two governorships at stake in New Jersey and Virginia, but could still point to a special congressional election pickup in upstate New York to argue that voters had not really turned on them.

That became more difficult to argue in January, as the Democrats were hit by a double whammy. In early January, veteran Democratic Senators Christopher Dodd of Connecticut and Byron Dorgan of North Dakota both announced their decisions not to seek reelection in 2010.

Many Democrats actually viewed the retirement of Dodd, the chairman of the Senate Committee on Banking, Housing, and Urban Affairs, as a political blessing. His popularity in Connecticut had fallen with the sinking economy, and the state's long-time attorney general, Richard Blumenthal, was ready to step in and take Dodd's spot on the Democratic ticket.

North Dakota, though, was another matter. Dorgan, a fiscal conservative, had been a member of Congress for three decades, rarely falling below two-thirds of the vote in the rural heartland, where the default position is to vote Republican. And Dorgan was still in his 60s, comparatively young by Senate standards. His decision to retire was greeted by an E. J. Dionne column in the *Washington Post* headlined, "A thunderclap over North Dakota."[2]

The Democratic concern with Dorgan's retirement was dwarfed by the unexpected outcome of the Senate contest in Massachusetts on January 19. It was considered the Democrats' election to lose. And they did.

Nothing in the early going altered the conventional wisdom that it would be an easy Democratic triumph. The state attorney general, Martha Coakley, handily won the Democratic primary in December 2009—a contest in which more than 650,000 ballots were cast. That was four times the number that participated in the Republican primary, in which a little-known state senator, Scott Brown, was nominated.

In the weeks that followed, the dynamic of the special election changed. Coakley acted as though the election were well in hand. She took some time off following the primary, and when she returned to the campaign trail she proved to be gaffe-prone. In one of her more prominent verbal missteps, she showed no familiarity with one of the state's cultural touchstones, the Boston Red Sox.

In contrast, Brown crisscrossed Massachusetts in his pickup truck, meeting voters in their places of work and play. His combative populist message helped to harvest voters dissatisfied with the ruling Democrats in both Washington and Boston. His feisty appeal resonated with conservative activists nationally. As the campaign wound down he was able to raise money easily.

In a state that Obama had swept in 2008 with 62 percent of the vote, Coakley could muster only 47 percent—a losing share. She won little more than the immediate Boston area and the lightly populated western part of the state, with its college towns and artistic communities. The bulk of the rest of the state—Boston's outer suburbs, towns from Cape Cod to the middle of Massachusetts, and even an old blue-collar mill town or two—bolted to Brown.

The Republican carried Lowell, a once thriving textile center and home to the late Democratic senator, Paul Tsongas. Brown won the town of Barnstable, which included the Kennedy homestead at Hyannis Port. He also swept independent-minded Marlborough, a town about 25 miles west of Boston that was featured in an election eve article in the *New York Times* as "the kind of place where many Massachusetts elections are won and lost these days."[3] Obama had carried Marlborough in 2008 with 57 percent of the vote. Brown won it in early 2010 with an identical 57 percent.

Compounding the problem for Coakley was that the turnout was generally low in traditional Democratic strongholds. This happened despite President Obama's eleventh-hour trip to Boston to fire up Democratic voters. His spirited speech served as Coakley's closing argument. As in New Jersey and Virginia two months earlier, the president's campaign efforts did not come close to producing a Democratic victory.

The Democrats' failure to rally their base was a precursor of a turnout deficit—popularly known as an "enthusiasm gap"—that would bedevil the party throughout 2010. The problem was exacerbated in Massachusetts by Brown's success in wooing the bulk of the state's large independent vote.

The loss of Ted Kennedy's former Senate seat left the Democrats with a crisis of confidence. For the first time, there was credible talk of the Republicans capturing the 10 seats that autumn, which would give them control of the Senate. There was even talk of the GOP capturing the three "trophy seats"—the ones formerly held by President Obama in Illinois and Vice President Biden in Delaware, as well as the Nevada seat occupied by Senate Majority Leader Harry Reid.

The situation did not get much better for the Democrats in the weeks that followed. In February, on the eve of the state's primary filing deadline, Sen. Evan Bayh of Indiana announced that he, too, was retiring. His decision turned what was a safe Democratic seat into one where the edge flipped to the Republicans.

In March, congressional Democrats pushed their health care overhaul through the House and Senate without a single Republican vote. It was the signature issue for the Obama administration in the 111th Congress (2009 to 2010), but the president and his Democratic allies garnered little credit for its passage. Like most of the other major Obama initiatives, the complex measure fared poorly in public opinion polls. It played easily into the Republican argument that the Democrats were intent on imposing expensive "big government" programs at a time when the nation could ill afford it.

The Primaries: A Cauldron of Volatility

Anti-incumbency was one of the main story lines during the 2010 campaign, even though, in the case of House and gubernatorial contests, in the long primary season it did not really merit the ink that it consumed.

Only four House members were defeated in the primaries, the same number as in 2008, and just one governor went down to primary defeat, the same number as in the previous midterm election in 2006. In the Senate, though, anti-incumbent sentiment was much more palpable. Three sitting senators were denied renomination—Republicans Robert Bennett of Utah and Lisa Murkowski of Alaska, as well as recently minted Democrat Arlen Specter of Pennsylvania. It was the highest number of Senate casualties in a single primary season since 1980, when four were defeated. (Murkowski, though, managed to hold her seat in the Senate by waging a successful write-in campaign in the general election.)

In addition, three other senators—Democrats Blanche Lincoln of Arkansas and Michael Bennet of Colorado, as well as Republican John McCain of Arizona—won their primaries with no more than 56 percent of the vote. In short, six of the 25 senators running for reelection in 2010 faced significant resistance from their party's primary voters.

The antipathy was bipartisan in nature. Liberal activists took on several Senate incumbents who had the backing of President Obama, and the burgeoning Tea Party movement actively challenged preferred candidates of the Republican establishment from the right.

The Tea Party was defined by its grassroots emphasis, its energy—which was higher than virtually any other element in the 2010 electorate—and members' anger with what they saw as an expansive federal government.

Although the movement had no formal national leadership, it was encouraged and guided by the "going rogue" element of the GOP, including Sen. Jim DeMint of South Carolina, former House majority leader Richard Armey of Texas, and former Alaska governor Sarah Palin. The latter, the charismatic Republican vice-presidential nominee in 2008, delivered highly watched "tweets" and Facebook postings of her candidate preferences throughout the primary season.

The strength of the Tea Party was evident by the spring of 2010, when its supporters dominated the GOP state convention in Utah, rejecting the renomination bid of three-term senator, Robert Bennett.

To ardent conservative activists, the veteran senator represented the "bad" side of Washington. He supported the 2008 economic bailout known as TARP (an acronym for Troubled Assets Relief Program) and committed the "sin" of reaching across the aisle to work with Democrats on issues such as health care reform. When Bennett appeared before the convention to make his case, many on the floor chanted, "TARP! TARP! TARP!"[4]

Successful Tea Party challenges to the GOP establishment continued throughout the Senate primary season. In May, Rand Paul (the son of 2008 libertarian Republican presidential candidate, Ron Paul) easily won the GOP Senate nomination in Kentucky over the choice of the state's senior senator, Minority Leader Mitch McConnell.

In June, Tea Party favorite Sharron Angle overcame a field of candidates, including the former state Republican chairman, to win the Nevada GOP Senate nomination.

In August, another favorite of conservative activists, Marco Rubio, formally won the Republican Senate nomination in Florida. His victory came nearly four months after his superior poll numbers had driven the early GOP front-runner, Gov. Charlie Crist, into an independent candidacy. Also in August, Sen. Lisa Murkowski of Alaska lost her bid for renomination to a political unknown, Joe Miller, whose campaign was backed by Palin and the Tea Party Express. However, Murkowski won reelection that fall on the strength of a write-in campaign.

In September, there was another Tea Party-assisted upset when Delaware Republicans chose Christine O'Donnell over the establishment favorite, Rep. (and former governor) Michael Castle.

While many of the higher-profile Republican Senate primaries had a theme of "the establishment versus the conservative grassroots," the more prominent Senate primaries on the Democratic side featured Obama-backed candidates against feisty challengers who refused to stand aside to accommodate the wishes of the White House.

Since Franklin D. Roosevelt's spectacularly unsuccessful effort to purge a number of conservative Democratic members of Congress in 1938, most presidents have shied away from extensive involvement in their party's primaries.

Obama's more active role was in part a reflection of the modus operandi of the then White House chief of staff, Rahm Emanuel, who played a hands-on role in recruiting electable House candidates while chairing the Democratic Congressional Campaign Committee in 2006.

It was also a reflection of Obama's own temperament. While a presidential candidate in 2008, he was not averse to making an endorsement in a Democratic congressional primary.

Obama's most prominent primary endorsements were meant to assist newly minted Democratic senators—appointed members such as Michael Bennet of Colorado and Kirsten Gillibrand of New York—as well as the party-switching Arlen Specter. Obama also lent his support to Blanche Lincoln, the beleaguered two-term Democratic incumbent in Arkansas.

Rather than regarding the president with "shock and awe," however, major challengers to his choices emerged in Democratic Senate primaries in Arkansas, Colorado, and Pennsylvania. In the latter, Rep. Joe Sestak defeated Specter by running an aggressive campaign that highlighted the incumbent's Republican past. In Arkansas, Lt. Gov. Bill Halter forced Lincoln into a runoff (which she ultimately won). In Colorado, the underfunded former state House Speaker Andrew Romanoff drew more than 45 percent of the vote against Bennet.

Obama's involvement in the primaries put him at odds, at least for some time, with major portions of his party. Elements of organized labor and the liberal netroots backed Halter in Arkansas. Former president Bill Clinton endorsed Romanoff in Colorado. In New York, the Obama team worked with other national and Empire State Democrats to prevent a significant primary challenge to Gillibrand. Three former or current Democratic congressmen had expressed interest in such a challenge but were effectively discouraged from taking on the appointed incumbent.

All in all, it was an eventful Senate primary season in 2010 for both the Democrats and the Republicans—one that could even be considered historic.

End Game

In the last few weeks of the 2010 campaign, the big question was whether Republicans would win the Senate. By October, political pundits were almost unanimous in their belief that the GOP would gain the 39 seats needed to win control of the House of Representatives. Throughout the year, it was assumed that Republicans would win a hefty majority of the nation's governorships, since they started the year with 24. Winning the Senate was another matter. It always looked as though it would require a bit of luck for the GOP to capture the 10 seats needed to win Senate control.

Election night, November 2, began well enough for Republicans. They picked off the Arkansas seat held by Democrat, Sen. Blanche Lincoln, the only one of the nine Southern Senate seats on the ballot in 2010 that was held by a Democrat.

The Republicans followed with a quintet of Senate victories across the Frost Belt from Pennsylvania to North Dakota. Democrat, Sen. Russell Feingold was ousted in Wisconsin. The other four GOP pickups came through the capture of open seats in Illinois, Indiana, North Dakota, and Pennsylvania. The Illinois seat was particularly prized, since it had been held by Obama before his election as president in 2008.

West of the Great Plains, Republicans hit a firewall of sorts. Major GOP challenges to Democratic senators in California, Colorado, Nevada, and Washington all fell short, with the Nevada loss probably the most frustrating of all for Republicans. There, they had Senate Majority Leader Harry Reid on the ropes throughout the year but he escaped with a fairly comfortable victory of nearly 6 percentage points.

In spite of the millions and millions of dollars poured into the Senate races and the high-stakes component of many of the contests, only five of the 37 races on the ballot in 2010 ended up being decided by a margin of less than 5 percentage points.

Democratic incumbents won a pair of these close elections. Patty Murray held off her Republican challenger by nearly 5 percentage points in Washington, while Michael Bennet prevailed by less than 2 points in Colorado.

Meanwhile, a pair of Republicans narrowly won two open Senate seats. Former representative Patrick Toomey in Pennsylvania and Rep. Mark Kirk in Illinois both registered victories that were no more than 2 points. In Wisconsin, GOP business executive Ron Johnson defeated Feingold by a margin of almost 5 points.

Sen. Lisa Murkowki's victory in Alaska could also be less than 5 percentage points once her write-in tally is certified. As of this writing, it was not. Several other high-profile Senate contests were expected to be close, but, in the end, were not.

In Florida, the race featuring Republican Marco Rubio, independent Charlie Crist, and Democrat Kendrick Meek was expected to be one of the top Senate contests of 2010. Instead, Rubio prevailed by a margin of nearly 20 percentage points over Crist, with election eve speculation focused on whether Meek would withdraw to allow the anti-Rubio vote to coalesce around Crist. Meek stayed in the race.

The Senate contest in Missouri featured a battle between two of the state's most prominent political families. Veteran Republican, Rep. Roy Blunt, whose son had been governor, trounced Democrat, Secretary of State Robin Carnahan, whose father had been governor, by nearly 15 points.

In Connecticut, the former chief executive of Worldwide Wrestling Entertainment (WWE), Linda McMahon, pumped tens of millions of dollars into her GOP Senate bid but still ended up losing to Democratic state attorney general, Richard Blumenthal, by more than 10 percentage points.

In West Virginia, Democrat, Gov. Joe Manchin recovered from a mid-fall campaign slump to ease past Republican business executive John Raese. Manchin's margin of victory: 10 points, in the special election for the Senate seat long held by the late Robert Byrd.

In California, Democrat, Sen. Barbara Boxer managed to fend off an aggressive Republican challenge from the former chief executive of Hewlett Packard, Carly Fiorina. Their race had been nip and tuck throughout much of the year, but opened at the end into a 9-point Boxer victory.

In Kentucky, Tea Party favorite Rand Paul followed his one-sided Republican primary victory over the choice of Senate Minority Leader Mitch McConnell with a solid 12 percentage point win over Democrat, State Attorney General Jack Conway in the general election.

As political observers reviewed the results, one of the main questions was whether the Tea Party had cost Republicans the Senate. Paul and Rubio were the movement's high-profile winners. But Tea Party favorites such as Christine O'Donnell in Delaware, Ken Buck in Colorado, Sharron Angle in Nevada, and Joe Miller in Alaska, all went down to defeat.

In the last few weeks of the campaign, the colorful O'Donnell seemed to become the public face of Tea Party Republicans. She famously declared in one TV advertisement, "I am not a witch"—a reference to a taped TV appearance years earlier in which she admitted that when she was younger, while on a date she had attended an event involving witchcraft.[5]

How much effect O'Donnell's candidacy had on other GOP candidates is an open question. In the end, she lost the Delaware race by more than 15 percentage points—and with it a Senate seat that many Republicans had expected to win before her upset victory in the Republican primary.

In a way, it was a fitting ending to a volatile political year—one in which Republicans won virtually everything, except control of the world's greatest deliberative body.

Endnotes

[1]Rhodes Cook, Alice V. McGillivray, Richard M. Scammon, *America Votes 28* (Washington D.C.: CQ Press, 2010).

[2]E. J. Dionne Jr., "A thunderclap over North Dakota," *Washington Post*, January 7, 2010.

[3]Michael Cooper, "In Senate Race, Massachusetts Bucks a Political Stereotype," *New York Times*, January 18, 2010.

[4]Amy Gardner, "For 'tea party,' victory at Utah GOP convention," *Washington Post*, May 9, 2010.

[5]Dan Farber, "Christine O'Donnell TV Ad: I'm Not a Witch . . . I'm You," posted October 5, 2010 at www.cbsnews.com/8301-503544_162-20018526-503544.html.

Chapter 4

The 2010 Gubernatorial Elections

by Dr. Thad Beyle

*Thomas J. Pearsall Professor of Political Science
at the University of North Carolina*

The 2010 gubernatorial elections hold special significance in our political system. These elections in 37 states mark the greatest number of gubernatorial races ever held in a single year. In this election, due to term limits on 15 incumbent governors and eight incumbents who decided not to seek another term, 23 of the 37 races were for open seats. This meant that there would be new governors elected in those states, along with 14 other seats in which incumbent governors lost their bid for another term in office. It is certainly the largest turnover of governorships we have seen.

These gubernatorial elections also took place during one of the worst economic crises that our country and the world have experienced in many decades, and there were many problems and programs the states were trying to address with not enough funds to do so. There was considerable discontent with our government and political leadership, making these elections almost a referendum on our system of government and living.

The States as the Base of the U.S. Election System

The states are the building blocks of our governmental system. As the American colonies went from being British-controlled to the independent states that formed a new nation, the leaders in these new states were critical to accomplishing the transition. They built the new nation on the state-based support system of government. Government leaders were to be elected on a state level. Representation in the new U.S. Congress was based on two senators per state, and the number of representatives from each state was apportioned according to state population. States would also determine the structure and functioning of local government.

At the state government level, the powers of government were divided into three branches mirroring the national design: the legislative, the executive, and the judicial. For the executive branch, each state created a governor, one who is elected rather than appointed or imposed, as they had been during colonial days. Over time, several trends have changed the way in which state governors are elected.

Table 4.1—Gubernatorial Terms: 1800–2010

Year	States	4-yr	3-yr	2-yr	1-yr
1800	13	2	3	2^1	6^2
1850	31	7	5	12	7
1900	44	19	1	22	2
1950	48	28	—	20	—
1980	50	46	—	4	—
2010	50	48	—	2	—

Source: Author's databases and *Congressional Quarterly*, 1998, "Gubernatorial Elections, 1987–1997."

Note: For more information, see endnotes 1 and 2, as indicated within the table.

First, by reviewing table 4.1, we see that by 1800, 13 states had set up a process for electing their governors, nine through the state's general election and four by having the popularly elected legislature in these states choose the governor. The legislative selection option slowly gave way to governors being elected by the voters in North Carolina in 1836, in Massachusetts in 1846, in Virgina in 1851, and in South Carolina in 1865.

Second, by reviewing the same table, we see that in the early years, governors served shorter terms: six with one-year terms, two with two-year terms, three with three-year terms, and only two with four-year terms. Over time, the trend has been toward four-year terms that mirror our presidential terms, so that now only two states—New Hampshire and Vermont—still have two-year terms.

Presidential Elections and Gubernatorial Elections

By looking at the years in which governors are elected we can see that many states have taken steps to separate these state-level elections from presidential election politics by shifting them to nonpresidential election years. This shift was facilitated, in part, by lengthening the terms governors served, so that now, governors in 48 states serve four-year terms. Some states also shifted these elections to nonpresidential election years. The pattern we now see in gubernatorial elections is best set out in a four-year span: Year 1 is presidential election year (even year, 2008); Year 2 is the first year of a presidential term (odd year, 2009); Year 3 is the second year of a presidential term (even year, 2010); Year 4 is the third year of a presidential term (odd year, 2011).

Looking over the past few four-year spans of gubernatorial elections leading up to the 2010 election, we can see several clear patterns. The first pattern is tied to the changes in gubernatorial terms and away from presidential elections. In Year 1, 11 states have held gubernatorial elections, while in Year 2 only New Jersey and Virginia have held their gubernatorial elections. Then, in Year 3, the midterm election year, 36 states have been holding their gubernatorial elections, while in Year 4, only three states—Kentucky, Louisiana, and Mississippi have held their elections.

A second pattern we have seen in recent four-year spans of gubernatorial elections is a rise in the number of candidates seeking the governorship, and a move away from the two major parties to third parties, and many now running as Independents. In the 1990 elections, there were 283 candidates for governors in the 36 states, split almost evenly between Democrats (41 percent) and Republicans (43.5 percent), with only 15.5 percent running as "Other" third-party or Independent candidates. The number and percent of these Other candidates continued to rise over the next elections so that by 2002 there was a higher percentage of Other candidates (36.8 percent) than Democratic (30.4 percent) or Republican (32.8 percent) candidates. In the 2010 gubernatorial elections, there were 410 candidates running for governor, with 27.6 percent Democrat, 37.6 percent Republican, and 34.9 percent Other. Clearly, to many of those getting into gubernatorial politics, the two major parties are no longer the only means of reaching their goals. This prospect also raises the issue that, if this trend continues, it may undermine our long-standing two-party system of politics.

Table 4.2 Candidates in the Midterm Gubernatorial Elections 1978–2010

		Candidates: number/percent				Number of States[3]	
Year	Races	All	Dem	Rep	Other	D/R	D/R/O
1978	36	298/100	136/45.6	105/35.2	57/19.1	27	9[4]
1982	36	305/100	137/44.9	100/32.9	68/22.3	25	11[5]
1986	36	294/100	127/43.2	125/42.5	42/14.3	27	9[6]
1990	36	283/100	116/41.0	122/43.5	43/15.5	15[7]	21
1994	36	336/100	130/38.7	131/39.0	75/22.3	8[8]	28
1998	36	279/100	114/40.9	86/30.8	79/28.3	6[9]	30
2002	36	345/100	105/30.4	113/32.8	127/36.8	3[10]	33
2006	36	286/100	92/32.2	105/36.7	89/31.1	7[11]	29
2010	37	410/100	113/27.6	154/37.6	143/34.9	6[12]	31[13]

Source: Compiled by the author.
Note: See information in endnotes 3–13, as indicated within the table.

A third pattern we have seen in the Year 3 elections over the past two decades is that the president's party gubernatorial candidates are generally put at a disadvantage in these midyear elections. In the 1990 midterm elections that followed the 1998 presidential election of Republican vice president George H. W. Bush, only 15 of the 36 gubernatorial races were won by Republicans. In the 1994 midterm elections that followed the 1992 presidential election of Democratic Arkansas governor Bill Clinton, only 11 of the 36 gubernatorial races were won by Democrats. In the 1998 midterm elections that followed the 1996 reelection of Bill Clinton, only 11 of the 36 gubernatorial races were won by Democrats. Then followed the two terms of Republican Texas governor George W. Bush, elected in 2000 and 2004. In the 2002 gubernatorial elections, his party candidates fared well—they won 32 of the 36 races. But in 2006, after his 2004 reelection to a second term, they also felt that negative impact as Republicans only won 16 of the 36 races. With the 2010 midterm election results final, a similar pattern was revealed regarding the presidential election of Democratic senator Barack Obama in 2008. Democrats won only 13 of the 37 gubernatorial races in 2010. The message is clear: There is a disadvantage for the party that wins the presidential election and then governs for the years before the Year 3 elections.

Money in Gubernatorial Races

Another pattern in these gubernatorial elections is not necessarily tied to when they are held, but to how the financing of these, and nearly all elections, have changed. What used to be party-led campaigns, and even Boss-run campaign politics, has changed considerably to become money-raising and spending campaigns. Since the total amount of money raised and spent in the 2010 midterm races is not known at the time of this writing, we can look at the previous elections and make reasonable predictions based on historical trends.

Table 4.3 Presidential Midterm, Even-Year Gubernatorial Elections, Money and Votes, 1978–2010

Year	Number of Candidates	TGE Votes[14]	2009$[15]	CPV-2009[16]
1978	299	47,180,492	326,641,079	6.92
1982	306	54,033,148	402,958,996	7.46
1986	296	51,494,871	531,225,199	10.32
1990	279	53,673,360	568,206,498	10.61
1994	336	60,168,543	607,338,573	10.09
1998	277	57,748,615	619,976,329	10.73
2002	319	62,696,370	1,006,246,484	16.05
2006	274	66,412,816	776,355,148	11.69

Source: Compiled by the author.

Note: There were 36 gubernatorial elections in every year up to 2006. In 2010, when Utah's governor, who was elected in 2008, began his new role as U.S. ambassador to China, a special election was held to validate the current governor's succession to office.

In the 1990 gubernatorial elections, candidates reported spending $344,508,344, or $6.42 per general election vote cast in the 36 campaigns.[17] In the 2002 elections, the amount of money spent in the 36 campaigns was $841,426,061, or $13.42 per general election vote.[18] It slipped slightly in the 36 races of the 2006 elections to $714,728,026, or $10.76 per general election vote.[19] These latter two races are important, as they point out another factor in these elections: Since most governors have the ability to serve a second or another term, they have an advantage of running for reelection rather than for an open seat. So, in the 2002 elections there were 20 open seats while 16 governors sought reelection; in 2006 there were only nine open seats while 27 governors sought reelection. Open seats increase the amount of money raised and spent because typically more candidates vie for the positions. In the 2010 midterm elections there were 24 open seats and only 13 governors seeking reelection.

The 2010 Gubernatorial Election Results

The first pattern to note in these 2010 elections is that, due to term limits on 15 incumbents, and eight incumbents who decided to not seek another term, there were 23 open-seat races. Because three of the incumbent governors seeking reelection were defeated, a record number of 26 new governors were elected: eight Democrats, 17 Republicans, and one Independent. Add to these numbers the five incumbent Democrats and six incumbent Republicans who won another term, and we see that Democrats won in 13 states, Republicans won in 23 states, and one Independent won in one state.

This set of Republican victories follows the pattern of the members of the president's opposition party faring quite well in these midterm Year 3 elections. Republicans won 23 of the 37 races (62 percent), Democrats won 13 of these races (35 percent), and an Independent won one of these races (3 percent). For 21 of these races (57 percent), the winning margin of the leaders was over 10 points (R: 15 races; D: six races). For six of these races (16 percent), the winning margin was between 5 and 10 points (R: four races; D: two races). And for 10 of these races (27 percent), the winning margin was less than 5 points (R: four races; D: five races; I: one race).

The second pattern to note is that, of the 14 incumbent governors seeking another term in office, 11 won their races, which is 78.6 percent (R: six; D: five). Only two Democratic incumbent governors seeking another term lost.[20] This is somewhat comparable to the 2006 races, when 25 of the 27 incumbents who ran won (93 percent), while only two Republican incumbent governors lost.[21] Incumbents did not fare as well in the 2002 races, in which 12 of the 16 incumbents who ran won (75 percent) and three Democratic and one Republican incumbent governor lost.[22]

The third pattern we see among the newly elected governors in 2010 is tied to their own political history. At the top of the list are those who have been successful in previous statewide election races: three former governors,[23] three former U.S. senators,[24] two state attorneys general,[25] and one lieutenant governor.[26] Then, at the substate political level, there were four former members of Congress who won,[27] four mayors or former mayors who won,[28] two state legislators who won,[29] and two county officials.[30] The other victors were two former U.S. court participants,[31] two businessmen,[32] and one medical doctor.[33]

Another situation tied to the 2010 elections is that two second-term governors, reelected in 2008, ran for an open U.S. Senate seat and won.[34] In early December, they resigned and left office to be sworn in as one of the state's two U.S. senators, and were replaced in office by new succession governors.[35]

Finally, we can see from table 4.4 that these gubernatorial races were spread rather evenly across the major regions of our country.

Table 4.4: 2010 Gubernatorial Races by Party, Region, and Margin of Victory

Region	Party		Races
Northeast	Democrats	6: [NY] [MD] (NH) (MA) {VT} {CT}	9
	Republicans	2: (PA) {ME}	
	Independent	1: {RI}	
South	Democrats	1: [AR]	8
	Republicans	7: [TN] [OK] [AL] [TX] [GA] {SC} {FL}	
Midwest	Democrats	2: {IL} {MN}	9
	Republicans	7: [NE] [KS] [SD] [MI] (IA)(WI) {OH}	
West	Democrats	4: [HI] [CO] [CA] {OR}	11
	Republicans	7: [WY] [UT] [ID] [AK] [AZ] [NV] (NM)	
Margin of Victory: [ ] +10 or more points; ( ) +5 points to less than 10 points; { } – less than 5 points			

Source: Compiled by the author.

In the Northeast, Democrats dominated the races, winning six of nine, and with an Independent winning in Rhode Island, the Republicans only won two states there. However, the Republicans dominated the remaining regions, winning seven in each of them while the Democrats only won only one in the South, two in the Midwest, and four in the West. It almost seems as if it might have been the Northeast versus the rest of the country.

Now, we will observe the transition of 26 newly elected governors into office and, conversely, the retirement of 26 incumbent governors. No matter who is sitting in that office, it will be a challenge, as the economy still reels from high unemployment and the states continue to have budgetary troubles. Some of these new governors may begin to wonder why they chose to become state leaders during such a tough time, once the initial thrill of winning gives way to the controversial, difficult decisions that must be made.

Endnotes

[1]In South Carolina, the earliest governors were chosen by the state legislature until 1865, when they were to be elected to two-year terms in the state's general election.

[2]In three of these states, the earliest governors were chosen or elected by the state legislature: Louisiana–by a joint vote of the two houses of the state legislature until 1846, when they were then to be elected by popular vote in the state's general election; North Carolina–by the general assembly until 1836, when they were then to be elected to two-year terms in the state's general election; and in Virginia–by the general assembly until 1851, when they were then to be elected to four-year terms in the state's general election.

[3]Number of States: D/R = those states with only Democratic and Republican candidates in the governor's race; D/R/O = those states with Democratic, Republican, and candidates from other parties, groups or independents in the governor's race.

[4]CA, KS, ME, MN, NH, OK, RI, SC, VT

[5]AK, AZ, CA, HI, MA, MI, NH, NY, OH, VT, WI

[6]AK, AZ, CO, CT, ME, MI, NY, OK, VT

[7]AL, AZ, FL, ID, IA, MD, NE, NM, OH, PA, RI, SC, SD, WI, WY

[8]AL, AR, FL, GA, KS, MD, MI, NE

[9]AL, FL, MD, MI, NE, NM

[10]CT, RI, SC

[11]NH, NM, OK, PA, RI, SC, WY

[12]AL, NE, NM, OK, PA, SD

[13]AK, AZ, AR, CA, CO, CT, FL, GA, HI, ID, IL, IA, KS, ME, MD, MA, MI, MN, NV, NH, NY, OH, OR, RI, SC, TN, TX, UT, VT, WI, WY

[14]"TGE Votes": Total votes cast in the general elections in these gubernatorial races.

[15]"2009$": Total amount spent in these campaigns converted into equivalent 2009$ using the CPI-U.

[16]"CPV 2009$": Cost Per Vote is the total amount spent, converted into 2009$, divided by the TGE Votes.

[17]In equivalent 2009$, these amounts would be $568,206,498 or $10.61 per GE vote.

[18]In equivalent 2009$, these amounts would be $1,006,246,484 or $16.05 per GE vote.

[19]In equivalent 2009$, these amounts would be $776,355,148 or $11.69 per GE vote.

[20]Chet Culver (D) in Iowa, and Ted Strickland(D) in Ohio.

[21]Frank Murkowski (R) in Alaska, and Robert Ehrlich (R) in Maryland.

[22]Donald Siegelman (D) in Alabama, Roy Barnes (D) in Georgia, Jim Hodges (D) in South Carolina, Scott McCallum (R) in Wisconsin.

[23]Jerry Brown (D) in California, Terry Branstad (R) in Iowa, and John Kitzhaber (D) in Oregon.

[24]Sam Brownback (R) in Kansas, and Lincoln Chafee (I) in Rhode Island (Chafee is also the former Republican U.S. senator from Rhode Island).

[25]Andrew Cuomo (D) in New York, and Tom Corbett (R) in Pennsylvania.

[26]Dennis Daugaard (R) in South Dakota.

[27]Nathan Deal (R) in Georgia, Neil Ambercrombie (D) in Hawaii, John Kasich (R) in Ohio, and Mary Fallin (R) in Oklahoma.

[28]John Hickenlooper (D) of Denver, Colorado; Daniel Malloy (D) of Stamford, Connecticut; Paul LePage (R) of Waterville, Maine; Bill Haslam (R) of Knoxville, Tennessee.

[29]Nikki Haley (R) state representative in South Carolina, and Peter Shumlin (D) state senate president in Vermont.

[30]Susana Martinez (R) district attorney in Dona Ana County, New Mexico; and Scott Walker (R) county executive in Milwaukee County, Wisconsin.

[31]Brian Sandoval (R) former U.S district court judge in Nevada, and Matt Mead (R) former U.S. attorney in Wyoming.

[32]Rick Scott (R) health company chief executive in Florida, and Rick Snyder (R) computer company executive.

[33]Robert Bentley (R) senior dermatologist in Alabama.

[34]North Dakota gov. John Hoeven (R), and West Virginia gov. Joe Manchin (D).

[35]The North Dakota new succeeding governor is former lt. gov. Jack Dalryple (R), and the West Virginia new succeeding governor is former state senate president Earl Ray Tomlin (D).

Chapter 5

Bringing Down the House: Reliving the GOP's Historic House Gains

by Isaac T. Wood

Director of Communications at University of Virginia Center for Politics; and House Editor of Sabato's Crystal Ball

L andslide. Avalanche. Tidal wave. Tsunami. The Republican gains in the U.S. House in November 2010 gave rise to as many natural disaster metaphors as new congressional careers. After the dust settled and the casualties were tallied, Republicans netted a gain of 63 House seats, the most in a half-century. In one night they tasted enough sweetness to extinguish the lingering bitterness of two straight election cycles of disappointment. These Republican leaders and congressional candidates established 2010 as the new pinnacle of conservative achievement.

Lost in their merriment and rejoicing was a clear understanding of how they reached such heights. Looking down from atop this new peak, the path they had taken was distant and hard to make out. The American people had sided with the GOP once and for all, some claimed. People were fed up with wishy-washy liberals and moderates, said others. It must have been the magic of Sarah Palin, a few suggested.

In fact, the secret elixir that gave Republicans their strength and delivered them electoral victory was a more complicated recipe. It contained bits of history, circumstance, strategy, and luck, which combined in a unique way not seen before in American politics.

Why They Won

On average, since the end of World War II, first-term presidents have surrendered 25 House seats to the opposing party in midterm elections. The fact that Barack Obama's presidency would also begin with a midterm setback should not have been a surprise, and never really was. This historical pattern, which has now held true for 11 of the 12 presidents since World War II, stems from a few reasons.

First, there is the fact that presidential elections often produce coattails, and midterms may represent a simple rebalancing as coattail victories are erased. Second, with a lower turnout in midterm elections, those who are most energized and likely to vote are those who are most upset with the status quo. When each party is out of power, it is looking for a way to express its opposition at the ballot box, while those who support the president may be more complacent. Lastly, there is a tendency of voters to prefer a divided or "balanced" government and they may choose to send additional House members to Washington who will check the president's power. These three theories—known as (1) *surge and decline theory*, (2) *negative voting theory*, and (3) *balancing theory*—all provide partial explanations for the midterm pattern that was repeated in 2010.[1]

In fact, Obama was also headed for a midterm letdown for another reason as well. The midterm election electorate is not only smaller, but also somewhat different from the presidential election universe of voters. In general, groups who vote at lower rates than the general population in presidential years show up in drastically lower numbers in midterm years. They can barely be bothered to vote once every four years in the election they consider to be most important, and are reluctant to exert the effort for a mere congressional midterm. These groups—particularly young voters and minorities—generally support Democrats, and their absence adds a handicap to the Democratic Party in midterm years.

In addition to the historical and demographic warning signs, Democrats were also at a high watermark entering 2010, following their significant pickups in 2006 and 2008. In those years—buoyed by the unpopularity of President George W. Bush and the Republican Party—they gained House seats across the country, including a large number of seats in normally Republican territory. Not only did this leave them devoid of opportunities to capture additional GOP seats, since they had picked the orchard clean over the past two elections, but it also left a lot of low-hanging fruit for Republicans to harvest if the winds shifted back in their favor.

There was a demographic component here as well. Many of the House seats Democrats gained in 2008 were won by candidates aided by Obama's presidential campaign and his coattails. Obama's historic candidacy excited large numbers of African American and young voters in particularly, who went to the polls to enthusiastically pull the lever for Obama and, while they were there, register their support for the local Democratic candidate, too.

With Obama off the ballot and the typical midterm malaise sitting in, Democratic freshmen in districts with high percentages of college-age or African American voters were particularly vulnerable. Steve Driehaus, for example, had ridden the Obama coattails to victory in Ohio's First District, which is 28 percent African American and, cast 16,000 more Democratic votes for president in 2008 than in 2004. Facing a rematch against the Republican incumbent he defeated in 2008, Driehaus's reelection odds were hampered by a drastically lower Democratic turnout just two years later, a story repeated in districts across the country.

By the time we at Sabato's Crystal Ball undertook our first full-scale ratings of all 435 House races, there were 106 contests that we considered to be competitive, and Democrats were on the defensive in 83—or 78 percent—of them. By May, the picture was coming into clearer focus with 85 Democratic-held seats in serious danger, 83 percent of the total number of competitive House races at that time.

Table 5.1—Competitive Districts as Rated by the Crystal Ball, February–November 2010

Totals include districts rated as "Likely Republican," "Likely Democratic," "Leans Republican," "Leans Democratic," and "Toss-up"

Date of Assessment	Total Competitive	GOP-Held	Dem-Held	% Dem-Held
February 25, 2010	106	23	83	78%
March 11, 2010	107	23	84	78%
May 27, 2010	103	17	85	83%
September 2, 2010	105	17	88	84%

September 9, 2010	108	17	91	84%
October 7, 2010	112	17	95	85%
October 14, 2010	116	17	99	85%
October 28, 2010	121	17	104	85%
November 1, 2010	122	17	105	86%

Source: Sabato's Crystal Ball, www.centerforpolitics.org/crystalball.

Before Labor Day, September 2, we wrote, "Republicans have a good chance to win the House." At that time we set our initial projection, 60 days out from Election Day, at a 47-seat gain for Republicans, although we cautioned, "If anything, we have been conservative in estimating the probable GOP House gains."[2] At that time, we saw 88 competitive Democratic-held House seats, but the number would leap up to 105 by our election eve update as more veteran Democrats became endangered and more GOP challengers gained traction.

The final election results bore out the predictions of a wide playing field that would allow the GOP to pick up the most House seats any party had gained since Democrats racked up 76 new congressional berths in 1948. A total of 80 House races were decided by 10 percent of the vote or less in 2010, the highest number since the mid-1990s. Similarly, 39 seats hosted contests where the winner and loser were separated by 5 percent of the vote or less, the most in a midterm since 1994.

Table 5.2—Competitive Race & Party Vote Totals for House Midterms, 1994–2010

Year	Races within 10%	Races Within 5%	Dem Votes	GOP Votes
1994	85	44	31,542,823	36,325,809
1998	42	17	31,391,834	31,983,612
2002	37	22	33,642,142	37,091,270
2006	61	36	42,316,631	35,866,160
2010	80	39	36,581,023	42,672,135

Sources: Office of the House Clerk, UVA Center for Politics Calculations.
Note: Race margins for purposes of this analysis are calculated as a function of the two-party vote.

Counting across the entire country, Republican candidates garnered 42.7 million votes for U.S. House in 2010, the most the party had ever won in a midterm year. For Democrats, it was a disappointing total of 36.6 million, nearly 6 million less than their record-setting 2006 tally. At least on a macrolevel, the election was something of a mirror image of 2006, when Democrats capitalized on voter disappointment with President George W. Bush and congressional Republicans. Nationwide, Republicans in 2010 won barely more House votes nationwide than Democrats did in 2006, while Democrats this year slightly outperformed the 2006 GOP slate.

It's the Economy, Stupid

While 2010 will likely be remembered for the Tea Party, the single greatest factor in the Republican victory was actually the economy, as exit polls would show overwhelmingly.[3] With national unemployment at 9 percent, the highest level in a federal election year since 1982, voters were growing impatient.[4] As Democrats controlled both the presidency and Congress, voters did not have to think too hard about which party deserved the lion's share of the blame.

As the exit polling data of those who voted in 2010 showed, the economy was the paramount issue of the election. Nearly two-thirds of voters (63 percent) called the economy the most important issue facing the country, and nearly half of those surveyed (49 percent) said they were "very worried" about the economic conditions, with only 13 percent "not too worried" or "not worried at all."

Other issues had the greatest impact when they related back to the economy. Republicans always felt their position to repeal the recently passed health care reform would be an electoral boon, but they actually gained greater traction by focusing on the expensive stimulus bill and cap-and-trade energy legislation, which they argued would increase utility costs for consumers and stifle American business.

Local issues, somewhat surprisingly, were mostly absent in congressional contests, which, after all, are an amalgamation of 435 different local elections. Just as in other wave years—like 1994 and 2006—voters across the country were casting their ballots based on the same sentiments. This was a big boost to the GOP. Instead of searching for dozens to hundreds of winning messages in individual competitive races, they could develop one strong national message for all their candidates to co-opt.

This national message focused on the economy, which was weak nationwide, and the Democratic leadership. Instead of taking on President Obama, the true head of the Democratic Party, Republicans smartly focused their fire on Nancy Pelosi, the House Speaker and leader of House Democrats. While Obama had pockets of popularity in some areas of the country, even in some GOP-targeted districts, Pelosi was unpopular among Republicans, independents, and conservative and moderate Democrats. Perhaps in part because she represented a district in San Francisco, seen as an out-of-touch liberal bastion, Pelosi lost control of her image and became a symbol of all that was wrong with Democrats in Washington.

Democrats tried their best to counter by changing the election from a "referendum" on the party in power to a "choice" between their party and the GOP. They highlighted moments when Republicans seemed to support privatizing Social Security, which seemed especially risky given the tumultuous stock market of the past few years, or when candidates refused to consider closing tax loopholes for companies that outsourced jobs.

Not unexpectedly, the Republican message won out. Voters were intrinsically suspicious of Democrats, who they saw as willing to say anything to keep their position of power, and they were not willing to listen to excuses about Republican obstructionism, which Democrats blamed for their failure to produce a more robust economy. The Republican message, on the other hand, matched voters' frustrations perfectly. Voters wanted the government to focus myopically on the economy and set aside all other goals for the time being. Republicans promised to cut spending and protect tax cuts, which seemed to match what voters were forced to do in their own households, and focused on the immediate concerns of most Americans.

The GOP Tide Lifts All Boats

The strength of the Republican message was able to compensate for even the least heralded of GOP candidates. A 30-second minor confrontation between seven-term Democratic representative Bob Etheridge and a pair of conservative college students was enough to catapult nurse Renee Ellmers, a newcomer to politics, over the 14-year incumbent, after a video of the incident was posted to YouTube.

Similarly, in Florida's Twenty-Second District, Republican challenger Allen West triumphed over Democratic incumbent Ron Klein, after losing to him by a 55 to 45 margin just two years earlier. West was a controversial figure, as his discharge from the military and association with biker groups made for attack-ad fodder. In 2010, however, he was able to parlay that controversy into a loyal following of Tea Party members who were skeptical of the media accounts.

The Republican wave was surging so high than even the second- and third-choice candidates of the National Republican Congressional Committee (NRCC), tasked with overseeing House races for the GOP—went on to victory in many races. In Idaho's First District, Raul Labrador defeated Sarah Palin-endorsed and NRCC-backed Iraq War veteran Vaughn Ward in the GOP primary, after Ward stumbled when faced with accusations of plagiarism. Labrador was never a strong fundraiser or a particularly well-known candidate, but he triumphed over conservative Democratic freshman Walt Minnick due to voters' revolt against the Democratic Party.

A similar storyline unfolded in Florida's Twenty-Fourth District, where eventual GOP nominee Sandy Adams was the third-string candidate in the eyes of many national Republicans, but after triumphing over a crowded field of GOP hopefuls, she unseated Democrat Suzanne Kosmas by a substantial 60-to-40 margin.

Even longtime Democratic incumbents who had survived the Republican wave of 1994, and had not faced a tough challenge in many years, became GOP targets as Election Day neared. Many of these veteran lawmakers represented conservative districts but had built a career on their moderate voting record and decades of constituent service, which caused many of them to believe that they would continue to win reelection as long as their name was listed on the ballot.

One example of this overconfidence was Virginia Democrat Rick Boucher, who served in Congress for 28 years. His defeat was an election night surprise and quite the stunning rebuke for a man synonymous with the district he had represented for nearly three decades. Boucher had not received under 55 percent of the vote—the standard yardstick for a competitive election—since 1984, but, by a 5 percent margin, he was defeated by a Republican candidate who did not even live within the district's borders.

Table 5.3—House Party Committee Fundraising, 2002–2010 Cycles

Total "Hard Dollar" Receipts through Post-General Reporting Period

Election Cycle	DCCC (Democratic)	NRCC (Republican)	Fundraising Gap
2001–2002	$58,067,160.22	$144,239,739.21	59.7%
2003–2004	$91,885,954.03	$175,072,854.55	47.5%
2005–2006	$137,022,484.47	$175,647,108.92	22.0%
2007–2008	$176,518,249.00	$118,226,373.00	33.0%
2009–2010	$104,813,088.00	$96,796,323.00	7.6%

Sources: Federal Election Commission Electronic Reports, www.fec.gov.

Just as Democrats won some unlikely victories in their 2006 wave, Republicans were able to capture seats in difficult districts, even without their top candidates on the ballot. Again turning the tables on the Democratic wave of 2006, the GOP managed to pick up these seats despite being outraised at the national congressional committee level. The GOP's NRCC—responsible for funding independent expenditures and assisting Republican House campaigns—was outraised by a margin of $97 million to $105 million, which is unusual, as Democrats typically have been outgunned at that level.

Making up for the narrow national committee deficit, Republican candidates raised $502 million to Democratic House candidates' mark of $465 million. Perhaps even more significantly, outside groups—emboldened by a series of court rulings relaxing campaign finance regulations—spent heavily in House races, mostly to boost GOP candidates. Particularly significant were the conservative U.S. Chamber of Commerce, which spent roughly $33 million overall on electioneering communications, and American Crossroads/Crossroads GPS, which spent just under $39 million in support of Republican candidates in Senate, House, and governor races. According to the Campaign Finance Institute, total spending on independent expenditures and electioneering communications by non-party groups rose by 130 percent from the 2008 level, due almost certainly to the new campaign finance rules which allowed a greater variety of expenditures with less disclosure requirements.[5]

Looking back at the races where incumbent Democrats were defeated by Republican challengers, the incumbents actually outspent the challengers even as they lost. The average losing incumbent raised $2.2 million by October 13, while the winning challengers raised just $1.5 million on average.[6] This pattern actually has occurred with some frequency in past House elections, and it seems the importance of challenger fundraising is in acquiring enough funding to make the race competitive, not necessarily in outspending the incumbent.

Counting the Casualties

As Democrats licked their wounds and tallied their losses after election night, there were a few categories where their losses were particularly apparent. Perhaps the clearest sign of how drastically the political sands shifted from 2008 to 2010 was the fate of freshmen Democrats who represented seats taken from Republican hands in the 2008 presidential election year. In 2008, Democrats captured a total of 26 seats that had been held by Republicans. Of those 26 freshmen Democrats who represented 2008 takeover districts, only five survived the GOP wave of 2010.

The story was similarly sad for sophomore Democrats representing some of the 30 seats picked up from the GOP in the 2006 Democratic wave. Of the 27 remaining sophomore Democrats from 2006 pickup districts, only 12 will be serving in the upcoming 112th Congress, as more than half either did not seek or were defeated for reelection.

Many of these Democratic losses are due to the nature of the districts that were picked up in those consecutive wave years of 2006 and 2008. Democrats took over many traditionally conservative districts and it was only a matter of time until the bill came due. Entering into the 2010 elections, there were 48 McCain Democrats—Democratic House members who represented districts won by Republican nominee John McCain in the 2008 presidential election. With that many incumbents representing unsteady territory, Democrats had a tough game of defense ahead of them. As it turned out, only 12 of the 48 McCain Democrats—a mere one-quarter—won their 2010 reelection battles and will continue their congressional careers.

As Republicans first began to sense the opportunity they were afforded in the upcoming midterm election, Democrats were skeptical that they could so easily lose the majority. Comparisons to 1994 abounded, and that was cause for at least a little optimism for Nancy Pelosi and her Democratic lieutenants. In particular, they noted that Republicans had picked up 24 open seats from Democrats in 1994—seats where the incumbent Democrat was no longer on the ticket, mostly due to retirements from Democratic members. In 2010, optimistic Democrats noted, they would only have to defend 20 open seats.

While it was true that Republicans would be forced to poach many more seats from members seeking reelection, the GOP also did quite well in winning open-seat contests. Of the 20 open seats left vulnerable by Democrats, a full 14 switched to Republican hands. By contrast, the GOP surrendered only one of their 23 open seats to Democrats.

More troubling for Democrats, however, was the number of first- and second-term members they would have to protect. In 1994, Republicans defeated 16 of the freshman Democrats who had been elected along with Clinton in 1992. In 2010, Democrats would have to defend 53 seats they had picked up in their 2006 and 2008 campaigns. Ultimately, Democrats would lose 23 of their freshman members, more than their 1994 losses, and much greater than the two GOP freshmen who were swept away by Democrats' 2006 wave.

Table 5.4—Characteristics of Districts Picked Up by Republicans in 1994

District	Democratic Incumbent	Terms	1992 percent*	District Tilt†
AZ-1	(Open Seat)	–	–	R + 13
AZ-6	Karan English	1	56%	R + 7
CA-1	Dan Hamburg	1	51%	D + 11
CA-19	Richard Lehman	6	50%	R + 11
CA-49	Lynn Schenk	1	55%	D + 6
FL-1	(Open Seat)	–	–	R + 31
FL-15	(Open Seat)	–	–	R + 18
GA-7	Buddy Darden	6	57%	R + 15
GA-8	(Open Seat)	–	–	R + 1
GA-10	Don Johnson	1	54%	R + 14
ID-1	Larry LaRocco	2	61%	R + 17
IL-5	Dan Rostenkowski	18	59%	D + 12

IL-11	(Open Seat)	–	–	D + 1
IN-2	(Open Seat)	–	–	R + 14
IN-4	Jill Long	3	62%	R + 21
IN-8	Frank McCloskey	6	54%	R + 4
IA-4	Neal Smith	18	63%	R + 2
KS-2	(Open Seat)	–	–	R + 6
KS-4	Dan Glickman	9	55%	R + 13
KY-1	Tom Barlow	1	61%	R + 1
ME-1	(Open Seat)	–	–	D + 2
MI-8	(Open Seat)	–	–	R + 2
MN-1	(Open Seat)	–	–	R + 2
MS-1	(Open Seat)	–	–	R + 14
NE-2	Peter Hoagland	3	51%	R + 21
NV-1	James Bilbray	4	60%	D + 6
NH-2	Dick Swett	2	63%	R + 3
NJ-2	(Open Seat)	–	–	R + 5
NJ-8	Herb Klein	1	53%	R + 3
NY-1	George Hochbrueckner	4	52%	R + 8
NC-2	(Open Seat)	–	–	R + 5
NC-3	Martin Lancaster	4	56%	R + 16
NC-4	David Price	4	66%	D + 4
NC-5	(Open Seat)	–	–	R + 16
OH-1	David Mann	1	100%	R + 6
OH-6	Ted Strickland	1	51%	R + 7
OH-18	(Open Seat)	–	–	D + 3
OH-19	Eric Fingerhut	1	53%	R + 3
OK-2	(Open Seat)	–	–	R + 0
OK-4	(Open Seat)	–	–	R + 15
OK-6	(Open Seat)	–	–	R + 15
OR-5	(Open Seat)	–	–	R + 1
PA-13	M. Margolies-Mezvinsky	1	50%	R + 1
SC-3	(Open Seat)	–	–	R + 22
TN-3	(Open Seat)	–	–	R + 6
TN-4	(Open Seat)	–	–	D + 2
TX-9	Jack Brooks	21	55%	D + 2
TX-13	Bill Sarpalius	3	60%	R + 13
UT-2	Karen Shepherd	1	52%	R + 13
VA-11	Leslie Byrne	1	53%	R + 7

WA-1	Maria Cantwell	1	57%	D + 4
WA-2	(Open Seat)	–	–	R + 0
WA-3	Jolene Unsoeld	3	56%	D + 3
WA-4	Jay Inslee	1	51%	R + 13
WA-5	Tom Foley	15	55%	R + 2
WA-9	Mike Kreidler	1	55%	D + 5
WI-1	Peter Barca	0.5	50%	R + 0

*"1992 percent" represents the share of the two-party vote the Democratic incumbent received in the 1992 election.

†"District tilt" gauges the district's party support in the 1992 presidential election versus the national average.

One area of unexpected gains that allowed Republicans to turn a good year into a great one was among veteran lawmakers. On Election Day 2010, the GOP defeated seven congressmen who had served 20 years or more. All of these longtime Democratic incumbents had survived the Republican rout of 1994 and many had been easily reelected year after year. With Republican fortunes rising, however, the GOP was able to put conservative districts into play, even where the incumbent had a long history with voters.

The most shocking examples of veteran lawmakers who were banished by GOP challengers in 2010 were a trio of Democratic committee chairmen: Ike Skelton in Missouri's Fourth District, John Spratt of South Carolina's Fifth District, and Jim Oberstar in Minnesota's Eighth District. Skelton was serving his seventeenth term and had not received less than 60 percent of the vote in an election since 1982. Although his district gave Obama only 38 percent of the vote in 2008, it seemed unlikely that the Armed Services Committee chairman and such a long-serving member could truly be in danger, even under a nightmare scenario for Democrats.

Similarly, Spratt had been seen as the odds-on favorite until a few months before his defeat at the hands of 43-year-old state senator Mick Mulvaney. The South Carolina Democrat's long winning record in the district, dating back to 1982, was outweighed by the overwhelming desire in the district to send a message to President Obama and Democrats in Washington. On election night, he lost by a 55-to-45 margin, a stunning 10 percent loss for such a well-known and long-tenured congressman.

Oberstar's defeat was the most surprising. After serving for 36 years, he had risen to the chairmanship of the Transportation and Infrastructure Committee. In all but one of his previous 18 House campaigns, he had received at least 60 percent of the vote and his district was actually Democratic at the presidential level, voting 53 percent both for Obama in 2008 and Kerry in 2004. Focusing on federal spending and the health care reform bill, retired airline and Navy pilot Chip Cravaack managed to defeat the venerable Oberstar by just over 1 percent of the vote.

Table 5.5—Characteristics of Districts Picked Up by Republicans in 2010

District	Democrat Incumbent	Terms	2008 percentage	District Tilt†
AL-2	Bobby Bright	1	50%	R+16
AZ-1	Ann Kirkpatrick	1	56%	R+9
AZ-5	Harry Mitchell	2	53%	R+6
CO-3	John Salazar	3	62%	R+5
CO-4	Betsy Markey	1	56%	R+4
FL-2	Allen Boyd	7	62%	R+8
FL-8	Alan Grayson	1	52%	R+1
FL-22	Ron Klein	2	55%	R+1
FL-24	Suzanne Kosmas	1	57%	R+4
GA-8	Jim Marshall	4	57%	R+10
ID-1	Walt Minnick	1	51%	R+17
IL-8	Melissa Bean	3	61%	D+3
IL-11	Debbie Halvorson	1	58%	D+0
IL-14	Bill Foster	1	58%	D+2
IL-17	Phil Hare	2	unopposed	D+4
IN-9	Baron Hill	5	58%	R+4
MD-1	Frank Kratovil	1	49%	R+13
MI-7	Mark Schauer	1	49%	R+1
MN-8	James Oberstar	18	68%	D+0
MO-4	Ike Skelton	17	66%	R+15
MS-1	Travis Childers	1	54%	R+15
MS-4	Gene Taylor	10	75%	R+21

NC-2	Bob Etheridge	7	67%	D+0
ND-AL	Earl Pomeroy	9	62%	R+8
NH-1	Carol Shea-Porter	2	52%	D+0
NJ-3	John Adler	1	52%	R+1
NM-2	Harry Teague	1	56%	R+4
NV-3	Dina Titus	1	47%	D+2
NY-13	Mike McMahon	1	61%	R+4
NY-19	John Hall	2	59%	R+2
NY-20	Scott Murphy	1	50%	R+2
NY-24	Michael Arcuri	2	52%	R+3
NY-25	Dan Maffei	1	55%	D+3
OH-1	Steve Driehaus	1	52%	D+2
OH-6	Charlie Wilson	2	62%	R+5
OH-15	Mary Jo Kilroy	1	46%	D+1
OH-16	John Boccieri	1	55%	R+5
OH-18	Zack Space	2	60%	R+8
PA-3	Kathy Dahlkemper	1	51%	R+4
PA-8	Patrick Murphy	2	57%	D+1
PA-10	Christopher Carney	2	56%	R+10
PA-11	Paul Kanjorski	13	52%	D+4
SC-5	John Spratt	14	62%	R+7
SD-AL	Stephanie Herseth-Sandlin	3	68%	R+8
TN-4	Lincoln Davis	4	59%	R+18
TX-17	Chet Edwards	10	53%	R+21
TX-23	Ciro Rodriquez	5	56%	R+2
TX-27	Solomon Ortiz	14	58%	D+0
VA-2	Glenn Nye	1	52%	R+2
VA-5	Tom Perriello	1	50%	R+5
VA-9	Rick Boucher	14	97%	R+13
WI-8	Steve Kagen	2	54%	D+1

†"District tilt" gauges the district's party support in the 2008 presidential election versus the national average.

Source: Compiled by the University of Virginia Center for Politics.

As Republicans cleared the decks of Democrats seated in moderate to conservative districts, they also washed away more than half of the Blue Dog Democrats. The Blue Dogs are a conservative consortium of Democratic House members who had become particularly well known during the health care reform battle, when many refused to go along with some of the more drastic Democratic proposals. Of the 54 self-identified Blue Dogs in Congress, only 26 survived the 2010 election, a shocking 44 percent casualty rate.[7]

Regionally, Republicans cleaned up in every corner of the country. After being shut out of New England in the previous Congress, Republicans picked up 15 seats in Northeastern states.[8] In New Hampshire, Republicans picked up both of the state's House seats, a dramatic swing that punctuated their regional revival. The GOP was also at an all-time low in New York, holding just two of the state's 29 House seats on Election Day 2010. After all the votes were tallied, however, the GOP picked up six new House seats across the state, a particularly strong showing considering how poorly the three Republicans running in statewide races performed. Republicans also cleaned up in Pennsylvania, winning five Democratic-held seats to take the majority in the state's House delegation, as they now hold 12 of the 19 seats.

Figure 5.1—2010 Republican Gains in the U.S. House of Representatives

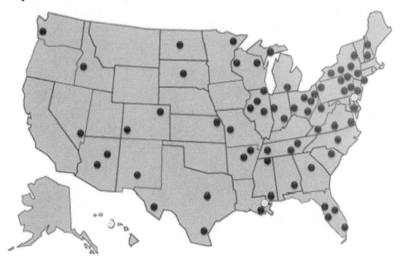

NOTE: Each dark dot indicates a seat picked up by Republicans. The three lighter dots in Hawaii, Louisiana, and Delaware represent the three seats picked up by Democrats.

Map credit: Joe Figueroa, University of Virginia Center for Politics.

The South, a traditional stronghold for the modern Republican Party, provided the largest share of the gains. The GOP picked up 21 seats, including four in Florida and three each in Tennessee, Texas, and Virginia. In Virginia, the Republican gains canceled out the Democratic pickups of 2008, when Democrats had managed to prevail in three Republican-held districts. Democrats had been successful across the South in 2006 and 2008 by running conservative candidates with strong local profiles, but Republicans highlighted their votes for Nancy Pelosi for Speaker as justification enough for booting them from office.

In the West, Democrats had some good news, as not a single one of California's 53 House seats switched parties in 2010. The West was certainly the strongest region for Democrats, but even there they lost a net seven seats—two in Arizona, two in Colorado, plus a seat each in Idaho, Nevada, New Mexico, and Washington while picking one up in Hawaii.

The Midwest was another bright spot for the GOP as they picked up a net total of 20 House seats, falling just a seat short of the South for the best Republican regional showing. The key states for Republicans were Illinois—where the GOP picked up four seats and held onto an open seat that looked quite vulnerable—and Ohio—where Republicans picked up a remarkable five seats, halving the number of Democratic congressmen in the state in just one election night.

A Winner's Circle Census

Now that we know who lost in 2010, the logical question remains, who won? In some ways, the crop of Republican freshmen looks different from past years, with a slate of Tea Party supporters and first-time candidates winning seats in Congress. In other ways, however, this year's freshman class will look similar to past years, with many state legislators winning promotions to Washington, and self-funding businessmen spending their way into congressional seats.

Nowhere are the similarities to the past more evident than with the group of "redshirt freshmen," Republican incumbents who had been defeated in past years but who won back their seats in this more favorable political climate. This year there were five of these comeback kids: Tim Walberg (Michigan's Seventh District), Steve Chabot

(Ohio's First District), Steve Pearce (New Mexico's Second District), Charlie Bass (New Hampshire's Second District), and Mike Fitzpatrick (Pennsylvania's Eighth District).

Three of these five congressmen were ousted in 2008—Walberg, Chabot, and Pearce—while the other two won back seats they lost in 2006 after they each sat out the 2008 election. Bass's victory came in an open-seat contest, but the other four each ousted the Democrat who had defeated them in their reelection bid loss.

In addition, there were several repeat candidates who had never won election to Congress before, but not for lack of trying. In total, five Republicans won races this year after having been denied in their 2008 bids. One of these rematch reversals was in Pennsylvania's Eleventh District, where Republican Lou Barletta defeated 13-term Democrat Paul Kanjorski in their third face-off, the first coming way back in 2002. In addition, Scott Tipton in Colorado defeated Democratic representative John Salazar, who he had faced in 2006 before taking a hiatus from congressional candidacy to run successfully for the state legislature in 2008.

On the other side of the coin was a healthy dose of first-time candidates, many of them motivated and supported by the Tea Party. Scott Rigell, who defeated Democrat Glenn Nye in Virginia's Second District, had spent his professional life as a car dealer before throwing his hat into the ring in 2010. Jon Runyan, who took the New Jersey Third District seat from John Adler, was a well-known football player for the Philadelphia Eagles before turning his attention to electoral politics. Other first-time Republican candidates had backgrounds as farmers, pizza parlor restaurateurs, and even a gospel singer.[9]

A statistical anomaly among this year's incoming Congress is a decline in the number of women serving in the House for the first time since 1979.[10] When the 112th Congress begins, only 72 women will be among the membership, just 17 percent of all House members. The new total represents one less congresswoman than in the 111th Congress, the first decline in female representation in over three decades. Some observers have suggested that the lack of winning women can be attributed to the diminished fortunes of Democrats, who typically have more female House members, although Republicans did have a large number of women running under their banner this year. In fact, of the 13 new women who were elected to Congress, nine were Republicans.

Republicans, for the first time since Oklahoman J. C. Watts left Congress in 2003, will have an African American member of their caucus—two in fact. One is Allen West, the controversial former army officer who defeated Ron Klein in Florida's Twenty-Second District after losing by almost 10 percent of the vote in 2008. The other African American Republican to join the House is Tim Scott, an insurance agent and state legislator. Scott won a heated Republican primary in South Carolina's First District, beating the son of former segregationist presidential candidate Strom Thurmond, in a runoff to capture the GOP nomination. Soon after, he easily won the general election in this heavily conservative district, he was elected as one of the two Republican freshman class representatives to the GOP leadership, highlighting a rising star that could help add some diversity to the party's image.

Gridlock Goes to Washington

If you want to understand the likely results of the 112th Congress, do not believe everything you see on television. Republican ads were filled with promises of tax cuts, budget balancing, and—most of all—repealing the "Obamacare" health care reform. Instead, the likely GOP achievement can be summed up in one word: gridlock. With Obama still in office for two more years and Democrats clinging to a slim Senate majority, anything significant Republicans manage to pass in the House will be sure to die a quick death as soon as it leaves the House chamber. As long as Obama sees health care reform as his signature achievement and his legislative legacy, why would he sign a bill that dilutes it in the slightest?

While gridlock may be frustrating for the new Republican House members, it actually seems to fit the wishes of the voters quite well. Since World War II, divided party control in Washington has been in place most of the time. The voters have added yet another check and balance to the constitutional ones dreamed up by the Founding Fathers.

Some undoubtedly remember the limited, but not insignificant, legislation that came out of the divided government following the Republican takeover in 1994, when Bill Clinton was still president. Might compromise allow that scenario to reoccur in the next two years? There are a few signs from the 2010 election that suggest it will not.

In order to have compromise you must first have some willingness on both sides of the aisle to come to the bargaining table. For Democrats, that willingness has been greatly diminished as the ranks of moderate and conservative Democrats have been decimated, with less than half of the Blue Dog Democrats returning to Congress in January. On the Republican side, cooperation with Democrats looks even more remote than it did before the 2010 elections got underway. One of the major storylines of this election cycle was the influx of conservative challengers to moderate Republican incumbents and candidates, in GOP primaries across the country. The greatest fear for some Republican members is no longer the general election, but the primary, ensuring that they will vote as they see fit to stave off any challenge from the right. Not only will this make them more conservative in their voting, but they will also be likely to heed the Tea Party rallying call of "no compromise" which was expressed loud and clear by conservative grassroots leaders both before and after the 2010 election.

As House Democrats were culled to their more liberal members and House Republicans are attempting to shore up their conservative credentials, there is now a much larger ideological gap in the Congress. When that is coupled with the mentality of "no compromise" and the reality of a divided government, the forecast for the next Congress consists of much more political posturing than policy production.

Gazing Into the "Crystal Ball": The 2012 House Elections

Already, diehard politicos and antsy politicians are asking, what is next? With the cacophony of the election still ringing in our ears, the question is, what can 2010 tell us about the next two years of American politics and what will be different in 2012, when all 435 House seats are once again on the ballot.

Seeing how quickly the pendulum swung from a Democratic year in 2008 to a Republican one in 2010, Democrats are naturally optimistic about their chances in the next election. Republicans, though, remember how Democrats were able to take the House majority in the midterm election in 2006 and expand on it in the presidential election of 2008, and they wonder whether they can pull off that trick themselves.

There are certainly a lot of unknowns as we look ahead to 2012 and attempt a preliminary forecast. The most glaring question mark is the economy. The political playing field will shift drastically depending on whether the economy is strong in November 2012 or whether it continues to languish. There is also the Tea Party, which emerged as a force for the first time in 2010, and has yet to take a permanent form. Will it continue to support conservative candidates within the Republican Party or, if the Tea Party voice is muffled in the House leadership, will it splinter off to run its own candidates in 2012?

There is also a huge difference between the two election years that is already apparent. While 2010 was a midterm year with no nationwide presidential race on the ballot, in 2012 there will be a Republican presidential candidate and a Democratic presidential candidate—and perhaps others—who will help to define their party in the eyes of voters. We do not yet know the identity of the Republican nominee and what message that candidate might send, but we do know that the presence of a presidential election will increase turnout across the nation. For Democrats who were burned by so-called "sporadic voters" in 2010, that sounds like quite the improvement. Republicans, however, could still achieve a significant victory in 2012 House races if their presidential candidate is able to win the presidency and usher in a cadre of congressional candidates on his or her coattails.

Neither party should get its hopes up for another wave of similar proportions to the GOP tsunami of 2010. Historically, midterm years have produced the greatest swings in the House. Over the past three decades, neither party has gained 25 House seats in a single presidential year, while that feat has been accomplished four times in midterm years over that same time period. While the average midterm House seat gain for the party out of power is around 24 seats, the victorious party in presidential election years has won a more modest average of 13 seats over the past 15 presidential elections.

Democrats in particular should take note and temper their optimism as they will need to gain 25 House seats in order to take the majority following the 2012 election, a tall order given historical precedent. The last time either party captured the House majority in a presidential year was way back in 1948. The last four switches of party control in the House have all occurred as a result of midterm elections instead.

Even without knowing some of the specifics of 2012, we can take stock of each side's vulnerability. Entering 2010, Democrats were hampered by the number of seats they held in Republican territory. In 2012, that danger is even greater for both sides, as it will be difficult to win a congressional race in a district that is voting for the other party's nominee for president. Using the 2008 presidential results as a yardstick, there are now 12 McCain Democrats—those Democratic House members who represent districts that voted for the Republican nominee for president in 2008—and 62 Obama Republicans—who represent districts that the Democratic presidential nominee carried. As each party drafts its target list over the coming months, expect to see these districts and incumbents make an appearance. If Obama repeats his coast-to-coast victory by a similar margin, there is certainly a cadre of House Republicans who could be vulnerable to Democratic challengers riding Obama's coattails.

A potential concern for Democrats, on the other hand, may be retiring members. Now that they have lost the House majority, some older members might consider retirement, rather than serve in the minority. For the most senior Democrats, a committee chairmanship holds a strong allure, but when the majority is lost and that is taken away, the incentive to serve out a few more years away from home can be much diminished. The problem from an electoral perspective is that open seats, where no incumbent is on the ballot, are much more difficult—and expensive—to retain than when a longtime House member is running for reelection. If Democrats are forced to defend a significant number of open seats in 2012, it would provide an opening for Republican candidates and would force Democrats to allocate valuable resources to defending their own districts, instead of playing offense against GOP members.

On the other side of the coin, there are Democrats who were defeated in 2010 who may not be ready to accept an early retirement. If the political winds shift and Democrats manage to find some momentum in the next year, defeated Democrats may sign up for rematch bids against the Republicans who defeated them, just as five Republican ex-congressmen did successfully in 2010.

Looking ahead to 2012, Democratic hopes will be pinned on the president, as their stock will rise and fall with his reelection odds. Republicans must hope for a strong GOP presidential nominee and work to avoid public relations disasters like the 1995 government shutdown, which arrested the party's momentum after their 1994 landslide: Bill Clinton took that opening and exploited it, winning a reelection plus a handful of House seats as well. As 2011 dawns, the chapter closes on the 2010 House elections and the opening lines of the 2012 election cycle are already being written.

Table 5.6—House Districts Picked Up by Republicans in 2010

District	Candidate	Percent Votes	Total Votes
AL-2	Martha Roby (R)	51%	111,332
	Bobby Bright (D)*	49%	106,465
AR-1	Rick Crawford (R)	52%	92,558
	Chad Causey (D)	43%	77,551
AR-2	Tim Griffin (R)	58%	119,962
	Joyce Elliot (D)	38%	79,183
AZ-1	Paul Gosar (R)	50%	106,423
	Ann Kirkpatrick (D)*	43%	92,681
AZ-5	David Schweikert (R)	52%	99,640
	Harry Mitchell (D)*	43%	82,225
CO-3	Scott Tipton (R)	50%	126,227
	John Salazar (D)*	46%	114,763
CO-4	Cory Gardner (R)	53%	129,919
	Betsy Markey (D)*	41%	99,907
FL-2	Steve Southerland (R)	54%	134,912
	Allen Boyd (D)*	41%	104,415
FL-8	Daniel Webster (R)	56%	123,464
	Alan Grayson (D)*	38%	84,036
FL-22	Allen West (R)	54%	115,411
	Ron Klein (D)*	46%	97,051
FL-24	Sandy Adams (R)	60%	145,932
	Suzanne Kosmas (D)*	40%	98,612
GA-8	Austin Scott (R)	53%	102,025
	Jim Marshall (D)*	47%	91,799

ID-1	Raul Labrador (R)	51%	126,055
	Walt Minnick (D)*	41%	101,870
IL-8	Joe Walsh (R)	49%	97,403
	Melissa Bean (D)*	48%	96,850
IL-11	Adam Kinzinger (R)	57%	128,250
	Debbie Halvorson (D)*	43%	94,939
IL-14	Randy Hultgren (R)	51%	111,808
	Bill Foster (D)*	45%	97,792
IL-17	Bobby Schilling (R)	53%	103,666
	Phil Hare (D)*	43%	84,820
IN-8	Larry Bucshon (R)	58%	115,778
	Trent Van Haaften (D)	37%	75,480
IN-9	Todd Young (R)	52%	118,055
	Baron Hill (D)*	42%	95,301
KS-3	Kevin Yoder (R)	59%	134,692
	Stephene Moore (D)	38%	87,920
LA-3	Jeff Landry (R)	64%	108,957
	Ravi Sangisetty (D)	36%	61,909
MD-1	Andy Harris (R)	55%	146,272
	Frank Kratovil (D)*	41%	111,237
MI-1	Dan Benishek (R)	52%	120,077
	Gary McDowell (D)	41%	94,805
MI-7	Tim Walberg (R)	50%	114,384
	Mark Schauer (D)*	45%	103,650
MN-8	Chip Cravaack (R)	48%	133,485
	James Oberstar (D)*	47%	129,083
MO-4	Vicky Hartzler (R)	50%	113,500
	Ike Skelton (D)*	45%	101,507
MS-1	Alan Nunnelee (R)	55%	116,036
	Travis Childers (D)*	41%	85,400
MS-4	Steven Palazzo (R)	52%	101,318
	Gene Taylor (D)*	47%	91,838

NC-2	Renee Ellmers (R)	50%	91,924
	Bob Etheridge (D)*	48%	89,829
ND-AL	Rick Berg (R)	55%	129,586
	Earl Pomeroy (D)*	45%	106,371
NH-1	Frank Guinta (R)	54%	120,588
	Carol Shea-Porter (D)*	43%	95,689
NH-2	Charlie Bass (R)	48%	108,550
	Ann Kuster (D)	47%	104,874
NJ-3	Jon Runyan (R)	50%	106,175
	John Adler (D)*	47%	100,069
NM-2	Steve Pearce (R)	55%	91,954
	Harry Teague (D)*	45%	73,995
NV-3	Joe Heck (R)	48%	128,703
	Dina Titus (D)*	47%	126,781
NY-13	Michael Grimm (R)	51%	59,346
	Michael McMahon (D)*	48%	55,056
NY-19	Nan Hayworth (R)	53%	104,154
	John Hall (D)*	47%	92,986
NY-20	Chris Gibson (R)	55%	123,511
	Scott Murphy (D)*	45%	99,255
NY-24	Richard Hanna (R)	53%	96,686
	Michael Arcuri (D)*	47%	86,037
NY-25	Ann Marie Buerkle (R)	50%	99,594
	Dan Maffei (D)*	50%	98,935
NY-29	Tom Reed (R)	56%	101,219
	Matthew Zeller (D)	44%	78,578
OH-1	Steve Chabot (R)	52%	101,691
	Steve Driehaus (D)*	45%	87,394
OH-6	Bill Johnson (R)	50%	101,558
	Charlie Wilson (D)*	45%	91,018
OH-15	Steve Stivers (R)	57%	137,441
	Mary Jo Kilroy (D)*	38%	93,578

OH-16	Jim Renacci (R)	52%	112,902
	John Baccieri (D)*	41%	89,008
OH-18	Bob Gibbs (R)	53%	105,727
	Zach Space (D)*	40%	79,257
PA-3	Mike Kelly (R)	55%	108,398
	Kathy Dahlkemper (D)*	44%	86,674
PA-7	Patrick Meehan (R)	55%	133,146
	Bryan Lentz (D)	43%	106,214
PA-8	Michael Fitzpatrick (R)	53%	126,404
	Patrick Murphy (D)*	46%	109,157
PA-10	Thomas Marino (R)	55%	109,603
	Christopher Carney (D)*	44%	89,170
PA-11	Lou Barletta (R)	54%	99,837
	Paul Kanjorski (D)*	45%	83,250
SC-5	Mick Mulvaney (R)	54%	119,776
	John Spratt (D)*	45%	99,034
SD-AL	Kristi Noem (R)	48%	153,683
	S. Herseth Sandlin (D)*	45%	146,571
TN-4	Scott DesJarlais (R)	57%	104,025
	Lincoln Davis (D)*	38%	70,329
TN-6	Diane Black (R)	67%	128,340
	Brett Carter (D)	29%	56,057
TN-8	Stephen Fincher (R)	59%	98,483
	Ray Herron (D)	38%	64,701
TX-17	Bill Flores (R)	61%	106,275
	Chet Edwards (D)*	36%	63,926
TX-23	Quico Conseco (R)	49%	74,761
	Ciro Rodriguez (D)*	44%	67,212
TX-27	Blake Farenthold (R)	48%	50,954
	Solomon Ortiz (D)*	47%	50,155
VA-2	Scott Rigell (R)	53%	88,007
	Glenn Nye (D)*	42%	70,306

VA-5	Robert Hurt (R)	50%	119,242
	Tom Perriello (D)*	47%	110,566
VA-9	Morgan Griffith (R)	51%	95,835
	Rick Boucher (D)*	46%	86,791
WA-3	Jaime Herrera (R)	53%	148,921
	Denny Heck (D)	46%	131,103
WI-7	Sean Duffy (R)	52%	132,248
	Julie Lassa (D)	44%	113,113
WI-8	Reid Ribble (R)	54%	144,050
	Steven Krogen (D)*	45%	118,617
WV-1	David McKinley (R)	50%	89,915
	Mike Oliverio (D)	49%	88,558

*Indicates incumbent.
Source: Compiled by the University of Virginia Center for Politics.

Table 5.7—House Districts Picked Up by Democrats in 2010

District	Candidate	Percent Votes	Total Votes
DE-AL	John Carney (D)	56%	173,443
	Glen Urquhart (R)	41%	125,408
HI-1	Colleen Hanabusa (D)	53%	93,930
	Charles Djou (R)*	46%	82,499
LA-2	Cedric Richmond (D)	64%	83,653
	Joseph Cao (R)*	33%	43,364

*Indicates incumbent.
Source: Compiled by the University of Virginia Center for Politics.

Endnotes

[1] Alan I. Abromowitz, "Forecasting the Midterm Election," Posted online by Sabato's Crystal Ball, www.centerforpolitics.org/crystalball/articles/aia20090 90301/.

[2]Larry J. Sabato, "Sixty Days to Go," Posted online by Sabato's Crystal Ball, www.centerforpolitics.org/crystalball/articles/ljs2010090201/.

[3]Exit polling data, www.cnn.com/ELECTION/2010/results/polls/#val=USH00p3.

[4]U.S. Bureau of Labor Statistics, data.bls.gov/PDQ/servlet/SurveyOutput Servlet.

[5]Campaign Finance Institute, www.cfinst.org/Press/PReleases/10-11-05 /Non-Party_Spending_Doubled_But_Did_Not_Dictate_Results.aspx.

[6]Ibid.

[7]Jon Ward, "Conservative Blue Dog caucus cut in half," Posted online by the Daily Caller, dailycaller.com/2010/11/03/conservative-democrat-blue-dog -caucus-cut-in-half/#ixzz14DhTzkID.

[8]For purposes of this analysis, regions are defined as follows:
Northeast: CT, DE, ME, MD, MA, NH, NJ, NY, PA, RI, VT, WV.
Midwest: IL, IN, IA, KS, MI, MN, MO, NE, ND, OH, SD, WI.
South: AL, AR, FL, GA, KY, LA, MS, NC, OK, SC, TN, TX, VA.
West: AK, AZ, CA, CO, HI, ID, MT, NV, NM, OR, UT, WA, WY.

[9]ABC News, "Vote 2010 Election: First-Time Candidates for House Are a Diverse Bunch," abcnews.go.com/WN/vote-2010-election-candidates-timers -diverse-backgrounds/story?id=12026698.

[10]Center for American Women and Politics, www.cawp.rutgers.edu/press _room/news/documents/PressRelease_11-23-10.pdf.

PART 2

Money and Media

Chapter 6

Money Worries: Campaign Financing and Spending in the 2010 Elections

by Dr. Michael Cornfield

The Michael Cornfield Company; Adjunct Professor of Political Management, George Washington and George Mason University

Introduction: The Story Line

Big flows of money into campaign communications, especially television advertising, became a prominent aspect of the election discourse in 2010. With prominence came considerable disagreement and disputation. Democrats cried foul at the waves of dollars, while Republicans trumpeted them as a sign of freedom. Political professionals, who rely on a percentage of that money for their income, worked hard on both sides of the partisan divide to raise and spend it on behalf of candidates and causes. Political activists on the progressive left and the Tea Party right, along with President Obama, expressed disgust with this "Washington" way of doing things; some of them worked the Internet, the pavements, and the press in order to advance their election favorites without giving into what they regarded as a corrupt culture of influence-peddling and vote-buying—even as others in their ranks raised big money precisely to fight a big-money culture.

When the topic is money in politics, it can be hard to disentangle the rhetorical smoke from the financial fire. But the basic story line of campaign spending in the 2010 elections is not subject to differences of interpretation. In retrospect, it divides neatly into the form of a three-act play:

1) Federal courts and regulators loosen legal and symbolic constraints on campaign spending with a series of decisions, of which the most notable is *Citizens United v. Federal Election Commission*, issued by the Supreme Court on January 21, 2010.

2) Record amounts of money are spent for a midterm election: an estimated $4 billion at the federal level, up from $1.61 billion in 1998, $2.18 billion in 2002, and $2.85 billion in 2006.[1] Some of this money comes from unidentified sources, some of it comes in unidentified amounts, and some of it runs through a new type of political organization, the "Super-PAC."

3) The Republicans win more House seats than any party in any midterm election since 1938, and gain seats in the Senate and state contests as well.

The obvious conclusion to draw from this sequence of events is that corporate power, unleashed by a sympathetic court, spent a lot of money to work its will on the electoral process. This occurred largely out of public view on behalf of the party of big business, the Republicans, who will now use their enhanced governmental authority to return the favor by pushing a pro-business policy agenda.

Throughout 2010, the story surfaced in bits and pieces on political blogs, talk shows, and newspaper pages. Some people drew the obvious conclusion; some even from the get-go. *Citizens United v. Federal Election Commission* became a touchstone for intense partisan argument; about the only thing that critics and defenders agreed on was that it opened the wallets of donors who wanted to remain anonymous and give in large amounts –but even that slender item of consensus took time to form.[2] Just how much money was contributed due to *Citizens United* is unknown almost by definition. But some spending figures were available before the election, and they showed that the dollar totals climaxed with a crescendo as the election neared. The Wesleyan Media Project, working with data compiled by the Campaign Media Analysis Group, reported that $250 million worth of national and cable television advertising was purchased between October 6 and October 20, more than the $220 million expended between January 1 and September 15. Of the $120 million spent by noncandidate campaigns on such ads between September 1 (a convenient starting point for measuring expenditures in general election campaigns) and October 20, $85 million supported Republicans.[3] The formal organizations of the two major parties and their candidates raised roughly the same amount of money in 2010.[4] Democratic House candidates spent $421.6 million, while their Republican counterparts spent $419.1 million. Democratic Senate candidates spent $288.7 million and Republicans $303.5 million. However, the $293 million attributed by the Center for Responsive Politics (CRP) to other sources, including those freed to give after *Citizens United*, broke for Republicans by a 2:1 margin.[5]

Close observers of American politics could read a portent of the pendulum swing out of the mid-October news that Texas home building magnate Bob Perry had donated $7 million to American Crossroads, a Super-PAC closely affiliated with stalwart Republican strategist Karl Rove. In 2004, Perry had been a principal donor for the controversial Swift Boat Veterans for Truth committee. Observers noting his big gift in the closing stages of the 2010 race might have also wondered how much Perry gave to the PAC's sibling organization, Crossroads GPS. (The "GPS" stands for Grassroots Political Strategies, not Global Positioning System, although perhaps its namers had the technological marvel in mind.) As a 501(c)4 "social welfare nonprofit," Crossroads GPS did not have to identify its donors.[6] The patently public coupling of the two campaign spending entities turned word of Perry's largesse into an ambiguous signal: simultaneously, "I've given much more," and "I just want you to think I've given much more." A few days earlier, meanwhile, the most famous benefactor of Democrats in recent years, billionaire financier George Soros, had been more blunt. He told a *New York Times* reporter that he was sitting out this cycle because "I don't believe in standing in the way of an avalanche."[7] The perception sparked by the news about these late money decisions by big donors ran to the Republicans' advantage. The election results confirmed this perception, particularly in the House races.

Seen as a whole or in parts, the spectacle of election campaign contributions poses basic questions about the impact of money on American politics, government, and public life. In trying to answer them, we encounter yet a third clash of perspective. It is not just Democrats and Republicans who view the money flows differently, and not just political insiders and outsiders. There are vocationally driven differences between journalists and political scientists which must be reconciled, or chosen between, in coming to grips with the implications of the often glaring disparities, amounts, and—oxymoronic though it may be—secrets bound up in the coursing of dollars through the campaigns and elections system.

Let's take up a few of these basic questions, FAQ style, in order to see where the obvious conclusion to the story is justified, and where it is not.

What's the Big Deal with *Citizens United*?

Citizens United overturned a key provision of the Bipartisan Campaign Finance Act of 2002 (BCRA), popularly known as the McCain-Feingold Act. (Senator McCain, an Arizona Republican, won reelection in 2010. Senator Feingold, a Wisconsin Democrat, lost his seat after three terms.) Before the decision, corporations, both for-profit and nonprofit, and unions had numerous ways to spend large amounts of money in order to affect the outcome of elections.

The decision legitimated several previously barred options for campaign spending:

- Money could now be spent more freely from general treasury funds.
- It could now be spent more freely on ads that ran on broadcast, cable, or satellite transmissions.
- More ads could now expressly advocate voting for or against a candidate.
- More ads could now run during the last 30 days before a primary election, or 60 days before a general election.

Meanwhile, if these new alternatives were not satisfactory, corporations and unions still could—and did—contribute money free from scrutiny by the Federal Election Commission (FEC), provided that they did so via a nonprofit entity organized under the tax code, subject to different regulations administered by the Internal Revenue Service. They could also, under the right circumstances, claim a news media exemption.

Citizens United retained requirements that BCRA-defined and FEC-regulated electioneering communications contain a disclaimer

("'Y' is responsible for the content of this advertisement"), and that PAC donors' identities be disclosed. Prohibitions remained in place on contributions from non-nationals, and direct donations from general treasuries to candidates and parties. Justice Anthony Kennedy, writing for the 5 to 4 majority, argued that "All speakers, including individuals and the media, use money amassed from the economic marketplace to fund their speech," and corporations and unions were no different in that regard. BCRA "was an outright ban, backed by criminal sanction." Thus, "the Court cannot resolve this case on a narrower ground without chilling political speech, speech that is central to the meaning and purpose of the First Amendment." Justice John Paul Stevens, writing for the minority, saw no such "outright ban." In his opinion, the majority had taken "a sledgehammer rather than a scalpel" to campaign finance law, overturning precedents and ranging beyond the case questions at hand. He jabbed at the "originalist" doctrine espoused by some in the majority by noting that the authors of the Constitution were greatly concerned with monetary corruption, and that they had limited corporate involvement through chartering. They would not find favor with this decision, he contended.[8]

Any doubt that *Citizens United* was a *cause célèbre* vanished six days after it was announced, when President Obama assailed the decision with the Supreme Court justices seated in front of him during his 2010 State of the Union Address. Justice Alito accepted the branch-to-branch glove slap. As soon as the president asserted his belief that the decision "reversed a century of law" and would "open the floodgates for special interests—including foreign corporations—to spend without limit in our elections," the television feed cut to Justice Alito, who shook his head and could be seen saying, "Not true."

The general public disapproved of the decision by wide and bipartisan margins. A *Washington Post* poll taken in early February 2010 found that 85 percent of Democrats, 81 percent of independents, and 76 percent of Republicans opposed *Citizens United*. The opposition was still lopsided in late October, when a CBS News/*New York Times* poll recorded 72 percent agreeing with the statement that the law should limit "groups not affiliated with a candidate" from spending money freely on campaign advertisements.[9] It should be noted that the distribution of opinion with respect to an issue tells us little about the relevance of those opinions to voting choices, grassroots activism, and trust in the political system. Historically, campaign finance has not been a high priority with voters. Published polling has yet to weigh in on whether the level of popular concern changed in the wake of the decision and controversy, and then as the rest of the story unfolded.

Did Money Make a Difference in the 2010 Election Results?

Numerous organizations certainly tried hard to affect election outcomes through smart and heavy spending. Two unions, the AFL-CIO (acronym for American Federation of Labor and Congress of Industrial Organizations) and AFSCME (acronym for American Federation of State, County and Municipal Employees), were the first to spend significantly under the expanded definition of permissible expenditures, most notably in a campaign against Senator Blanche Lincoln of Arkansas before the June 8 Democratic primary.[10] During the summer, the Club for Growth, a Republican PAC whose former head, Pat Toomey, would soon be elected to the Senate from Pennsylvania, and Commonsense Ten, a just-launched Democratic counterpart, sought and received FEC approval to collect unlimited funds from corporations, unions, and individuals in order to make independent expenditures. These became known as "SuperPACs." By mid-September, 33 SuperPACS had registered with the FEC.[11] By Election Day, according to CRP estimates of attributable spending, conservative SuperPACs and other outside-the-party and candidate expenditures topped $190 million, more than twice the $85 spent by "outside" liberal groups and individuals.[12]

A cautionary episode occurred in the summer involving the Target Corporation. The retail giant spent $150,000 in support of business policy positions taken by Tom Emmer, the Republican candidate for governor in its home state of Minnesota, only to hear severe criticism from company stakeholders large and small regarding the candidate's anti-gay stance. Several institutional investors openly questioned the company's procedure for campaign spending decisions. Activists videotaped a Minnesota woman who has a gay son-in-law as she returned $226.32 in merchandise and her cut-up Target credit card to her local store. Target's CEO tried to quell the incident by offering a public apology, but a boycott ensued nevertheless.[13]

In mid-October, the president's State of the Union comment about foreign dollars in campaign spending came back into play. *Think Progress*, a blog run by the liberal think tank, Center for American Progress, reported that the general accounts fund of the U.S. Chamber of Commerce, the biggest spending conservative trade advocacy organization in the cycle, included money from foreign sources.[14] This suggested illegal and unpopular activity had occurred. The Chamber and Republican leaders took quick and vigorous exception, arguing that its institutionalized procedures prevented dues and contributions paid by multinational corporations based outside the United States from being used for electioneering.[15] A furious volley of ads, speech remarks, talk-show comments, and blog posts ensued. Since the Chamber did not open its accounting books—a legal choice given its status as a not-for-profit—the controversy ended with the *Think Progress* report slammed as desperate partisan rhetoric, but its assertion and implied accusation left unrefuted.

Newsmaking events like these provide extra impetus to the perennial and supervening question about the power of money to decide election results. (For the record: Lincoln won the primary but lost her Senate seat, and the Minnesota governor's race remains undecided at this writing.) Political scientists frequently attempt to answer the overarching question with the help of mathematical models. They devise a formula to predict the number of House seats that will switch, based what has happened in previous midterm elections under a range of discrete recurring conditions (notably, indicators of the state of the macroeconomy, party identification, presidential popularity, and incumbency). The predicted and actual outcomes are then compared, and the difference may be attributed to other factors, including campaign spending. By this method, the Republicans indeed over-performed in act three of the 2010 story, winning at least 10 to 15 more seats then quantitatively forecast by a collection of models.[16] Campaigning made a difference.

Adequate funding is vital to effective campaigning, especially for challengers.[17] But the best campaigners of 2010, like their predecessors, did more than just raise and spend money. They conducted audience research, devised and tested messages, selected messengers and media channels, and adjusted the contents and placements based on sophisticated analysis (including, yes, more modeling) of the early results. They competed against opponents doing similar things, in view of a vocal audience of activists and commentators whose reactions reached voters in most of the very same channels carrying the campaign messages. The multitude of factors that determine electoral victory, only some of which are calculable as variables and are subject to the influence of campaigners, make it practically impossible to answer the morally charged question of whether one can buy an election victory. Those with certain answers about the power of money in an election are probably confirming biases they held in advance of the campaign cycle.

Was Too Much Money Raised and Spent?

The latest statistics documenting the spiraling of campaign spending regularly generate headlines and headshakes. Trend data is particularly impressive. We know already, for instance, that the receipts of House and Senate race winners doubled in a dozen years, from a respective mean of $650,000 and $4.1 million in 1998 to $1.2 million and $8.3 million in 2010.[18] But in politics, as in most marketplaces, money is wrongly spent only when it does not yield appropriate value. So before we can answer this question, we must be precise about what the money is being spent on.

Contrary to some beliefs and accounts, campaign money does not purchase votes. The common journalistic format of calculating the "cost per vote" for big-spending candidates and groups reinforces this misconception. One recent example, following the formula of dividing the amount a campaign spends by the number of votes it garners, concluded that the top spenders in the 2010 federal elections were Senate Republican candidates Sharron Angle in Nevada and Linda McMahon in Connecticut. The headline: "At $97 per vote, top spenders lost."[19] Yet, plainly, votes were not being bought. Those who voted for Angle and McMahon did not get a Benjamin for their act (factoring in a slight bonus). In those exceptional cases where voters do get paid, they should of course be prosecuted along with those paying for and implementing the bribe, just as candidates should be sanctioned when they divert campaign money into personal use.

Campaign money does not go to voters or candidates, but to media, consultants, and staff, for the purpose of telling voters about the candidates. As obvious and complex as this is, the summary statistic does not reflect it. The proper indicator for the cost of campaigns is "cost per potential voter," the amount a campaign spends divided by the number of people eligible to respond favorably and vote for the candidate. Given a 40 percent turnout rate in midterm elections, the number falls considerably, to approximately $39 per vote in the two races cited. More importantly, using the proper statistic avoids aggravating a generally inappropriate worry about vote-buying in America. But the adjustment still does not answer the value question.

Some reject the idea that campaign spending is worthwhile, on the grounds that the messages are typically of low and even mischievous quality. Indeed it is hard to defend the demagoguery, personal attacks, mind-numbing repetitions of banalities, and robocalls that go off in the middle of the night. There is no hard correlation between message quality and expenditure. It must be admitted, as well, that the growth of information clutter makes it more costly for any message, good or bad on content terms, political and nonpolitical, to get through to its intended audience.

There are other spending drivers from the campaign insiders' point of view. The winner-take-all structure of most American elections motivates campaigns to go all-out; losing campaigns with unspent money elicit reactions of disgust from the cognoscenti. Candidates also collect and spend as much money as they possibly can because of the personal costs of losing. Many incumbents want to stay in their jobs (all right, they want to keep their jobs in the worst way), and, again, this is not for monetary rewards, because they would make much more money the minute they left office. The close partisan division of seats over time, compounded by the polarized intensity of debate, boosts the stakes. Finally, the monumental scale of the financial crisis and the record of recent governments in coming to grips with it has spurred more interest and more spending.

These factors should be considered when citizens reckon the value of campaign spending. It is respectable, if not downright compelling, to take the position that even Meg Whitman gave democracy good value from a message-per-potential voter perspective. Through October 16, the Republican nominee for governor of California had spent an eye-popping, non-presidential race record-setting $140 million of her own money, plus $20 million that her campaign raised.[20] That is a lot of cash to people with household money worries. The sight of big self-financed candidates losing brings private satisfaction to them and others—one reason journalists love to report it. (The Center for Responsive Politics has calculated that fewer than one in five of the 58 federal candidates in 2010 who spent more than $500,000 on their race won, so happy day.[21]) From a civic perspective, however, $160 million at an arbitrary price of $.10 per eligible voter would bring the 28 million in the California electorate approximately one message a week for one year. Too much, for too long? Perhaps. Then again, this is the spending record-setter for message saturation for non-presidential campaigns. The point to remember when judging the expensiveness of campaigning is that money buys candidates an audience. The California audience needed to hear from its first-time candidate for governor given the parlous conditions of California government. That counts as value for them.[22]

What Does Secrecy Cloak?

The dominant presumption fed by the campaign discourse is that where there is secrecy, there is corruption. *Citizens United* triggered a flurry of finger-pointing at the existence of obvious secrecy in campaign financing and spending. Public attention was directed to unknown names funding known entities, which contributed unknown amounts to known candidates and messages. The partisan voices and media businesses engaged in this practice know that calling attention to a secret simultaneously attracts attention for oneself.

Sometimes, the public is served by secret-proclaimers. The watchdog catches a burglar, as was most famously, and literally, the case in the Watergate scandal. Even when inquiries find no criminal ring reaching from campaign operatives to party leaders and elected officials, the uncovering of secrets benefit the democratic republic by bringing to light neglected aspects of the campaign money scene. This was exemplified in 2010 by Jane Mayer's reportage in *The New Yorker* about the extensive political underwriting activities of multibillionaire energy industrialists Charles and David Koch.[23]

On other occasions, railing against secrets stretch evidence so thin that it becomes tantamount to linguistic corruption. A front page story in the *New York Times* "Week In Review" section run late in the campaign year spun a tale of speculation, insinuation, and guilt by association out of the fact that Fred Malek, a deputy director in Richard Nixon's notorious reelection organization, was now the founder of the American Action Network, a two-pronged nonprofit engaged in campaign spending whose donors are unknown. The article, entitled "Return of the Secret Donors," presented no information indicative of wrongdoing by Malek or his Network. But it referenced Watergate in 16 of its 29 paragraphs, capped with a photomontage of Nixon and his secretary, Rose Mary Woods, keeper of the secret list of donors to his campaign. The closing quote equated secret funding with "guaranteed corruption."[24] Readers could not help but worry.

Corruption certainly exists, but so do false positives, where all secrecy masks is aboveboard negotiating and strategizing. In order to deter corruption, campaign finance law prohibits certain types of coordination between party personnel and funders operating independently. As the FEC guidebook puts it, "When financing communications in connection with federal elections, it is important to understand that the rules differ significantly depending on whether the communication is coordinated with a candidate or party committee or is produced and distributed independently. In general, amounts spent for coordinated communications are limited, but independent expenditures are unlimited."[25] The mandated self-segregation of political actors seems like a poor solution to the genuine problems of public affairs, including corruption. Besides, coordination can be achieved tacitly. For example, party committees can simply publish their advertising buys, enabling independent or outside spenders to spot gaps and opportunities.[26]

What Does Disclosure Accomplish?

Congressional Democrats introduced legislation to blunt the impact of *Citizens United* on April 29, 2010. The DISCLOSE Act (acronym for Democracy Is Strengthened by Casting Light On Spending in Elections), as its acronymic and full titles suggested, relied heavily on the power of public information to fix what its backers regarded as a rupture in the election system. It required organizations that spent money on political campaigns not just to identify large donors in public, but in the ads their money funded. The DISCLOSE Act passed the House. However, even after a more modest version was introduced, it fell one vote short in the Senate of attaining a filibuster-proof majority.

The disclosure system for national campaigns consists today of compliance data compiled by candidates, PACs, parties, and independent spenders, delivered to and released by the Federal Election Commission, and arranged for ready public consumption by a few journalism companies and, chiefly, the nonprofit, foundation-funded Center for Responsive Politics. There are a few glaring black holes and speed bumps, most egregiously the Senate's refusal to adopt electronic filing. But this system improves with each cycle, thanks to database integration tools and efforts.

There is a disjunction between the disclosure system and the expectations it arouses. The compound of shame and guilt that exposure crystallizes can be a power for good, but that depends on the popular mood, the psyches of those involved, and other ineffable factors. As a rule, however, sunshine is not a political disinfectant with anything like the automatic chemical effect the famous mixed metaphor implies.[27] Instead, disclosure is frequently necessary, but probably an insufficient means to create an informed electorate, honest government, and morally sound politics. The rest of the work to reach these ends entails providing would-be corruption-checkers with context specifics so that they understand campaign financial data from several perspectives. It has been the goal of this essay to illustrate these perspectives and their importance in drawing story and data lessons. Acting on disclosure to curb and deter corruption also requires that its civic agents possess adequate time to verify and discuss a charge, as well as the capacity to respond. None of these arrive in public with the regularity and ease of access like information from an instituted disclosure program. Because they do not, disclosure can be infuriating for not empowering as much as it appears to promise.

What Wasn't Emphasized in the 2010 Story?

Every narrative leaves out details and minimizes themes—sometimes for political reasons, always with political implications. The basic story line describing the role of money in the 2010 midterm election, preoccupied with and configured by the court case drama as it was, neglected several aspects of the topic. Here are three concerns that did not make the cut.

First, the suspicion that campaign contributions buy the recipient officials' allegiance, as later manifest in policymaking commitments (speeches, bill cosponsorships, votes, and, the most prominent symbol of late, earmarks) is so worrisome that it need not be stoked by the charge of secrecy. This is too complex a subject to be addressed here. It involves a comparably large flow of money into lobbying over periods of years, if not decades, to determine results. There was a case in point to be made involving BP and the oil and gas industry, and less recent and vivid cases involving the parties to financial regulation and health care legislation. But they were not part of this story.

Second, there is procedural corruption (legal, but corrosive) in that incumbents fail to adequately perform oversight and negotiating activities because they pour so much time into fundraising. This is an opportunity-cost argument suited to political scientists, a hard story for journalists and partisans to tell. The corruption charge surfaced as Republicans and Tea Party exponents railed at Congress for acceding to the president's agenda, but those were purportedly corrupt acts of commission, not omission. As for legal corruption, two cycles earlier, the Democrats could harp on Jack Abramoff and Tom DeLay; in 2010 the scandals involving Charlie Rangel and Maxine Waters were not pursued with similar attention.

Third, in as much as donating to a campaign is associated with attentive interest and participation in politics, the low number of Americans who contribute money to election campaigns is a legitimate worry.[28] Only 14 percent of registered voters, or roughly 10 percent of citizens eligible to vote, donated money to campaigns in 2010. That is up slightly from 2006, and relatively even in donations to both Democrats and Republicans.[29] It is a chronic concern nonetheless, one masked by the discourse predilection to focus on the money and the big money-givers instead of the disengaged.

Conclusion: More Than a Language Game

Money attracts attention in politics for a variety of reasons. It offers metrics of success to campaigners and clues of culpability to investigative journalists and their audiences. Its distribution patterns across sources and destinations are conducive to data analysis that can illuminate how politics is working and what Americans want from politicians. Its movements from sources to destinations are signs of influence. But the versatility of money as an enabler of action and a mark of power also renders it a tricky subject. "Outside money" will seem heroic or intrusive, depending on whether the recipient is an ally or opponent. "Independent expenditures" are instruments of free and autonomous citizens, or unjust and unaccountable powers, again depending on one's view of the side to which they are directed.

Does this mean that the topic of money in politics is a pure language game; a competitive exercise in argumentation and narration with no firm basis for judgment apart from one's ideological and class predilections? Not if one believes in the rule of law (even as it changes, sometimes radically). It is worth a few false positives undergoing scrutiny and due process to better apprehend cheaters and deter their ilk. Not if one believes in popular sovereignty and the benefits of robust debate to good government, for then policies should be pursued which amplify "small money" and "cheap speech" as counterweights to "big money."[30] Matching programs, whereby public or private funds may be contributed to the extent they correspond to citizens making small donations, hold promise in this regard.

A good case can be made that money is legitimate when it comes from outside formal party and campaign organizations and outside the district where a race is occurring. A good case can be made against spending limits. However, the use of general treasury fund money seems wrong. A shopper in a store and an employee in a closed shop should not have to worry about their purchase and dues dollars finding their way into campaign politics. The campaign discourse seems doomed to occasionally get bogged down in trench warfare-style arguments pegged to the fungibility of money, but sanctioning general fund money as a source makes that worse than necessary. Only by hiving off general funds can organizations operate in a global economy without being unfair or unfairly accused. Finally, and most importantly, money in politics should be money for politics. Justice Kennedy's logic needs to be inverted: It is not that GE should be as free as Soros and Perry to draw down their general accounts, but that Soros and Perry need to be as limited as GE once was. Perhaps we should require individuals to form PACs to distribute money, and abide by what remains of the rules governing PACs.

New spending records seem all but certain to be set in the 2012 cycle. Scarcely a week had elapsed after the election before one of President Obama's top political aides, David Axelrod, floated a fundraising target for the reelection campaign: "If they [referring to the "outside" Republican groups] spent $200 million on Senate races, they are capable of adding a half-billion to a billion in a race for control of the presidency."[31] There will be more rules changes, partisan wrangles, irresistible stories, and sharper resonance with the money worries of Americans about the financial precariousness of their households and their national future. We must work for full explications of what gets disclosed to keep our heads and preserve our core values as the cash zooms around our campaigns. For that, we have three places to look: civic education, including journalistic coverage; the policymaking issue network; and the campaign marketplace, which incubates innovative techniques and technologies to raise and spend money.

Endnotes

[1]OpenSecrets.org Blog, "Election 2010 to Shatter Spending Records as Republicans Benefit from Late Cash Surge," October 27, 2010, www.open secrets.org/news/2010/10/election-2010-to-shatter-spending-r.html .

[2]Michael Luo, "Money Talks Louder Than Ever in Midterms," New York Times, October 8, 2010, www.nytimes.com/2010/10/08/us/politics/08donate .html?emc=eta1.

[3]Erika Fowler, Wesleyan Media Project press release, "Ad Spending in Federal and Gubernatorial Races in 2010 Eclipses $1 Billion; $250 Million in Last Two Weeks Alone," election-ad.research.wesleyan.edu/2010/10/27 /spending-update/.

[4]Through FEC filings up to October 13, there had been approximately $1.4 billion raised on behalf of Republican candidates for federal office, and $1.3 billion for Democrats. OpenSecrets.org blog, "Bad News for Incumbents, Self-Financing Candidates in Most Expensive Midterm Election in U.S. History," November 4, 2010, www.opensecrets.org/news/2010/11/bad-night -for-incumbents-self-finan.html.

[5]Ibid.

[6]For an example of a news article reporting Perry's donation while also mentioning Crossroads GPS, see Holly Bailey, "Swift Boat donor gives $7 M to American Crossroads," Yahoo! News *The Upshot* blog, October 21, 2010. news.yahoo.com/s/yblog_upshot/20101021/el_yblog_upshot/swift-boat-donor -gives-7-million-to-american-crossroads.

[7]Sewell Chan, "Soros: I Can't Stop a Republican 'Avalanche,'" *New York Times*, October 11, 2010, thecaucus.blogs.nytimes.com/2010/10/11/soros-i -cant-stop-a-republican-avalanche/.

[8]*Citizens United v Federal Election Commission*, 130 S.Ct. 876 (2010). Full text at www.scribd.com/doc/25537902/Citizens-Opinion.

[9]Both polls may be found at www.pollingreport.com/politics.htm.

[10]T. W. Farnam, "Unions outspending corporations on campaign ads despite court ruling," *Washington Post*, July 7, 2010, www.washingtonpost.com/wp-dyn /content/article/2010/07/06/AR2010070602133.html.

[11]Michael Beckel, "The Rise of 'SuperPACs' Continues, Leaving Voters in Dark as Attack Ads Fill Airwaves," *OpenSecrets* blog, September 22, 2010, www.opensecrets.org/news/2010/09/the-rise-of-super-pacs.html.

[12]Michael Beckel, "Led by Karl Rove-Linked Groups, 'Super PACs' and Nonprofits Significantly Aid GOP in Election 2010," *OpenSecrets* blog, November 5, 2010, www.opensecrets.org/news/2010/11/led-by-karl-rove-linked -groups-nonp.html.

[13]Eric Kleefeld, "Target Faces Backlash for Supporting Tom Emmer in Post-Citizens United World, *TPMDC* blog, July 30, 2010, tpmdc.talking pointsmemo.com/2010/07/target-faces-backlash-for-supporting-tom-emmer -in-post-citizens-united-world.php#more.

[14]Lee Fang, "Exclusive: Foreign-Funded 'U.S.' Chamber of Commerce Running Partisan Attack Ads," *ThinkProgress* blog, October 5, 2010, thinkprogress.org/2010/10/05/foreign-chamber-commerce/.

[15]See, for example, Ed Gillespie, "Democrats' desperation tactics on campaign finance,' *Washington Post*, October 12, 2010, www.washingtonpost .com/wp-dyn/content/article/2010/10/11/AR2010101103054.html.

[16]See the special section edited by James E. Campbell, "Forecasts of the 2010 Midterm Elections," *PS: Political Science & Politics*, 43:4, pp. 625–641, journals .cambridge.org/action/displayJournal?jid=PSC.

[17]Alan S. Gerber, "Does Campaign Spending Work?" *American Behavioral Scientist* 47:5, January 204, 541–574, abs.sagepub.com/content/47/5/541 .short, p. 558.

[18]Campaign Finance Institute press release, "Non-Party Spending Doubled in 2010 But Did Not Dictate the Results," November 5, 2010, Table 3, www.cfinst.org/Press/PReleases/10-11-05/Non-Party_Spending_Doubled_But_Did_Not_Dictate_Results.aspx.

[19]T. W. Farnam, "At $97 per vote, top spenders lost," *Washington Post*, November 9, 2010, www.washingtonpost.com/wp-dyn/content/article/2010/11/09/AR2010110900153.html.

[20]Lance Williams, "How Whitman Spent $160 Million," California Watch blog, californiawatch.org/watchblog/how-whitman-spent-160-million-6292.

[21]OpenSecrets.org blog, "Bad News for Incumbents, Self-Financing Candidates in Most Expensive Midterm Election in U.S. History," November 4, 2010, www.opensecrets.org/news/2010/11/bad-night-for-incumbents-self-finan.html.

[22]A related question asks whether television station owners deserve to get so much of that money, especially since they are licensed oligopolists in terms of broadcast spectrum. It is true that they do not bilk candidates and by extension their contributors by gouging political ad-placers with artificially high prices; if anything they can and in some cases must offer lower prices than the market will bear. Even so, they do not deserve the money. Or they don't without providing the public more than they give them in terms of public interest programming, including free airtime for qualified candidates. But even if justice were served here, and candidates got that free time, they would still spend above that if they had it.

[23]Jane Mayer, "Covert Operations," *New Yorker*, August 30, 2010, www.newyorker.com/reporting/2010/08/30/100830fa_fact_mayer.

[24]Jill Abramson, "Return of the Secret Donors," *The New York Times*, October 17, 2010, www.nytimes.com/2010/10/17/weekinreview/17abramson.html.

[25]Federal Election Commission, *Coordinated Communications and Independent Expenditures*, www.fec.gov/pages/brochures/indexp.shtml. As of this writing in early November 2010, the guidebook had not been updated to reflect *Citizens United*.

[26]Jeanne Cummings, "Republican groups coordinated financial fire power," *Politico*, November 3, 2010, www.politico.com/news/stories/1110/44651.html.

[27]The eminent lawyer, future supreme court justice, and quintessential progressive Louis Brandeis wrote that "Sunlight is said to be the best of dis-

infectants" in a *Harper's Weekly* magazine article that became a chapter in his 1914 book *Other People's Money.*

[28]Four political scientists make the case for policies that will encourage more Americans to donate to campaigns on these grounds in Anthony J. Corrado, Michael J. Malbin, Thomas E. Mann, and Norman J. Ornstein, *Reform in an Age of Networked Campaigns: How to foster citizen participation through small donors and volunteers.* www.brookings.edu/reports/2010/0114_campaign_finance_reform.aspx. Report released January 14, 2010. (Before the *Citizens United* decision was announced.)

[29]Pew Research Center for the People & the Press survey report, "Ground War More Intense Than 2006, Early Voting More Prevalent," people-press .org/report/666/, October 21, 2010, Section 2. Calculation of donors as a percentage of eligible voters based on a 71% registration rate as reported by the U.S. Census Bureau, "Voting and Registration in the Election of November 2008," July 20,2009, www.census.gov/hhes/www/socdemo/voting /publications/p20/2008/index.html, Table 1.

[30]Richard L. Hasen, "Political Equality, the Internet, and Campaign Finance Regulation," p. 7. Loyola-LA Legal Studies Paper No. 2008–11. Available at SSRN: ssrn.com/abstract=1116774.

[31]Jeanne Cummings, "White House open to Democratic outside groups in 2012," Politico.com, November 9, 2010, www.politico.com/news/stories/1110 /44868.html.

Chapter 7

The Impact of the Federal Election Laws on the 2010 Midterm Election

by Michael E. Toner

Former Chairman of the Federal Election Commission;
currently Head of the Election Law and Government Ethics
Practice Group at Bryan Cave LLP in Washington, DC

and Karen E. Trainer

Senior Reporting Specialist at Bryan Cave LLP

The 2010 midterm election, only the second midterm election conducted under the McCain-Feingold campaign finance law, witnessed record-breaking fundraising by congressional candidates and outside interest groups. The 2010 election was the most expensive midterm election on record, with candidates, political parties, and outside groups collectively spending a reported $4 billion.[1] To put that figure in perspective, this amount was 33 percent larger than the total spent on the 2006 midterm election, which, prior to 2010, was the most expensive midterm election in history. The historic 2010 election spending figure was also more than was spent on the 2000 presidential election, and nearly as much as was spent on the 2004 presidential election.[2] Of the $4 billion that was expended on the 2010 elections, over $564 million[3] was reportedly spent by outside groups and $2 billion by congressional campaign committees.[4]

However, perhaps the most important campaign finance trend to emerge in 2010 was the full flowering of outside interest groups, which spent hundreds of millions of soft-dollar funds on hard-hitting advertisements and aggressive get-out-the-vote efforts in targeted U.S. House and U.S. Senate races. Taking advantage of favorable federal court rulings, and operating outside of the hard-dollar fundraising restrictions of the McCain-Feingold campaign finance law,[5] outside group spending in 2010 dwarfed the expenditures of the national party committees and, in many races, even exceeded the spending of the candidates themselves.[6]

Outside entities first came to the fore in the 2004 presidential election, when groups such as the Swift Boat Veterans for Truth and Americans Coming Together spent tens of millions of dollars in support of George W. Bush and John Kerry. Yet, in the aftermath of the U.S. Supreme Court's landmark ruling in early 2010 in *Citizens United v. FEC*—which struck down legal restrictions on the content and timing of corporately financed advertisements in connection with federal elections—outside group spending played an even larger role in the 2010 midterm election. Absent major changes to the federal election laws in the future, significant outside group spending will likely be a permanent part of the federal campaign finance landscape and may play a key role in the 2012 presidential election.

Congressional Candidates Raised Record-Breaking Amounts of Money in 2012 and Republican House Challengers Posted Particularly Strong Fundraising Numbers

U.S. House and U.S. Senate campaign committees spent an estimated $2 billion in connection with the 2010 elections. This aggregate total is 43 percent more than the $1.4 billion that was spent by House and Senate campaigns in connection with the 2006 and 2008 elections. Republican House and Senate candidates as a whole raised more than their Democratic opponents, which is highly unusual given that the Democratic Party controlled both the House and Senate during the 2010 election cycle.

Table 7.1 compares House and Senate campaign fundraising in the 2010 election cycle with the fundraising figures for the 2008 and 2006 elections.

Table 7.1—Comparison of House and Senate Campaign Committee Fundraising, 2006–2010[7]

2010			
Republican House	$502 Million	Democratic House	$465 Million
Republican Senate	$356 Million	Democratic Senate	$294 Million
Republican Total	$858 Million	Democratic Total	$759 Million
2010 Total Campaign Fundraising: $1.64 Billion			
2008			
Republican House	$441 Million	Democratic House	$533 Million
Republican Senate	$193 Million	Democratic Senate	$217 Million
Republican Total	$634 Million	Democratic Total	$750 Million
2008 Total Campaign Fundraising: $1.39 Billion			
2006			
Republican House	$454 Million	Democratic House	$415 Million
Republican Senate	$244 Million	Democratic Senate	$289 Million
Republican Total	$698 Million	Democratic Total	$704 Million
2006 Total Campaign Fundraising: $1.43 Billion			

Source: Center for Responsive Politics 2010 Stats at a Glance, www.opensecrets .org/overview/index.php; 2008 Price of Admission, www.opensecrets.org/bigpicture /stats.php?cycle=2008; 2006 Price of Admission, www.opensecrets.org/bigpicture /stats.php?cycle=2006.

As table 7.1 indicates, Republican Senate candidates as a whole outraised their Democratic opponents by 17 percent during the 2010 election cycle, and Republican House candidates collectively outraised their Democratic opponents by 7 percent.

Although the amount of money federal candidates raise and spend is often a key factor in determining who wins and loses on Election Day, higher-spending candidates are by no means assured of electoral success, particularly in a wave election such as the 2010 election. In fact, as table 7.2 and table 7.3 indicate, just over half of the candidates who spent the most funds in the 10 most expensive House and Senate races were victorious in 2010.

Table 7.2—Campaign Spending in the Most Expensive Senate Races

State	Who Spent the Most?	Did the Candidate that Spent the Most Win?
AZ	McCain	Yes
CA	Boxer	Yes
CT	McMahon	No
FL	Greene	No
IL	Kirk	Yes
MO	Blunt	Yes
NV	Reid	Yes
PA	Toomey[8]	Yes
WA	Murray	Yes
WI	Feingold	No

Sources: Center for Responsive Politics Most Expensive Races, www.opensecrets.org/overview/topraces.php, CQ MoneyLine District Profiles.

Table 7.3—Campaign Spending in the Most Expensive House Races

State	Who Spent the Most?	Did the Candidate that Spent the Most Win?
FL-08	Grayson	No
FL-22	Klein	No
MN-6	Bachmann	Yes
NY-1	Altschuler	No
NY-20	Murphy	No
NY-23	Doheny	No
OH-8	Boehner	Yes
SC-2	Wilson	Yes
TX-17	Flores	Yes
WA-8	DelBene	No

Sources: Center for Responsive Politics Most Expensive Races, www.opensecrets.org/overview/topraces.php, CQ MoneyLine District Profiles.

A number of congressional candidates were prolific contributors to their own campaigns in 2010, but the vast majority of these self-funding candidates were defeated.[9] Only one of the eight federal candidates who contributed in excess of $3.5 million to their own campaign was victorious on Election Day,[10] and only four of the 15 federal candidates who contributed $1 million or more to their own campaigns were elected. Connecticut Senate candidate Linda McMahon loaned or contributed $49.1 million to her campaign.[11] This amount made McMahon the second-largest congressional self-funder in history, behind only Jon Corzine, who contributed $60.2 million to his Senate campaign in 2000.[12] Tables 7.4 and 7.5 below identify the amounts contributed by the top self-funding congressional candidates in 2010; only three of the 20 top self-financing candidates were ultimately elected to office.

Table 7.4—U.S. Senate Candidate Contributions and Loans[13]

Candidate	Party	State	Amount	Election Result
McMahon	R	CT	$46,600,161	Lost
Greene	D	FL	$23,788,077	Lost
Pagliuca	D	MA	$7,590,643	Lost
Johnson	R	WI	$6,764,184	Won
Binnie	R	NH	$6,587,594	Lost
Fiorina	R	CA	$5,511,080	Lost
Raese	R	WV	$4,660,113	Lost
Blumenthal	D	CT	$2,269,607	Won
Lowden	R	NV	$1,924,985	Lost
Malpass	R	NY	$1,600,500	Lost

Source: Center for Responsive Politics, "Self-Funded Candidates Face Tough Odds in Election 2010," www.opensecrets.org/news/2010/10/self-funded-candidates-face -tough-o.html.

Table 7.5—U.S. House Candidate Contributions and Loans[14]

Candidate	Party	State	Amount	Election Result
Flinn	R	TN	$3,500,000	Lost
Rigell	R	VA	$2,424,364	Won
DelBene	D	WA	$2,284,033	Lost
Ganley	R	OH	$2,213,417	Lost
Altschuler	R	NY	$2,010,213	Lost
Hartman	R	KS	$1,995,025	Lost
Doheny	R	NY	$1,690,000	Lost
Iott	R	OH	$1,673,100	Lost
D'Annunzio	R	NC	$1,397,445	Lost
Moise	D	FL	$1,386,540	Lost

Source: Center for Responsive Politics, "Self-Funded Candidates Face Tough Odds in Election 2010," www.opensecrets.org/news/2010/10/self-funded-candidates-face -tough-o.html.

Democratic National Party Committees Outraised Their GOP Counterparts but Party Spending Was Less Significant in 2010 Than in Past Election Cycles

Although the national political party committees collectively raised more funds for the 2010 election than they did during the last mid-term election cycle in 2006, there are growing indications that party committees are becoming less relevant as spending increasingly shifts to outside groups that are not subject to the hard-dollar requirements that apply to the national party committees.[15] As figure 7.1 demonstrates, total spending by national party committees during the 2010 election cycle comprised a much smaller proportion of overall federal election-related spending than was the case during the 2006 election cycle.

Figure 7.1—Comparison of Outside Spending in 2006 and 2010

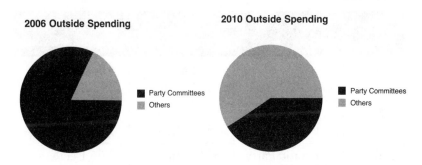

Source: Paul Blumenthal, "Court Rulings Change Elections, Independent Spending Dwarfs Party Spending in Midterm," Sunlight Foundation, blog.sunlight foundation.com, October 15, 2010.

National party committee fundraising data indicates that total contributions to Republican national party committees have dropped in recent years, while total contributions to Democratic national party committees have increased. Between 2006 and 2010, contributions to the three Republican national party committees decreased by 15 percent, while contributions to the Democratic national party committees increased by 30 percent. Tables 7.6 and 7.7 detail national party committee contributions for the 2009–2010 cycle and changes in national party contributions over time.

Table 7.6—2009–2010 National Party Committee Receipts

DNC	$195 Million	RNC	$170 Million
DSCC	$107 Million	NRSC	$93 Million
DCCC	$129 Million	NRCC	$107 Million
Total Democratic	**$432 Million**	**Total Republican**	**$370 Million**

Source: CQ MoneyLine National Party Committee Financial Summaries 2009–2010.

Table 7.7—National Party Committee Fundraising Trends
Over Time[16]

Year	Party	Amount	Change from Previous Cycle
2010	Democratic Party	$432 Million	6% Decrease
2010	Republican Party	$370 Million	29% Decrease
2008	Democratic Party	$462 Million	40% Increase
2008	Republican Party	$519 Million	19% Increase
2006	Democratic Party	$331 Million	27% Decrease
2006	Republican Party	$435 Million	22% Decrease

Sources: CQ MoneyLine National Party Committee Financial Summaries
2009–2010, 2007–2008, 2005–2006, and 2003–2004.

In 2010, party committee fundraising continued to be aided by extensive use of joint fundraising activities. Under FEC regulations, candidates and political parties may simultaneously raise hard-dollar funds through joint fundraising committees (JFCs), which permit candidates and parties to combine the per-recipient contribution limits and solicit greater amounts of money from donors at any one time.[17] More than 700 JFCs were registered with the FEC for the 2009–2010 election cycle, which is double the number of JFCs that were registered for the 2006 election cycle.[18] JFCs often raise millions of dollars, which are then transferred to the various fundraising participants. In 2009 and 2010, JFCs reportedly transferred approximately $9.5 million to the Republican national party committees and $5.7 million to the Democratic national party committees.[19]

Third-Party Groups Had a Significant Impact on the 2010 Election and Likely Will Be Even More Influential in the Future

Prior to the enactment of McCain-Feingold campaign finance law, the national political party committees spent hundreds of millions of dollars of soft money each election cycle on issue advertisements attacking and promoting their candidates as well as on ticket-wide get-out-the-vote operations in key states and congressional districts.[20] With the national party committees subject to the soft-money ban for the first time in the 2004 presidential race, soft-money spending migrated from the national parties to a number of prominent Section 527 organizations. Section 527 organizations get their name from the section of the federal tax code under which they operate.[21] All told, 527 groups reportedly raised and spent approximately $409 million on activities designed to influence the 2004 presidential race.[22] Of this amount in 2004, Democratic-oriented 527s reportedly spent $266 million, or 65 percent of the total, and Republican groups spent $144 million, or 35 percent of the total.[23] Although Democrats in 2004 were the first to make major use of 527 groups as soft-money vehicles, Republicans quickly joined suit, and the Republican-oriented Swift Boat Veterans for Truth became perhaps the most influential outside group during that election cycle.

However, following the 2004 election, the FEC found that a number of 527 organizations had broken the law by failing to register with the FEC as political committees and by failing to adhere to hard-dollar contribution limits. As a result, when the 2008 presidential campaign began, it was uncertain whether 527 organizations would be as active in raising and spending soft-money funds as they had been four years earlier. By Election Day 2008, it was clear that federally-oriented 527 groups had spent significantly less than they had during the 2004 election, but it was also clear that greater amounts of soft-money had been spent by various 501(c) organizations.[24]

Recent federal court decisions, including the U.S. Supreme Court's ruling in *Citizens United v. FEC*, helped outside interest groups flourish even more during the 2010 election cycle. 501(c) organizations, corporations and labor unions—as well as a new type of political committee known as Super PACs—spent significant funds in connection with the 2010 midterm election. A study by the Campaign Finance Institute notes that independent spending in the 2010 congressional elections, not including spending by national political parties, totaled $147.5 million, compared with only $32 million in 2006.[25] Table 7.8 provides detail on the amount of funds spent by top outside groups in connection with the 2010 elections.

Table 7.8—Top Outside Spenders in 2009–2010[26]

Entity	Entity Type	Dollar Amount
AFSCME	Labor Union	$87 Million
U.S. Chamber of Commerce	501(c)	$75 Million
American Crossroads and Crossroads GPS	Super PAC/501(c)	$65 Million
SEIU	Labor Union	$44 Million
NEA	Labor Union	$40 Million

Source: Brody Mullins and John D. McKinnon, "Campaign's Big Spender," *Wall Street Journal*, October 22, 2010.

Under the federal campaign finance laws, 501(c) entities are required to disclose spending for advertising that expressly advocates the election or defeat of federal candidates, but are only required to disclose spending for other types of television and radio advertisements if the advertisements refer to federal candidates, and air shortly before a federal election. However, an analysis of reportable 501(c) activity, combined with other publicly available information such as tax filings, found that 501(c) organizations, other entities, and non-campaign political committees were on track to spend $564 million on the 2010 congressional election, which was an increase of 153 percent from 2006.[27]

Labor organizations also spent significant funds in connection with the 2010 midterm election in the wake of the *Citizens United* Supreme Court decision. In one stark example, AFSCME (acronym for America Federation of State, County, and Municipal Employees) spent a reported $91 million on the 2010 congressional elections, which is 80 percent more than AFSCME spent in connection with the 2006 midterm elections.[28] AFSCME was the largest outside group spender in the 2010 elections, reportedly spending approximately $16 million more than the U.S. Chamber of Commerce.[29]

None of the top five outside group spenders in the 2010 election cycle was a corporation. However, many corporations chose to make contributions to Super PACs or other entities for the purpose of funding their election-related communications. For example, NewsCorp made contributions of $1 million each to the U.S. Chamber of Commerce and the Republican Governors Association.[30] Other corporations chose to fund election-related advertisements through their political action committees. For example, the National Association of Realtors PAC funded mailings supporting three Republican congressional candidates and also television advertisements supporting Democratic Congressman Paul Kanjorski.[31]

In *SpeechNow vs. FEC*, a federal appeals court struck down limits on contributions from individuals to political committees funding only independent expenditures. In Advisory Opinions issued after the *SpeechNow* ruling, the FEC concluded that political committees formed strictly to make independent expenditures supporting or opposing federal candidates could accept unlimited contributions from individuals, corporations, and labor organizations. These new political committees, which are prohibited from making contributions to federal candidates and other federal political committees, are commonly referred to as Super PACs.

Because Super PACs are not subject to contribution limits or source restrictions, many entities that made independent expenditures in connection with the 2010 congressional elections opted to register Super PACs with the FEC rather than creating 527 organizations. This strategic decision allowed these groups to run independent expenditures at any time, attacking or promoting federal candidates, while using unlimited contributions from individuals, corporations, and other entities, and without running the risk of an FEC finding that the entities involved had illegally failed to register with the FEC as a political committee.

In the 2006 midterm election, 36 percent of independent spending through mid-October of the election year supported Republicans, compared with 71 percent in the 2010 election cycle.[32] A large portion of outside group spending in 2010 took place through Super PACs, many of which supported Republican congressional candidates. American Crossroads, a Super PAC associated with Karl Rove, was the largest Super PAC of the 2010 cycle. FEC records indicate that 55 Super PACs were registered as political committees as of Election Day 2010. These Super PACs spent approximately $63 million in connection with the 2010 election.[33] Table 7.9 lists the top 10 Super PACs based on the amount spent. Of these top 10 Super PACs, the Super PACs supporting Republican congressional candidates spent approximately $30 million, while the Super PACs supporting Democrats spent $22 million.

Table 7.9—Top 10 Super PACs by Amount Spent[34]

American Crossroads	$21.6 Million
America's Families First Action Fund	$5.9 Million
Club for Growth Action	$5.0 Million
NEA Advocacy Fund	$4.2 Million
Women Vote!	$3.6 Million
Commonsense Ten	$3.3 Million
Our Future Ohio PAC	$3.1 Million
Patriot Majority PAC	$2.0 Million
Super PAC for America	$1.6 Million
New Prosperity Foundation	$1.5 Million

Source: Center for Responsive Politics, "2010 Outside Spending by Groups," www.opensecrets.org/outsidespending/summ.php?disp=O.

Despite the proliferation of outside spending by Republican-leaning Super PACs in the course of the 2010 election, data on traditional PAC contributions has shown a shift in contributions from Republican to Democratic candidates and parties since the 2005–2006 election cycle.[35] As table 7.10 indicates, during the 2005–2006 election cycle, 56 percent of PAC contributions were made to Republican candidates, party committees, and political committees. However, during the 2007–2008 cycle, after the Democratic Party had captured control of the U.S. House and U.S. Senate, PAC contributions to Republican candidates and committees dropped to 44 percent, and in the 2009–2010 cycle the figure dropped even further to 40 percent. With the Republican takeover of the U.S. House and significant GOP gains in the U.S. Senate, Republican candidates will likely receive more PAC contributions than Democratic candidates following the 2010 election.

Table 7.10—Party Breakdown of PAC Contributions[36]

	2009–2010 Election Cycle	2007–2008 Election Cycle	2005–2006 Election Cycle
Republican	40%	44%	56%
Democratic	59%	56%	44%

Source: CQ MoneyLine, PAC Contributions by Industry.

During the 2009–2010 election cycle, eight out of 10 of the largest PACs (based upon contributions made) were so-called "connected" PACs associated with corporations, trade associations, labor organizations, and membership organizations. Table 7.11 identifies the 10 largest PACs during the 2010 election cycle.

Table 7.11—2009–2010 Largest PACs[37]

PAC Name	Total Contributions Made
ActBlue	$46,800,372
Moveon.Org Political Action	$5,731,413
Honeywell International PAC	$5,013,600
International Brotherhood of Electrical Workers PAC	$4,553,550
National Association of Realtors PAC	$4,458,794
AT&T Inc. Federal PAC	$4,270,725
American Federation of Teachers, AFL-CIO PAC	$4,049,750
Service Employees International Union PAC (SEIU COPE)	$3,974,100
American Association for Justice PAC	$3,526,500
National Beer Wholesalers Association PAC	$3,461,500

Source: CQ MoneyLine Top PAC Contributors to PACs, Candidates, and Party Committees 2009–2010.

Online Political Activity Continued to Play an Important Role in 2010 and Remained Largely Unregulated by the FEC

The Internet came of age politically in 2008 as the Obama Campaign developed an unprecedented web-based strategy and involved millions of Americans in the presidential race through sophisticated and cutting-edge online technologies. In the 2010 election cycle, federal candidates, PACs and outside interest groups once again developed and implemented new Internet technologies to disseminate political information in real time to millions of voters and raised increasing amounts of campaign funds online. A new fundraising program operated through Twitter is the latest online innovation that federal candidates and committees used to raise funds during the 2010 election cycle.

One key factor that has contributed to the rapid growth of the Internet in American politics in recent years has been the FEC's deregulatory approach to online activities. In 2006, the FEC adopted regulations, which remain in place today, concerning use of the Internet in federal elections. The FEC's regulations exempt the Internet from the various prohibitions and restrictions of the McCain-Feingold law with only one exception: paid advertising placed on another person's website.[38] The practical effect of the FEC's regulations has been that individuals, volunteers, and anyone else with access to a computer can conduct a wide range of Internet activities on behalf of federal candidates—such as setting up and maintaining websites, blogging, emailing, linking, and posting videos on YouTube—without fear that the FEC will monitor or restrict their activities. Although it is difficult to measure or gauge precisely, there is no question that the FEC's hands-off regulatory approach to online political activities has helped the Internet play a growing and vital role in American politics.

ActBlue, a website that raises funds for Democratic campaigns and political committees, announced in 2009 that it would begin accepting contributions through Twitter.[39] In order to participate, a contributor must first create an account through the ActBlue website. The contributor may then contribute by tweeting "donate $amount @candidate via @actblue." For example, a contributor making a $25 contribution to the Joe Sestak for Senate Campaign would tweet "donate $25 @JoeSestak via @actblue."[40] Contribution totals are not yet available for ActBlue's fundraising program through Twitter. However, given the growing popularity of Twitter—particularly among economically upscale and politically active voters who are more predisposed to make political contributions—this latest online fundraising strategy bears watching in the future. As one published report recently noted, the Twitter fundraising technology "turns Internet giving into a mobile enterprise. Lots of people tweet from their phones and BlackBerrys—something, presumably, supporters with ActBlue accounts might find themselves doing from rallies."[41]

Several recent studies have examined the use of social media such as Facebook and Twitter by federal candidates and officeholders. According to one report, 91 out of 100 U.S. senators have YouTube channels, 87 have Facebook pages, and 56 have Twitter accounts.[42] Another study found that Republican candidates for the U.S. Senate in 2010 had significantly more Facebook fans and Twitter followers than did their Democratic opponents. Republican candidates in 2010 had on average four times as many Facebook fans and five times as many Twitter followers than did Democratic candidates.[43] Table 7.12 illustrates the Facebook and Twitter disparities that existed in 2010 between Republican and Democratic U.S. Senate candidates, even after omitting data for Senator John McCain and Senate candidate Carly Fiorina, who had the largest number of Facebook friends and Twitter followers.

Table 7.12—Average Facebook Fans and Twitter Followers for U.S. Senate

Candidates by Party		
Party	Average Facebook Fans	Average Twitter Followers
Democratic Candidates	8,260	2,591
Republican Candidates	38,718	14,009
Republican Candidates Excluding McCain/Fiorina	20,985	5,891

Source: HeadCount, "GOP Winning Social Media Battle by Wide Margin," www.headcount.org/wp-content/uploads/2010/09/VIEW-REPORT1.pdf.

Further detail on the number of Facebook fans and Twitter followers for specific U.S. Senate candidates and their opponents appears in table 7.13.

Table 7.13—Comparison of Fans and Followers for Specific U.S. Senate Candidates[45]

State	Republican Candidate	Followers/ Fans	Democratic Candidate	Followers/ Fans
California	Fiorina	312,578	Boxer	57,997
Delaware	O'Donnell	24,808	Coons	6,893
Florida	Rubio	138,736	Meek	25,688
Louisiana	Vitter	50,014	Melancon	13,901
Nevada	Angle	74,978	Reid	17,638
Washington	Rossi	44,318	Murray	19,524

Source: HeadCount, "GOP Winning Social Media Battle by Wide Margin," www.headcount.org/wp-content/uploads/2010/09/VIEW-REPORT1.pdf.

The Internet dominance of Republican congressional campaigns in 2010—at least as measured by the number of Facebook friends and Twitter followers—stands in stark contrast with the online advantage that Barack Obama enjoyed during the 2008 presidential race. On Election Day in 2008, the Obama Campaign had nearly 2.4 million Facebook friends, while the McCain Campaign had only 620,000.[46] The Obama Campaign also outpaced the McCain Campaign in a number of other online indicators, including the number of Twitter followers, the number of campaign YouTube videos, and the number of unique campaign website videos.[47]

Much was written after the 2008 presidential election about the Democratic candidates' natural advantage in online communications and fundraising. However, the impressive online performance of Republican congressional candidates during the 2010 election cycle casts serious doubt on this conclusion. It increasingly appears that neither political party has a unique advantage in online political activities. Rather, the Internet can best be seen as amplifying the political energy and excitement that exists at the grassroots level on both the left and the right, which can shift dramatically between elections, as we saw between President Obama's election in 2008 and the Republican takeover of the House of Representatives in 2010.

Early Voting Continued to Play a Key Role in 2010

The number of Americans voting prior to Election Day grew steadily during the 1990s and 2000s, reaching 16 percent of voters in 2000 and 22 percent of voters in 2004.[48] Analysts estimate that up to one-third of all Americans cast their ballots prior to Election Day in 2008, which far surpassed the number of early voters in previous presidential elections. Some studies indicate that more than half of votes for recent elections in several states were cast through early voting.[49] In 2010, this trend continued in several states, including states such as Nevada and California, which had high-profile Senate races. Reportedly 65 percent of votes cast in Nevada for the 2010 elections were cast early. Published reports estimate that approximately 29 percent of votes cast across the country in the 2010 election were early votes.[50]

For many years, voters who expected to be absent from their home communities on Election Day could apply for an absentee ballot to cast prior to the election. However, in order to obtain an absentee ballot, many jurisdictions required voters to show cause or otherwise explain why they were not able to vote on Election Day in their local precincts, which reduced the number of people who voted absentee.[51] However, in 1978, California amended its laws to permit voters to cast ballots before Election Day without providing any excuse or showing any cause.[52] In recent years, many more states have permitted voters to vote prior to Election Day, either in person or by mail, without cause. The National Conference of State Legislatures has indicated that for the 2010 elections, 35 states offered no-excuse absentee voting, no-excuse in-person voting, or both.[53] In some states, in-person early voting for the 2010 elections began as early as September 20.[54] The early-voting states provide voters with locations to vote early in-person or by mail.[55] Early voting has historically been most prevalent in a number of western states, including Colorado, Nevada, and New Mexico.[56] Some states allow voters to become "permanent" absentee voters and automatically receive absentee ballots for each election without having to submit a request.

The availability of no-excuse early and absentee voting in 2010 caused some campaigns to change their strategies based on the timing of early voting. For example, a Senate debate in Nevada was cancelled because the campaigns could not agree on a date. A major source of the disagreement between the campaigns was reportedly whether the debate should take place prior to the start of early voting in Nevada, which commenced on October 16.[57] Similarly, Ohio Senate candidate Lee Fisher cast an early ballot in front of media onlookers in September instead of voting on Election Day in November.[58] With the rise of early voting, campaigns can no longer focus their efforts just on Election Day, but rather must sustain their campaign activities for weeks in numerous states. In many ways, we no longer have a single Election Day in America, but rather an election window that lasts for a month or even longer in some jurisdictions.

Looking Ahead to 2012

The race to the White House began in earnest the day after the midterm election, and the 2012 presidential election will almost certainly be the most expensive in American history.

In 2008, we witnessed the first billion-dollar presidential election as both President Obama and Senator McCain raised record-breaking amounts of money for their campaigns. Obama became the first presidential candidate since 1972 to run without public funds for either the primary or the general-election campaign. Obama raised an unprecedented $750 million for his campaign, including $414 million for the primaries alone. McCain raised $221 million for the primaries and received another $85 million of public funds for the general election, for a total campaign war chest of $306 million. To put these figures in historical perspective, George W. Bush, who was a prolific campaign fundraiser, raised $100 million for the primaries in 2000 and $270 million four years later, which were record-breaking totals at the time.[59]

As impressive as President Obama's fundraising performance was in 2008, history suggests that Obama likely will exceed that extraordinary total in 2012. Since the advent of the public financing system in 1976, every sitting president who has run for reelection has raised more campaign funds the second time around than he did when first winning the presidency.[60] If history is any guide, Obama's campaign fundraising totals in 2012 may approach, or even exceed, $1 billion. However, Obama's fundraising strength likely will be even more daunting given that Obama in 2008 was forced to burn through more than $400 million of his $750 campaign war chest just to win the Democratic nomination. If no credible primary opponent runs against Obama in 2012, Obama will likely be able to roll over hundreds of millions of dollars of excess primary funds directly into his general election campaign.

Given President Obama's decision in 2008 to turn down public funds, not only for the primaries but for the general election as well— and the near certainty that Obama will do so again in 2012—all of the top-tier Republican candidates will likely follow suit. Once a Republican candidate clinches enough convention delegates to become the GOP's presumptive nominee, the putative nominee may enjoy a fundraising burst much like Senator Kerry experienced in 2004 when he ran against the well-heeled Bush-Cheney Campaign.[61] Nevertheless, there is no question that all of the candidates who seek the presidency in 2012 will confront an extraordinary campaign fundraising arms race that will require them to raise well in excess of $500 million, just to be competitive with Obama. The stage is thus set for the 2012 presidential race to be the most expensive in history.

Endnotes

[1]Center for Responsive Politics, "Election 2010 to Shatter Spending Records as Republicans Benefit from Late Cash Surge," www.opensecrets.org/news /2010/10/election-2010-to-shatter-spending-r.html, October 27, 2010.

[2]Center for Responsive Politics, "Election 2010 to Shatter," www.opensecrets .org/news/2010/10/election-2010-to-shatter-spending-r.html.

[3]Campaign Finance Institute, "Election-Related Spending by Political Committees and Non-Profits Up 40% in 2010," cfinst.org/Press/PReleases /10-10-18/Election-Related_Spending_by_Political_Committees_and_Non -Profits_Up_40_in_2010.aspx, October 18, 2010.

[4]Dan Eggen, "Price Tag of Midterm Campaign Likely to hit $4 Billion," *Washington Post*, October 27, 2010.

[5]Under the McCain-Feingold law, which went into effect in 2003, the national political parties are prohibited from raising and spending soft

money for any purpose. "Soft money" is defined as funds raised and spent outside of the prohibitions and limitations of federal law. Soft money includes corporate and labor union general treasury funds as well as individual donations in excess of federal contribution limits. Funds raised in accordance with federal law come from individuals and federally registered political action committees and are harder to raise; accordingly, these funds are known as "hard money."

[6]Paul Blumenthal, "Court Rulings Change Elections, Independent Spending Dwarfs Party Spending in Midterm," Sunlight Foundation, blog.sunlight foundation.com/2010/10/15/court-rulings-change-elections-independent -spending-dwarfs-party-spending-in-midterm/, October 15, 2010.

[7]2010 election cycle totals include fundraising data reported to the Federal Election Commission (FEC) through October 13, 2010. 2006 and 2008 election cycle totals include fundraising data reported to the FEC through December 31 of the election year. Campaign fundraising totals for the cycle may not add up exactly because of additional fundraising by third-party candidates and because of rounding.

[8]Based on total disbursements, Arlen Specter's campaign committee spent more than Pat Toomey's in the Pennsylvania Senate race. However, if the Specter Campaign's contribution refunds are deducted from its spending totals, the Toomey Campaign outspent the Specter Campaign over the course of the campaign.

[9]Federal law allows federal candidates to contribute or loan unlimited amounts of personal funds to their own campaigns.

[10]Jeanne Cummings, "Self-Funders Strike Out Big Time," *Politico*, November 5, 2010.

[11]Federal Election Commission data, images.nictusa.com/cgi-bin/fecgifpdf /?_18070+10020924492.pdf, (data as reported to the FEC through October 13, 2010).

[12]Steve Peoples, "Connecticut's McMahon No. 4 All-Time Self Funder," *CQ Politics News*, July 31, 2010.

[13]Data as reported to the FEC through October 13, 2010.

[14]Data as reported to the FEC through October 13, 2010.

[15]The Republican national party committees are the Republican National Committee (RNC), the National Republican Senatorial Committee (NRSC), and the National Republican Congressional Committee (NRCC). The Democratic national party committees are the Democratic National Committee

(DNC), the Democratic Senatorial Campaign Committee (DSCC), and the Democratic Congressional Campaign Committee (DCCC). National political party committees are prohibited from accepting corporate and labor union contributions and may accept contributions from individuals of up to $30,400 per calendar year.

[16]Data as reported to the FEC through October 13, 2010. Data from election cycles prior to 2009–2010 adjusted to exclude fundraising after mid-October of the election years based on FEC filings.

[17]For example, if a JFC included a U.S. Senate campaign, a national party, and two state parties, donors could contribute up to $55,200 to the JFC— including up to $4,800 to the U.S. Senate Campaign ($2,400 for the primary and $2,400 for the general election), $30,400 to the national party, and $10,000 each to the two state parties. Any prior contributions donors made to any participating entities would count against what could be contributed to the JFC.

[18]Alex Knott, "Politicians Create Record Number of Joint Fundraising Committees," *Roll Call*, September 17, 2010.

[19]Knott, "Politicians Create Record," (Reflecting fundraising data reported to the FEC through late September 2010).

[20]"Issue advertisements" are public communications that frequently attack or promote federal candidates and their records, but which refrain from expressly advocating the election or defeat of any clearly identified federal candidate (which is referred to as "express advocacy"). "Vote for McCain" and "Vote Against Obama" are examples of express advocacy. The Supreme Court established the express advocacy standard in *Buckley v. Valeo*, 424 U.S. 1 (1976).

[21]Under the Internal Revenue Code, groups may organize under Section 527—and therefore shield many of their activities from taxation—if their exempt function is "influencing or attempting to influence the selection, nomination, election, or appointment of any individual to any Federal, State, or local public office or office in a political organization, or the election of Presidential or Vice-Presidential electors," 26 U.S.C. § 527(e)(2). Thus, 527 entities are partisan political organizations as a matter of law.

[22]Eliza Newlin Carney, "Rules of the Game: The 527 Phenomenon: Big Bucks for the Upstarts," *NationalJournal.com*, December 13, 2004.

[23]Carney, "Rules of the Game: The 527 Phenomenon."

[24]501(c) organizations are entities that are organized and operate under Section 501(c) of the Internal Revenue Code. They include 501(c)(4) enti-

ties (social welfare organizations) and 501(c)(6) entities (business leagues including trade associations). 501(c)(4) and 501(c)(6) organizations are permitted to engage in partisan political activities, provided that such activities are not their primary purpose. By contrast, the activities of 527 organizations may be entirely partisan. 527 organizations are legally required to disclose their donors; 501(c) organizations are not.

[25]Campaign Finance Institute, "Election-Related Spending by Political Committees and Non-Profits Up 40% in 2010," cfinst.org/Press/PReleases /10-10-18/Election-Related_Spending_by_Political_Committees_and_Non -Profits_Up_40_in_2010.aspx, October 18, 2010. Data as reported to the FEC through mid-October 2010.

[26]Data as reported to the FEC through late October 2010. Published reports indicate that the American Federation of State, County, and Municipal Employees (AFSCME) ended up spending a total of $91 million on the 2010 election. Steven Greenhouse, "Union Spends $91 Million on Midterms," The New York Times Caucus, thecaucus.blogs.nytimes.com, October 26, 2010.

[27]Campaign Finance Institute, "Election-Related Spending by Political Committees and Non-Profits Up 40% in 2010," cfinst.org/Press/PReleases /10-10-18/Election-Related_Spending_by_Political_Committees_and_Non -Profits_Up_40_in_2010.aspx, October 18, 2010.

[28]Brody Mullins and John D. McKinnon, "Campaign's Big Spender," Wall Street Journal, October 22, 2010. Data as reported to the FEC through late October 2010.

[29]Steven Greenhouse, "Union Spends $91 Million on Midterms," The New York Times Caucus, thecaucus.blogs.nytimes.com, October 26, 2010.

[30]Ben Smith, "NewsCorp gave pro-GOP Group $1M," Politico, September 30, 2010.

[31]Brody Mullins and Devlin Barrett, "Businesses Step Up Political Ads," Wall Street Journal, September 30, 2010.

[32]Campaign Finance Institute, "Election-Related Spending by Political Committees and Non-Profits Up 40% in 2010," cfinst.org/Press/PReleases /10-10-18/Election-Related_Spending_by_Political_Committees_and_Non -Profits_Up_40_in_2010.aspx, October 18, 2010.

[33]Center for Responsive Politics, "2010 Outside Spending by Groups," www.opensecrets.org/outsidespending/summ.php?cycle=2010&disp=o&type =S. Data as reported to the FEC through mid-October 2010.

[34]Data as reported to the FEC through mid-October 2010. As was noted above, published reports indicate that American Crossroads (combined with its 501(c) and Crossroads GPS) spent a total of $65 million in connection with the 2010 election.

[35]Traditional PACs, unlike Super PACs, may make contributions to federal candidates and other federal political committees. Traditional PACs are prohibited from accepting corporate and labor union contributions and may accept contributions from individuals of up to $5,000 per calendar year. Traditional PACs are referred to herein as "PACs."

[36]Percentages for the 2005–2006 and 2007–2008 election cycle are based on data including contributions through December 31 of the election year. Percentages for the 2009–2010 cycle are based on data including contributions through October 13, 2010.

[37]Data as reported to the FEC through October 13, 2010.

[38]For example, if an individual spends money to take out an advertisement for a federal candidate who appears on the home page of Yahoo.com or CNN.com, the transaction will be subject to regulation in a fashion similar to television, radio, and other mass-media advertising. However, messages that individuals create on their own websites or post without charge on other websites such as YouTube are not subject to FEC regulation.

[39]Chris Good, "Democrats to Raise Money on Twitter," *The Atlantic*, www.theatlantic.com/politics/archive/2009/07/democrats-to-raise-money-on-twitter/20518/.

[40]ActBlue, "Twitter Integration," www.actblue.com/twitter.

[41]Chris Good, "Democrats to Raise Money on Twitter." *The Atlantic*, www.theatlantic.com/politics/print/2009/07/democrats-to-to-raise-money-on-twitter/20518. Very little academic research exists on the amount of success that campaigns have had with tweeting links to fundraising websites. Some analysts estimate that the click-through rate for a tweet with a campaign fundraising website is between 4 and 10 percent. David Herbert, "Will Twitter Add a New Wrinkle to Campaign Fundraising?," *National Journal online*, www.nextgov.com/nextgov/ng_20090407_4752.php.

[42]L2, "Digital IQ Index: U.S. Senate," www.docstoc.com/docs/51232277/L2-Digital-IQ-Index-US-Senate, August 18, 2010.

[43]HeadCount, "GOP Winning Social Media Battle by Wide Margin," www.headcount.org/wp-content/uploads/2010/09/VIEW-REPORT1.pdf, September 23, 2010.

[44]Data as of September 21, 2010.

[45]Data as of September 21, 2010.

[46]Andrew Rasiehj and Micah Sifry, "The Web: 2008's Winning Ticket," *Politico*, November 12, 2008, 24.

[47]Rasiejh and Sifry, "The Web."

[48]Stephen Ohlemacher and Julie Pace, "A Third of Electorate Could Vote Before Nov. 4," Associated Press, September 22, 2008.

[49]Early Voting Information Center, "Frequently Asked Questions," earlyvoting .net/faq.

[50]United States Elections Project, "2010 Turnout Rate and Early Voting Rate Forecasts," elections.gmu.edu/2010_vote_forecasts.html, November 3, 2010.

[51]For example, scholars estimate that only about 5 percent of the nation's voters cast absentee ballots in 1980. June Krunholz, "Forget Election Day— Early Voting for President Has Started," *Wall Street Journal*, September 23, 2008.

[52]Domenico Montanaro, "Can Early Voting Ease Election Day Drama?," www.msnbc.com, September 24, 2008.

[53]National Conference of State Legislatures, "Absentee and Early Voting," www.ncsl.org/?tabid=16604. By contrast, in 1996 only 11 states provided for early voting; by 2004, the number had climbed to 26. Domenico Montanaro, "Can Early Voting Ease Election Day Drama?," www.msnbc.com, September 24, 2008.

[54]Early Voting Information Center, "Early Voting Calendar 2010," www.early voting.net/calendar.

[55]In Oregon voting is done entirely by mail and there are no physical precincts.

[56]For example, in the 2004 presidential election, 53 percent of the ballots were cast early in Nevada, with 51 percent in New Mexico, 47 percent in Colorado, and 36 precent in Florida. June Krunholz, "Forget Election Day— Early Voting for President Has Started," *Wall Street Journal*, September 23, 2008.

[57]Associated Press, "Nevada Broadcasters Cancels Harry Reid-Sharron Angle Debate," www.lasvegassun.com/news/2010/aug/20/nevada-broadcasters -cancels-us-senate-debate/, August 20, 2010.

[58]Sean J. Miller and Shane D'Aprile, "Early Voting Has Campaigns Scrambling to Gain Support," *The Hill*, September 29, 2010.

[59]Bush raised $100 million for the 2000 race under the pre-McCain-Feingold $1,000-per-person contribution limit. The McCain-Feingold law doubled the individual contribution limit to $2,000 per election for the 2004 election and indexed the contribution limit for inflation going forward. The individual contribution limit was $2,300 per election in 2008 and may increase to $2,500 per election for the 2012 presidential race.

[60]Campaign Finance Institute, "Participation, Competition, Engagement: How to Revive and Improve Public Funding for Presidential Nomination Politics," www.cfinst.org/pdf/federal/president/TaskForce1_Fullreport.pdf, table A.3.7, and CQ Moneyline, US Presidential Candidate Committees with 1999–2000 activity and US Presidential Candidate Committees with 2003–2004 Activity.

[61]Kerry amassed enough delegates to win the Democratic Party nomination on March 11, 2004. CNN, "Primary Results: Delegate Scorecard," www.cnn.com/ELECTION/2004/primaries/pages/scorecard/graphical.html. Between mid-March and Kerry's nomination at the Democratic National Convention in the end of July, the Kerry campaign raised approximately $170 million.

Chapter 8

Midterm Media Explosion

by Dr. Diana Owen

Associate Professor of Communiction, Culture, and Technology at Georgetown University

A merican election media reached new levels of ubiquity during the 2010 midterm contests. A multilayered election media system has emerged, where people can access news via large information gateways as well as through increasingly specialized sources. Voters were exposed to an abundance of election information from mainstream media outlets. They also could engage the campaign through an array of new media and social media platforms that have grown in scope and prominence since the 2008 presidential contest. Citizens had better access to vital election information than ever before. At the same time, they endured months of the multimedia circus that has come to characterize American election campaigns.

While the lines between traditional media, new media, and social media are becoming increasingly conflated, the mainstream press remains a strong and identifiable force in American politics. The *mainstream press* consists of communications media that are formally associated with established organizations that practice professional journalism, such as newspapers and news magazines, television network news, and radio news programs. The mainstream media have had to make serious adjustments as the economic model for journalism has changed, and the delivery system for news has been radically transformed. Severe budget cutbacks over the past few years have meant that there are fewer professional print journalists on the ground getting the story firsthand. Journalists increasingly rely on information culled from other communication outlets, blogs, and social media. Yet, there are key elements of the mainstream news product that continue to set it apart from new media content. In an era of increasingly fragmented media representing specific partisan and ideological perspectives, mass audiences still rely on mainstream media for the big picture.

Concurrently, new media have continued their novel forays into political territory. *New media* can be defined broadly as communication forms that enhance users' ability to develop political content, provide opportunities for discussion and the expression of opinion, and facilitate interaction among audience members. Old media platforms can be adapted to new media applications, such as call-in political talk radio and television programs. New media also consist of entirely novel entities that are supported by technological innovations, like political websites.[1] *Social media* are a subset of new media that take particular advantage of the interactivity and accessibility of digital technology to facilitate sharing of political content, conversation and debate, and community building. Networking sites, including Facebook; videosharing platforms, like YouTube; and microblogging sites, such as Twitter have quickly developed into campaign mainstays.

Although the mainstream media persist, and may by some measures be thriving as they adapt to the current communication environment, they have been significantly affected by new media. The relationship between traditional and new media has shifted from adversarial to symbiotic over the course of 20 years. Traditional media have tacked new media components onto their repertoire of election reporting techniques. Blogs, Facebook sites, Twitter feeds, and videosharing abound on mainstream media websites. During the midterm elections, some of the most well-established news organizations unveiled innovative applications for providing campaign information. The *New York Times* and the *Wall Street Journal* made election information available through iPad apps, and the *Washington Post* was a mainstream media Twitter pioneer. Perhaps a more striking, but less transparent, development is that mainstream media have become delivery systems for new media content that originates from independent sources, including political party websites, candidate Twitter feeds, and voters' homegrown videos. By the same token, new media rely on mainstream press coverage for publicity and validation. New media can break stories, but the mainstream media often set the agenda for new media, establishing the broader context for campaign news.

This chapter begins with a discussion of the characteristics of midterm election coverage, taking into account both traditional and new media. It examines the audiences for the broad range of campaign media, and demonstrates that mainstream media still attract the lion's share of voters. The discussion then turns to coverage of candidates in the midterm campaign to illustrate some major trends, including the focus on celebrity politicians, coverage of candidates that run against the media, and feeding frenzies that are fueled by new media.

Midterm Election Media Coverage

Press coverage of midterm elections is typically less prolific than reporting on presidential campaigns. Voters are less interested in midterm elections, which lack the galvanizing presence of candidates for the nation's highest office. They become weary of the protracted campaigns that have become the norm in American politics, especially when there are multiple races to follow and unfamiliar candidates to track. A Pew Research Center study indicated that approximately 30 percent of the public followed news about the congressional elections very closely in the week before Election Day 2010. In contrast, 58 percent of the public reported following the 2008 presidential election very closely in the week before balloting. Turnout is substantially lower in midterm elections than in presidential years, especially among young voters. A November 2010 study by the Center for Information and Research on Civic Learning and Engagement (CIRCLE) indicates that 21 percent of 18- to 29-year-old voters cast a ballot in the 2010 midterm elections compared to 51 percent in the 2008 presidential contest.

While voter attention to the midterm elections was far from robust, stories about the campaign began to appear more than a year in advance of the election and dominated the news agenda during

October 2010. The Project for Excellence in Journalism (PEJ) found that campaign coverage increased from 6 percent of the newshole in July to 42 percent just prior to the election, which was comparable to the amount of coverage devoted to the health care debate. The midterm election results received more coverage than any other story in over two years. According to a November 2010 PEJ study, the election results and postmortems filled 57 percent of the newshole for the week including Election Day.

Media coverage of the midterm elections was heavily negative. Stories and commentary reflected the pessimistic tone of candidate rhetoric and the politically polarized perspectives of media commentators. A study released by the Center for Media and Public Affairs (CMPA) in October 2010 found that close to 70 percent of nightly news coverage of Democrats and Republicans was negative while only around 30 percent of coverage was positive. The Tea Party received slightly better treatment, with 63 percent negative and 37 percent positive coverage. Campaign content on blogs and online news sites, such as Huffington Post and *Politico*, also was highly negative. According to a report by PEJ, the blogosphere was preoccupied with partisan debate and candidate blunders. Between October 18 and 22, 17 percent of blog links were to heated discussions about comments made by Delaware Republican Senate candidate Christine O'Donnell during a debate, in which she asked, "Where in the Constitution is the separation of church and state?"

The type of midterm election information voters accessed differed depending upon the platform. The mainstream media provided general reports about the election context, key races, issues, and the political process. According to PEJ, newspapers provided a clear synthesis of the main election stories, while television news incorporated more speculation into its coverage through its prominent use of pundits. The new media spectacle, including how citizens can use social media in elections, has become a storyline for the mainstream media, if not an entirely new category of news. Online news sites developed during the new media era, such as Huffington Post, featured more sensational news stories, opinionated blog posts, and politainment content. Political websites, including candidate, political party, and nonpartisan sites were rich in campaign information, providing logistical details about how to register and polling locations.

Blogs specialized in often heated ideological commentary, partisan debate, and scrutiny of the electoral process. Social media, especially Twitter, focused more on influencing vote choice, encouraging people to get involved in the campaign, and getting out the vote.

Local and National News Coverage

Local and regional newspapers, television news, and radio programs are in the best position to cover individual races for state legislature, Congress, and governor. Local news organizations have a handle on the key storylines and personalities. Election coverage varies widely across campaigns and localities, and tends to be more extensive for close or controversial races. Local news can set the agenda for national news coverage, especially in the digital era when journalists have ready access to local online media. National issues are integral to election coverage even at the local level, as many incumbent candidates attempt to downplay controversial local issues.[2]

National news coverage provides a general context for the election, identifies issues of widespread concern, establishes core election themes, and places a spotlight on consequential races. Local news stories can fit into the key news frames that national news employs. Dominant media frames characterize midterm elections as (1) a report card on the sitting president, (2) a referendum on incumbent officeholders, (3) a barometer on the state of the political parties, (4) a contest to determine the balance of power in Congress, (5) an indicator of partisan trends in the states, and (6) a trial run with implications for the next presidential race. In 2010, these frames were heavily in evidence, especially as the policies of President Obama and the Democratic Party came under fire. The active presence of the Tea Party, a conservative/libertarian grassroots movement, provided a high-profile challenge to the typical two-party scenario. According to the *New York Times*, 129 House candidates and 9 Senate candidates had Tea Party backing.[3] An NBC News/Wall Street Journal poll conducted in October indicated that 35 percent of voters were Tea Party supporters.[4] Initially, coverage of the Tea Party was heaviest in the blogosphere, but caught on in the mainstream media as candidates began to contest seriously for the Republican nomination in states across the nation.

Other media frames highlight strategy and campaign dynamics. The horserace frame that has come to dominate campaign coverage was prevalent in 2010, especially as polling has proliferated. The usual barrage of surveys conducted by media organizations, professional pollsters, think tanks, political parties, and candidate organizations was supplemented by an array of convenience polls facilitated by digital media. Instant polls conducted via computers, iPads, and handheld devices quickly tracked voter sentiments, and the results made it into the news stream. Many news organizations played up the notion of the "angry voter," a standard news frame that is justified by polling data indicating public dissatisfaction with the way government and politicians are doing their job. Another perennial news frame focuses on money in the election and the specter of candidates "buying seats." The 2010 midterm elections were the most costly in history. The Center for Responsive Politics reported that the average cost of winning a House seat in 2010 was $1.09 million compared to $8.28 million for a Senate seat. The number of self-financing candidates reached new heights, with 58 candidates contributing at least a half million dollars of personal money to their own campaigns. Groups outside of party and candidate organizations funded campaign ads and other communication efforts in more than two-thirds of the election contests. Mainstream media and the blogosphere had lots of raw material to craft into story lines as they followed the money trail.

New Media

The midterm elections marked another significant step in pushing forward new media frontiers. As Lee Rainie, director of the Pew Internet and American Life Project observes, "This is the election when [social media] became more deeply embedded in the rhythms of campaigning."[5] Candidates on both sides of the aisle embraced social media as a means of targeting voters, controlling their message, and appealing to constituents in new ways. Parties and candidates innovated with new applications, including iMedia applications that capitalize on Americans' heavy use of mobile devices. Voters turned to new media to engage with campaigns and get information quickly from selected sources.

Despite these developments, the 2010 midterm elections demonstrated that new media alone are not sufficient for creating an informed electorate. A new media-dominant electoral strategy is not enough to produce a victorious candidacy, and it can backfire. The audiences for social media in elections are still not extensive, and tend to consist of people who already are interested in politics and candidate supporters. Candidates spent less than 5 percent of their budgets on social media, while the bulk of expenditures went to the old media standby—television advertising.

Mainstream Media Still Matter

Politics Daily analyst Steve Friess observes, "The big winners of the 2010 midterm elections were, in this order: the House Republicans, the unsinkable Senate Majority Leader Harry Reid, the media," by which he means the mainstream press.[6] The public turns most often to the mainstream media for midterm election news. Candidates who ignored or ran against the mainstream media did so at their own peril. As a Neiman Journalism Lab report on election media notes, "Traditional media still paves the way for journalistic standards and political coverage."[7]

The public relied far more heavily on traditional media sources during the 2010 midterm elections than on new media sources. However, Internet use has cut into the audience for mainstream media since 2006. Table 8.1 depicts data from the Pew Research Center indicating public reliance on media sources for information over the course of the past three midterm elections and the previous two presidential contests. Online campaign content was in its nascent stages in 1992, when candidate Bill Clinton established a rudimentary website that received little traffic from the public or the press. The percentage of people consulting Internet sources for campaign information climbed from 3 percent in the 1996 presidential contest to 7 percent in the 2002 midterm election, and has remained steady at around 20 percent over the past two midterm election cycles.

Before the Internet era, reliance on television was overwhelming, with 82 percent of the public tuning in during the 1992 campaign. Television, which includes reliance on local news, network evening news, and cable news, remained the main source of election news for 66 percent of the public in 2010, down only slightly from 69 percent in the 2006 midterm contests and consistent with 2002 levels. The percentage of people who rely on print sources—newspapers and magazines—for midterm election information has dropped precipitously as Internet sources have become more popular. Newspaper use reached an all-time low in 2010; only 31 percent relied on newspapers compared to 60 percent in 1996. Reliance on magazines also has dropped from a high of 11 percent in 1996 to 3 percent in 2010. The drop in reliance on traditional print media tracks with the increase in online journalism, including websites and blogs. Radio use during midterm elections has fluctuated slightly over time, with 17 percent of the public treating radio as a main campaign news source. Conservative talk radio tends to attract more followers during election contests. In 2010, right-leaning candidates, including those endorsed by the Tea Party, turned to talk radio to reach out to constituents.

Table 8.1—Public Reliance on Media Sources During Election Campaigns

Source	2010	2006	2002	1996	1992
Television	66%	69%	66%	72%	82%
Newspapers	31%	44%	39%	60%	57%
Internet	20%	19%	7%	3%	—
Radio	17%	18%	13%	19%	12%
Magazines	3%	3%	1%	11%	9%
Other	5%	6%	5%	4%	6%
Visited a Candidate's Website or Followed a Candidate Through Email, Facebook, or Twitter	19%	—	—	—	—

Respondents could name multiple sources.
Source: Pew Research Center for the People and the Press, October 2010 Political Survey.

The number of people who turned directly to social media for campaign information in 2010 paled in comparison to those relying

on mainstream media. This is consistent with trends in the 2008 presidential election, where the publicity surrounding social media was
more expansive than the audience. The Pew Research Center found
that 19 percent of the public visited a candidate's website or followed
a candidate through email, Facebook, or Twitter in 2010. There are
indications that the use of Facebook as a political tool has waned
since its emergence as the social media of choice in the 2008 campaign. Users were less inclined to use Facebook as a hub for campaign
information dissemination, organizing, outreach, and fundraising.
Instead, the most prominent use of Facebook in the campaign was a
massive get-out-the-vote appeal to users over age 18. Videosharing
sites were popular during the campaign, as approximately 450 candidates had official YouTube channels and many traditional and new
media platforms supported outlets for video distribution. It is important to note that the figures describing social media use do not take
into account the fact that many people are exposed to new media
content through traditional media venues. The campaign itself provided an opportunity for some mainstream media organizations to
expand their new media offerings. The *Washington Post* became the
first major news organization to feature a "promoted trend" on
Twitter with the hash tag "Election." The *New York Times* created a
Twitter visualization that highlighted the number of posts related to
candidates running for governor or the Senate.

Candidate Coverage

National media elevate particular story lines that they perceive will
appeal to audiences beyond the state and local districts from which
they originate. Issue coverage in the election focused heavily on the
economy, which resonated with the majority of voters. Other issue
concerns, such as unemployment, immigration, education, and
health care, were fragmented across the electorate. While the issues
in particular states may not have broad appeal to a national audience,
controversial, unconventional, or intriguing personalities do.
Political celebrities can command substantial press coverage even if
they are not running for office. A handful of candidates out of the
hundreds contesting in state, congressional, and gubernatorial elections managed to capture the attention of the national media in

2010—for better or worse. Four Tea Party candidates running under the GOP banner received ample national media coverage, including Christine O'Donnell, who ran for Senate in Delaware; Rand Paul, who won a Senate seat in Kentucky; Sharron Angle, who challenged Senate Majority Leader Harry Reid in Nevada; and Carl Paladino, who ran against Andrew Cuomo for governor of New York. The California gubernatorial race was in the media spotlight in large part due to the candidate matchup. Republican Meg Whitman, a successful businesswoman who spent over $100 million of her own money in the campaign, made headlines for allegedly employing an undocumented worker, which contradicted her strong stance on immigration. Democrat Jerry Brown had a colorful political history that included a run for president and a stint as a liberal talk-radio host. He had been the youngest governor in California history and in 2010 became the oldest after winning the election. A number of candidates drew significant mainstream media attention by running against the media, a strategy which seemed to backfire.

Celebrity Politicians

High-profile political personalities stumping for candidates attracted significant national media attention. Especially prominent were celebrity politicians who served as lightening rods for both intense political support and opposition. According to the Project for Excellence in Journalism, President Barack Obama garnered far more news coverage than any candidate running for office, as his presidency was at the center of much campaign debate. He received a tremendous amount of press attention when he hit the campaign trail to rally support for Democratic contenders in the closing days of the election. While much of the coverage focused on his message, other stories centered on his inability to connect personally with voters. An op-ed in the *Washington Post* by Michael Gerson on October 19 labeled Obama an "intellectual snob," a characterization that became widespread among bloggers and other new media practitioners. First Lady Michelle Obama, who was portrayed in the media as "the closer" and her husband's "deadliest weapon," received almost as much press attention for her fashion sense as for her stump speeches as she crossed the country to promote the Democratic cause. Former Democratic president Bill

Clinton was active on the campaign trail, but gained the most press attention for a perceived gaffe. He allegedly asked Democrat Kendrick Meek, a Florida Senate candidate, to withdraw from the race and throw his support behind his moderate Republican opponent, Charlie Crist, in an effort to stop Tea Party-backed Republican candidate, Marco Rubio, who ultimately won the election.

Politicians considering a presidential bid in 2012 sought to gain political favor from candidates and party officials by working on their behalf during the midterm contests. Former Alaska governor and vice-presidential candidate Sarah Palin, who publicly pondered a presidential bid in 2012 commanded the media spotlight throughout the campaign. Other potential Republican presidential contestants, including former Massachusetts governor Mitt Romney, Minnesota governor Tim Pawlenty, former House Speaker Newt Gingrich, and Mississippi governor Haley Barbour, endorsed and raised funds for midterm election candidates, but failed to capture a fraction of the press attention that Palin drew. Palin was a fixture on the midterm election media circuit largely due to her celebrity appeal, which straddles the line between politics and entertainment. She simultaneously made headlines as a Fox News commentator, campaign activist, proud supporter of daughter Bristol's appearance on *Dancing with the Stars*, and for plugging her upcoming TV reality series, *Sarah Palin's Alaska*. Palin endorsed over 100 conservative candidates for state and federal office during the primary and general election periods. The endorsements were highlighted on her grizzly-bear-themed website, Organize4Palin.com, and advertised via her Facebook and Twitter accounts. Despite her disdain for the "lamestream media," a term originated by ultraconservative bloggers that she popularized, the most significant effect of Palin's endorsement was the ability to draw mainstream media coverage to candidates, especially those who were unknown to voters and flew under the radar of journalists. Mainstream press stories about the candidates Palin endorsed tended to quote liberally from her social media sites. Of the 77 candidates Palin endorsed during the general election, nearly 50 were successful, although candidates she supported in high-profile races, including Sharron Angle in Nevada, Christine O'Donnell in Delaware, and John Raese in West Virginia, lost their election bids. Election media postmortems honed in on the fact that Senate candidate Joe Miller, her protégé in her native Alaska, was unable to defeat Republican write-in candidate Lisa Murkowski.

Running From the Press

A number of candidates made the risky decision to flaunt the mainstream media in favor of conducting their campaigns predominantly through new media. The move catapulted some of the candidates into the national media spotlight, where they received more than their share of mainstream press coverage. Candidates who made a point of running against the mainstream press, including Tea Party-supported contestants Sharron Angle, Joe Miller, and Christine O'Donnell, failed in their election bids. The approach backfired for a variety of reasons. Voters have faith in their local news outlets and rely on them for midterm election information. Mainstream media coverage of these candidates was unremittingly negative, and at times bordered on parody. Relying exclusively on new media often means preaching to the choir in tight elections where expanding the base of electoral support is imperative. While the case can be made that these candidates may not have won even with more positive media coverage, they made more than their fair share of national headlines.

The anti-media strategy, adapted from Sarah Palin's playbook, assumes that public loathing and distrust of the press runs so deep that vilifying, selectively engaging, and antagonizing the media will translate into votes. Like Palin, these candidates relied heavily on alternative media to get their message across, especially ideological talk radio and television programs, as well as social media like Facebook, Twitter, and YouTube channels. Angle, who was defeated by Democrat, Senate Majority Leader Harry Reid, alleged that the press was "unprofessional" and that candidates should teach the media a lesson whenever they have the opportunity. She refused to give in-depth interviews with local newspapers and television stations throughout the campaign. At one point, she held a three-minute press conference, and then promptly bolted out the back door, where she was followed by reporters yelling out questions, including one who was six months pregnant. The press relentlessly followed her, ostensibly to confirm her positions on issues. They tracked her down in airports and parking lots, prompting her to employ decoys to evade the media during public events. Press accounts, backed by YouTube video evidence, of Angle's "signature move"—running away from reporters—ridiculed her. A July 22, 2010 *Newsweek* article entitled, "Sharron Angle Perfects Dodges Reporters," opened with: "It's not a bird. It's not a plane. That worried-looking blur reporters keep seeing in Nevada is Republican Senate candidate Sharron Angle." In a final act of defiance, Angle banned mainstream media reporters from her election night festivities, although there wasn't much to celebrate.

Feeding Frenzies and Gotcha Journalism

Many candidates embraced new media in an effort to control their message and energize their supporters. However, the new media environment is open and volatile, which makes it difficult to harness. Candidates faced more aggressive and invasive scrutiny than in previous elections due to digital technology. Journalists, bloggers, and average citizens dug deep into digital archives with the goal of exposing candidates' past transgressions. They kept a careful watch on candidates, recording their every move and quickly publicizing their blunders through social media and videosharing platforms. In a previous era, these kinds of activities were performed by a relatively small cadre of campaign operatives. Today, media feeding frenzies are as likely to be sparked by a citizen's cell phone video uploaded to YouTube as by journalists or political activists.

Christine O'Donnell, who won the Delaware Republican Senate primary with Tea Party support and the endorsement of Sarah Palin against congressman and two-time governor Mike Castle, was the second most prominent newsmaker in the midterm cycle behind Barack Obama (PEJ, 2010). She made heavy use of social media while disparaging the mainstream press, although new media did not always prove to be an ally. O'Donnell was haunted by statements that she made on television in 1999 on Bill Maher's *Politically Incorrect*, where she alleged that she had "dabbled into witchcraft" when she was in high school. A clip from the show went viral on the Internet as O'Donnell prepared for national television appearances. Karl Rove, a Republican operative and former advisor to President George W. Bush, stated that O'Donnell's win would cost the Republicans the

Senate seat, which had formerly been held by Democratic Vice President Joe Biden. O'Donnell replied, "There's been no witchcraft since. If there was, Karl Rove would be a supporter now." She further responded with a YouTube campaign ad where she proclaimed, "I'm not a witch." The video received millions of hits, was parodied on *Saturday Night Live*, and mashed up by numerous YouTube fans.

Conclusion

Since the advent of new media almost a quarter century ago, the election communication environment has evolved in novel ways with almost every contest. During the 2010 midterm elections, the mainstream media reinforced their solid position in the media hierarchy with broad-based coverage and traditional reporting styles supplemented by expanded new media applications. The social media election experiment that began with the 2008 presidential contest pressed on as candidates, media organizations, and citizens continued to innovate. Some applications that debuted during the campaign, including those instituted on mainstream news sites, have become regularized components of political news coverage. These developments set the stage for the media blitz that is certain to surround the 2012 presidential campaign.

Endnotes

[1]Richard Davis and Diana Owen, *New Media and American Politics* (Oxford University Press, 1999).

[2]Douglas R. Arnold, *Congress, the Press, and Political Accountability* (Princeton: Russell Sage Foundation, 2004).

[3]Kate Zernike,"Tea Party Set to Win Enough Races for Wide Influence," *New York Times*, October 14, 2004.

[4]Jonathan Weisman, "GOP in Lead in Final Lap," *Wall Street Journal*, October 20, 2010.

[5]Jake Coyle, "In Social Media Election, the GOP Capitalizes," AP, November 3, 2010, www.pewinternet.org/Media-Mentions/2010/In-social -media-election-the-GOP-capitalizes.aspx.

[6]Steve Friess, "Another Midterm Winner—the Mainstream Media," Politics Daily, November 6, 2010, www.politicsdaily.com /2010/11/05/another-midterm -winner-the-mainstream-media/.

[7]Matt Diaz, "It's Election Night: Here's What Some News Orgs (Old & New) Have Planned," Nieman Journalism Lab, November 2, 2010, www.niemanlab.org/2010/11/its-election-night-heres-what-some-news-orgs -old-new-have-planned/.

PART
3

Senate and Gubernatorial Races

Chapter 9

California:
The Great Exception

by Dr. John J. Pitney Jr.

Roy P. Crocker Professor of American Politics
Claremont McKenna College

*C**alifornia: The Great Exception* was the title of Carey McWilliams's classic 1949 analysis of the state's history. It would also sum up the state's role in the 2010 midterm election. While the rest of the country was moving toward the GOP, California was voting Democratic.

Republicans ran Meg Whitman for governor and Carly Fiorina for senator, both former corporate CEOs who hoped to exploit their status as political outsiders. But in 2010 California, "insiderism" was in. Jerry Brown, the Democratic victor in the gubernatorial race, had won his first statewide office 40 years earlier. Barbara Boxer, the incumbent who defeated Fiorina, was finishing her third term in the Senate and had served a decade in the House before that.

So what accounted for these outcomes? Did they reflect strengths and weaknesses of the candidates, or did they stem from the state's peculiar political characteristics?

The Backdrop

One big question is why candidates ran at all. The state's economic position had been on a jagged downward path for decades, with its share of overall U.S. employment dropping 10 percent since 1990.[1]

As of May 2010, its jobless rate (12.4 percent) was the nation's third worst. As the poor economy deepened the state's budget problems, Governor Arnold Schwarzenegger's approval fell from a near-record high of 65 percent in 2004 to a near-record low of 23 percent in early 2010.[2] It did not seem likely that the next governor could fare better. There was speculation that the popular Senator Dianne Feinstein would seek the governorship. But after 18 years in the Senate, she had finally achieved the political trifecta of seniority, majority status, and a president of the same party. She was not going to give it up for the mess in Sacramento. Senator Barbara Boxer, who had first won her seat at the same time as Feinstein, was enjoying the same trifecta.[3] She would surely seek reelection, but what sensible Republican would challenge her? Though less popular than Feinstein, she was a strong fundraiser who had won her last race by nearly 20 points. No Republican had won a Senate election in California since 1988, and in the 2008 presidential election, Barack Obama carried the state with 61 percent.

Nevertheless, candidates did emerge for both offices. With the governorship, some had the high self-confidence (or ego) to think that they could fix the policy problems that had overwhelmed the "Terminator." With the Senate seat, a few Republicans saw glimmers of opportunity.

To understand who ran—and who did not run—for governor and senator, we should first look at some basic features of the state's political landscape. The most striking is its sheer size: 37 million people covering 156,000 square miles and a dozen media markets. House members and state legislators may make good gubernatorial or senatorial candidates elsewhere, but California is just too big for them to make a statewide impression. No sitting House member has won the governorship in living memory, and only four have won Senate seats. It has been decades since a sitting state legislator won either office.

Big-city mayors and statewide officeholders enjoy a better launching pad, and have long provided Democrats with gubernatorial and senatorial candidates. Republicans, however, have seldom occupied such posts in recent years. In 2006, the only Republican to win a downballot race was Steve Poizner, who defeated an inept Democrat for insurance commissioner. As for Governor Schwarzenegger, term limits would have prevented him from seeking reelection even if he had kept his popularity.

Like Senator George Murphy and Governor Ronald Reagan before him, Schwarzenegger used his Hollywood visibility to compensate for lack of elective experience. But as of 2010, the roster of Republican movie stars was tiny and the number who could plausibly run for governor or senator was about zero. So if Republicans could not find their champion in the pages of *Variety*, they would look in *Fortune*. What rich businesspeople lack in glitz, they can make up for in advertising. Although self-financing is hardly a sure route to victory, cash-strapped California Republicans liked the idea of running candidates who could pay much of their own way.[4]

The Candidates

As the party's only statewide elected official not named Schwarzenegger, Steve Poizner should have been the favorite to win the Republican primary for governor. In his business career, he founded a high-tech company that he sold for a billion dollars in 2000. Though he said that he was not a billionaire in 2010, he had enough wealth to launch a serious campaign.

Unfortunately for Poizner, another Republican had even deeper pockets. Meg Whitman, former chief executive officer of eBay, had built a net worth of about $1.2 billion.[5] For most of her business career, she had not been active in Republican politics except as a donor—and she had even given to Democrats. In the 2008 presidential primary campaign, she became a major supporter of Mitt Romney. She reportedly grew "fascinated" with politics, and as early as January 2008 was already exploring a gubernatorial race.[6] In the general election campaign, her appearances for McCain got favorable reviews from state Republicans.

Even before Poizner or Whitman announced, Tom Campbell filed for the race. He had a splendid résumé, including stints as a House member and state finance director, and two previous statewide races had given him visibility among politically attentive voters. And as a fiscal moderate and social liberal, he was a good fit for a California general election. The primary would be another matter, since conservative Republican voters balked at his support for legal abortion and same-sex marriage. Even so, he ran a close second to Whitman in some early polls. But by January 2010, it was clear that he could not compete financially with her, and he switched to the Senate race.

Whitman's wealth shaped the other party's primary as well. No Democratic billionaires emerged, so the party needed a candidate who did not have to buy name identification. That candidate was Jerry Brown. He, or a member of his family, had been on the California statewide ballot in 13 of the 16 midterm elections between 1946 and 2006. His father served as state attorney general and governor, while his sister served as state treasurer and was a Democratic nominee for governor. Brown himself won a race for secretary of state in 1970 and then served two terms as governor before losing a Senate campaign to Pete Wilson in 1982. He stayed in public life as state Democratic chair, candidate for the 1992 Democratic presidential nomination, and two-term mayor of Oakland. In 2006, he easily won election as state attorney general. In 2010, he was eligible to return to the governorship because service prior to 1990 does not count against California's term limits.[7]

Some leading figures, such as Los Angeles mayor Antonio Villaraigosa, declined to run against Brown. San Francisco mayor Gavin Newsom briefly entered the race, then ran for lieutenant governor instead. Both mayors had personal liabilities, but as journalist Timm Herdt explained, their biggest problem was financial: "Democratic Party leaders and donors were well aware that they would have to husband all their resources for a fall campaign, so they closed their checkbooks to potential Brown challengers, who dropped out of the race one by one. . . . It was Meg Whitman's shadow as much as Brown's that chased them away."[8]

Money was a major theme of the race for the Republican Senate nomination. As with the governor's race, the wealthy candidate was a woman who had led a high-tech company, played a high-profile role in the McCain campaign, and lacked a clear ideological background. Carly Fiorina, former CEO of Hewlett Packard, announced her interest in the post early in 2009. A bout with breast cancer slowed her down for much of the year, but by November she was well enough to make a formal declaration. Despite some striking similarities between Whitman and Fiorina, there were differences. Whereas Whitman had won praise for her leadership of eBay, Fiorina had made many enemies at HP, whose board fired her in 2005. As a McCain spokesperson, she had not fared nearly as well as Whitman. (At one point, she said that neither John McCain nor Sarah Palin had the experience to run a major company.)[9] Most importantly, Fiorina's net worth was less than one-tenth of Whitman's. She could give a lot, but could not pay for the whole campaign herself.

Before Campbell's unexpected jump to the Senate race, the only other major GOP candidate was Assemblyman Charles DeVore. Like Campbell, he was a policy wonk with strong qualifications. Unlike Campbell, he was an across-the-board conservative. Though his affluent home base in southern Orange County included many executives, he ran not as a corporate insider, but as a Tea Party outsider. His candidacy would test the movement's grassroots strength in California.

The Primary Campaigns

Right after Campbell switched races, his support split between Whitman and Poizner, leaving Whitman with a double-digit advantage. When Whitman began her ad campaign in February (a very early start for a June primary), she gained further momentum. The Field Poll showed her lead increasing from 45 to 17 percent in January to 63 to 14 percent in March.[10]

Meanwhile, Campbell took an early lead in the Senate race, though many voters were undecided. Fiorina may have hoped to corner moderate-to-conservative primary voters and isolate DeVore on her right. But with moderates going to Campbell, she took a different approach. Fiorina spokeswoman Julie Soderland said of Campbell's entry, "In some ways, it helps us define Carly for Republican primary voters," as a mainstream conservative and political outsider.[11]

Fiorina's campaign ran a strange web video—"Demon Sheep"— depicting Campbell as a tax-hiking, budget-busting wolf in sheep's clothing. The ad drove home the message with video of a person crawling around a pasture in a sheep costume with glowing, demonic eyes. Initially, the ad struck journalists as a bizarre mistake, but it had a purpose. Embedded within the video was a standard attack ad on Campbell's record as state finance director.[12] Standing alone, the attack might have flopped, but the garish wrapping guaranteed attention. The ad may have played a part in tightening the race. In late March, a survey by the Public Policy Institute of California showed Fiorina leading Campbell 24 to 23 percent, with just 8 percent for DeVore.[13]

A remarkable feature of the primary races was the effort of Republican candidates to tie each other to Schwarzenegger. Though "Demon Sheep" omitted the governor's name, its premise was that his fiscal policy had been a disaster. In the gubernatorial race, Poizner ran a television spot morphing Schwarzenegger's face into Whitman's. (By coincidence, the word "morphing" had entered everyday language directly from a Schwarzenegger movie, *Terminator 2: Judgment Day*.) Representative Tom McClintock, a Poizner endorser, appeared onscreen to warn that Whitman would represent Schwarzenegger's third term. Such ads were a sign of how far GOP sentiment had swung. Four years earlier, both Poizner and McClintock had been Schwarzenegger's running mates, as candidates for insurance commissioner and lieutenant governor. And in a 2004 race for state assembly, Poizner had even called himself a "Schwarzenegger Republican."[14] The Whitman camp liked reminding reporters of that label.[15]

Whitman and Poizner went after each other's conservative credentials. On both sides, the attacks had some basis: Their conservative garments still had the tags on them. A few years earlier, Poizner had been a liberal Republican, and Whitman had voiced no discernable ideology. In fact, she had often skipped voting. Poizner was having a tough time differentiating himself from Whitman until the Arizona immigration law put illegal aliens on the national agenda. Poizner endorsed the Arizona law and flayed Whitman for saying such a measure would not be appropriate for California.

Around the same time, the Securities and Exchange Commission (SEC) filed a civil fraud case against investment bank Goldman Sachs. Whitman had been a member of the firm's board. Although she had no direct involvement in the misconduct, the publicity provided Poizner with an opening for an attack ad. Over video images of circling vultures, the narrator says, "For most Californians, the financial crisis was a disaster. For Meg Whitman, it was easy money."[16]

The immigration and Goldman Sachs issues apparently drew blood, and polls showed Whitman's lead shrinking. She then poured more resources into the campaign, filling primary voters' mailboxes with anti-Poizner flyers and deploying former governor Pete Wilson to affirm that she would be "tough as nails" on illegal immigration.

During May, Newt Gingrich and Dick Cheney both endorsed her. (The Cheney endorsement had an element of payback. In an op-ed, he noted that Poizner had contributed $10,000 to the Gore-Lieberman Recount Committee in Florida.)[17] Though their support would carry little weight with independents, they were probably helpful with Republican base voters. By the end of May, she had regained an edge in the polls.

Fiorina had her own endorsement from a polarizing figure— Sarah Palin. Although she did not have the same financial advantage as Whitman, she pulled ahead in the polls as she outraised Campbell and DeVore put together. She could afford a modest television ad buy, while Campbell ran only a few spots and DeVore ran none at all. In spite of his limited budget, DeVore had hoped that Tea Party activists would put him into contention. For the most part, however, the self-styled "peasants with pitchforks" never showed up. The California coordinator for a Tea Party umbrella group explained, "Just from the distance perspective, it truly is like herding cats in California."[18]

Campbell's social liberalism proved a drawback. The conservative National Organization for Marriage sponsored ads and robocalls highlighting Campbell's support for same-sex marriage. According to the group's polling, many GOP primary voters said that his stand influenced their decision not to support him.[19]

Both Campbell and DeVore were hoping that the Internet would help them make up for their low television profile, but they were mostly tweeting to the converted. Just before the primary, Campbell ran a web ad arguing that he had the best chance of defeating Boxer. It drew only a few thousand views. Over on the Democratic side, blogger Mickey Kaus ran a quixotic campaign against Boxer. Relying on web videos and online issue papers, Kaus broke with party orthodoxy by opposing amnesty for undocumented aliens and criticizing public employee unions.[20] Kaus's effort attracted kind words from columnists and almost no support from Democratic voters.

The June 8 primary results were not close. Whitman crushed Poizner, 64 to 27 percent. Fiorina won 56 percent to Campbell's 22 percent, and DeVore's 19 percent.[21] Whitman's heavy spending on mail voters proved to be a wise investment: 58 percent of the vote came by mail instead of precinct polling places.

Campaigning in the primaries did provide valuable experience to novice candidates Whitman and Fiorina. On balance, though, tough nomination battles left them at a disadvantage. Since neither Brown nor Boxer had serious primary opponents, they could save their resources as the Republicans were burning through millions of dollars. And while Boxer had an 18-year voting record to defend, Brown enjoyed the luxury of remaining vague on the budget and other key issues. If he had fought Newsom or Villaraigosa, he would have had to stake out positions appealing to Democratic primary voters, and then try to modulate them for the general electorate.[22]

The Republican candidates now had to handle a good deal of residue. Their business records had come under criticism during the primary campaign, and Democrats picked up this line of attack. Unions immediately started running ads accusing Whitman of hiding profits in the Cayman Islands and making personal use of corporate jets. Meanwhile, the Boxer campaign reposted a Campbell web ad lambasting Fiorina's record at HP.[23] More important, both Whitman and Fiorina had courted conservative Republicans in ways that might limit their appeal to other voters, including Hispanic Americans. Whitman tried to shift by advertising in Spanish-language media and by stressing her opposition to a 1994 ballot measure to deny government benefits to illegal aliens. Yet she soon learned that her "tough as nails" stance on immigration had set her up for a stumble.

The General Election Campaign

As the campaign got under way, Democrats led Republicans both in party identification and formal party registration.[24] Notwithstanding some high-profile Republican victories, the Democratic Party has had a strong position in the state for decades.[25] It got even stronger in the 1990s, thanks in part to the loss of GOP-leaning aerospace workers and the increase in Democratic-leaning Hispanics. The state went Republican in all six presidential elections between 1968 and 1988. It went Democratic in all five presidential elections between 1992 and 2008.

Nevertheless, California Republicans thought that they had a chance. Whitman said that she would dig deep into her own bank account to finance the campaign, and other GOP candidates hoped to clutch her coattails. Moreover, Jerry Brown initially reinforced his reputation for eccentricity by making unguarded comments comparing Whitman to Nazi propaganda minister Josef Goebbels and—potentially more harmful to party unity—disparaging his old rival, former president Clinton.

During the early weeks, most polls showed a tight race for governor, with Whitman sometimes in the lead. On September 28, the gubernatorial candidates had their first debate. It produced no major gaffes or rallying cries, but it did show Brown at his best: well informed, spontaneous, and proud of being 72 years old. (He had been the state's youngest governor of the 20th century, and if elected, he would now be its oldest governor ever.) Whitman stuck to her talking points too carefully: At times she sounded overly scripted. Nevertheless, she turned in a credible performance that gave mild encouragement to her supporters.

The next day brought the kind of moment that campaigns dread. Attorney Gloria Allred, a notorious publicity-seeker, charged that Whitman had long employed an illegal alien as her housekeeper. At Allred's press conference, the housekeeper tearfully said that Whitman had mistreated her and coldly fired her when she asked for immigration help. After Whitman responded that she had not known that the housekeeper was undocumented, Allred produced a 2003 letter from the Social Security Administration informing Whitman and her husband that the housekeeper's Social Security number did not match their files. Whitman's husband had written on the letter, "Nicky, please check this. Thanks."[26] Such "no-match" letters are a well-known red flag, so Whitman's credibility came into question. More broadly, the issue opened this "tough-as-nails-on-immigration" candidate to the charge of hypocrisy.

The following Saturday, she had her second debate with Brown, on Spanish-language Univision. Immigration was a major topic, of course, and Brown hammered her for wanting to bring in "semi-serfs" to do the dirty work for affluent people.[27] And two days after that exchange, California counties started sending out vote-by-mail ballots. The timing of the housekeeper revelation was so hurtful that Republicans suspected collusion between Allred and the Brown campaign, though no hard evidence emerged. (It later turned out that the pro-Brown California Nurses Association had helped put the housekeeper in touch with Allred.)

Whitman did well in a third debate, talking about the need for pension reform and other fiscal issues. But by this time, the controversy had done its damage and most surveys put Brown in the lead. Between late September and late October, the Field Poll showed Whitman holding steady among white non-Hispanic voters at 44 percent, but plunging 13 points among Hispanic voters, from 40 to 27 percent.[28]

The governor's race tended to eclipse the senatorial race, with the candidates debating only twice, once on television and once on radio. In the debates, Boxer and Fiorina mostly stuck with standard party positions on social and economic issues. Most of the action took place in 30-second television spots, with Fiorina attacking Boxer as an arrogant and ineffectual career politician. Boxer went after Fiorina's corporate record, and toward the end of the campaign aired a dramatic spot featuring emotional testimony by laid-off HP workers.

Boxer led in most polls throughout the fall, though some showed Fiorina within striking distance and a couple even gave her a slight lead. These numbers encouraged pro-Republican outside groups such as Crossroads GPS to put some money into the state. Fiorina also hoped that Whitman's massive spending—more than $140 million by Election Day—would have the side effect of putting her over the top.

Nevertheless, Democrats retained their longstanding advantage in the ground game. To the extent that there was any grassroots activism in the state, it was mostly the work of organized labor, especially public employee unions. Despite Whitman's spending on "microtargeting" operations, Republicans had nothing comparable. The religious right and the nebulous Tea Party movement, highly significant elsewhere, barely registered.

The Results

On election night, the Republican tide stopped on the far side of the Sierras. Brown defeated Whitman 53 to 42 percent and Boxer beat Fiorina 52 to 42 percent. In much of the country, challengers ousted career politicians by casting themselves as rebels. But when the pollsters asked Californians whether they would rather have an insider or an outsider for governor, they preferred the insider by 54 to 36 percent.[29]

Demographics hurt the Republicans. Hispanics made up 22 percent of the state's voters, compared with only 8 percent nationwide.

African Americans and Asian Americans also sided with the Democrats, leaving Republicans to vie for white voters, who account-ed for 62 percent of the state electorate. Whitman and Fiorina did win the white vote, but not by the numbers that they needed. Religion was one reason. White evangelicals vote strongly Republican but account for only about 15 percent of Californians. By comparison, the percentage is three times as great in such GOP strongholds as Oklahoma.[30] White Californians tend to be more socially liberal than whites in other states, and thus less sympathetic to today's GOP.

Democrats had a 13-point party identification advantage among California voters, compared with an even split in the nation. Whereas voters in the national exit poll disapproved of President Obama's job performance by 55 to 44 percent, California voters went the opposite way, with 53 percent approving and 44 percent disapproving. It made sense that Boxer put the president in one of her last campaign ads: California was a rare spot where his support could help.

Whitman advisor Rob Stutzman succinctly summarized California's demographic and political characteristics: "Too damn blue."[31]

But is that the whole story? In the previous decade, after all, Republicans had won gubernatorial elections in other deep-blue states: New York, Connecticut, Hawaii, and Rhode Island, among others. In 2010, Republican Scott Brown won a Senate seat in Massachusetts. Any explanation of the results in California must take account of the candidates and their campaigns. Brown and Boxer were both veteran politicians who knew how to win Californians' votes. Whitman and Fiorina were newcomers who had to answer for business decisions that they had made before running.

Whitman in particular suffered for her late entry into political life. Someone with political experience would have been more care-ful about hiring domestic help, or at least would have found a way to defuse the housekeeper issue before it exploded. And while maintain-ing message discipline, a veteran politician would have varied her rhetoric to sound more spontaneous. (The old joke is that sincerity is everything, and if you can fake that, you have it made). At a women's forum toward the end of the campaign, television journalist Matt Lauer challenged the candidates to stop negative ads. The audience booed Whitman when she refused. She could have turned the situation around by noting that the unions would continue their attack ads against her even if Brown stopped his. But she froze.

Sometimes wealthy candidates have great natural talents that help them overcome their lack of campaign experience. Nelson Rockefeller was a spectacular example, winning the governorship of New York in 1958 and becoming a star of an otherwise dismal GOP midterm. Whitman did not display such innate talent. It cost her $43 a vote to prove that money cannot buy everything.

Endnotes

[1] Joel Kotkin, "The Golden State's War on Itself," *City Journal* 20 (Summer 2010), at www.city-journal.org/2010/20_3_california-economy.html.

[2] Mark DiCamillo and Mervin Field, "Voter Ratings of Schwarzenegger and the State Legislature Equal Historic Lows," The Field Poll, March 21, 2010, at field.com/fieldpollonline/subscribers/Rls2333.pdf.

[3] In 1992, Feinstein won a special election to complete the last two years of Pete Wilson's Senate term. She defeated John Seymour, whom Governor Wilson had named as his interim successor in the Senate. During that year, Boxer won a full term, succeeding Democrat Alan Cranston.

[4] On the surprisingly poor record of self-financed candidates in California and other states, see Anne Bauer, "The Efficacy of Self-Funding a Political Campaign," National Institute on Money in State Politics, June 22, 2010, at www.followthemoney.org/press/PrintReportView.phtml?r=429.

[5] "The 400 Richest Americans #326 Margaret Whitman," *Forbes*, September 30, 2009, at www.forbes.com/lists/2009/54/rich-list-09_Margaret-Whitman_5AW7.html.

[6] Joe Mathews, "EBay Chief May Run for Governor," *Los Angeles Times*, January 25, 2008, at articles.latimes.com/2008/jan/25/local/me-whitman25.

[7] The only other living former governor in that category was Republican George Deukmejian, 82 years old and long retired from active politics.

[8] Timm Herdt, "The Shadow of Meg's Money," *Ventura County Star*, April 20, 2010, at www.vcstar.com/news/2010/apr/20/the-shadow-of-meg-whitmans-money/.

[9] Brian Montopoli, "McCain Adviser Says McCain, Palin Unprepared to Run Major Company," CBS News, September 16, 2008, at www.cbsnews.com/8301-502163_162-4453258-502163.html.

[10]Mark DiCamillo and Mervin Field, "Whitman Widens Her Lead over Poizner in GOP Primary and Is Now Leading Brown in Simulated General Election Match-Ups," The Field Poll, March 17, 2010, at field.com/fieldpollon line/subscribers/Rls2330.pdf.

[11]Debra J. Saunders, "Meg's Money Has Power to Change the Game," San Francisco Chronicle, March 28, 2010, at www.sfgate.com/cgi-bin/article.cgi?f= /c/a/2010/03/28/INSQ1C12AN.DTL.

[12]John Guardino, "In Defense of Demon Sheep," Frum Forum, February 6, 2010, at www.frumforum.com/in-defense-of-demon-sheep.

[13]Mark Baldassare et al. "PPIC Statewide Survey: Californians and Their Government," Public Policy Institute of California, March 2010, at www.ppic .org/content/pubs/survey/S_310MBS.pdf.

[14]Kevin Yamamura, "Poizner No Longer a 'Schwarzenegger Republican,'" Sacramento Bee, August 19, 2010, at www.sacbee.com/2010/04/29/2713919 /poizner-no-longer-a-schwarzenegger.html.

[15]Stu Woo, "GOP Rivals Bash California Icon," Wall Street Journal, May 26, 2010, at online.wsj.com/article/SB100014240527487033419045752668216 81457474.html.

[16]Joe Garofoli, "Hard-Hitting New Poizner TV Ad: Whitman's 'Vulture'-Like Dealings With Goldman Sachs," San Francisco Chronicle, April 30, 2010, at www.sfgate.com/cgi-bin/blogs/nov05election/detail?entry_id=62542.

[17]Dick Cheney, "Whitman Stronger Republican Candidate," Orange County Register, May 14, 2010, at www.ocregister.com/articles/california-248902 -bush-poizner.html.

[18]Maeve Reston, "DeVore, Fiorina Actively Court 'Tea Party' Vote," Los Angeles Times, May 31, 2010, at articles.latimes.com/2010/may/31/local/la-me -tea-party-20100531.

[19]National Organization for Marriage, "National Organization For Marriage Poll Finds Pro-Gay Marriage Stance Hurt Tom Campbell's Campaign," June 11, 2010, at "www.nationformarriage.org/site/apps/nlnet/content2.aspx?c=om L2KeN0LzH&b=5075187&ct=8437245&notoc=1.

[20]Robin Abcarian, "Mickey Kaus Versus the Box," Los Angeles Times, May 28, 2010, at latimesblogs.latimes.com/california-politics/2010/05/mickey -kaus-vs-the-box.html.

[21]California Secretary of State, Statement of Vote: June 8, 2010, Direct Primary Election, at www.sos.ca.gov/elections/sov/2010-primary.

[22]See Dan Schnur's comments in Cathleen Decker, "Whitman Scoots Right on a Two-Edged Sword," *Los Angeles Times*, May 30, 2010, at www.latimes .com/news/local/la-me-theweek-20100530,0,4210214.story.

[23]"Internal Affairs: Barbara Boxer Recycles . . . Tom Campbell's Campaign Ads!" *San Jose Mercury News*, June 20, 2010, at www.mercurynews.com/bay -area-news/ci_15330202.

[24]Jeffrey M. Jones, "Party ID: Despite GOP Gains, Most States Remain Blue," Gallup Poll, February 1, 2010, at www.gallup.com/poll/125450/Party -Affiliation-Despite-GOP-Gains-States-Remain-Blue.aspx; California Secretary of State, "15-Day Report of Registration," May 24, 2010, at www.sos.ca .gov/elections/ror/ror-pages/15day-prim-10/hist-reg-stats.pdf.

[25]Sean Trende, "The Politics of Arizona's Immigration Law," *RealClearPolitics*, July 8, 2010, at www.realclearpolitics.com/articles/2010/07/08/the_politics _of_arizonas_immigration_law_106221.html.

[26]Ken McLaughlin and Steve Harmon, "Lawyer: Whitman's Husband Told Housekeeper to `Check This' Government Letter," *San Jose Mercury News*, October 1, 2010, at www.mercurynews.com/ci_16221008.

[27]John Ellis, "Housekeeper Issue Heats up Fresno Gov. Debate," *Fresno Bee*, October 1, 2010, at www.fresnobee.com/2010/10/01/v-textonly/2101070 /hispanic-issues-loom-large-in.html.

[28]Mark DiCamillo and Mervin Field, "Brown and Whitman in a Dead Heat in the Race for Governor," The Field Poll, September 3, 2010, at field.com/fieldpollonline/subscribers/Rls2353.pdf; Mark DiCamillo and Mervin Field, "Increased Support from Women, Latinos, Non-Partisans and L.A. County Voters Propelling Brown to a Ten-Point Lead over Whitman in Governor's Race," The Field Poll, October 28, 2010, at field.com/fieldpollon line/subscribers/Rls2362.pdf.

[29]Exit poll data from Edison Research, November 2, 2010, at www.cnn.com /ELECTION/2010/results/polls.main/.

[30]Compilation of survey data by John Green at www.beliefnet.com/Faiths /2004/11/State-By-State-Percentage-Of-White-Evangelicals-Catholics-And -Black-Protestants.aspx.

[31]Seema Mehta and Maeve Reston, "Whitman, Fiorina losses raise questions about their political futures in California," *Los Angeles Times*, November 8, 2010, at articles.latimes.com/2010/nov/08/local/la-me-whitman-fiorina-20101108.

Chapter 10

The Perils of Holding a Tea Party at High Altitude: Colorado's Senate and Gubernatorial Races in 2010

by Dr. Seth E. Masket

*Associate Professor of Political Science
at the University of Denver*

Introduction

Colorado's top-ballot races were anything but predictable in 2010. The Tea Party movement was particularly powerful during these races, leading to defeats of candidates favored by Republican Party elites during the primaries. The general election for Senate was one of the most expensive and closely watched in the country. The gubernatorial general election, meanwhile, featured Republican leaders abandoning their own nominee in favor of a third-party candidate. Despite the general rout of Democrats across the country and within Colorado, the Democratic nominees in these two contests prevailed. The results demonstrated the strengths of the Tea Party movement during 2010, but also revealed the risks that a party faces when a populist movement takes over its nomination process.

The Primaries

During the party nominations stage, party elites went about doing what they normally do—picking candidates they like and giving them enormous advantages (money, expertise, endorsements) for the nomination (Cohen et al. 2008; Masket 2009). In most years, these advantages prove insurmountable to all but a handful of lucky challengers. 2010 was not like most years, however.

To say that 2010 was an anti-incumbent/antiestablishment year (Beam 2010) is a bit too simplistic. As Sides (2010a) and Abramowitz and Sabato (2010) note, despite the media attention on incumbents being in trouble in primaries, only six members of Congress actually lost their jobs during the primary season—about average historically. While the casualties did include such presumably safe incumbents as Sen. Bob Bennett (R-UT), they nonetheless represent only a tiny fraction of the members of Congress actually up for reelection in 2010, with the vast majority retaining their seats. Yet it does seem fair to say that incumbents and party-favored candidates had to work harder than usual to win this year. Colorado's senatorial and gubernatorial primaries provide rich examples of this phenomenon.

The U.S. Senate Race

Of the four top-ballot statewide races, only the Democratic contest for U.S. Senate actually featured an incumbent seeking to defend his seat. And Sen. Michael Bennet was not a typical incumbent; Gov. Bill Ritter had appointed him to the position in January of 2009, after Sen. Ken Salazar accepted a position as President Obama's secretary of the interior. This was, according to many observers, a most unusual appointment, as Bennet—then the superintendent of the Denver Public School district—had no prior electoral experience. Having previously served as chief of staff to Denver's mayor, John Hickenlooper, Bennet was no stranger to politics, but he had no automatic allies within the state's Democratic Party. Thus, many of the advantages incumbents usually enjoy—political experience, a seasoned staff, a network of party allies—were missing from Bennet's quiver.

Indeed, Bennet's appointment to the Senate laid the seeds for his most serious challenge in the primaries. Among the list of prominent Democratic candidates suggested to Governor Ritter for the appointment was former statehouse Speaker Andrew Romanoff, who had just recently been termed out of office. Others mentioned for the job, including Mayor Hickenlooper and Reps. John Salazar and Ed Perlmutter, already had jobs in which they appeared to be safe.[1] Romanoff was extremely popular among the state's active Democrats, many of whom felt that the Senate seat was a perfectly timed opportunity for the state to continue to utilize Romanoff's skills. When the governor passed on appointing Romanoff to this position, Romanoff and his supporters became incensed and began looking for other avenues for him to hold office.

In September 2009, Romanoff announced his intention to challenge Bennet for the Senate seat. From the start, Romanoff enjoyed some advantages over the incumbent, including significant electoral and legislative experience, a network of Democratic friends and allies across the state, and a more comfortable public speaking style. Yet Bennet had two things Romanoff did not—substantial financial resources—and the ability to raise more—and the energetic support of the president of the United States. Within a day of Romanoff's announcement, Obama stated his preference for Michael Bennet.

Colorado's system for party nominations is unusual and multi-tiered. While the nomination is ultimately determined by a primary held in early August, the first contest is traditionally a precinct caucus, held in March of the election year. At these caucuses, attendees must perform two tasks—register their support for one candidate or another, and elect attendees for the next stage of the process, the county conventions and assemblies, usually held a month or two later. The same process repeats itself there, with attendees voting on their preferences and electing delegates to the state assembly and convention.

While the precinct caucuses are open to all registered party voters, turnout is usually much lower than in primaries. Thus it would not be terribly shocking to find that the preferences of caucus attendees are significantly different than those of primary voters (although see Hersh 2010). By their nature, those who attend the caucuses and stick through the process to attend the county and state convention and assembly are the most committed partisans, usually with many years of party experience and service under their belts.

In the Democratic Senate race, these caucus attendees picked Andrew Romanoff over Michael Bennet by a vote of 50 to 42 percent, with the rest voting uncommitted. The party faithful, it seemed, had made a choice. The endorsement by Barack Obama, who remained greatly popular among party activists, proved far from influential on this select electorate. Yet this stage of the nominations process is far from determinative. It ensured only that both Romanoff and Bennet would have a primary contest and that Romanoff's name would appear first on the ballot.[2]

The primary itself was a very different contest. When competing for the favor of a few thousand convention attendees, Bennet's vast financial resources made little difference; most forms of advertising at that stage were pretty useless. When trying to win over a primary electorate, however, the funds proved quite helpful. This electorate contained many who were only marginally familiar with either Romanoff—the former state legislator from Denver—or Bennet—the incumbent who had been appointed just over a year earlier.

Romanoff surely raised a respectable amount of money—nearly $2 million overall—and his campaign was bolstered by the endorsement of former president Bill Clinton.[3] However, Obama's endorsement of Bennet was not just in name. It came with several presidential fundraisers and the activation of the Obama For America (OFA) organization, which was essentially a rebranding of the president's 2008 campaign (Catanese 2010). With this help, Bennet ultimately raised more than $7 million prior to the primary.

Romanoff did succeed in raising questions about Bennet, particularly when it came to his ties to Wall Street. Yet it was difficult to overcome Bennet's advantages. The one thing that could have affected many primary voters—a *New York Times* article tying Bennet to a financially questionable decision regarding the pensions of Denver Public Schools employees—arrived a bit late for Romanoff's purposes.

On Election Day, Bennet prevailed over Romanoff 54 to 46. His support was remarkably widespread; while Romanoff held his hometown of Denver and took a handful of counties in the southeast region of the state, Bennet took the majority of the vote in 51 of the state's 64 counties, 21 of them by more than 60 percent. A geographical depiction of the vote can be seen in figure 10.1.

Figure 10.1—County-Level Vote in 2010 Colorado Democratic U.S. Senate Primary

Source: *Denver Post*
Note: Shaded counties are those in which Michael Bennet received the majority of the vote. Others were won by Andrew Romanoff.

To what extent did Bennet owe his commanding win to the work of the Obama For America organization? In theory, if the Obama organization influenced the 2010 primary vote in Colorado, we should see similarities in the voting patterns between that election and the state's presidential caucuses two years earlier. I test this in table 10.1, regressing Bennet's share of the county-level 2010 primary vote on Obama's share of the 2008 caucus vote. I include census measures to control for county demographic disparities, including urbanization, education, income, race, and religion. I also include the 2008 presidential general election vote as a control for county liberalism-conservatism.[4]

Table 10.1—Variables Predicting Bennet Primary Vote in 2010

Variable	Coefficient
Obama share of Clinton + Obama caucus vote, 2008	0.305** (0.103)
Percent urban	1.405 (3.713)
Percent with college degree	36.36 (21.74)
Percent making more than $75,000	–33.65 (16.93)
Percent African American	–44.72 (53.61)
Percent Latino	19.54 (15.47)
Percent Evangelical	–2.628 (12.61)
Percent Catholic	–5.137 (9.659)
Obama share of two-party vote, 2008 general election	–33.77* (13.97)
Constant	39.52** (13.11)
Observations	60
R-squared	0.293

Notes: Cell entries are ordinary least squares coefficients. Standard errors appear in parentheses (*$p \le .05$, **$p \le .01$, ***$p \le .001$).

Source: Compiled by author.

The table shows a strong relationship between the Obama caucus vote from 2008 and the Bennet primary vote in 2010; each percentage-point increase in the Obama vote was associated with a 0.3 percentage point increase in the Bennet vote. This result is statistically significant at the .01 level. The implication is that Bennet won, at least in part, because of the influence of the Obama organization. The control variables, meanwhile, showed little relationship to the primary vote with the exception of the measure of county ideology. This suggests that Bennet did better in the more conservative counties across the state.

The Republican contest for Senate saw considerable competition as well. Although Democrats had been doing well in statewide elections since 2004, they had only controlled both Senate seats since 2008. Most polling, meanwhile, suggested that the president's party, which tends to lose congressional seats in midterm elections, was looking particularly vulnerable for 2010, and the Senate incumbent whose term was up in Colorado was an appointee with almost no electoral experience. (Unlike most incumbents, Senate appointees have a tough time in elections; only about a third of appointees have won voters' permission to keep their seats since the passage of the Seventeenth Amendment (Reed 2008). Thus this race looked like a strong potential pickup opportunity for the Republicans, and the right nominee could seal the deal.

Many Republican Party leaders settled early on their choice for nominee. Partly at the urging of Sen. John McCain (R-AZ), many elite Republicans backed Jane Norton, who had previously been Colorado's lieutenant governor. The idea of Republican Party elites converging on a preferred candidate long before the primary is hardly a new in Colorado. Many of these same party figures had helped clear the field for Senate candidates Bob Schaffer in 2008 and Pete Coors in 2004, as well as for gubernatorial candidate Bob Beauprez in 2006.

Many of these activists, brought into politics through the nascent Tea Party movement, expressed an early liking for Ken Buck, the district attorney of Weld County in the north-central part of the state. Buck seemed to attract activist support in part due to political stances that were more conservative and more provocative than those of Jane Norton. Buck, for example, had previously described Social Security as a "horrible policy" and advocated for its privatization (Miller 2010).

The Norton campaign was concerned enough about Buck's challenge that it chose not to contest Buck in the caucuses. By skipping the contest altogether, she would avoid the potential embarrassment of a caucus loss or, worse, being barred from the primary by failing to secure 10 percent of the vote. Buck's caucus victory would thus be an empty one.

After the convention, Norton generally trailed Buck by 10 to 15 points in polls. While she maintained an advantage in terms of both endorsements and funds, she was never able to overtake Buck, who ultimately won the primary by just over 3 points. A map of the primary vote (seen in figure 10.2) shows that Buck's support was widespread, limiting Norton's wins to the Denver metro area, a handful of mountain counties, and her home county of Mesa, the home of Grand Junction on the state's western border. Buck, meanwhile, won not just in his own Eastern Plains region, but also in the Western Slope and along much of the Front Range.

Figure 10.2—County-Level Vote in 2010 Colorado Republican U.S. Senate Primary

Source: *Denver Post*
Note: Shaded counties are those in which Ken Buck received the majority of the vote. Others were won by Jane Norton.

The Governor's Race

By the summer of 2010, things were looking good for Denver mayor John Hickenlooper's bid to become Colorado's next governor. Indeed, a prominent Colorado political blog confidently claimed, "There's no realistic scenario where [Hickenlooper] loses anymore" (ColoradoPols 2010). This outcome would have been quite difficult to predict just eight months earlier. Although Hickenlooper had a quiet primary day in August, having avoided any challengers to his nomination, the path that led him to the Democratic nomination was circuitous.

At the beginning of 2010, Colorado's political observers were focused on Gov. Bill Ritter's odds for reelection. His polling situation looked difficult, if not insurmountable; a December 2009 Rasmussen poll showed Ritter trailing likely Republican nominee Scott McInnnis 48 to 40. With slow economic growth and high unemployment, combined with political actions that had undermined his support among organized labor (Bartels 2009), Ritter announced on January 5 that he would not run for a second term (Bartels 2010).

This left the Democrats scrambling to find a new gubernatorial nominee less than a year before the election. To a remarkable degree, the party managed to avoid internal strife, with the leading possible Democratic candidates quietly coordinating and apparently deferring to each other in order of declining electability. Eyes first turned to Interior Secretary Ken Salazar, who had won his U.S. Senate seat with broad support in 2004. Salazar received tacit endorsements from President Obama and Mayor Hickenlooper. When Salazar demurred, Hickenlooper agreed to run, and Democrats quickly rallied around him (Kraushaar 2010). No other Democrat challenged Hickenlooper's candidacy, and the Denver mayor won his party's nomination for governor by acclamation at the state convention.

The Republican contest for governor remained contentious from the beginning. Scott McInnis, with his congressional experience and strong name recognition throughout the Western Slope, seemed a popular early choice. He drew two challengers for the nomination, one from a little-known Evergreen businessman named Dan Maes, the other from McInnis's own former protégé, state senator Josh Penry. Penry, all of 33 years old, had previously worked in McInnis's congressional office, and offered a challenge somewhat from McInnis's right. Penry won early press attention through a campaign that was sharply critical of both political parties (Bonham 2009), and even won a September 2009 party straw poll held at Keystone Resort. Yet by November, Penry had decided to abandon the race. Conservative donors were assembling a 527 committee on behalf of McInnis, threatening to overwhelm Penry's own fundraising abilities (Crummy 2009).

Penry's departure at the end of 2009 left Scott McInnis, a well-known former congressman with numerous endorsements and half a million dollars cash on hand, facing only Dan Maes, who had little name recognition or experience and less than $8,000 in the bank. Perhaps McInnis could be forgiven at this point for not taking Maes's challenge more seriously. Maes, however, continued to press his case with Tea Party groups across the state, raising concerns that McInnis was not sufficiently conservative and that only someone from outside the system could fix it. With the support of these activists, Maes managed to win nearly 40 percent of the vote on caucus night in March and actually defeated McInnis in the Republican Assembly in May by a slender margin of 49.4 percent to 48.9 percent.

McInnis still had the lion's share of funds and endorsements by this point, and convention winners rarely go on to win the primary. The environment might have remained safe for McInnis had it not been for the emergence of a scandal. In mid-July, the *Denver Post* and other news organizations aired allegations that Scott McInnis had, while writing on water policy for a newsletter owned by the Hasan Family Foundation, extensively borrowed from a 1984 article by Gregory Hobbs, who later served on the Colorado Supreme Court. McInnis was paid $300,000 for these articles but did not attribute the text to Hobbs or anyone else (Crummy 2010a). McInnis initially tried to blame the incident on subordinates and on a water policy analyst, but ultimately owned up to the error and sought to pay back the income. The scandal proved damaging to McInnis; while he'd been leading Hickenlooper in matchup polls earlier in the summer, post-scandal polling showed him down by 5 points to the Democrat (Booth and O'Connor 2010).

At this point, the situation looked daunting for Republicans who, less than a year earlier, saw the Colorado governor's mansion as low-hanging fruit for 2010. Their handpicked front-runner suddenly looked weak against the Democrat and was facing a surprisingly strong primary challenge from a poorly funded relative extremist who had scandals of his own (Fender 2010). This situation was apparently too much for former U.S. representative Tom Tancredo (R-Littleton). Arguing that neither of the Republican candidates could win in November, he publicly demanded that both drop out of the race, or else he would run against them. When neither dropped out, Tancredo followed through on his threat, enlisting as the gubernatorial nominee of the American Constitution Party.

Tancredo, one of the most conservative members of the House of Representatives, had a sharp impact on the race for governor. Polls suggested he would split the Republican electorate in two, virtually guaranteeing the Democrats a win should he stay in the race. Maes, meanwhile, showed little interest in moderating his views prior to the primary. During a late July campaign rally, Maes warned his supporters that Denver's popular public bicycle-sharing program was "converting Denver into a United Nations community" (Osher 2010).

Figure 10.3—County-Level Vote in 2010 Colorado Republican Gubernatorial Primary

Source: *Denver Post*
Note: Shaded counties are those in which Dan Maes received the majority of the vote. Others were won by Scott McInnis.

It was in this environment that Colorado Republicans went to vote in the August 10 primary. Republican voters, by a 2-point margin, picked Maes as their nominee. The county-level results show a strong regional pattern in the vote (figure 10.3), with McInnis winning the western part of the state, including his home county of Garfield, handily. Maes, however, dominated the Eastern Plains and the Denver metro area.

In many ways, Dan Maes and Ken Buck shared similar campaign narratives, fighting long odds to claim their party's nominations. To what extent were their candidacies fueled by the same insurgency? I seek to address this question in table 10.2, where I have regressed Maes's county-level vote on Buck's, using the same control variables used in table 10.1. Although none of the control variables' coefficients reaches statistical significance, there is a strong relationship between the Maes and Buck votes, with each 1-point increase in Buck's primary vote corresponding with a .55-point increase in Maes's primary vote share. The implication is that both candidacies were backed by the same sort of newly energized Tea Party voters. Buck and Maes were both part of the same insurgency.

Table 10.2—Variables Predicting Maes Gubernatorial Primary Vote in 2010

Variable	Coefficient
Buck share of Republican Senate primary vote, 2010	0.556** (0.192)
Percent urban	7.106 (4.080)
Percent with college degree	36.18 (24.18)
Percent making more than $75,000	−0.445 (18.51)
Percent African American	98.36 (59.54)
Percent Latino	8.955 (17.03)

Percent Evangelical	1.765 (13.52)
Percent Catholic	7.587 (10.61)
Obama share of two-party vote, 2008 general election	−21.98 (14.79)
Constant	−2.694 (19.72)
Observations	60
R-squared	0.259

Notes: Cell entries are ordinary least squares coefficients. Standard errors appear in parentheses (*p≤.05, **p≤.01, ***p≤.001).
Source: Compiled by author.

The General Election

Typically, even bizarre primary contests give way to relatively predictable general elections, with the nominees of the two major parties sparring to control a plurality of the electorate. This did not happen in Colorado's gubernatorial race in 2010. Tom Tancredo's quixotic bid as the nominee of the little-known American Constitution Party did not fade away, unlike so many other third-party campaigns. The opposite happened—Tancredo was increasingly perceived as the more credible and electable of the two conservative candidates.

This trend was abetted by a string of Republican Party elites issuing endorsements for Tancredo. Former U.S. representative and 2006 Republican gubernatorial nominee, Bob Beauprez, former state Senate president John Andrews, state senator Josh Penry, state representative Marsha Looper, and former state representative Rob Witwer were among the broad ideological range of Republican officials endorsing Tancredo for governor, considering Maes unelectable (Crummy 2010c). Even Ken Buck, running under the Republican banner for the U.S. Senate, withdrew his earlier endorsement of

Maes (Strogoff and Luning 2010). All this occurred amidst a strong but unsuccessful effort by party leaders to convince Maes to withdraw as the party's nominee. It is an interesting reflection on the peculiar nature of the 2010 midterm elections that Tom Tancredo—who once called President Obama a greater threat to the Constitution than Al Qaeda, and referred to the Council of La Raza as a "Latino KKK without the hoods or the nooses"—was considered the pragmatist's candidate. Not all Republican leaders found Tancredo an acceptable alternative, however; Mary Smith, the chair of the Denver County Republican Party, announced her endorsement of Democratic nominee John Hickenlooper (Strogoff and Luning 2010).

Figure 10.4—Polling in Colorado Gubernatorial Race During General Election

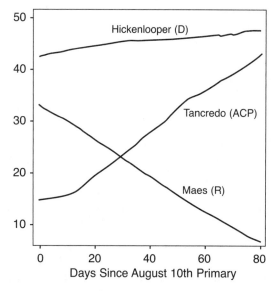

Note: Graph depicts lowest running averages of polls between John Hickenlooper (D), Dan Maes (R), and Tom Tancredo (American Constitution Party) during the general 2010 election cycle. Data compiled by Pollster.com.

So many party leaders lining up against Maes severely dampened his fundraising potential. During the first two weeks of September, while Hickenlooper raised $218,000 and Tancredo raised $120,000,

Maes only raised $14,000, much of which went toward paying a penalty for a previous campaign finance violation (Crummy 2010b). The result of all this activity was that Maes's support continued to drop throughout the fall. As figure 10.4 suggests, Maes's support transferred almost perfectly to Tancredo. By November, voters had largely settled on two main candidates for governor, with the Republican appearing as little more than a third-party spoiler. Indeed, prominent Republicans feared that Maes would finish below 10 percent of the vote, which, under Colorado law, would have rendered the Republicans a minor party for the next four years, severely hampering its fundraising abilities. In the end, Maes managed to eke out just over 11 percent of the vote, while Tancredo pulled 37 percent. Hickenlooper, who stayed relatively quiet during much of the campaign season and ran only a handful of positive advertisements, managed to win with 51 percent of the vote.

Figure 10.5—Polling in Colorado U.S. Senate Race During General Election

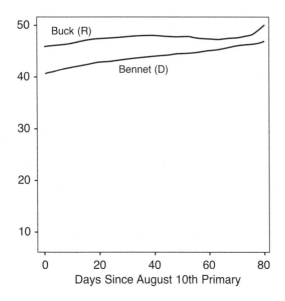

Note: Graph depicts lowest running averages of polls between Ken Buck (R) and Michael Bennet (D) during the general 2010 election cycle. Data compiled by Pollster.com.

By comparison, the race for U.S. Senate was much more typical of statewide elections, with the two major party candidates running within a handful of points of each other throughout the fall (see figure 5). The candidates began the general election season by trying to distance themselves somewhat from some of the stances they took during their difficult primary battles. Democratic nominee Michael Bennet, who had relied upon very explicit and public support from President Obama during the primary, decided that Obama's support might not be so helpful for the general election (Stephanopoulos 2010). Bennet further distanced himself from the president by opposing a second stimulus measure and urging action on the national debt (Kane 2010).

Republican nominee Ken Buck, meanwhile, sought to walk back several stances he had taken during his primary against Jane Norton, including opposition to the Seventeenth Amendment and support of Colorado's "personhood" amendment initiative, which would have defined life as beginning at the moment of conception.

Both candidates engaged in a blistering ad war. Bennet sought to define Buck as simultaneously an extremist ("Ken Buck's ideas are too extreme") and a flip-flopper ("Who is Ken Buck?"). For his part, Buck sought to describe Bennet as one of Obama and Pelosi's foot soldiers. A National Republican Senatorial Committee (NRSC) ad showed a picture of Bennet with the president and the Speaker, with the voiceover saying, "We need a senator for us, not them."

Bennet largely outmatched Buck financially, raising over $11 million to Buck's $3 million by mid-October. That difference was somewhat mitigated by outside money, which tended to favor Buck. The NRSC and the DSCC (Democratic Senatorial Campaign Committee) were heavily involved in the race, as well. Outside funding for the Senate race topped $30 million, making it the number one destination for outside money during the entire cycle (Attkisson 2010).

It was one of these outside funding efforts that ended up shaping the final days of the general election contest. During his primary with Jane Norton, Buck made the comment that Republicans should vote for him because he doesn't wear high-heeled shoes. This was a reference to an earlier comment by Norton's campaign that she would use her high-heeled shoes to kick Senate Majority Leader Harry Reid in the shins. Buck's comment, however, drew complaints of sexism during the primary. A Democratic-leaning group called Women's Voices Women's Votes revived these criticisms during the general election. They spent nearly $1 million running an advertisement featuring a woman explaining to the camera, "Colorado women deserve respect. We need leaders who will stand with us, whether we're in high heels or cowboy boots." The ad also referred to comments Buck had made as the Weld County district attorney, when he had refused to prosecute a rape case, suggesting that the victim had "buyer's remorse" (Peoples 2010).

It is difficult to say whether those ads *per se* caused the race to tighten up in the final weeks. However, it is interesting to note that the gender gap in the Senate race was historically massive. According to CNN exit polls, men preferred Buck to Bennet 54 to 40, while women preferred Bennet to Buck 56 to 39—roughly 15 points across gender lines. By comparison, the national House vote in 2010 only saw a 6-point gender gap. Similarly, there was only a 6-point gender gap in the U.S. Senate race between Mark Udall (D) and Bob Schaffer (R) in Colorado in 2008. It is certainly conceivable that the activation of gender issues in the final weeks of the campaign helped produce Michael Bennet's narrow victory.

Conclusion

Colorado's altitude did not place the state out of reach of the Republican wave of November 2010. Republicans took over the secretary of state and treasurer positions and retained their hold on the attorney general's office. Two of the state's seven congressional districts—those held by John Salazar and Betsy Markey—flipped from Democratic to Republican control. The GOP also made substantial inroads in the Colorado State Senate and managed to take over the state House by a single seat. Victories by John Hickenlooper and Michael Bennet ran very much counter to these trends and marked some of the very few bright spots for Democrats.

The results suggested that the Tea Party movement, which certainly energized Republican voters and activists and may have boosted the vote shares of conservative House candidates (Sides 2010b), had a considerable downside in some races—the nomination of less-electable Republicans. Dan Maes was very much the creature of

Colorado's Tea Party movement; it is difficult to conceive of his nomination in a different year. And he proved to be such a flawed candidate that many lifelong Republican leaders chose to actively work against their own nominee. We obviously cannot know whether a scandal-tainted Scott McInnis would have won the election had he won the primary, but it seems fair to suggest he would have done better than Maes.

Ken Buck, while certainly a more experienced politician than Maes, also rose to prominence with the aid of the state's Tea Party activists. It is less clear in Buck's case whether he was a superior or inferior candidate than Jane Norton, whom he defeated in the primary. However, a Norton candidacy likely would not have activated gender politics in the way Buck's did, possibly enabling Norton to defeat Michael Bennet. Whether fair or not, Buck is now spoken of in the same sentence as Sharron Angle of Nevada and Christine O'Donnell of Delaware—Tea Party candidates who may have cost the Republican Party control of the Senate.

References

Abramowitz, Alan, and Larry Sabato. 2010. "The Myth of the Angry Voter." *Politico*, May 24, www.politico.com/news/stories/0510/37662.html.

Alvarez, R. Michael, Betsy Sinclair, and Richard L. Hasen. 2010. "How Much Is Enough? The 'Ballot Order Effect' and the Use of Social Science Research in Election Law Disputes." *Election Law Journal* 5 (1):40–56.

Attkisson, Sharyl. 2010. "Outside Money Rules in Colorado Senate Race." *Political Hotsheet*, October 26.

Bartels, Lynn. 2009. "Ritter Rebuts Critics of Labor Bill Veto." *Denver Post*, June 6.

———. 2010. "Sources: Ritter Expected to Withdraw from Governor's Race." *Denver Post*, January 5.

Beam, Christopher. 2010. "Anti-Anti-Incumbency." *Slate*, August 4, www.slate.com/id/2262668.

Bonham, Nick. 2009. "Candidate Josh Penry: Republicans Deserve Another Chance." *Pueblo Chieftain*, October 11.

Booth, Michael, and Colleen O'Connor. 2010. "Maes Holds Slight Edge over McInnis, Poll Says." *Denver Post*, August 1.

Catanese, David. 2010. "How Michael Bennet Made It Look Easy." *Politico*, August 11, www.politico.com/news/stories/0810/40971.html.

Cohen, Marty, David Karol, Hans Noel, and John Zaller. 2008. *The Party Decides: Presidential Nominations before and after Reform*. Chicago: University of Chicago Press.

ColoradoPols. 2010. "Governor Line." *ColoradoPols.com*, weblog, August 17, coloradopols.com.

Crummy, Karen. 2009. "Penry Intends to Leave Governor's Race." *Denver Post*, November 9.

———. 2010a. "Judge's Water Essay Copied. Expert: McInnis' Work, Submitted as 'Original,' Plagiarizes Words, Ideas." *Denver Post*, July 13, A-01.

———. 2010b. "Maes' Fund-Raising Struggle Continues." *Denver Post*, September 21.

———. 2010c. "Republicans Come out for Tancredo over G.O.P. Nominee Maes." *Denver Post*, September 8.

Fender, Jessica. 2010. "Maes Agrees to Fine for Alleged Campaign-Finance Issues." *Denver Post*, July 13.

Hersh, Eitan. 2010. "Primary Voters Vs. Caucus Goers and the Peripheral Motivations of Political Participation." Paper read at the annual conference of the Midwest Political Science Association, April 7, at Chicago, Illinois.

Kane, Paul. 2010. "Bennet, in Tough Colo. Senate Race, Opposes Obama's Infrastructure Plan." *Washington Post*, September 8.

Kraushaar, Josh. 2010. "Salazar Not Running for Governor; Backing Hickenlooper." *Politico*, January 7, www.politico.com/blogs/scorecard /0110/Salazar_not_running_for_governor_backing_Hickenlooper.html.

Masket, Seth E. 2009. *No Middle Ground: How Informal Party Organizations Control Nominations and Polarize Legislatures*. Ann Arbor: University of Michigan Press.

Miller, Elizabeth. 2010. "Political Polygraph: A Fact Check on Ken Buck." *Denver Post*, August 14.

Osher, Christopher N. 2010. "Bike Agenda Spins Cities toward U.N. Control, Maes Warns." *Denver Post*, August 4, A01.

Peoples, Steve. 2010. "Women's Group Spends $800k to Attack Ken Buck's 'High Heels' Comment." *CQ Roll Call*, October 21.

Reed, Bruce. 2008. "The Wisdom of Crowds." *Slate*, December 17, www.slate .com/id/2207046.

Sides, John. 2010a. "Feel the Anger, People." *The Monkey Cage*, weblog, June 8, www.themonkeycage.org/2010/06/feel_the_anger_people.html.

———. 2010b. "How Much Did the Tea Party Help G.O.P. Candidates?" *The Monkey Cage*, weblog, November 4, www.themonkeycage.org/2010 /11/how_much_did_the_tea_party_hel.html.

Stephanopoulos, George. 2010. "Sen. Bennet Appreciates Obama's Help, Not Sure He Wants Him Back." *George's Bottom Line*, weblog, August 11, blogs.abcnews.com/george/2010/08/sen-bennet-appreciates-obamas -help-not-sure-he-wants-him-back.html.

Strogoff, Jody Hope, and Ernest Luning. 2010. "Defiant Maes Stays in Race as State G.O.P., Top Business Leaders Pull Support." *Colorado Statesman*, September 3.

Endnotes

[1]Salazar ended up losing his 2010 reelection bid, although Perlmutter easily won reelection.

[2]Top ballot placement may be worth roughly a percentage point of the vote, or maybe nothing at all (Alvarez et al. 2010).

[3]Clinton was possibly repaying a favor here, as Romanoff had endorsed Sen. Hillary Clinton's presidential run in 2008, while Bennet was an early Obama supporter.

[4]Broomfield, Jackson, Pitkin, and Rio Bravo counties are excluded from the analysis due to insufficient census data.

Chapter 11

Of Witches' Brew and Tea Party Too!: 2010 Delaware Senate Race

by Dr. Samuel B. Hoff

George Washington Distinguished Professor of History and Political Science; Department of History, Political Science, and Philosophy at Delaware State University

An Unexpected Vacancy

Delaware was not supposed to have a U.S. Senate election in 2010. Six-term incumbent Joseph R. Biden Jr. briefly ran for the Democratic nomination for president in 2008 before bowing out. He then announced his intention to seek a seventh term in the Senate, but instead was tapped by Barack Obama as his vice-presidential nominee. Biden simultaneously ran for vice president and U.S. senator from Delaware, winning the latter race by a 65 to 35 percent margin, even though he virtually ignored his Republican challenger. Biden accepted election as vice president and announced his intention to resign his Senate seat.

Two weeks after the 2008 presidential election, Delaware governor Ruth Ann Minner surprised many political observers by appointing long-time Biden aide Edward "Ted" Kaufman to the vacated seat. According to law, a special election would have to be held in 2010 to fill Biden's unexpired term. Immediately after his appointment, Kaufman declared that he would not seek election to the seat. Though Biden was sworn in for his seventh term as U.S. senator from Delaware on January 3, 2009, he officially resigned his seat on January 15, setting the stage for events that followed.

Delaware as a Blue State

Delaware's long political history is highlighted by alternating periods of dominance by one of the major political parties. Since 1992, the Democratic Party has ascended in the state. For instance, the majority of Delaware citizens have voted for Democratic candidates for president over the last five elections. Further, Democrat Thomas Carper joined Joe Biden in the Senate after defeating veteran Republican senator William Roth in the 2000 Senate race. During the 2008 presidential election cycle, a large number of citizens registered to vote for the first time, and the majority identified with Democrats. In the general election, the Barack Obama–Joe Biden ticket enjoyed its fifth-largest margin of victory among all states by trouncing the John McCain–Sarah Palin team in Delaware. At the state level, Democrats gained a majority in the Senate, and therefore controlled both legislative chambers for the first time in over a decade.

Opening Round: Waiting for Beau

When Delaware governor Ruth Ann Minner declined to appoint Lieutenant Governor John Carney to the vacant Senate seat and selected Ted Kaufman instead, speculation began over whether Kaufman was appointed simply to keep the seat warm for Joseph R. Biden III, better known as Beau. The oldest son of Joe Biden, Beau had gained national prominence through his introduction of his father at the 2008 Democratic National Convention and as an activist attorney general for the state of Delaware. After Kaufman stated his intention to step down from the Senate seat following the 2010 election, the drumbeat for a Beau Biden candidacy reached a fever pitch. But several factors eventually led the younger Biden to decide against entering the Senate race. First, Beau Biden's Army National Guard unit was deployed to Iraq for a year-long tour in

October 2008. Second, after Attorney General Biden returned from Iraq in September 2009, a large amount of his attention was required to prosecute the case of Dr. Earl Bradley, a Lewes-area pediatrician accused of sexual abuse of hundreds of infants and toddlers. Third, by the beginning of 2010 the political landscape had changed for Democrats, such that it was no longer a certainty that Beau would win the Senate seat in a cakewalk. In fact, a poll asking about prospective candidates showed him slightly trailing veteran U.S. House member Michael Castle, a moderate Republican who had served the state in one capacity or another for more than 40 years. Castle had entered the Senate race in October 2009. Still, Beau Biden's January 25, 2010 announcement that he would forego a campaign for the U.S. Senate sent shockwaves through the state and changed the dynamics of the Senate race.

Advantage Republican: Castle in Front

Following Beau Biden's decision not to contest the Senate seat in the 2010 special election, Delaware Democrats had to find another suitable candidate to take on Michael Castle. In early February 2010, second-term New Castle County executive Christopher Coons agreed to run for the Democratic nomination for the open Senate seat. From that point until the September 14, 2010 primary election in Delaware, Coons trailed Castle by double digits in the polls and struggled to keep up with Castle's fundraising. As it turned out, Castle's real competition came not from Coons, but from a challenger within his own party: Christine O'Donnell. O'Donnell, a conservative commentator who had competed in the previous two Senate elections in Delaware, entered the 2010 Senate race in March. Largely regarded as a fringe candidate with little chance to win, O'Donnell nonetheless challenged Castle to debates and promised to vigorously oppose the Democratic agenda if elected. By July 2010 she was answering questions about her personal finances and had raised only $55,000 for her Senate bid.

Then another lightning bolt hit the Delaware Senate race. In late July, Christine O'Donnell earned the endorsement of the Tea Party Express, a Sacramento, California group that promotes smaller government and lower taxes. Similar organizations associated with the Tea Party movement had lent their support to Republican candidates in other states' primaries, helping them to score huge upsets against establishment candidates in Kentucky (May) and Nevada (June). When another Tea Party-backed candidate won a Senate primary in Alaska in August and the Tea Party Express committed up to $250,000 to O'Donnell's campaign, a noticeable shift in campaign momentum occurred. In the final major public opinion poll released before the September 14 primary in Delaware, Michael Castle retained his large lead over Democrat Chris Coons, who ran uncontested for the Democratic nomination. Yet Castle's lead over O'Donnell vanished; he actually trailed her by 3 points.

Enter the Dog Catcher: O'Donnell Triumphant

By the evening of the primary in Delaware, it became apparent that Christine O'Donnell had scored a political upset of titanic proportions. She had defeated nine-term U.S. House member and political icon Michael Castle by a 53 to 47 percent margin, receiving a total of 30,561 votes to Castle's 27,021. O'Donnell won two of three counties, losing only in upstate New Castle but doubling Castle's total in Sussex and winning easily in Kent.

There were certainly many reasons for O'Donnell's stunning victory over the highly favored Castle. First, the infusion of Tea Party-based support added to the national momentum of that movement and excited indigenous conservative groups within Delaware, such as the 9-12 Delaware Patriots. Second, while it was logical for Castle to ignore O'Donnell during the fight for the Republican nomination, given his large lead in the polls, that strategy upset stalwarts who at least wanted the candidates to debate. When the Republican Party endorsed Michael Castle at the party's May 2010 convention and the state Republican Party chair took sides on behalf of Castle during the summer months, many O'Donnell supporters openly questioned the direction of the party. Third, though his moderate approach to politics made Michael Castle a favorite among Delaware voters of both parties for decades, his record contrasted sharply from O'Donnell's strident conservatism. Calling Castle a "RINO"—Republican In Name Only—O'Donnell criticized his support for the $700 billion bailout plan, stem cell research, and for environmental legislation.

A fourth explanation for O'Donnell's victory in the Republican Senate primary in Delaware can be traced to turnout patterns. Republican turnout exceeded Democratic turnout in the 2010 primary by an almost 3-to-1 ratio. The 32 percent turnout among registered Republicans doubled the turnout among voters in the party's primary that occurred in 2008 and quadrupled the turnout from 2006. However she did it, Christine O'Donnell—whom the Republican Party state chairman claimed could not be elected as dog catcher—was the party's nominee for the U.S. Senate.

Post-Primary Drama for Republicans

In the two weeks after the September 14 primary in Delaware, state Republicans had to respond to several developments emanating from O'Donnell's upset. For one, because the party had officially endorsed Michael Castle in its pre-primary convention, many wondered whether the party would recognize O'Donnell's achievement and rally around her. A few days after the election, the state party gave O'Donnell a tepid pledge of support. Further, Castle himself contemplated a write-in candidacy for the Senate, a result of losing the primary and bad feelings left over from the campaign. Although Castle decided against that move at the beginning of October, he continued to deny O'Donnell his backing.

Advantage Democrat: Coons in Front

When he first entered the Senate race, Chris Coons was viewed as a suitable foil for Michael Castle. Coons trailed Castle through the spring and summer. But in the first wave of polling that was done immediately after the primary, Coons held a consistent lead of 15 percentage points over Christine O'Donnell. Part of the reason for this advantage can be traced to Delaware's blue state status. But perhaps another reason has to do with Ms. O'Donnell's telegenic past.

Throughout the previous two decades, O'Donnell had appeared on a series of television programs in which she asserted a variety of bizarre positions and personal views, from disbelieving evolution to preaching abstinence to dabbling in witchcraft. While snippets from programs like Bill Maher's *Politically Incorrect* dribbled out shortly before the primary, the unflattering stories flooded the airways after the primary. The negative publicity from these stories contributed to a change in campaign strategy by the O'Donnell team. Instead of appearing on national media shows, she began opting for regional and local media coverage to get her message out. However, that revision of strategy led to criticism that she was inaccessible and afraid of responding to incessant questions about her past.

In mid-October, Democrat Chris Coons and Republican Christine O'Donnell met in a nationally televised debate sponsored by the Delaware First Media group and the University of Delaware. While neither candidate committed a serious error, Ms. O'Donnell's inability to identify any recent Supreme Court decision she disagreed with did not help her case.

Further, her indirect answer to a question about evolution made it appear that she was backing off from her previous controversial remarks on that topic. At another debate at Widener Law School, Ms. O'Donnell rejected the contention that the separation of church and state concept is found explicitly anywhere in the Constitution or amendments. Overall, the debates probably helped Mr. Coons more, in that Ms. O'Donnell's extreme views on certain social policies were exposed. Subsequently, public opinion polls showed Mr. Coons with a lead as large as 21 points and as low as 10 points; the actual election outcome was in between these parameters.

Election Outcome: Democrats Retain Seat

On November 2, 2010, 49 percent of registered voters cast ballots in the midterm election in Delaware. In the U.S. Senate race, Chris Coons defeated Christine O'Donnell by more than 50,000 votes, garnering 56.6 percent of the vote to O'Donnell's 40 percent. Ms. O'Donnell actually won two of three counties in the state, but could not make up the 70,000 vote advantage that Coons accumulated in New Castle. Though turnout in Delaware increased by 4 percent over that in the 2006 midterm election, the fact that it did not reach 50 percent worked against Ms. O'Donnell.

The Senate victory was part of a good night for Democrats in Delaware. For instance, the single U.S. House seat was won by Democrat John Carney, making it one of few in the nation where a House seat switched control to the Democrats. In state legislative contests, the net +1 pickup for Democrats was the only instance where any state legislature gained Democratic seats in 2010, according to the National Conference of State Legislatures. Finally, Democratic candidate Chipman Flowers won a close statewide race for treasurer, leaving auditor Tom Wagner as the only Republican holding a statewide elective office. The Senate outcome in Delaware meant that the Democrats held the seat vacated by Joe Biden in 2009, one of 13 states where Democrats retained the Senate seat in 2010. Though Democrats lost six U.S. Senate seats, they retained control of that chamber while losing more than 60 U.S. House seats and control of the latter chamber of Congress. Nationally, 2010 witnessed the worst midterm election performance by Democrats since 1938.

Back to the Future

A confluence of factors coalesced to produce an enormously interesting U.S. Senate race in Delaware, one that was followed extensively by national and international media alike. Much of it had to do with Christine O'Donnell's personality, issue positions, Tea Party affiliation, and upset of Republican Michael Castle in the Senate primary. According to the Pew Research Center's Project for Excellence in Journalism, O'Donnell was the biggest story of the midterm elections in the U.S. news media, and ranked second behind President Obama in total media coverage since the beginning of 2010. Yet all that name recognition and Ms. O'Donnell's $3 million advantage in funds raised resulted in her receiving only 5 percent more of the total vote than she did in the U.S. Senate race in 2008.

While Ms. O'Donnell's boast that her campaign forever changed the Delaware Republican Party was validated, the impact of that change remains uncertain. What is not in dispute is that Delawareans largely rejected the challenge posed by Tea Party insurgents in the 2010 general election, and that the First State is now among the bluest of Democratic states.

General References

Michael Barone and Richard E. Cohen, *The Almanac of American Politics 2010* (Washington, DC: National Journal Group, 2009).

Samuel B. Hoff, "Delaware," chapter in *State Party Profiles: A 50-State Guide to Development, Organization, and Resources*, eds. Andrew M. Appleton and Daniel S. Ward (Washington, DC: *Congressional Quarterly*, 1997), 52–57.

Samuel B. Hoff, "Delaware's Changing Political Landscape," *Delaware Lawyer*, (Fall 2009): 32–31.

Chuck Todd and Sheldon Gawiser, *How Barack Obama Won: A State-by-State Guide to the Historic 2008 Presidential Election* (New York: Vintage Books/Random House, 2009).

Chapter 12

Florida: A "Red Tide" Beaches All Democrats Running Statewide; U.S. Senate and Gubernatorial Races Highly Nationalized

by Dr. Susan A. MacManus

Distinguished Professor of Government and International Affairs at the University of South Florida

(With the assistance of Mary L. Moss, Undergraduate Researcher, USF Honors College; and David J. Bonanza, Research Assistant and USF Graduate)

Introduction: Florida's Faltering Economy Dashes Democrats' Hopes

Although Democratic registrants have outnumbered Republicans in Florida for years, Republicans frequently win statewide offices by pulling in independents and conservative Democrats living in the state's more rural Panhandle. Heading into the 2010 midterm election, Democrats had 600,000 more registered voters than Republicans.[1] Democrats had high hopes of winning back the governor's mansion, just in time for redistricting. They were equally optimistic about electing another Democrat to the U.S. Senate to join Senator Bill Nelson. It was not to be.

Democrats' Dreams Fade

As Florida's unemployment and foreclosure rates continued to creep up, animosity toward the majority party in Washington did as well. The voting enthusiasm gap between Republicans and Democrats widened as Tea Party activists and sympathizers gained momentum and independents increasingly leaned toward "the party out of power in Washington" and sought new faces in high places. It was a highly nationalized midterm election at every level—from the top to the bottom of the ticket. The sagging economy, TARP (an acronym for Troubled Asset Relief Program), the economic stimulus package, bailouts, the exploding national debt, and the health care reform plan, nicknamed "ObamaCare," made Democrats easy targets in a state experiencing unusually high levels of economic stress.

Citizen Anti-Washington Activism Escalates

For well over a year before the fall 2010 election, anger had been at a fever pitch against elected officials at all levels for their inability to reverse Florida's economic slide. Early warning signs included a record number of first-time candidates filing to run, an upswing in intraparty competition as challengers rose up against long-serving incumbents, and citizen activism on the rise.

Early on, Republican Marco Rubio became a favorite of the anti-Washington, anti-incumbent, Tea Party activists.[2] Later, so did Republican Rick Scott, a first-time candidate for political office who upset establishment candidates on both sides of the aisle on his way to becoming Florida's 45th governor.

A Clean Sweep for Republicans

Republicans ended up winning both the U.S. Senate and gubernatorial races (see table 12.1), along with all three statewide cabinet post contests, four congressional seats held by Democratic incumbents, two state Senate seats, and five state House seats.

Table 12.1—2010 Election Results: Florida (Major Party Candidates)

Primary (August 24, 2010)					
	U.S. Senator				Florida Governor	
	Democrat				Democrat	
Total	Kendrick B. Meek 528,266	Jeff Greene 284,948	Glenn A. Burkett 59,840	Maurice A. Ferre 45,219	Alex Sink 669,630	Brian P. Moore 201,705
% Votes	57.5	31	6.5	4.9	76.9	23.1
	Republican				Republican	
Total	Marco Rubio 1,069,936	William Billy Kogut 112,080	William Escoffery, III 82,426	Rick Scott 599,909	Bill McCollum 563,538	Mike McCalister 130,991
% Votes	84.6	8.9	6.5	46.3	43.5	10.1
General (November 2, 2010)					
	U.S. Senator			Florida Governor	
Total	Marco Rubio (R) 2,644,539	Kendrick Meek (D) 1,092,059	Charlie Crist (NPA) 1,606,726	Rick Scott (R) 2,618,419	Alex Sink (D) 2,556,453
% Votes	48.9	20.2	29.7	48.9	47.8

Note: NPA = No Party Affiliation.
Source: Florida Division of Elections.

An Older, More Conservative, Less Diverse, and Impatient Electorate

Plummeting turnout rates among younger voters and, to a lesser extent, African American and Hispanic voters, contributed to Democratic defeats. The older, more conservative electorate in 2010 was more receptive to anti-Washington messages, particularly those focusing on the rising national debt and out-of-control spending. Such issues tapped into baby boomers' fears of a vanishing pension and a less-than-rosy retirement, and senior citizens' concerns about the economic futures of their children and grandchildren.

Among the candidates for the U.S. Senate, Republican Marco Rubio's "Reclaim America" theme, with its multigenerational dimension, resonated with these voters more than did Democrat Kendrick Meek's "I'll fight for the middle class," or independent Charlie Crist's "I'll be a voice for the people and be above party politics in Washington."

Among married voters and those with young children, the fear of losing their jobs and/or their homes made Republican gubernatorial candidate Rick Scott's "Let's Get to Work" slogan more appealing than Democrat Alex Sink's "Accountability and Integrity" theme. The theme differential was one factor cited by distraught Democrats in post-election analyses for their party's losses. So, too, was the lack of a consistent message from Democratic candidates up and down the ballot.[3]

Economic Recovery Demands + Wealthy Outsider Challengers = Negative Campaigns

Throughout the long campaign season, the top issue priority of every senatorial and gubernatorial candidate was clearly economic recovery and job creation. In a year when polls showed many voters were angry with the economic status quo, campaigns took on a highly negative tone that escalated as the campaigns evolved.

The record-setting television ad wars, which began in spring,[4] were largely driven by the entry of two self-financed multimillionaire newcomers (Democrat Jeff Greene; Republican Rick Scott) running as outsiders against party establishment candidates. Greene ran against Congressman Kendrick Meek in the Democratic primary for the U.S. Senate; Scott opposed Bill McCollum, the state's attorney general and a former congressman, in the Republican primary for governor. Greene ended up losing; Scott won.

But it was the U.S. Senate race that first captured the nation's attention and held it the longest.

The U.S. Senate Race: An Independent's Day?

"Expect the unexpected." That simple phrase describes Florida's U.S. Senate race from start to finish. The drama began December 2, 2008 when Republican U.S. senator Mel Martinez shocked Floridians by announcing he would not run for reelection in 2010. Rumors immediately began circulating that popular Republican governor, Charlie Crist, would make a run for the Senate in spite of being seen as a shoo-in for reelection as governor. On May 5, 2009 Republican Marco Rubio, former Florida House Speaker, beat Crist to the punch by announcing his candidacy, forcing Crist to decide more quickly than he might have wanted.

On May 12, 2009 Crist finally confirmed his candidacy. He stressed the need for more bipartisanship in Congress: "Regardless of party, we have to work together to get things done, and that's what I'd like to take to Washington, D.C."[5]

One reason for the bipartisan theme may have been to help stem the fallout Crist was getting from his embrace of Barack Obama at a rally in Fort Myers (February 10, 2009) to promote the president's $787 billion economic stimulus plan. What became known as "the hug" cost Crist much-needed support among the state's conservative Republicans, and ultimately became a widely used photo in campaign ads promoting his opponent.

The Republican Primary Fight Ends Abruptly; Crist Turns Independent

For months, with Crist leading in the polls, political pundits labeled Rubio's campaign a long shot at best. It was not until late January 2010 that a poll showed Rubio had inched ahead. (See figure 12.1.) Seven months earlier, Rubio had trailed Crist by 31 points.[6] So what contributed to Rubio's gains? For months, Rubio had crisscrossed the state, visiting local party organizations and speaking to any group he could. He caught the attention of conservative groups like the Club for Growth, which endorsed him relatively early. Conservative columnist George Will endorsed him in September 2009. In October, he reported raising nearly $1 million—an impressive figure for a long shot. In January 2010, Rubio appeared on the cover of the *New York Times Magazine*, with the headline "First Senator From the Tea Party?" In February, he gave the opening address at the Conservative Political Action Conference (CPAC) in Washington. The standing ovation he received led Fox News to pronounce, "A Political Star Is Born."

From then on, Rubio had a cable platform to reach Floridians and conservative donors across the United States.

The campaign road continued to get rockier for Crist as the Tea Party movement, including lightning rod Sarah Palin, gained steam and threw its support behind Rubio. On April 29, 2010, Crist made national headlines by announcing he was leaving the Republican Party to run as an independent (no party affiliation). At the time, he was trailing Rubio in one poll by more than 20 points.[7]

Crist's decision abruptly ended[8] what up to that point had been a contentious GOP primary. Suddenly, it was the Democratic primary that was dominating the news.

Figure 12.1—Rubio Pulls Ahead in Three-Way U.S. Senate Race

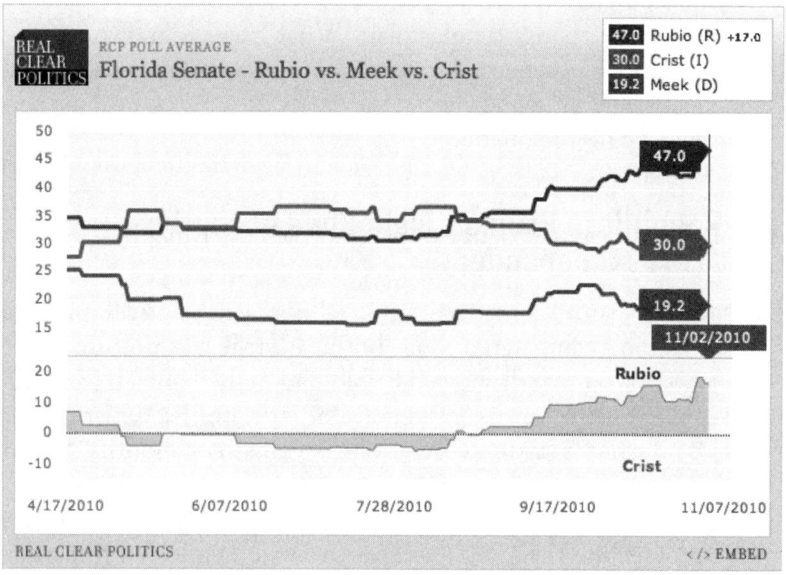

Source: www.realclearpolitics.com/epolls/2010/senate/fl/florida_senate_rubio_vs_meek _vs_crist-1456.html.

The Democratic Party Primary Heats Up; A Billionaire Enters the Race

Democratic Congressman Kendrick Meek[9] from Miami announced his candidacy for the U.S. Senate on January 13, 2009, making him the first major party candidate to jump into the race. An African American, Meek was convinced he could replicate Obama's victory in Florida via a coalition of moderate and liberal Democrats and independents with higher-than-average turnout by young and minority voters.

Without formidable primary opponents, Meek spent a lot of time collecting voter signatures to allow him to qualify by petition rather than by paying a fee. He was the first statewide candidate to qualify by this method, collecting more than 140,000 signatures (112,000 were required). Much to his chagrin, Meek got little publicity for this petition drive. An April 10, 2010 *Miami Herald* headline accurately summed up Meek's campaign to that point: "Overshadowed by GOP Primary Feud, Democratic Senate Candidate Meek Works and Waits."

Late in the campaign, conventional wisdom strongly suggested that Meek could not win. (Meek had trailed Rubio and Crist in every poll taken after the contest became a three-way race.) That perception would ultimately prompt former president Bill Clinton to discuss with Meek the possibility of dropping out and allowing Democrats to vote for Crist as a way of stopping Rubio and preventing the GOP from gaining control of the Senate. It was a controversial move that some analysts believe dampened minority turnout in the general election and ultimately caused Democrats up and down the ballot to lose.[10]

The lack of enthusiasm for Meek's candidacy among some Democrats undoubtedly played a role in billionaire real estate developer Jeff Greene's decision to enter the primary on April 30, 2010. He was a California transplant with colorful friends (boxer Mike Tyson, Hollywood madam Heidi Fleiss) and great wealth generated from a controversial source (credit default swaps).

Like many self-financed candidates in 2010, Greene immediately cast himself as the outsider and labeled Meek, Rubio, and Crist as insiders: "I want to give you a different choice, between three career politicians on one side and an outsider who is willing to shake things up in Washington on the other." [11]

Greene spent millions of dollars—$6 million through July—on television ads and on direct mail pieces before Meek ever ran a TV ad.[12] Greene's ads and mailers attacked Meek for steering federal contracts to a failed developer in Liberty City, one who gave Meek's mother, former congresswoman Carrie Meek, a $90,000 contract and a Cadillac Escalade.[13]

With the late campaign help of Obama and Bill Clinton, Meek surged and handily beat Greene for the Democratic nomination despite being outspent by Greene by 5 to 1.[14]

The Three-Way Race Captures National and International Attention

The U.S. Senate race was fascinating for a number of reasons. First, it was the only race in the country featuring a prominent African American (Meek), Cuban American (Rubio), and the grandson of a Greek immigrant (Crist). Florida's racial/ethnic mix has long mirrored the nation's more than any other large battleground state.

Second, the race raised the question of whether a popular statewide elected official (Crist) could abandon a major party and successfully win an important statewide office as an independent. Had Crist's independent run been successful in the nation's fourth largest state at the same time more voters are labeling themselves independents, it would likely have prompted independent candidacies to spring up in other states. Political parties fear such a trend, while independents would cheer it.

A Close Race at First, But a Landslide Victory for Rubio

Initially, Crist led in the polls, but soon Rubio took the lead and never lost it. With each poll showing him ahead, more money poured into his campaign coffers,[15] giving him a significant funding advantage. A record number six debates gave Floridians many opportunities to see the three candidates side by side. Rubio claimed to be the outsider who would oppose the Obama agenda, Meek pledged to support Obama and Democratic policies aimed at helping the middle class, and Crist pledged to turn his back on partisan politics and "fight for the people of Florida." Rubio's strong anti-Washington, fiscally conservative message won out.

Rubio won with 49 percent of the vote. In addition to solid Republican support, he captured a majority of the state's sizeable independent vote. Crist and Meek divided up the liberal and moderate Democratic and independent vote that did not go to Rubio. The Republican former House Speaker did best in the rural Panhandle, whose residents were still stinging from the Obama administration's handling of the oil spill in the Gulf of Mexico and BP's slow reimbursement rates. Rubio also won many of the state's suburban counties with their higher-than-state-average home foreclosure rates. Crist carried four counties (Palm Beach, Broward, Leon, and Pinellas). Meek won only one—Gadsden—the state's lone majority black county. Crist's better showing in South Florida's large Democratic strongholds is evidence of the schism within the party over the Meek candidacy.

In a state suffering from job losses and record home foreclosures, it was hardly surprising that Rubio was strongly supported by voters with worsening family finances, worries about foreclosures, and fear of a long-term decline in the U.S. economy.

The election dashed the hopes of the eternally optimistic Crist, who wanted to make history as an independent, and the dreams of Meek, who would have been Florida's first African American U.S. senator. In the end, "With uncompromising conservatism, Rubio proved to be the perfect candidate at the perfect time," wrote Adam Smith, political editor of the *St. Petersburg Times*.[16]

The Governor's Race: Two CEOs Slug It Out; The Outsider Wins, But Barely

Florida's gubernatorial race was closely watched because of the key role the governor's veto power can play in the congressional redistricting process that begins in 2011. Redistricting took on added importance once it was announced that the state is likely to gain two new congressional seats and thereby increase the state's presence on the national political stage. At one point, President Obama even remarked that winning the governor's race in Florida was more important to the administration than capturing the U.S. Senate seat.

Initially, everyone presumed that Governor Crist would seek and easily win reelection, as would two other statewide elected officials— Republican Bill McCollum, the state's attorney general, and Democrat Alex Sink, Florida's chief financial officer. All that changed on May 12, 2009, when Crist announced his candidacy for the Senate. Suddenly, Democrats thought they had their best chance in years to win the governorship; it had been 16 years since they last won the state's top office.

Party Establishment-Backed Candidates Take Early Lead

First Sink, then McCollum, threw their hats into the governor's race. Predictably, each party's leaders and major contributors immediately threw their support to Sink and McCollum—the establishment candidates.

Both major parties pushed hard to limit the field of candidates, knowing full well the high costs of running statewide elections in Florida, and fearing the advantage a divisive primary might give to the other party's candidate. Yet, both parties saw mavericks enter the race.

Mavericks Buck the Major Parties

The last thing Florida Democrats expected was for Lawton "Bud" Chiles III—son of one of Florida's most revered Democratic governors—to turn his back on the party and run as an independent. Democrats throughout the state feared he would split the party vote and hand the governorship to Republican McCollum. Chiles promised to run a grassroots, bottom-up campaign by replicating his father's famous walk across Florida. On September 1, having realized that television ads were a more effective way to build support and that he lacked the funds to mount such a campaign, he abandoned the run and threw his support to Sink, much to the relief of Democrats.

Florida Republicans had their own share of maverick candidates lining up to challenge McCollum. On November 2, 2009, Paula Dockery, a feisty state senator from Polk County, who had led the defeat of a commuter-rail project favored by many GOP legislators, announced she would run against McCollum.

Another Republican maverick was Rick Scott, an unknown multimillionaire first-time candidate from Naples, in southwest Florida. He spent $5 million of his own money on a television ad campaign with the clever theme, "Let's Get to Work," which drew him even in the polls with McCollum and left Dockery trailing badly. Dockery withdrew and later threw her support to fellow maverick Scott and ended up serving on his transition team.

Scott's candidacy shook the Republican Party establishment to the bones. They feared his tainted business background would paint all the GOP candidates as crooks. Even more, they resented anyone standing in the way of McCollum, a loyal Republican, whose lifelong dream was to become governor.

A Divisive GOP Primary; Sink Stays Above the Fray

The GOP gubernatorial primary turned out to be "a bitter, expensive battle"[17] fought on TV with negative ads and combative debates.[18] It was every bit as contentious and divisive as the Democratic U.S. Senate primary.

The outsider Scott immediately put insider McCollum on the defensive by running ads painting the attorney general as just another career politician with strong ties to Washington. (McCollum had served 20 years in Congress.) Scott also tagged McCollum as opposed to an Arizona-type immigration law in a state where Rasmussen polls were showing 61 percent of voters favoring such legislation. The claim, which fact-checking sites had found to be a misrepresentation, hurt McCollum, who had to spend time and resources explaining his actual position,[19] effectively keeping the issue alive.

McCollum spent more than $10 million on attack ads of his own, lambasting Scott for having presided over Columbia/HCA, the giant health care company that was assessed a record $1.7 billion fine for Medicare and Medicaid fraud. The Saturday before the primary, McCollum released records of a deposition Scott gave in 2000 in which he invoked his Fifth Amendment right against self-incrimination 75 times. Scott retorted that the deposition had nothing to do with the Columbia/HCA case, and was a desperate political stunt.

Throughout the campaign, McCollum struggled financially against his self-financed opponent. McCollum suffered a blow when the U.S. Court of Appeals for the Eleventh District upheld Scott's legal challenge to the portion of the state's public financing law that imposes a $24.9 million spending cap on candidates for governor just 24 days before the election.[20] Under this rule, if one candidate spends more than the cap amount, the state gives each of his or her opponents a dollar-for-dollar match of the funds spent over that amount.

Polls taken the weekend before the primary election actually had McCollum in the lead.[21] But when the returns rolled in on August 24, Scott had narrowly won. Double-digit margins in many high-turnout rural and suburban counties, areas wracked financially, gave him the edge. (McCollum did better in large urban counties but turnout there fell below average.)

And so ended what some described as "the most expensive primary—and one of the ugliest—in Florida history."[22] The candidates spent an estimated $70 million—$50 million by Scott. A third relatively unknown GOP candidate who had spent less than $8,000 got 10 percent of the vote, which many interpreted as voter disgust with both Scott and McCollum.

Table 12.2—2010 U.S. Senate Race Returns by Media Market

Region	Marco Rubio (REP)	Kendrick Meek (DEM)	Charlie Crist (NPA)	Other
Media Market (% of Florida Votes Cast)	%	%	%	%
North Florida				
Pensacola (3.9%)	64.3	13.5	20.5	1.8
Panama City (2.2%)	69.3	12.8	15.6	2.3
Tallahassee (3.1%)	39.2	25.1	34.5	1.2
Jacksonville (9.7%)	58.8	20.6	19.4	1.2
Gainesville (1.8%)	44.9	25.6	27.7	1.8
Central Florida				
Tampa/St. Petersburg (24.6%)	45.4	16.2	37.1	1.3
Orlando/Daytona Beach (19.9%)	53.0	21.5	24.1	1.3
South Florida				
Naples/Ft. Myers (6.7%)	58.2	10.3	30.4	1.1
West Palm Beach/Ft. Pierce (10.6%)	44.4	18.2	36.5	0.9
Miami/Ft. Lauderdale (17.5%)	38.9	30.2	30.2	0.7
Total	48.9	20.2	29.7	1.2

Note: NPA = No Party Affiliation.
Source: Florida Division of Elections.

The primary left a schism within the GOP ranks that made the race between Scott and Sink closer than it might have been. A Scott ad linking McCollum to the disgraced former Florida Republican

Party chairman Jim Greer (who had misused state party funds) greatly offended party leaders, who saw the ad as an unnecessary and unfair potshot at the whole party.[23] While many GOP insiders ultimately came around to Scott, some of McCollum's backers never did. In the general election, they voted for neither Scott nor Sink.

While Republicans were watching their primary returns, Democrat Alex Sink coasted to victory in her party's primary in a race that got almost no media attention. She began the general election campaign as the frontrunner in the polls,[24] having been able to spend her time fundraising and campaigning with little primary opposition.

Sink v. Scott, At Last!

The governor's race quickly turned into a real nail-biter. Throughout the campaign, a flurry of polls continually showed the race to be a dead heat, varying only in who was on top. (See figure 2.) The general perception was that "a poll a day keeps Florida in play."

Figure 12.2—2010 Governor's Race A Toss-Up All The Way

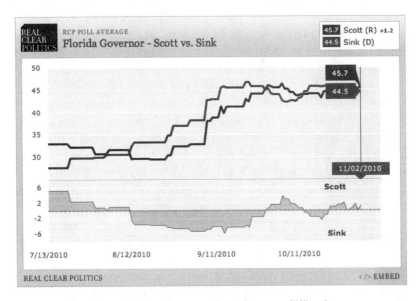

Source: www.realclearpolitics.com/epolls/2010/governor/fl/florida_governor_scott
_vs_sink_vs_chiles-1607.html#polls.

Alex Sink had already run her first general election ad before the primary was over. It featured two men punching each other, one yelling "Let's get it on," the other, "Let's get to work." Her punch line? "Let's get real" about tackling Florida's challenges. The ad raised hopes that she would stay above the fray and run a positive campaign. This did not happen. She took every opportunity to label Scott a crook, while he cast her as a Tallahassee insider—a liberal Democrat joined at the hip with President Obama, in lockstep with his economic policies (the stimulus plan, higher taxes, and "ObamaCare").

Sink's attacks on Scott's business practices simply intensified those McCollum had initiated. At every turn, she questioned Scott's integrity and raised the issues of the record-level Medicare fraud fine paid by his former company. Her campaign theme of honesty and accountability was well grounded in polling data. The 2010 Sunshine State Survey (conducted in February by Leadership Florida and the Nielsen Company) found that the quality Floridians want most in their leaders is integrity.

Scott went after Sink's business practices as well. He accused her of failing to rein in NationsBank's (later Bank of America) scams against the elderly and of poor oversight of the state's pension fund as chief financial officer. Scott was, in effect, betting that voters would be more critical of a banker than of a hospital CEO, since a hospital still provides help in bad times.

The candidates participated in three televised debates hosted by Univision, Florida PBS stations/Leadership Florida, and CNN/St. Petersburg Times/University of South Florida. For the most part, their answers to moderators' questions mirrored the content of their television ads. It was in the third and final debate, just a week away from the election, that both candidates stumbled. In a highly embarrassing moment, neither candidate (both wealthy CEOs) could accurately identify the current minimum wage, which was $7.25 per hour, yet both were running on a job-creation platform. But it was the simple glance at a text message by Alex Sink that created a post-debate storm broadcast across the nation. During a break, a Sink aide had sent her a cell phone via her makeup artist. Sink read the text message displayed on the Droid, which was a tip on how to respond to Scott. It was a clear violation of debate rules and it was captured on video for all to see—over and over. Dubbed "iCheat," "Debate-Gate," or "Message-Gate," it was a devastating moment for a candidate running on an integrity platform.

Whether the incident mattered or not is unclear. What is clear is that the race became the closest governor's race in Florida history. Fewer than 62,000 votes (1 percent of all votes cast) separated the two candidates. The winner was not known until mid-morning the day after the election. But the tally was not close enough (half of 1 percent) to trigger an automatic recount on the 10th anniversary of the famous 2000 Florida recount.

Sink was the lone Democrat running statewide who came close to victory. She attributed her loss to Scott's money—he had poured more than $73 million of his own money into the campaign—and to his success in casting her as an Obama clone at a time when the president's approval ratings were slipping among Floridians.

Early voting statistics (absentee and in-person) showed 271,000 more Republicans than Democrats had voted—a sharp reversal from 2008. Republicans won the turnout game in spite of the Democrats' coordinated voter mobilization program. This simply reflected the enthusiasm gap between the two parties.

What helped make the Scott–Sink race so close was that, because of the candidates' negative advertising, some Floridians just could not bring themselves to vote for either candidate. Over 50,000 fewer Floridians voted in the governor's race than voted in the U.S. Senate contest. Overall, turnout was a modest 48.7 percent, up slightly from 46.8 percent in 2006.

Sink lost among the same group of voters and generally for the same reasons that Crist and Meek lost to Rubio. The vote patterns (demographic, geographical, policy preference) for Rubio and Scott were similar. (See tables 12.4–12.6.) Like Rubio, Scott did considerably better than Sink in the suburban and rural areas, particularly in the Panhandle, where residents were still suffering financially from the BP oil spill and critical of the Obama administration's handling of the crisis.[25] (See table 12.3.) Scott got strong support from older voters, whites and Hispanics, males, married couples, middle- and upper-income voters, and those with children. He also did considerably better among Floridians upset with the direction of the country, those personally experiencing economic stress, and citizens pessimistic about the pace of economic recovery. For these voters, Scott, the outsider, had more appeal with his "Let's Get to Work," anti-Washington message than Sink, the insider, with her honesty, integrity, and accountability message. In the words of one Florida journalist: "In a normal election year, Scott's baggage might have been too much to overcome, even with his record-shattering personal spending ... But this is a year when Republicans and independents alike are so angry and fed up that such issues [had] little traction."[26]

Table 12.3—2010 Governor's Race Returns by Media Market

Region	Rick Scott/ Jennifer Carroll (REP)	Alex Sink/ Rod Smith (DEM)	Other
Media Market (% of Florida Votes Cast)	%	%	%
North Florida			
Pensacola (3.9%)	63.6	30.9	5.5
Panama City (2.2%)	62.3	32.4	5.2
Tallahassee (3.1%)	37.2	60.2	2.5
Jacksonville (9.7%)	57.3	39.8	2.9
Gainesville (1.8%)	42.8	53.9	3.2
Central Florida			
Tampa/St. Petersburg (24.6%)	49.5	46.4	4.1
Orlando/Daytona Beach (19.9%)	50.3	45.8	3.8
South Florida			
Naples/Ft. Myers (6.7%)	59.8	36.6	3.6
West Palm Beach/ Ft. Pierce (10.6%)	43.6	53.4	3.0
Miami/Ft. Lauderdale (17.5%)	38.3	59.8	1.9
Total	**48.9**	**47.7**	**3.4**

Source: Florida Division of Elections.

Table 12.4—2010 Election: Candidate Preferences by Voter Demographics

Demographic Characteristic	US Senate				Governor		
	Meek (D) %	Rubio (R) %	Crist (NPA) %	Other/ No Answer %	Sink (D) %	Scott (R) %	Other/ No Answer %
Age							
18–24 (4%)	27	36	37	N/A	57	39	4
25–29 (4%)	40	32	27	1	62	36	2
30–39 (10%)	25	44	28	3	48	48	4
40–49 (16%)	21	50	26	3	46	51	3
50–64 (30%)	20	51	28	1	46	51	3
65+ (35%)	17	50	31	2	46	50	4
Race							
White (74%)	12	55	32	1	41	56	3
African American (11%)	76	4	19	1	92	6	2
Latino (12%)	21	55	23	1	48	50	2
Asian (1%)	N/A	N/A	N/A	N/A	N/A	N/A	N/A
Other (2%)	N/A	N/A	N/A	N/A	N/A	N/A	N/A
Sex							
Male (44%)	18	54	27	1	43	54	3
Female (56%)	23	44	31	2	52	45	3
Income							
< $50,000 (46%)	28	41	29	2	52	44	4
$50,000-$100,000 (35%)	17	55	28	N/A	43	55	2
$100,000 + (19%)	13	55	29	3	44	53	3
College Graduate							
Yes (47%)	19	47	32	2	52	46	2
No (53%)	23	50	26	1	44	52	4
Marital Status							
Married (61%)	16	56	26	2	40	57	3
Unmarried (39%)	29	36	33	2	59	37	4
Children Under 18							
Yes (26%)	23	49	26	2	44	52	4
No (74%)	20	48	30	2	49	47	4

Note: NPA = No Party Affiliation.
Source: National Exit Poll, Florida.

Table 12.5—2010 Election: Candidate Preferences by
Voter Political Leanings

	U.S. Senate				Governor		
	Meek (D)	Rubio (R)	Crist (I)	Other/ No Answer	Sink (D)	Scott (R)	Other/ No Answer
Political Leanings	%	%	%	%	%	%	%
Party ID							
Democrat (36%)	49	8	42	1	89	9	2
Republican (36%)	1	86	11	2	10	88	2
Independent (29%)	10	51	35	4	42	52	6
Ideology							
Liberal (18%)	39	10	50	1	84	15	1
Moderate (42%)	24	36	38	2	60	37	3
Conservative (40%)	7	81	10	2	16	80	4
Consistency in Vote (U.S. Senate)							
Sink (48%)	41	11	48	N/A			
Scott (49%)	2	86	11	1			
Consistency in Vote (Governor)							
Meek (21%)					94	5	1
Rubio (48%)					11	88	1
Crist (29%)					78	19	3

Note: NPA = No Party Affiliation.
Source: National Exit Poll, Florida.

Table 12.6—2010 Election: Candidate Preference by Voter Economic Concerns & Priorities

Economic Concern/ Priority	U.S. Senate				Governor		
	Meek (D)	Rubio (R)	Crist (NPA)	Other/ No Answer	Sink (D)	Scott (R)	Other/ No Answer
	%	%	%	%	%	%	%
Family Financial Situation							
Better (11%)	39	24	35	2	70	27	3
Worse (44%)	15	61	23	1	35	63	2
Same (44%)	21	45	32	2	53	45	2
Worried About Foreclosure for You or Relative							
Yes (45%)	21	55	20	4	41	55	4
No (54%)	20	43	35	2	55	42	3
Worried About Economic Conditions							
Yes (86%)	17	53	29	1	42	55	3
No (13%)	47	15	38	N/A	83	14	3
Economy as Most Important Issue							
Yes (69%)	20	50	29	1	47	51	2
No (29%)	22	46	31	1	49	46	5
U.S. Economy Is in . . .							
Normal Downturn (23%)	34	25	39	2	73	23	4
Long-Term Decline (73%)	16	58	24	2	39	58	3
Highest Priority for Next Congress							
Cut Taxes (18%)	11	73	13	3	24	73	3
Reduce Deficit (34%)	13	63	22	2	36	62	2
Spending to Create Jobs (42%)	32	27	40	1	68	30	2

Note: NPA = No Party Affiliation.
Source: National Exit Poll, Florida.

An Unusual Year: Bring in the New

In 2010, it was largely Republicans and independents' animosity toward Washington's handling of the economy that led them to support anti-Washington candidates like Republican Marco Rubio and Rick Scott. When you are facing the loss of a job and a home, as many Floridians were in 2010, the need for new faces in leadership posts, whether in Washington or Tallahassee, is quite compelling.

Endnotes

[1] Democrats made up 41 percent of all registrants, Republicans 36 percent, independents (no party affiliation) 20 percent, and minor party members, 3 percent. Republicans have *never* outnumbered Democrats in Florida.

[2] Mark Lebovich, "The First Senator From the Tea Party?" *New York Times Magazine*, January 6, 2010; Beth Reinhard, "Marco Rubio Becoming Star on Tea-Party Circuit," *Miami Herald*, January 13, 2010.

[3] George Bennett, "Florida Democrats Blame Lack of Unified Message in Election-Day Beat-Down," *Palm Beach Post*, November 7, 2010.

[4] Florida's primary election was held on August 24, 2010. These two unknowns had to spend millions early on to build up their name recognition to be competitive against their better known, more experienced primary opponents.

[5] FOXNews.com, "Florida Gov. Crist Announces Senate Run," May 12, 2009.

[6] Rich Jones, "Major Reversal in Florida Senate Race," WOKV.com, January 26, 2010. Cites Quinnipiac University poll.

[7] Associated Press, "Crist Announces Independent Bid for Senate," April 29, 2010.

[8] Rubio still faced an opponent in the Republican primary but he was not a serious challenger.

[9] Prior to running for the Senate, Meek had been a Florida Highway Patrol trooper before serving eight years in the state legislature and three terms in Congress.

[10] *PBS NewsHour*, "Florida's Senate Race Leaves Democrats Divided," October 15, 2010; Jane Musgrave, "Are Democrats Taking the Black Vote For Granted?" *Palm Beach Post*, October 23, 2010.

[11]Christopher Weber, "More Florida Drama: Billionaire Jeff Greene Enters Senate Race," *Politics Daily*, April 30, 2010.

[12]News Service of Florida, "Meek and Greene Blame Each Other for Negative Campaign," August 11, 2010.

[13]George Bennett, "Dems Greene, Meek Trade Salvos Over Meek's Ties to Accused Developer," *Palm Beach Post*, May 16, 2010.

[14]John Fritze, "Kendrick Meek Wins Democratic Primary in Florida," *USA Today*, August 24, 2010. Greene spent more than $23 million of his own money; Meek spent just over $4.7 million, according to the article.

[15]One estimate was that Rubio raised more than $26 million, a sizeable portion from interest groups like the U.S. Chamber of Commerce and Karl Rove's American Crossroads PAC and from the National Republican Party. William March, "Independent Cash Aids Rubio," *Tampa Tribune*, October 31, 2010.

[16]Adam Smith, "A Wild Ride Nobody Envisioned," *St. Petersburg Times*, October 31, 2010.

[17]Lloyd Dunkelberger, "McCollum, Scott Bring Divergent Experience to Governor's Race," *Ocala Star Banner*, August 15, 2010.

[18]The candidates debated each twice—once on Univision, the Spanish language cable network aired in Miami, Orlando, and Tampa; the other on the Fox affiliate in Tampa.

[19]"McCollum said he opposed the original version of the legislation—which he said would have led to racial profiling—but supports the final version of the law." See endnote 17, Dunkelberger, "McCollum, Scott Bring Divergent Experience."

[20]B. Shaw, "Appeals Court Upholds Scott's Challenge to Public-Finance Law," *Orlando Sentinel*, July 30, 2010.

[21]Mary Ellen Klas, "McCollum, Meek Surge Ahead of Rivals Scott, Greene in New Poll," *Miami Herald*, August 22, 2010.

[22]Aaron Deslatte and Jennifer Gollan, "Rick Scott Beats Bill McCollum to End Nasty GOP Governor's Primary Fight," *Orlando Sentinel*, August 25, 2010.

[23]Brandon Larrabee, "Can Rick Scott Win Over the Florida GOP?" *Florida Times-Union*, August 25, 2010.

[24]Aaron Deslatte and Jennifer Gollan, "Rick Scott Beats Bill McCollum to End Nasty GOP Governor's Primary Fight," *Orlando Sentinel*, August 25, 2010. The fact that Sink's opponent got 23 percent did raise some eyebrows until it was pointed out that he is a perennial candidate in statewide races.

[25]In a post-election interview with Politico.com, Sink strongly criticized Obama for failing to respond to her warnings about the Panhandle region slipping away from Democrats. Her opinions were seconded by Rod Smith, Sink's lt. gov. running mate. (Nathan Crabbe, "Back in Gainesville, Rod Smith Reflects on a Tough Loss," *Ocala Star Banner*, November 6, 2010.)

[26]Adam C. Smith, "A Wild Ride Nobody Envisioned," *St. Petersburg Times*, October 31, 2010.

Chapter 13

As Far as Politics and Governance Goes... Illinois' Governor and Senate Races

by Dr. Paul Green

Arthur Rubloff Professor of Policy Studies
at Roosevelt University

As far as politics and governance goes, to paraphrase the number from the Broadway musical, *South Pacific*, "There is nothing like Illinois." Since 1960, the "Land of Lincoln" has elected several governors—three have gone to jail, one has just been convicted and, after his appeal, will become the fourth. At the same time, Illinois has been the only state to elect African Americans to the United States Senate in the last several decades, one of whom is currently living in the White House. Furthermore, since 1989 its largest city—Chicago—has had as its mayor one of the most dominant and dynamic municipal leaders in the nation, Richard M. Daley.

If Illinois politics is considered "over the top," the state's financial situation is "under the bottom." No state has a higher per capita debt. Illinois' pension system is near the lowest of any of the other 49 underfunded states, and in Springfield, the state capital, it is believed that most of the state's budget experts are graduates from the University of Houdini (by some magic, they claim Illinois has had a balanced budget every year, meanwhile the state has sunk deeper into debt—currently $13 billion).

Given these facts, one would think little could shock the brave souls who call themselves Illinoisans, but 2010 statewide politics made even legendary hard-nosed political pundits and professors grunt, grimace, and groan.

The Primary

Illinois held the first midterm primary in the nation on February 2, 2010. Why? Prior to the 2008 primary season the Democratic-controlled state legislature moved up the state's traditional primary date from the third week in March to Super Tuesday—the first Tuesday in February. No obtuseness here: Illinois Democratic legislative leaders openly admitted they wanted to help their former colleague, Senator Barack Obama, in his presidential nomination struggle against Senator Hillary Clinton. The plan worked—Obama easily crushed Clinton in most parts of the state—as Illinois gave him his only big state victory on that crucial day.

Following the Obama presidential triumph, these same Democratic Party leaders recognized the value of keeping the early primary date for 2010: Ballot petitions would have to be filed by Halloween, which meant that Thanksgiving, Christmas, and New Years would curtail campaign time. And it would be cold. All of these factors were critical parts of a political strategy to help incumbents win renomination against outsider party challenges. Remember, this is Illinois. For the most part, the plan was successful except for a few top-of-the-ticket shockers in both party primaries.

The Democrats

Two races dominated the 2010 Illinois Democratic primary campaign—governor and United States senator. As most of the country knows, former Illinois governor Rod Blagojevich was impeached and ousted from office by the state legislature in January 2009 (more on Blagojevich later in this chapter). His lieutenant governor, Pat Quinn, a longtime politician and reformer, assumed the state's top job. Quinn had never been "leader of the band" and his uncertainty and awkwardness as the state's chief executive, together with the state's miserable financial situation, found him being challenged for the gubernatorial nomination by state comptroller, Dan Hynes.

Hynes was a three-term state officeholder from a very prominent Chicago political family. (It is important to note that Chicago Democratic domination of Illinois statewide offices is so great that only Senator Dick Durbin is not a current Chicago resident.) Hynes, an earnest and serious politician, went after Quinn in a good old-fashion political grudge match. Quinn, who had served as Illinois state treasurer and a Cook County officeholder, was placed in the unfamiliar role of not being on the offensive, but rather, he now had to defend his short time as governor.

The race went down to the wire, and probably turned in Quinn's favor on a controversial Hynes television ad late in the campaign. Hynes's commercial depicted former Chicago mayor Harold Washington (the city's first African American mayor) attacking Quinn's performance as Chicago revenue director. It was a brutal condemnation of Quinn. The governor quickly returned fire with a television ad featuring former Washington staffers and allies claiming that Hynes was playing the race card against Quinn. Incredibly, neither Quinn nor his supporters refuted any of Washington's specific comments about Quinn's capabilities.

Quinn's counterattack worked—barely. The geopolitical breakdown of the results revealed that Quinn's strength in Chicago and suburban Cook County (won by 40,000 votes) was greater than Hynes's support in the rest of the state (32,000 vote margin). The 8,000-vote difference maker was Quinn's strength in predominantly black Chicago wards and suburban townships.

Compared to the gubernatorial primary, the U.S. Senate race was a mild affair—until all hell broke loose in the final weeks of the Senate campaign. State Treasurer Alexi Giannoulias, an Obama protégé, was considered a strong favorite to win the Senate nomination from the outset. His two leading opponents had never held public office and could not match Giannoulias's campaign war chest. However, late in the campaign a series of newspaper stories appeared concerning Giannoulias's family-owned Broadway Bank and some of its questionable loans to alleged mob figures. Juicing the story was the fact that Broadway was not going to survive as a community bank.

In the end, Giannoulias won a solid, but not spectacular, victory over his nearest opponent, former Chicago inspector general, David Hoffman (39.0 percent to 34.0 percent, a 47,445-vote margin). Victory came at a price for Giannoulias—as Broadway Bank's former vice president, he would be vulnerable to Republican attack ads for the rest of the campaign.

Both the gubernatorial and U.S. Senate Democratic battles were interesting and even exciting, but they were soon overwhelmed by the party's lieutenant governor contest. In Illinois, until recently, candidates for governor and lieutenant governor ran separately in the primary (the law has now been changed so that in 2014 governor and lieutenant governor candidates will run as a team for the nomination). The lieutenant governor's office has no real duties, so, in 2010, as in the past, the media and almost everyone else ignored the multi-candidate contest for this office.

On election night, Scott Lee Cohen, a political unknown, defeated a group of several state legislators for the lieutenant governor nomination. Cohen was the only Democratic lieutenant governor candidate who put on a real campaign, with outstanding media, almost fully self-financed. Cohen was now Pat Quinn's running mate—or was he?

Stories broke immediately that Cohen was a pawnbroker who had some serious problems with domestic abuse and involvement with prostitutes. Party leaders and other Democratic influentials demanded Cohen withdraw from the ticket. Cohen refused. Only when his former girlfriend, who was once arrested for prostitution, said he was unfit for office did Cohen fold his hand. He dropped out Chicago-style—in a saloon during half-time of the Super Bowl, an event that was covered by all local media. But this is Illinois. After further political reflection some weeks after his withdrawal, Cohen announced his independent candidacy for governor—and yes, he was on the November ballot.

The Republicans

The Illinois Republican Party has won only a single statewide race in the 21st century. In fact, most of these GOP losses have been by landslides, as party disunity and the rise of Barack Obama has turned

Illinois into a very dark blue state. Nevertheless, the Democratic double whammy of Blagojevich and budget deficits inspired and motivated several GOP heavy-hitters to run for the gubernatorial nomination.

A wide-open, seven-man race ensued, with most of the candidates doing their utmost to be the "rightest" of them all. Though most of the candidates sounded alike (I can vouch for this fact since I moderated a pre-primary GOP gubernatorial debate at the City Club of Chicago), one fact did show some major separation—it was geographical and not philosophical. State senator Bill Brady, an unsuccessful 2006 gubernatorial primary candidate, was the only 2010 candidate not originally from "Chicagoland." In the end, Brady's residential home base proved to be the difference maker.

Brady's eyelash victory over his nearest competitor, state senator Kirk Dillard, was by 193 votes, or 20.3 percent to Dillard's 20.2 percent. Dillard had been endorsed by former Republican governor Jim Edgar, a downstater and the last Illinois governor not to be indicted; it was thought that he would give Dillard some downstate help. But in the end, it was not enough. Brady, who received less than 10 percent of the vote in Chicago and its suburbs, crushed Dillard and his other rivals downstate.

The GOP U.S. Senate primary was a virtual "walk in the prairie" for Tenth District congressman, Mark Kirk, compared to the other contests discussed. Kirk destroyed his five little-known opponents, winning 57 percent of the vote. Undoubtedly, Kirk tacked to right during the campaign as he fended off attacks from social conservatives who labeled him as a RINO (Republican In Name Only). To be sure, Kirk's moderate voting record had given him enough "oomph" to win two hotly contested and expensive reelection campaigns (2006 and 2008) in his high-income north side congressional distinct. However, it was the fact that Kirk could win in November that won over any conservatives, who wanted a Republican to take back Obama's Senate seat.

Again—but this is Illinois. Just when it seemed that Kirk was the real deal, press reports appeared revealing that the congressman had either misspoken, exaggerated, or lied about crucial parts of his résumé. Specifics about these episodes are less important than the political impact—it resurrected a disheartened Giannoulias back into the general election battle. In the post-primary period, Kirk went on the defensive as he attempted to explain away the "Walter Mitty" aspects of his biography. (James Thurber's 1939 short story, "The Secret Life of Walter Mitty," became a popular film in 1947 and soon the term "Mittyesque" entered the English language, meaning an ordinary person who indulges in fantastic daydreams of personal triumphs, or, more darkly, someone who tries to fake an impressive career.)

The Endless Campaign

The eventual brutal general election races for Illinois governor and U.S. senator started off as a crawl. As one irreverent professor put it, "A baby could have been conceived on primary night and been born full-term prior to the Election Day." Imagine a contest that started before the Chicago Cubs and White Sox went to spring training camp and ended after the World Series.

Race for Governor:
Pat Quinn (D) versus State Senator Bill Brady (R)

The national economic recession has staggered most states but Illinois was "wobbly" even before the big hit. In simple terms, the state has a structural deficit problem. Each year it gets worse as expenditures outpace revenues and only "magic accounting" allows the state to claim its budget is balanced. The current deficit ranges from $9 to $13 billion dollars.

Added to this number is the state debt—most of it linked to the state's pension system. One conservative Illinois think tank figured out that 91 percent of the state's total debt is due to pensions and retiree health care. The total debt dollar amount using "Illinois accounting" ranges from $80 to $100 billion. Unless something happens soon, the Illinois pension system will run dry by 2018. Even the much-publicized bleak California state fiscal condition has its pension system in far better shape than Illinois.

Brady immediately tried to put Quinn in the deficit trick bag. Because of the early primary, the state legislature was in full session and the Republican nominee hit the governor on three corollary fronts. First, since the Democrats had controlled the governorship and both chambers of the legislature—the deficit/debt was their fault.

Second, Brady claimed he could cut this monster deficit without raising taxes (though his rhetoric contained few specifics). Third, Blagojevich! Brady stretched the truth, claiming that Quinn was a loyal ally and running mate of the disgraced former governor. In reality, Brady and almost every other player in Springfield knew "Blago" and Quinn had an ice-cold relationship.

Quinn's response to these attacks was tepid at best. The term "Quinn organization" became an oxymoron. The governor roamed the state, talking of the need for new revenue (tax increases). He found an ally in the state senate president, John Cullerton, but any tax hike hope was stopped cold by House Speaker Mike Madigan, who undoubtedly is the shrewdest state legislator in Illinois history.

As spring turned to early summer, Quinn fired his consulting team (folks connected to President Obama's chief political advisor, David Axelrod). Early polls showed Brady ahead as his downstate strength increased, while Quinn's expected Chicago vote power showed little oomph. And then came Rod Blagojevich's trial.

Race for United States Senate: Illinois State Treasurer Alexi Giannoulias (D) versus Tenth District Congressman Mark Kirk (R)

The Kirk versus Giannoulias contest was bizarre—even by Illinois standards. Following his tight primary victory, Giannoulias was hit by both the media and Kirk on his role at his father's Broadway Bank in Chicago. This issue dominated the early Giannoulias campaign. He was asked about bank loans that he approved to members of organized crime; about his total bank involvement since the institution was about to be closed; and whether or not other members of his family were involved in these sordid operations. Giannoulias, a young, personable, and attractive candidate, was simply in a political vice and everyone was squeezing. His carefully worded response showed that he would not and could not blame his family and the bank for being less than vigilant in their loan procedures, nor could he explain away why they happened in the first place.

Kirk was on a roll until his campaign strategy emphasized his personal history. His Mittyesque tendencies were revealed as he expanded, exaggerated, and finally "misrepresented" (his word) his military and teaching records, as well as his life-changing experience on a boat in Lake Michigan. Amazingly, for a politician who had won two barn-burner congressional reelection contests—his over-the-top résumé pumping seemed amateurish and embarrassing. Like his opponent, Kirk spent most of the early campaign "defending his life"—and like Giannoulias, he said very little about national issues that affected the country and Illinois. In sum, the U.S. Senate race for Barack Obama's seat was, for months, boring and banal.

Campaign "Interruptus"

Blago

Former governor Rod Blagojevich's federal trial was a combination of Roman gladiator match and Monty Python skit. The former governor and his brother faced a combined 24 federal felony charges that included trying to sell Barack Obama's vacant U.S. Senate seat. However, to look at Blago entering and leaving the Everett M. Dirksen Federal Building, you would have thought he did not have a care in the world and, in fact, appeared to be enjoying himself.

Adding to the circus atmosphere were Blago's father-and-son lawyer team—Sam Adam Sr. and Sam Adam Jr. These men were in-your-face Cook County criminal court lawyers who had little experience in or concern for federal court trial procedures and protocols. And they showed it.

Needless to say, the Blago trial dominated summer political news, and, though both the Illinois Senate and governor races were called toss-ups—few people paid attention to the candidates. In short, it was wall-to-wall Blago. When the day of the verdict dawned, every major media outlet in Illinois had their top political guns at the federal building, and not on the candidates' campaign trails.

For the record, Blago was found guilty on half of one count and the jury was hung on the other 23 counts. Thus, R.B.-1 ended, and these same media outlets eagerly anticipate the sequel, R.B.-2, scheduled to start in April, 2011.

Daley

Just when one thought Illinois campaign politics would return to normal following the Blago verdict—another bombshell hit. In early

September, six-term Chicago mayor, Richard M. Daley (elected first in 1989) announced he would not seek a seventh term. It shocked and awed Chicagoans and almost everyone else. This surprise development once again minimized 2010 state campaign stories in both the print and electronic media. Questions were asked—Why did Daley do it? Were there hidden reasons? Was it his wife's illness? Was there some kind of deal? The last questions reached crescendo proportions when former congressman and President Obama's chief of staff, Rahm Emanuel, announced that he would leave Washington, D.C. and run for mayor of Chicago.

For weeks, mayoral politics dominated Chicagoland political news (the mayoral election will not actually take place until late in February 2011) and only by late September did most Illinoisans begin to focus on the tight gubernatorial and Senate races. Thus, despite having the nation's longest general election campaign season—in reality due to Blago and Daley—the marathon campaign had become a sprint.

The 2010 Illinois Campaign Final Days

Governor

October 2010 saw Brady and Quinn engage in a no-holds-barred street fight. Instead of punches, the candidates used 30-second paid TV advertising funded by their own campaigns and outside sources. Polls showed Brady still clinging to a narrow lead; major newspaper endorsements were about evenly split; and their televised debates were filled with more smoke than fire.

Both men stuck to their ongoing campaign themes, leaving voters bored by the repetition. Suddenly late in the campaign, Quinn caught a small tailwind. First, his television advertising shifted to himself and his long career as a political outsider fighting for the average citizen. Second, Illinois state senator Ricky Hendon, an African American from Chicago's west side, known for his bravado and bluster, called Republican Brady "racist, sexist, and homophobic," based on his colleague's legislative record. All political hell broke loose. Hendon not only refused to apologize for his comments, but added more, saying, "Brady is a dangerous extremist and people need to know that." Lastly, President Obama made a visit to Chicago on the weekend before the election—mainly for his friend Giannoulias, but Quinn shared in the spotlight.

All three of these late-breaking developments were mainly aimed to energize Chicago and suburban Cook County African American voters who were lukewarm to Quinn. It worked, though there was some downside to Hendon and Obama—especially Hendon—in downstate counties. At the end, the Brady–Quinn contest remained incredibly tight, though the incumbent finally seemed to have hit his campaign stride.

U.S. Senator

The Giannoulias and Kirk homestretch resembled the governor's race minus the Hendon rant. Their last televised debate, less than a week before the election, was largely a replay of their personal TV ad attacks on each other. On the issues, both candidates sounded similar, due to the fact that Kirk had shifted back to his centrist political comfort zone for the general election.

The Republican clung to his lead in the polls but his strategists worried about the impact of the high-profiled Chicago visits of the president and first lady, and by former president Bill Clinton—all on behalf of Kirk's opponent. Like the governor's race, this Senate battle was going down to the wire with no sure winner.

The Results

On Election Day, Illinois voters produced a political split decision. Quinn was elected governor by a mere 19,000 votes out of nearly 3.7 million votes cast. At the same time, Kirk edged past Giannoulias with a 70,000-vote margin. Unofficial returns (the only returns available at the time of this writing) reveal that both hotly contested races mirrored each other for the most part, except for two critical differences.

First, in the governor's contest, it appears the third-party candidates (Rich Whitney, Green Party; Lex Green, Libertarian; and Scott Lee Cohen, Independent) tallied over a quarter of a million votes statewide with only about 37 percent of these votes coming from Quinn's Cook County powerbase. These third-party numbers suggest Brady's downstate total votes were impacted far more than Quinn's Cook County totals. Second, the irony of it all. Geography keyed Brady's photo-finish victory for the GOP gubernatorial nomination by being the only downstater in the race, but in the general election his downstate roots worked against him. Part of his loss is due to his performance in suburban Chicagoland. Brady's monster downstate strength came close to giving him a victory, but, in the end, it was unable to overcome his suburban vote percentages. A brief example: In suburban Cook County, Kirk garnered 43.6 percent of the vote while Brady tallied 39.7 percent. This 3 percent vote differential between these two Republican candidates helped determine a winner and a loser on election night.

The above analysis largely explains Kirk's 2 percent victory over Giannoulias. Overall, Kirk ran well downstate. Conservative Republicans who were lukewarm at best about Kirk voted heavily for him, and he was a suburbanite. Giannoulias's Chicago landslide numbers were not enough to keep his slight suburban vote erosion (slight, compared to his ticket-mate Quinn) from costing him the election.

Here are two final thoughts: First, this election should have been a huge GOP victory in Illinois. To be sure, Chicago remains undeniably heavily Democratic (Quinn and Giannoulias both received over 76 percent of its vote), but the rest of Illinois was up for grabs. Obviously, it was a good night for the Illinois GOP—they took a U.S. Senate seat, won two lesser statewide offices (treasurer and comptroller), and unseated four incumbent Democratic congressmen. Still, the Democrats retained control of the governorship and both chambers of the Illinois General Assembly—which means 2012 redistricting will see a Democratic map. The man most responsible for this Democratic "hold the line" outcome is House Speaker Michael Madigan. Despite an all-out effort to discredit him by certain media and the GOP, he remains the shrewdest and ablest politician in Illinois.

Second, immediately following the election—Brady was unwilling to concede—saying all the votes (absentee, etc.) had to be counted. As the numbers rose against him, he still would not admit defeat. This promoted deputy editorial writer John McCormick of the *Chicago Tribune* to write that perhaps Brady was waiting for the "lost county of Atlantis" to be found and have its votes recorded. Brady quickly caved. What a state!

Chapter 14

Indiana Senate: Bayh Dominoes

by Brian A. Howey

Brian A. Howey is Editor of Howey Politics Indiana; *and is Writer-in-Residence at the Franklin College Pulliam School of Journalism. He publishes from Indianapolis and Franklin, Indiana.*

Seated in the Oval Office before the president in early September 2009 was Sen. Evan Bayh. "Are you 100 percent sure?" President Obama asked.

"I'm 98 percent sure," Bayh responded to his one-time Senate colleague and rival for the Democratic nomination. If the Indiana senator had been selected as a running mate for Obama's 2008 ticket, Bayh would be speaking to the man who would have been his boss. The news Bayh brought to Obama was that he planned to retire from the Senate in 2010.

The implications were vast. A virtually "safe" Democratic Senate seat would almost certainly come into play in red state Indiana, despite Obama's stunning once-in-a-generation breakthrough. And the young president and his political team knew that the sprawling policy agenda they were in the midst of hammering out would create treacherous political currents for Obama's first midterm election.

No one was predicting then that Obama's Democrats would lose control of Congress and, most improbably, the Senate. Certainly Evan Bayh defending his Indiana seat was part of the calculus. While his father, former U.S. senator Birch Bayh, had never won the seat by more than 5 percent, the younger Bayh was a landslide artist, winning twice with more than 63 percent of the vote.

It was on President's Day—February 15, 2010—that Bayh dropped his bombshell, after the Obama team had spent the intervening time since September 2009 trying to keep him in the fold. After months of Bayh's self-admitted "procrastination," the Earth was shaking. Republican Scott Brown had won the late Ted Kennedy's Senate seat in January. Within hours, Bayh was projecting a catastrophe for the Democratic Party. Bayh told ABC News, "If you lose Massachusetts and that's not a wake-up call, there's no hope of waking up."

Thirteen days before, in his Senate office, Bayh had met with Indiana constituents on energy issues. When the meeting ended, he had sighed and said, "Now I've got to go deal with a German ambassador." That night, word leaked out that former Republican senator Dan Coats, who had become ambassador to Germany on September 10, 2001, was preparing to join the race with Bayh, which Coats had ducked in 1998. Democrats had figured Bayh would face a second-tier challenger like former congressman John Hostettler or state senator Marlin Stutzman after Republican House Conference Chairman Mike Pence and Secretary of State Todd Rokita declined the challenge.

U.S. senator, John Coryn, and members of the National Republican Senatorial Committee watched with growing apprehension as the Indiana Republican field, which included Winchester businessman Don Banks Jr. and Tea Party-backed candidate Richard Behney, a plumber from Carmel, raised less than $250,000 combined. When Pence did not take the bait, Coryn told Coats, "We have an outside shot to take the Senate, but there's no chance if we can't win in Indiana. And you give us the best chance." Coats accepted.

Thirteen days later, the decision looked prescient. "No one—not one person—gave me any inkling that Evan wasn't going to run," Coats said. "People very close to him—both politically and financially—told me they didn't have a clue." On the morning of February 15, political operative Anne Hathaway dialed Coats up, saying, "There's a story that Bayh will retire." Coats replied, "Anne, welcome to the age of bloggers. This stuff is all over all the time. If you've got something serious, call me back." Twenty minutes later, she did. "It's true," Hathaway said. After a long pause, Coats finally said, "I can't believe it."

Coats, too, had confounded his party as Bayh angled for a challenge to recapture his father's old Senate seat in 1998: Coats had abruptly dropped out, saying 18 years in Congress with the constant need to raise money had jaded him. But in a farewell interview, he walked away before returning to tell this writer, "I could have beat Evan Bayh." Asked if his return in 2010 was "unfinished business," Coats acknowledged, "To be candid with you, a little bit. I had committed to term limits. I wanted to honor that commitment. But I did feel bad that in a sense I opened the door and turned a Republican seat into a Democratic seat."

Coats premised his resurfacing by saying he had become increasingly alarmed and frustrated by the failure of Washington leaders to listen, while creating what he called "staggering debt" with "no regard for future generations."

With the Tea Party movement swirling around Republican circles and devouring some of his old colleagues, the reemergence of Coats teemed with ironies. He had not been on a ballot since 1992. But in the Senate, he had championed the Line Item Veto Act of 1996, outmaneuvering Senate lion Robert Byrd, getting it passed and and getting President Clinton's signature. Line-item veto was the law of the land until the U.S. Supreme Court ruled it unconstitutional.

Hoosier Democrats, however, were in shock at Bayh's "bugout." U.S. representative Baron Hill was flying 30,000 feet over Afghanistan on Feb. 15, 2010 when a soldier on the plane showed him his BlackBerry with reports of Bayh's retirement. U.S. representative Brad Ellsworth, another Democrat from the class of 2006 that brought three new Indiana seats into the party's fold, was just beginning a series of town hall meetings near Evansville when the news hit. As the party hierarchy began sorting out the new era, and as the filing deadline approached within hours, the dynamic sometimes turned surreal. A Facebook drive even commenced pushing Hoosier rocker John Mellencamp to run for Bayh's Senate seat.

By the following weekend, after primary candidate filing had passed, the Democratic dominoes tumbled. Ellsworth, the telegenic former Vanderburgh County sheriff, withdrew from the Eighth Congressional District (8th CD) and positioned himself for the Senate nomination that would not come until a week after the May 4 primary, with a vote from the 30-person state Democratic Central

Committee. Hoosier Democrats would find no Senate nominee on their primary ballot. State representative, Trent Van Haaften, had filed for the 8th CD seat just before the deadline. State senator Bob Deig enlisted for Van Haaften's legislative seat. All were politically doomed. As a GOP wave approached, ripples that included Coats's lackluster 39 percent primary win and a $1.06 million FEC report of cash-on-hand on June 30 had become rip tides. The Obama–Biden "summer of recovery" became an Indiana jobless rate of 10.3 percent. Obama had saved General Motors and Chrysler (and up to 140,000 Indiana jobs, including its vast supplier network), but Gov. Mitch Daniels and Indiana treasurer, Richard Mourdock, had scoffed at the fast-tracked bankruptcies. (Mourdock would go on to spend $2 million suing to overturn the Chrysler-Fiat merger in the U.S. Supreme Court, saying the deal perverted centuries of bankruptcy law. He lost).

These were strange twists in a state in love with the internal combustion engine, with Coats lashing out at the Obama auto bailouts and stimulus money that was seeding the state's emerging electric car sector. Inexplicably, Ellsworth and Indiana Democrats barely raised the issue.

Polls consistently showed Coats with big leads. A July Rasmussen Reports survey had Coats leading 51 to 30 percent, and on September 15, the Republican maintained a 50 to 34 percent lead.

The Coats–Ellsworth race quickly came down to two major issues: Coats's role as a Washington lobbyist, and the Obama health reforms. Ellsworth and Indiana Democrats had hoped to turn the debate away from health care and instead focus attention on Coats's lobbying efforts on behalf of King & Spaulding, an international law firm. A web video released in July tied Coats to Bank of America, recipient of a $15 billion TARP bailout.

On health reform, Rasmussen Reports polling showed Indiana voters favoring repeal of the Affordable Care Act by 62 percent on September 14–15, almost 10 percent above the national average. For Ellsworth, the reforms were a minefield. It was an Indiana health plan company—WellPoint—that revived the flagging legislation when it raised policy premiums for some by up to 39 percent in February. Yet on health reform, Rasmussen Reports polling showed Indiana voters favoring repeal, possibly influenced by the warnings of Governor Daniels, "It will raise by trillions the crushing debt we are already leaving young Americans. Any claims to the contrary are worse than mistaken, they are knowingly fraudulent."

A "no" vote on the health reforms would be damaging to the Democratic base Ellsworth needed to be competitive. Between March 4 and 16, Ellsworth was mute. The campaign was not returning calls. He finally put out a statement on March 16 saying, "I am looking carefully at the current language of the bill to ensure it meets my pro-life principles, and I will continue to work to ensure pro-life concerns are addressed."

Three days later, Ellsworth announced his decision: "After assurance from the Catholic Health Association, Catholic nuns and pro-life advocates I am confident in my heart that this bill meets my pro-life principles and upholds the policy of no federal funding for elective abortions." The news had hit as Rep. Bart Stupak was still trying to forge a compromise that would lead to Obama's executive order.

In a June interview with Howey Politics Indiana, Ellsworth explained, "I've had mixed reaction. I have had no less than hundreds of meetings and thousands of phone calls and correspondence going back and forth. It was a diverse response: people who were all for it, people who were all against it. And so that became my goal to dissect it and make the best decision I could on what I felt was best for the state and the country." Ellsworth added, "I would have liked to have seen something more incremental. When you have something that big it becomes ripe for misinformation and when people get misinformation they get scared."

On October 11, 2010, when the issue surfaced in the first Coats–Ellsworth debate in Indianapolis, Ellsworth said that when he first ran for Congress in 2006, he heard from hundreds of constituents about their escalating health care costs. "I am proud that we took it on," he said. "Is it perfect? No. It was a good first step." Coats said it as a 2,000-page behemoth that would cost "a trillion dollars" and not contain costs, characterizing it as a "pent-up, 23-year liberal wish dream."

As Ellsworth entered the homestretch, he was facing fear and anger. Rasmussen's September poll described 74 percent of Indiana voters as "angry at the current politics of the federal government, including 47 percent who are very angry." Ellsworth's fav/unfavs stood at 38/44 percent (compared to 56/35 percent for Coats).

During the first debate, Coats came off as rambling, while Ellsworth went on the offensive, seizing on the long-simmering residency issue that Coats was no longer a true Hoosier, and digging deep into Coats's lobbying career to justify the attack. Ellsworth quoted Coats from a 1992 debate with Democrat Joe Hogsett: Coats had said, "You go home and work in the private sector [after leaving Congress]." Ellsworth repeatedly reminded voters that Coats did just the opposite, leaving Indiana to become a lobbyist "Instead," Ellsworth said, "he hasn't paid taxes in Indiana, hasn't voted here in 10 years. He has houses in Virginia and North Carolina."

Within minutes of Coats's political resurfacing on Groundhog Day, Indiana Democrats assessed and assigned a negative tag to him: Lobbyist. It was a theme of most of Ellsworth's TV ads and dozens of press releases. It just did not work.

By a resounding 55 to 40 percent, Coats defeated Ellsworth on November 2, winning 84 percent of the Tea Party vote. He carried 84 of 92 counties, and 15 of 18 in Ellsworth's 8th CD, including Ellsworth's home county. Coats carried every demographic.

"Hoosiers have every reason to be proud because with your help, we have done our part by turning a U.S. Senate seat from one that is fundamentally supportive of the Obama regime to one that firmly opposes it," Coats told Republicans at Indianapolis' historic Union Station that Tuesday night, about 90 minutes after his victory became the first congressional Democratic seat to flip to the GOP.

Asked two days after the election if Coats thought he could have defeated Evan Bayh, he responded, "I would not have entered if I didn't think that. It was the right thing to do. It would have been a very contested race and it would have come down to a narrow margin. Evan Bayh's record was enabling the Obama agenda. He was not representing the Indiana I know."

Ellsworth was philosophical about his defeat, noting that some candidates spend a lifetime planning a Senate race. "We did it in eight months," he said. Ellsworth, along with the other "Bayh dominoes" tumbled to defeat.

No wonder Ellsworth would stand with Tim Kaine, the DNC chairman, at the Indiana Democratic Editorial Association Convention just before Labor Day at French Lick, quipping, "I would like to thank Evan Bayh—I think—for this opportunity."

Chapter 15

Iowa's 2010 Gubernatorial Race: Money, the Economy, and Same-Sex Marriage

by Amanda Frost-Keller and Dr. Caroline Tolbert

University of Iowa

Introduction

The 2010 Iowa gubernatorial election featured two extremely qualified candidates, both with previous state-level elected office experience. It was a unique race with an incumbent Democratic governor
running against a former four-term Republican governor; a race in
which both candidates were well known and ran well-financed campaigns. We argue that factors internal to the state of Iowa shaped the
outcome of the 2010 election, rather than national trends, in which
the Republican Party gained a historic 60 seats in the U.S. House of
Representatives and took control of two-thirds of the nation's governorships. Of Iowa's five U.S. House seats, neither the Republican nor
Democratic parties lost or gained seats, and besides the governor,
only one statewide office (secretary of state) changed party control.
Rather, the status quo ruled. Chet Culver, Iowa's incumbent governor, was held accountable not only for a poor state economy[1] but
also the decision by Iowa's Supreme Court to legalize legal same-sex
marriage the previous year. Culver also faced an opponent with considerable fundraising prowess. The result was a loss to Republican

challenger Terry Branstad by 10 percentage points on Election Day. We argue the gubernatorial race was a referendum on internal factors related to Iowa politics.

While the last governor, Chet Culver, was a Democrat, Iowa is by no means a safe Democratic state. The partisan majority has tended to swing between the Democrats and the Republicans, often resulting in a divided government due mainly to Iowa's long history of electing Republican governors. In recent presidential elections, Iowans have split their support for Democrats and Republicans, making it a true swing state. In 1998, Iowa elected its first Democratic governor since 1969, and in 2000 Iowa had a Republican majority in both houses of the legislature. While the Democrats have held the governorship through 2010, they were not able to win majorities in the state legislature until 2006. Although Iowa voters reelected a Democrat in 2002, they voted to give their electoral votes to George W. Bush in 2004, but chose Barak Obama four years later, with united Democrat control of both houses of the legislature in 2008. In sum, there is no clear partisan trend in Iowa; elections over the last decade have given victories to both Democratic and Republican candidates, at all levels of government.

Gubernatorial incumbent Chet Culver was a first-term governor, having been first elected as the Iowa executive in 2006. He succeeded two-term Democratic governor Tom Vilsack, who chose not to run for governor again. Before running for governor, Culver was twice elected Iowa secretary of state. In September of 2009, he had only a 41 percent job approval rating.[2]

The Republican nominee for governor, challenger Terry Branstad, faced two challengers in a competitive primary on June 8, 2010. Branstad out-fundraised his closest opponent almost 2 to 1,[3] and won by nearly 10 percentage points. Branstad has a long career in Iowa politics. He was first elected to the Iowa House in 1972, where he served three terms. Following this, he successfully ran for lieutenant governor in 1978. After Robert D. Ray, a popular Republican incumbent, chose not to seek reelection in 1983, Branstad was elected governor. He served four terms as governor, making him the longest-serving governor in Iowa history before he chose to step down in 1999. In terms of service in office in Iowa, Branstad was more of an incumbent than Culver.

Prior research on elections tells us that incumbents are very likely to beat challengers for a variety of reasons, including increased name recognition and fundraising. The more popular the incumbent, the more likely they are to win.[4] In typical elections, the incumbent, in this case Culver, would be predicted to beat the challenger, Branstad. However, the 2010 Iowa gubernatorial election was anything but typical given both candidate and electoral factors. Culver began the campaign as a not very popular incumbent. Branstad won the Republican primary as a popular former governor. At the same time, historic campaign expenditures, the economy, and the perpetually divisive issue of gay marriage altered the electoral landscape.

Campaign Financing and Spending

In gubernatorial elections, incumbents typically have many advantages over challengers, including more money. Gubernatorial challenger Branstad was unique in his ability to raise more money than his incumbent challenger, Culver, in large part because of individual campaign contributions.

In the 1970s, less than two-thirds of the total amount of money donated to congressional campaigns was from individual donations.[5] By the 2004 election, the vast majority of donations to political parties came from individuals.[6] In 2002, the Bipartisan Campaign Reform Act (BCRA) banned soft money donations to parties while increasing the limit on hard money donations to candidates to $2,000 per election.[7] This was an attempt to limit the influence of corporations and special interests, and force parties and candidates to rely more on donations from individuals.[8]

By refusing public financing and focusing on small private donations made largely over the Internet, Obama raised over $600 million dollars in 2007 through 2008.[9] Ordinary individuals are more likely to make campaign donations than they have been in the past, and their impact on elections can be large, as evidenced by the Obama campaign.

After winning the Republican primary on June 8, Branstad was able to raise more money than Culver. The total funds raised in the period leading up to the primary[10] (see box 15.1) remained relatively equal. However, the primary created momentum in campaign fundraising for Branstad due to the competitiveness of the primary, which activated and galvanized Republican voters. Culver, in contrast, faced no opponent in the June 8 primary. Overall, through October 26, Branstad raised over $2 million more than Culver. While Culver raised much of his money though large PAC donations, Branstad was able to attract a large number of individual donors, those donating small amounts. Raising money from individuals rather than interest groups (PACs) is an important form of voter mobilization.

Box 15.1—Candidate Fundraising

Amount of Money Raised as of June 1, 2010
Culver: $3,757,311—45.9% ($1,726,211) from 2,103 individuals Branstad: $3,537,380—95% ($1,493,027) from 3,070 individuals
Amount of Money Raised as of October 26, 2010
Culver: $6,058,102—from 4,000 individuals Branstad: $8,175,020.32—from 13,306 individuals

Source: National Institute of Money in State Politics, 2010.

While claiming credit and the delivery of pork are important advantages, name recognition continues to be a major benefit to incumbents.[11] As the governor of Iowa, Culver's name recognition was very high. However, Branstad was able to overcome this incumbent advantage in two ways. First, as an extremely popular former Iowa governor he already had name recognition with older voters. Second, he was able to successfully fundraise and buy advertising, the most effective way of increasing name recognition. The amount of money spent by the challenger significantly alters their chances of winning.[12] Specifically, the more the challenger spends in the election, the closer the final outcome.

Culver began the general election campaign with low approval numbers and there was little improvement over the course of the campaign, whereas Branstad outpolled Culver by up to 20 percentage points (see figure 15.1). Culver's low approval numbers led to lower levels of donating than if he were more popular, and spending more on campaigning does little to change the minds of voters in the case of unpopular governors.[13] Branstad, however, had high approval ratings throughout the campaign, and was able to translate this into more money and more votes. Branstad raised much more than Culver (see figure 15.2), and displayed much broader public support by attracting three times the number of individual donors.[14]

Figure 15.1—Job Approval Rating through Public Opinion Polling Data, and Distribution of Votes

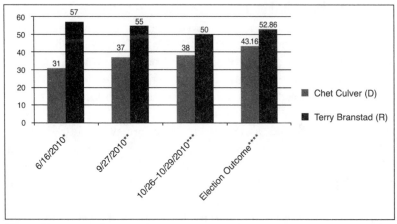

Note: *Rasmussen Reports, June 16, 2010a. **Rasmussen Reports, September 27, 2010b. ***Des Moines Register, October 26–29, 2010b. ****Iowa Secretary of State.

Figure 15.2—Campaign Finance Data

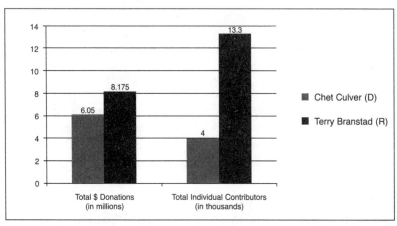

Note: *National Institute of Money in State Politics, 2010; Des Moines Register. **Terry Branstad Webpage.

Referenda on Iowa's Economy

Chet Culver governed during the worst economic crisis since the Great Depression and, to balance the budget, was responsible for an unpopular 10 percent across-the-board cut in state government spending. Research shows that governors, as state executives, are held accountable for perceived state economic conditions.[15] Given the poor economic health of the United States, as well as Iowa specifically, the 2010 governor's race may have been decided by retrospective economic evaluations. In short, Chet Culver may have been held accountable for the poor economic conditions of the state.

Polling data in the months leading up to the election finds mixed support for this idea. When asked who deserved "a lot of the blame" for the current condition of the economy, the most popular answer was Wall Street banks, as 79 percent of Iowans polled in September believed this to be true.[16] A majority, 51 percent, claimed President Obama deserved blame, and a majority also disapproved of the president's job performance. While Iowans were willing to assign much, or even most, of the blame to figures outside of Iowa, 46 percent believed Culver deserved blame for the state of the economy. Even more problematic, 51 percent believed Branstad was better equipped to improve the economy than was Culver. Even while they are willing to blame Culver for the poor economy, Iowans disagreed about how to fix it. Only 14 percent believed the state government would be able to fix the economy, while the plurality, 29 percent, suggested it was individual action that was necessary.

Issue Spillover: Judicial Retention Elections and Gay Marriage.

The headline story of the Iowa 2010 elections was not the dueling governors, but that Iowans had overwhelming voted to not retain three Iowa Supreme Court judges who had ruled in a unanimous decision to legalize same-sex marriage one year prior. Never in the 60 years since retention elections were instituted in the state had the judges not been retained. Hundreds of thousands of dollars in external funds from religious organizations were diverted to Iowa and 527s, including the National Organization of Marriage, to air negative campaign ads about same-sex marriage and the Iowa Supreme Court. Polls reveal many turned out to vote in the midterm election because of the judicial retention elections, not the candidates for elected office.[17] The judicial elections became a referendum, akin to the politics of direct democracy, on the court's ruling to legalize gay marriage.

In March 2009, the state's supreme court ruled that the state's constitution guarantees gays and lesbians the right to wed. At the time, a 2009 University of Iowa Hawkeye Poll found 26 percent supporting gay marriage, 28 percent opposing gay marriage but supporting civil unions, and 37 percent opposing both gay marriage and civil unions. Only 9 percent of conservatives supported gay marriage, while 56 percent of liberals did; a gap of 47 points. The court's ruling was controversial, and depending on how one reads the polling numbers, was not consistent with public opinion.

Ballot propositions on salient policy issues can have spillover effects on other candidate races in a state, shaping the policy agenda and voting decisions.[18] State ballot measures on same-sex marriage, for example, increased the salience of gay marriage as an issue that voters used when evaluating the 2004 presidential candidates.[19] The issue was also a more important factor in affecting voter choice for president in states where gay marriage bans were on the ballot (13 states). The results provide empirical evidence that the same-sex marriage-ban ballot measures may have helped reelect George W. Bush in the 2004 presidential elections.[20] High-profile ballot propositions ending social services for illegal immigrants (Proposition 187) and affirmative action (Proposition 209) have been linked to Republican gubernatorial successes in California.[21]

In a similar way, the issue of same-sex marriage and the judicial retention elections may have effected voting in the 2010 Iowa gubernatorial race. Nicholson argues candidates are often linked to measures on statewide ballots for which they are not responsible, or have not taken a formal position.[22] Rather, ballot measure campaigns can indiscriminately prime individual voting decisions up and down the ballot because voters use partisan stereotypes to link their preference on a policy (e.g., same-sex marriage) to the party best able to deal with that issue.[23] Readers must wonder whether those mobilized to throw out the three supreme court judges went to vote for the political party most capable of dealing with conservative moral issues (i.e., Branstad and the Republican Party). The survey data suggests that this was the case.

Support and opposition to the supreme court judges divided along partisan lines. Forty percent of Republicans surveyed in a 2010 Iowa poll said they planned to vote to remove all judges up for retention elections, and an additional 18 percent said they would vote to remove some of them.[24] In contrast, 54 percent of sampled Democrats planned to vote to retain all judges.[25] The same poll found 37 percent of those sampled planned to vote to remove all judges, 34 percent planned to vote to retain all, 10 percent planned to vote to retain some. Of those who said they wanted to retain all or some—69 percent said they thought the justices were being targeted because of the gay marriage ruling, and they agreed with the ruling.[26] Of those who wanted to remove all or some—73 percent said this was the voters' chance to say they disagreed on the gay marriage ruling. These data provide evidence that Iowa voters were informed of the importance of the judicial retention elections and had tied the vote to the issue of same-sex marriage.

Conclusion: Three Stories of Why Culver Lost to Branstad

We have presented three stories of how challenger Branstad was able to unseat incumbent Culver to lead the state of Iowa. The first was based on the Branstad's fundraising; the second, the poor economy; and the third, the unique judicial retention elections that became a referenda on same-sex marriage. If raising contributions from individuals is necessary for broad-based support like it was to Obama's campaign in the 2008, it may be an important trend for congressional and presidential elections alike. We provide some evidence that all three explanations have validity. However, the explanations are rooted in unique Iowa experiences, rather than nationwide trends. Iowa remains a battleground state and either political party could win the hearts and souls of Iowans in 2012. As the presidential primaries begin with the Iowa caucuses in January 2012, Iowa will once again be a national stage for testing the presidential candidates for both parties.[27]

References

Albrecht, Tim. 2010. "Governor Branstad 2010 Committee Eclipses $8 Million Funds Raised." GovernorBranstad2010.com. October 28. governor branstad2010.com/governor-branstad-2010-committee-eclipses-8-million -funds-raised/.

Atkeson, Lonna Rae and Randall W. Partin. 1995. "Economic and Referendum Voting: A Comparison of Gubernatorial and Senatorial Elections." *American Political Science Review* 89:634–47.

Bardwell, Kedron. 2005. "Reevaluating Spending in Gubernatorial Races: Job Approval as a Baseline for Spending Effects." *Political Research Quarterly* 58(1):97–105.

Barnett, Guy. 2008. "Huge campaign gives bang for bucks." *Hobart Mercury* (Australia). November 5.

Cillizza, Chris. 2008. Obama: The $150 Million Man. *Washington Post*. October 19.

Des Moines Register. 2010a. "Who Deserves Blame?" *DesMoinesRegister.com*. September 29. www.desmoinesregister.com/article/20100929/NEWS /9290356.

Des Moines Register. 2010b. "Iowans Plan to Split Tickets." *DesMoines Register.com*. October 31. www.desmoinesregister.com/article/20101031 /NEWS09/10310349.

Des Moines Register. 2010c. "Iowans Split Over Retaining Supreme Court Justices." *DesMoinesRegister.com*. October 31. www.desmoinesregister.com /article/20101031/NEWS09/10310356.

Donovan, Todd, Caroline Tolbert, and Daniel Smith. 2008. "Priming Presidential Votes by Direct Democracy." *Journal of Politics* 70:1217–31.

Gibson, Rachel K. 2008. "New Media and the Revitalization of Politics." Paper presented at the Revitalizing Politics Conference, London, England. November 5–6.

Glantz, Stanton A., Alan I. Abaramowitz, and Michael P. Burkart. "Election Outcomes: Whose Money Matters?" *The Journal of Politics* 38(4):1033–1038.

Iowa Secretary of State. 2010. "2010 General Election Unofficial Results." www.iowaelectionresults.gov/.

Jacobson, Gary C. and Samuel Kernell. 1981. *Strategy and Choice in Congressional Elections*. New Haven, CT: Yale University Press.

King, James D. 2001. "Incumbent Popularity and Voter Choice in Gubernatorial Elections." *The Journal of Politics* 63(2):585–597.

Luo, Michael. 2008. "Obama Recasts the Fundraising Landscape." *New York Times*. October 20.

Malbin, Michael J. 2008. "Thinking About Reform." in *Life After Reform: When the Bipartisan Campaign Reform Act Meets Politics*. ed. Michael Malbin. Lanham, MD: Rowman & Littlefield Publishers, Inc.

National Institute of Money in State Politics. 2010. "Iowa 2010." *FollowTheMoney.org*. www.followthemoney.org/database/grid.phtml?s =IA&y=2010&c=116521&t=0#c116521.

Nicholson, Stephen. 2005. Voting the Agenda: Candidates Elections and Ballot Propositions. Princeton, NJ: Princeton University Press.

Patterson, Kelly D. 2006. "Spending in the 2004 Election." In *Financing the 2004 Election*. Ed. David B. Magleby, Anthony Corrado, and Kelly D. Patterson. Washington D.C.: Brookings Institution Press.

Rasmussen Reports. 2010a. "Iowa Governor: Branstad (R) 57%, Culver (D) 31%." *RasmussenReports.com*. June 16. www.rasmussenreports.com/public _content/politics/elections/election_2010/election_2010_governor _elections/iowa/iowa_governor_branstad_r_57_culver_d_31.

Rasmussen Reports. 2010b. "Election 2010: Iowa Governor." *Rasmussen Reports.com*. September 27. www.rasmussenreports.com/public_content /politics/elections/election_2010/election_2010_governor_elections/iowa /election_2010_iowa_governor.

Redlawsk, David P., Caroline J. Tolbert, and Todd Donovan. 2010. *Why Iowa? How Caucuses and Sequential Elections Improve the Presidential Nominating Process*. Chicago, IL: University of Chicago Press.

Stone, Walter J and L. Sandy Maisel. 2003. "The Not-so-Simple Calculus of Winning: Potential U.S. House Candidates' Nomination and General Election Prospects." *The Journal of Politics* 65(4):951–77.

Survey USA. 2009. "Iowa." SurveyUSA.com. September 30. www.survey usa.com/client/PollReport.aspx?g=69056e58-7f60-4f2f-b17e-89a3c 7276249.

Tolbert, Caroline and Rodney Hero. 1996. "Race/Ethnicity and Direct Democracy: An Analysis of California's Illegal Immigration Initiative." *Journal of Politics* 58: 806–818.

Tolbert, Caroline and Rodney Hero. 2001. "Dealing with Diversity: Racial/Ethnic Context and Social Change Policy." *Political Research Quarterly* 54: (3) 571–604.

Wilcox, Clyde, Alexandra Cooper, Peter Francia, John C. Green, Paul S. Herrnson, Lynda Powell, Jason Reifler, Mark J. Rozell, and Benjamin A. Webster. 2003. "With Limits Raised, Who Will Give More? The Impact of BCRA on Individual Donors." In *Life After Reform: When the Bipartisan Campaign Reform Act Meets Politics*. Ed. Michael J. Malbin. Lanham, MD: Rowman & Littlefield Publishers, Inc.

Endnotes

[1]Lonna Rae Atkeson and Randall W. Partin. 1995. "Economic and Referendum Voting: A Comparison of Gubernatorial and Senatorial Elections." *American Political Science Review* 89:634–47.

[2]Survey USA. 2009. "Iowa." SurveyUSA.com. September 30. www.survey usa.com/client/PollReport.aspx?g=69056e58-7f60-4f2f-b17e-89a3c 7276249.

[3]National Institute of Money in State Politics. 2010. "Iowa 2010." *FollowTheMoney.org.* www.followthemoney.org/database/grid.phtml?s=IA&y =2010&c=116521&t=0#c116521.

[4]James D. King. 2001. "Incumbent Popularity and Voter Choice in Gubernatorial Elections." *The Journal of Politics* 63(2):585–597.

[5]Gary C. Jacobson and Samuel Kernell. 1981. *Strategy and Choice in Congressional Elections.* New Haven, CT: Yale University Press.

[6]Approximately 78 percent of donations to Democratic Parties, and 84 percent of donations to Republican Parties.

Kelly D. Patterson. 2006. "Spending in the 2004 Election." In *Financing the 2004 Election.* Ed. David B. Magleby, Anthony Corrado, and Kelly D. Patterson. Washington D.C.: Brookings Institution Press.

[7]Michael J. Malbin. 2008. "Thinking About Reform." in *Life After Reform: When the Bipartisan Campaign Reform Act Meets Politics.* ed. Michael Malbin. Lanham, MD: Rowman & Littlefield Publishers Inc.

[8]Clyde Wilcox, Alexandra Cooper, Peter Francia, John C. Green, Paul S. Herrnson, Lynda Powell, Jason Reifler, Mark J. Rozell, and Benjamin A. Webster. 2003. "With Limits Raised, Who Will Give More? The Impact of BCRA on Individual Donors." In *Life After Reform: When the Bipartisan Campaign Reform Act Meets Politics.* Ed. Michael J. Malbin. Lanham, MD: Rowman & Littlefield Publishers, Inc.

[9]In addition to raising the most money ever in a presidential election ($639.2 million, Barnet 2008), Obama also set a one-month fundraising record in September of $150 million (Luo 2008), and attracted a record 3 million individual donors to his campaign (Cilliza 2008). Ron Paul also focused on individual donations and raised a record $6 million in online donations, a new one-day record (Gibson 2008).

[10]Funds raised from January 1, 2009 through June 1, 2010.

[11]Walter J. Stone and L. Sandy Maisel. 2003. "The Not-so-Simple Calculus of Winning: Potential U.S. House Candidates' Nomination and General Election Prospects." *The Journal of Politics* 65(4):951–77.

[12]Stanton A. Glantz, Alan I. Abaramowitz, and Michael P. Burkart. "Election Outcomes: Whose Money Matters?" *The Journal of Politics* 38(4):1033–1038.

[13]Kedron Bardwell. 2005. "Reevaluating Spending in Gubernatorial Races: Job Approval as a Baseline for Spending Effects." *Political Research Quarterly* 58(1):97–105.

[14]Final campaign finance data was not yet available at press time.

[15]Atkeson and Partin, 1995.

[16]Poll was conducted for the *Des Moines Register* by Selzer & Co., Inc. of Des Moines, September 19-22. The sample includes 803 Iowans 18 and older, with a margin of error of 3.5 percent.

Des Moines Register. 2010a. "Who Deserves Blame?" *DesMoinesRegister.com.* September 29. www.desmoinesregister.com/article/20100929/NEWS/9290356.

[17]Poll was conducted for the *Des Moines Register* by Selzer & Co., Inc. of Des Moines, October 26–29. The sample includes 1,093 Iowans 18 and older, with a margin of error of 3.5 percent.

[18]Stephen Nicholson. 2005. Voting the Agenda: Candidates Elections and Ballot Propositions. Princeton, NJ: Princeton University Press.

[19]Todd Donovan, Caroline Tolbert, and Daniel Smith. 2008. "Priming Presidential Votes by Direct Democracy." *The Journal of Politics* 70:1217–31.

[20]Ibid.

[21]Caroline Tolbert and Rodney Hero. 1996. "Race/Ethnicity and Direct Democracy: An Analysis of California's Illegal Immigration Initiative." *Journal of Politics* 58: 806–818. Tolbert, Caroline and Rodney Hero. 2001. "Dealing with Diversity: Racial/Ethnic Context and Social Change Policy." *Political Research Quarterly* 54: (3) 571–604. Nicholson, 2005.

[22]Nicholson, 2005.

[23]Ibid.

[24]*Des Moines Register*, 2010a.

[25]Independents were split, 30 percent retain all, 31 percent remove all, 9 percent retain some.

[26]Poll was conducted for the *Des Moines Register* by Selzer & Co., Inc. of Des Moines, October 26–29. The sample includes 1,093 Iowans 18 and older, with a margin of error of 3.5 percent.

Des Moines Register. 2010c. "Iowans Split Over Retaining Supreme Court Justices." *DesMoinesRegister.com.* October 31. www.desmoinesregister.com/article/20101031/NEWS09/10310356.

[27]David P. Redlawsk, Caroline J. Tolbert, and Todd Donovan. 2010. *Why Iowa? How Caucuses and Sequential Elections Improve the Presidential Nominating Process.* Chicago, IL: University of Chicago Press.

Chapter 16

"Not That Expensive, but Certainly Nasty and Weird": the 2010 Kentucky Senate Race[1]

by Dr. Laurie A. Rhodebeck

Associate Professor of Political Science
at the University of Louisville

The 2010 Kentucky Senate race opened with speculation that Republicans would lose a seat if incumbent Jim Bunning ran for reelection and closed with the victory of a Tea Party favorite, Rand Paul. Paul transformed a race that ordinarily would have focused on local issues into a contest that challenged established Republican leaders and raised questions about national government. Paul was an unusual candidate in an unusual election year. He had never held elected office, seemed unfamiliar with the issues that generally drive politics in Kentucky, and promoted ideas that run contrary to the material interests of many voters in a relatively poor state that depends on federal help.[2] Nonetheless, he easily won office, most likely because he espoused a philosophical message that resonated with an increasingly conservative electorate.

The Primary Election Takes Shape

Bunning was vulnerable enough for analysts to call the 2010 race a toss-up before any Democrat announced plans to challenge him.[3] Besides having low approval ratings,[4] Bunning had raised only a fraction of the money he needed for his campaign (table 16.1), and he was behaving in ways that alienated colleagues he needed for support.[5] Ending months of speculation, Bunning announced in July 2009 that he would not seek another term.

While Bunning was sending mixed signals about his candidacy, two serious Democratic candidates emerged. Lieutenant Governor Dan Mongiardo declared his candidacy in January; Attorney General Jack Conway launched his campaign in April. Mongiardo and Conway had previously run as underdogs in high-profile contests. Mongiardo nearly unseated Bunning in the 2004 Senate race,[6] and Conway narrowly lost to three-term House incumbent Anne Northup in the 2002 congressional election.[7] Results from a Public Policy Polling survey conducted in early April showed that either Conway or Mongiardo would beat Bunning in hypothetical matchups.[8]

Soon after Bunning withdrew, two serious Republican candidates emerged: Secretary of State C. M. "Trey" Grayson III, a rising star in the Kentucky Republican Party, and Rand Paul, an ophthalmologist, founder of Kentucky Taxpayers United, and son of Representative Ron Paul (R-TX). The differences between the two candidates were immediately apparent. Grayson was the establishment candidate who launched his career in elective office in 2003 by becoming the nation's youngest secretary of state. He hired professional staffers, relied upon the assistance of Kentucky Republican Party leaders, and sought funds in traditional Republican-sponsored forums. Paul sought to set himself apart from the career politicians he frequently criticized during his campaign. He appointed novices to his campaign staff, reached out to a national network of his father's supporters, and raised money via Internet "money bombs."

The dynamics of the Republican primary race shifted quickly. A SurveyUSA poll[9] conducted in mid-August placed Grayson ahead of Paul, but by mid-autumn a new poll showed Paul edging past Grayson (table 16.2). Paul was also rapidly filling his campaign coffers, raising slightly more money than Grayson had by the end of 2009 (table 16.1).

The same two polls showed more stagnant preferences among likely Democratic voters, who consistently preferred Mongiardo over Conway (table 16.2), but Conway's fundraising efforts (table 16.1) suggested that the dynamics of the Democratic primary race might soon change.

Table 16.1—Campaign Finance in the 2010 Kentucky Senate Race

Quarter/Year	Bunning[a]	Grayson	Paul	Conway	Mongiardo
Election cycle-to-date[b]	519,000	—	—	—	—
1/2009[c]	263,000	—	—	—	430,000
2/2009	287,000	595,000	111,000	1,330,000	303,000
3/2009	—	643,000	1,011,000	546,000	514,000
4/2009	—	443,000	650,000	327,000	226,000
Totals, 2009	—	1,682,000	1,772,000	2,203,000	1,472,000
1/2010	—	728,000	607,000	211,000	309,000
April 1–28	—	328,000	310,000	114,000	98,000
Apr 29–June 30	—	147,000	822,000	894,000	164,000
2/2010[d]	—	476,000	1,132,000	1,008,000	261,000
3/2010	—	—	2,607,000	1,631,000	—
October 1–13	—	—	459,000	333,000	—
01/01/2009–04/28/2010:					
Total receipts[e]		2,767,000	2,701,000	2,666,000	1,886,000
Total disbursements[f]		1,947,000	2,532,000	1,991,000	1,389,000
01/01/2009–10/13/2010:					
Total receipts[e]			6,727,000	5,027,000	
Total disbursements[f]			6,069,000	4,370,000	
Contributions from:					
Individuals			6,172,000	4,188,000	
PACs			395,000	298,000	
Party			43,000	0	
Candidate			615,000	444,000	
Other			–497,000	97,000	

Sources: www.fec.gov and www.opensecrets.org/races/summary.php?id=KYS2& cycle=2010.

Notes: Entries are dollar amounts rounded to the nearest thousand. Entries for total amounts may differ from the sums due to rounding.
[a]Bunning left the race on July 27, 2009.
[b]Total reported as of December 31, 2008.
[c]Quarterly entries are net contributions for that period.
[d]Second quarter 2010 entries are the sums of the entries for April 1–28 and April 29–June 30.
[e]Total receipts include total contributions, transfers from authorized committees, loans from the candidate or others, operating expenditures offsets, and other receipts.
[f]Total disbursements include operating expenditures, transfers to authorized committees, loan repayments to the candidate or others, refunds, and other disbursements.

The Primary Election in Full Swing

A few issues were prominent in the primary, and the candidates took predictable positions on them. Grayson and Paul opposed the health care reform legislation, abortion rights, and the Employee Free Choice Act. Conway and Mongiardo expressed support for health care reform (although both raised minor reservations), a woman's right to make reproductive health choices (although Mongiardo said he personally opposed abortion), and the Employee Free Choice Act. The candidates agreed on their support for federal fiscal responsibility and their opposition to cap-and-trade legislation. Paul offered the most extreme approach to controlling federal spending: He pledged to reject all earmarks. The other candidates favored various balanced budget measures. All four candidates also pledged to support Kentucky's mining industry and investment in clean-coal technology, although they quibbled about who would be coal's best friend.

The candidates aired their views in campaign ads, televised debates, and public forums. Attack ads were the norm. Grayson's ads portrayed Paul as unfriendly to the mining industry, soft on national security issues, and too far out of the mainstream to represent Kentucky voters. Paul ran response ads to challenge Grayson's claims, and portrayed Grayson as a career politician with ties to big government. The Democratic candidates ran ads that raised questions about each other's ethics. Conway's ads accused Mongiardo of abusing taxpayers' money; Mongiardo's ads accused Conway of influencing utility rates after accepting campaign contributions from utility interests.

The need to finance these ads motivated impressive levels of fundraising. By the end of March, Conway led all candidates with $2.5 million; Grayson, Paul, and Mongiardo followed with $2.4 million, $2.3 million, and $1.7 million, respectively (table 16.1).

Did the money and the ads they bought affect the dynamics of the election? In the months preceding the May 18 primary, voter support shifted. Results of a March SurveyUSA poll showed Paul leading Grayson among likely Republican voters and Mongiardo leading Conway among likely Democratic voters (table 16.2). While Paul's lead over Grayson remained constant at about 15 percentage points, support for the Democratic candidates moved in opposite directions in subsequent polls. Mongiardo's numbers dropped while Conway's rose, leaving the Democrats in a statistical tie one week before the primary election (table 16.2).

As the first fully contested primary in both parties since the popular election of senators began in Kentucky, the election generated considerable interest in the state.[10] It also caught the attention of the nation, thanks primarily to Paul's candidacy. Paul ran as a representative of the Tea Party movement, which enjoys strong support in Kentucky.[11] Portraying himself as an "independent Republican" who would stand up to the Washington establishment, his candidacy was a challenge to mainstream Republican leaders. The intraparty division was especially apparent in the high-profile endorsements the Republican candidates received: Mitch McConnell, Dick Cheney, Rudy Giuliani, and Rick Santorum for Grayson; Jim Bunning, Sarah Palin, and Jim DeMint for Paul. In contrast, the Democratic primary maintained a more local character, with Conway and Mongiardo focused on policy issues specific to Kentucky and each other's alleged ethical lapses as state officeholders.

On May 18, Republican voters picked Paul over Grayson, 59 percent to 35 percent, while Democratic voters chose Conway over Mongiardo, 44 percent to 43 percent. Paul won in 108 of Kentucky's 120 counties. Conway and Mongiardo split the state, with Conway taking the urban central counties and Mongiardo taking the rural western and eastern counties.[12]

Intermezzo

As the first Tea Party candidate to win a statewide primary, Paul achieved instant celebrity status. The media attention was not flattering. Paul found himself under scrutiny for his views on racial desegregation, his comments about the BP oil spill in the Gulf of Mexico and a recent mining accident, and his opposition to citizenship for children born in the U.S. to parents who are illegal immigrants. On the advice of Republican leaders, Paul began staying closer to home and appearing before friendlier audiences. He also added professional staff to his campaign and participated in a Washington fundraiser sponsored by several of the "insiders" he had previously criticized. Bringing Paul into the party fold may have been as uncomfortable for the Republican establishment as it was for Paul; nonetheless, the Republican Party wasted no time in holding a unity rally shortly after the primary. Nor did Grayson hesitate to endorse his former opponent.

Table 16.2—Polling in the 2010 Kentucky Senate Race

	Republicans		Democrats	
	Grayson	Paul	Conway	Mongiardo
August 15–17, 2009 Undecided/Other N = 516 Republicans (±4.4) N = 647 Democrats (±3.9)	37	26 17/20	31	39 14/17
October 30–November 2, 2009 Undecided/Other N = 448 Republicans (±4.7) N = 602 Democrats (±4.1)	32	35 18/16	28	39 16/18
March 1–3, 2010 Undecided/Other N = 454 Republicans (±4.7) N = 590 Democrats (±4.1)	27	42 19/11	27	45 19/9
April 9–11, 2010 Undecided/Other N = 446 Republicans (±4.7) N = 659 Democrats (±3.9)	30	45 19/6	32	35 21/11
May 9–11, 2010 Undecided/Other N = 440 Republicans (±4.8) N = 662 Democrats (±3.9)	33	49 11/7	37	38 12/13
May 25–27, 2010 Undecided N = 569 (±4.2)		51 4	45	
July 27–29, 2010 Undecided N = 568 (±4.2)		51 5	43	
August 30–September 1, 2010 Undecided N = 561 (±4.2)		55 5	40	
September 21–23, 2010 Undecided N = 611 (±4)		49 4	47	
October 24–25, 2010 Undecided N = 637 (±4)		52 4	43	

Source: SurveyUSA polls sponsored by the Louisville *Courier-Journal* and WHAS-TV. All data and cross-tabulations can be found at www.surveyusa.com. Table is based on the following polls: #15674, #16002, #16314, #16441, #16533, #16614, #16858, #17033, #17120, #17489.

Notes: Entries are percentages of "likely voters" who supported a major candidate, collectively supported minor candidates, or were undecided. Figures in parentheses are margins of error.

Unity among the Democrats proved elusive. Mongiardo, who lost by 0.7 percent, said he would request a recanvass. Although he quickly changed his mind, he waited until August to endorse Conway. Democratic leaders voiced concern that Mongiardo's delayed endorsement might have tacitly signaled to his supporters that they should consider crossing party lines to vote for Paul in the fall.[13]

In the 2010 primary, Conway won more votes than Grayson and Paul combined; however, this margin offered no guarantee of victory in the fall. Kentucky is solidly Democratic in voter registration,[14] but the state tends to support Republicans in federal races.[15] The first SurveyUSA poll after the primary put Paul ahead of Conway, and the July poll showed little change in voters' preferences (table 16.2).

The General Election

The fall campaign in Kentucky opened at Fancy Farm, a lively meeting held in August at the St. Jerome Catholic Church in Graves County. The 130-year-old event usually attracts little attention beyond Kentucky, but in 2010 the state's high-profile Senate race brought national media coverage. Conway and Paul offered the larger-than-usual crowd of 15,000 previews of their upcoming campaigns. Conway focused on his record as state attorney general and criticized Paul for having "out-of-touch, radical views that are risky and even scary."[16] Paul barely mentioned his opponent, choosing instead to attack President Barack Obama, House Speaker Nancy Pelosi, and Senate Majority Leader Harry Reid. These were the two sets of messages that played repeatedly during the fall campaign in the candidates' television ads and public appearances, which included five formal debates.

Paul nationalized the Kentucky Senate race by coupling his attacks on Washington and Democratic leaders with the Tea Party platform of smaller government and lower taxes. Some of Paul's ads portrayed Conway as Obama's "yes man," suggesting that Conway would support more spending, higher taxes, and bigger government. Other ads portrayed Paul, in contrast, as "a physician, not a career politician" who would fix Washington's ills. Parallel ads run by the National Republican Senatorial Committee (NRSC), the U.S. Chamber of Commerce, and the Crossroads organizations reinforced Paul's attacks on Conway. Paul and his supporters appeared to have a winning strategy, opening up a 15-point lead over Conway by Labor Day (table 16.2).

Table 16.3—Selected Exit Poll Results in the 2010 Kentucky Senate Race

Voter Groups	Conway	Paul
Male (50%)	39	60
Female (50%)	49	51
White (90%)	41	59
African American (6%)	86	13
18–29 years old (13%)	51	48
30–44 years old (23%)	43	57
45–64 years old (44%)	44	56
65+ years old (20%)	42	58
Income less than $50K (45%)	51	49
Income $50K+ (55%)	39	60
No high school (5%)	52	48
High school graduate (25%)	46	54
Some college (29%)	38	61
College graduate (23%)	40	60
Postgraduate (18%)	52	47
Urban residence (21%)	59	41
Suburban residence (26%)	34	66
Rural residence (52%)	43	56
Democrat (38%)	83	16
Republican (40%)	8	91
Independent (22%)	42	58
Liberal (16%)	83	16
Conservative (42%)	16	84
Moderate (42%)	57	43
Household lost job in last two years (27%)	51	48
No job loss in household (72%)	39	61
Country going in right direction (25%)	88	12
Country on wrong track (71%)	25	74

Voter Groups	Conway	Paul
Approve how Obama is handling job as president (36%)	87	12
Disapprove how Obama is handling job as president (63%)	19	81
Senate vote expressed support for Obama (18%)	92	8
Senate vote expressed opposition to Obama (40%)	14	85
Obama not a factor in Senate vote (41%)	61	39
Supports Tea Party (43%)	11	89
Neutral toward Tea Party (27%)	45	54
Opposes Tea Party (28%)	90	9
Senate vote expressed favor for Tea Party (26%)	12	87
Senate vote expressed opposition to Tea Party (22%)	90	10
Tea Party not a factor in Senate vote (47%)	45	54
Satisfied/enthusiastic about federal government (26%)	82	17
Dissatisfied/angry about federal government (73%)	32	67
Highest priority for next Congress cutting taxes (21%)	25	73
Highest priority for next Congress reducing deficit (35%)	33	67
Highest priority for next Congress spending to create jobs (37%)	71	29

Source: CNN Exit Polls www.cnn.com/ELECTION/2010/results/polls/#val=KYS01p1.

Notes: Entries are the percentages of groups that voted for Jack Conway or Rand Paul. The relative size of each group is shown in parenthesis. Total N = 2212.

Conway fought back by putting his opponent on the defensive, often using Paul's public statements about various issues, including his support for a $2,000 increase in the Medicare deductible, his support for a proposal to replace federal payroll taxes with a 23 percent sales tax, and his dismissal of illegal drug use as a pressing issue. Several of Conway's ads touted his record as attorney general, creating the image of a "law and order" candidate who would protect citizens from all kinds of crime. Ads run by the Democratic Senatorial Campaign Committee

(DSCC), the National Education Association, MoveOn.org, and People for the American Way buttressed the messages in Conway's ads.

By late September, Conway had moved into a statistical tie with Paul (table 16.2). In an effort to gain ground, the Conway campaign took a bold step in mid-October: It aired an ad that raised questions about Paul's involvement with a secret society when he was a student at Baylor University, and reminded voters that Paul had suggested ending federal faith-based initiatives and deductions for religious charities. The ad revived the "Aqua Buddha" story,[17] reaped bipartisan criticism, poisoned the fourth debate,[18] and spurred response ads from Paul and the NRSC that condemned Conway for attacking Paul's Christian faith. The ad and its attendant controversy seemed to reverse Conway's progress. A week after the ad's first appearance, Paul's lead widened significantly (table 16.2).

Paul carried his advantage all the way to Election Day, beating Conway 55.8 percent to 44.2 percent.[19] Paul won easily among men, whites, voters aged 30 or over, voters earning $50,000 or more, suburban and rural voters, and all but the least- or most-educated voters. Most telling, he received especially high levels of support from voters who expressed disapproval of Obama or dissatisfaction or anger with the federal government (table 16.3), a pattern that emerged throughout the nation's midterm races.[20]

Conway blamed his loss on the money spent by outside groups to attack him,[21] but other factors were also at work. Conway was slow to define himself to voters, and he did not place enough emphasis on the economy or jobs.[22] Although he said he had no regrets about the "Aqua Buddha" ad, the collective wisdom is that it contributed to Paul's late surge.[23]

The 2010 general election in Kentucky was a clash between national issues and local interests. Paul advocated a smaller role for federal government and fiscal restraint, even challenging the earmarks that have been so important to Kentucky. Conway emphasized Kentucky's concerns as a poor state, stressing that he would "always put Kentucky first." In 2010, the majority of voters in Kentucky did not seem to care whether anyone put Kentucky first. Anti-Washington, and especially anti-Obama, sentiment ran so high in the state that conducting a campaign against the federal government ultimately proved to be a winning strategy.

Endnotes

[1]With apologies to Howard Fineman, who described the 2010 election season as "expensive, nasty and weird," www.huffingtonpost.com/2010/10/19 /tv-ad-avalanche_n_768799.html. Bill Goodman of Kentucky Educational Television introduced the final debate between Jack Conway and Rand Paul by calling the Kentucky Senate race one of the "expensive, nasty and weird" contests, www.c-span.org/Politics/All/5051.aspx. The *New York Times* described the race as "childish and nasty," "Boiling point in Kentucky," *New York Times*, October 27, 2010, A32.

[2]According to 2008 U.S. Census data, 17.3% of Kentuckians live below the poverty level, compared to 13.2% of all Americans, quickfacts.census.gov/qfd /states/21000.html. According to 2009 U.S. Census data, Kentucky receives federal aid in amounts higher than the U.S. average, www.census.gov/prod /2010pubs/fas-09.pdf.

[3]Joseph Gerth, "Bunning has only $175,045 for reelection," *Courier-Journal*, November 23, 2008, 1.

[4]A Public Policy Polling survey conducted in early April 2009 showed Bunning's approval rating at 28%, www.publicpolicypolling.com/pdf/surveys /2009_Archives/PPP_Release_KY_408.pdf.

[5]Bunning was inexplicably absent from the Senate for most of January 2009. He threatened to sue the National Republican Senate Committee if it backed a primary challenger, he made insulting comments about Senate Minority Leader Mitch McConnell, and when pressured to discuss the progress of his campaign he retorted that he might quit to let Democratic Governor Steve Beshear appoint a replacement to the junior Senate seat.

[6]Bunning: 50.7% (873,507 votes), Mongiardo: 49.3% (850,855 votes). 2004 election results reported at elect.ky.gov/NR/rdonlyres/3A2A50FF-35A2-44ED -BCFD-EFA7028E14EC/0/2004state.txt.

[7]Northup: 51.6% (118,228 votes), Conway: 48.4% (110,846 votes). 2002 election results reported at elect.ky.gov/NR/rdonlyres/923B8096-2858-46DC -B908-5EAE046D079E/0/2002state.txt.

[8]www.publicpolicypolling.com/pdf/surveys/2009_Archives/PPP_Release_KY _408.pdf.

[9]To simplify the presentation of the dynamics of public opinion about the candidates, I rely primarily on SurveyUSA polls. They are generally consistent with polls that other organizations conducted during the race.

[10]Al Cross, "Grayson, Paul put Senate race in spotlight," *Courier-Journal*, May 2, 2010, H1.

[11]According to a SurveyUSA poll taken May 25–27, 2010, 36% of Kentucky adults have a favorable opinion of the Tea Party movement, and 45% either agree with what the Tea Party stands for (41%) or are active members (4%). In a May 28–29, 2010 survey, Rasmussen Reports found that 31% of Kentucky voters consider themselves part of the Tea Party movement, compared to 16% of voters nationwide who do so, www.rasmussenreports.com/public_content /most_recent_videos/2010_06/where_is_the_tea_party_strongest.

[12]Two minor Democratic candidates, Darlene Price and James Buckmaster, each picked up their home county. Maurice Sweeney was the fifth candidate on the Democratic ballot. The Republican primary included four minor candidates: Bill Johnson, Gurley Martin, Jon Scribner, and John Stephenson. Election results reported at results.enr.clarityelections.com/KY/15261/30235 /en/summary.html.

[13]Joseph Gerth, "Democrats' grudges may ease way for Paul," *Courier-Journal*, June 21, 2010, B1.

[14]As of November 2, 2010 there were 1,624,361 registered Democrats and 1,067,537 registered Republicans, (elect.ky.gov/NR/rdonlyres/9B962D0A -E25D-43DE-8DE6-8603346E3433/241387/statconggen.txt).

[15]During the past 12 years the state has been represented by two Republican senators, and at least four of the six House members have been Republicans. Since 2000 the Republican presidential candidates have won their elections by margins of at least 15 percentage points (elect.ky.gov/results/).

[16]Joseph Gerth, "Barbs fly at Fancy Farm," *Courier-Journal*, August 8, 2010, 1.

[17]The story was originally reported on August 9, 2010, at GQ.com, www.gq.com/blogs/the-q/2010/08/gq-exclusive-rand-pauls-crazy-college-days -hint-theres-a-secret-society-involved.html.

[18]During the debate Paul expressed outrage over the ad and refused to shake Conway's hand; Conway defended the ad and refused to apologize, www.cspan.org/Watch/Media/2010/10/17/HP/A/39564/Kentucky+Senate +Debate.aspx.

[19]Election results reported at elections.nytimes.com/2010/results/senate.

[20]Jackie Calmes and Megan Thee-Brenan, "Democrats lose support among women and independents, polls show," *New York Times*, November 3, 2010, P7.

[21]In his concession speech Conway said he was outspent 5-to-1 by Republican-allied groups, www.c-spanvideo.org/program/296377-1. Although Conway may have exaggerated the ratio, the numbers did favor Paul. As of October 28, the NRSC had spent $1,846,957, and other outside groups supporting Paul had spent $4,149,854. The DSCC had spent $1,586,482, and other groups supporting Conway had spent $876,382, Stephenie Steitzer, "Groups spend $8 million on Senate race," *Courier-Journal*, October 30, 2010, 1. Excluding contributions from the party committees, the Center for Responsive Politics ranked the Kentucky Senate race as tenth in attracting outside spending, www.opensecrets.org/outsidespending/index.php. The candidates themselves spent only a bit more than the outside groups did (table 16.2). Based on candidate spending alone, the 2010 Kentucky Senate race was not characterized by especially high levels of spending, www.open secrets.org/overview/topraces.php. And the $10.4 million that Conway and Paul spent pales by comparison to the $31.9 million spent in the 2008 Kentucky Senate race. In relative terms, the 2010 Kentucky Senate race was not that expensive.

[22]Jack Brammer and Bill Estep, "Rand Paul wins U.S. Senate race in Kentucky," *Lexington Herald-Leader*, November 3, 2010, www.kentucky.com /2010/11/02/1506746/rand-paul-wins-us-senate-race.html.

[23]Al Cross, "GOP wave ran deep in local elections," *Courier-Journal*, November 7, 2010, H1.

Chapter 17

The Maryland Governor's Race: The Old Line State Bucks the National Tide

by Dr. Paul S. Herrnson

*Director of the Center for American Politics and Citizenship;
and Distinguished Scholar-Teacher at the
University of Maryland, College Park*

and Dr. Thomas F. Schaller

*Professor of Political Science at the
University of Maryland, Baltimore County*

In 2009, the Republicans won the governorships in New Jersey and Virginia. In a 2010 special election, they claimed the Massachusetts U.S. Senate seat that had been held for 47 years by liberal icon Ted Kennedy. In the 2010 general elections, the GOP was expected to make big gains in the U.S. House, the U.S. Senate, and statehouses across the country. This momentum, and the national mood leading up to November 2010, allowed Maryland Republicans to hope that former GOP governor Robert Ehrlich would be able to ride the nationwide anti-incumbent, anti-taxes, anti-big government wave back into office. Conversely, Democrats were optimistic that their state would be insulated from the national tide and enable Governor Martin O'Malley to remain in the governor's mansion.

The 2010 Maryland governor's race can be best characterized as a high-spending, high-profile, no-holds barred rematch that ended with O'Malley emerging victorious by a convincing 13.5 percentage point

283

margin. Although Ehrlich ran a respectable campaign, he could overcome neither the more powerful effort launched by O'Malley nor the partisan advantages that have benefited Democratic candidates for decades.

The Setting

Democrats have dominated Maryland politics for much of the state's history. Beginning with Reconstruction, they have elected 24 of the state's 30 governors. Indeed, the last Republican to serve in Maryland's governor's office prior to Ehrlich's 2003–2007 term was Spiro Agnew, who was elected in 1966 when Democrats were sharply divided over civil rights. Democratic control of the state legislature has also been longstanding. The Democrats have held majorities in both chambers of the state legislature since at least 1950, and Maryland has supported the Democratic nominee for president in the last five elections.

Maryland is a geographically, economically, and demographically diverse state with strong Democratic inclinations. Most of its population resides in the Baltimore–Washington, D.C. urban-suburban corridor, which leans strongly Democratic. The state's western and eastern regions are largely rural and Republican. Just over 65 percent of all Marylanders are white, 30 percent are African American, and 5 percent are of Asian descent. Maryland residents enjoy incomes and educational levels above the national average, in part, because of the availability of many good-paying jobs provided by the federal government and government contractors and a significant share of union workers.[1]

Most objective indicators suggested that the setting for the 2010 election would favor Governor O'Malley. His party held 33 of 47 seats in the state senate, and 105 of 141 seats in the state house of delegates. Maryland's delegation in the U.S. House of Representatives comprised seven Democrats and only one Republican, and both of its U.S. senators were Democrats. During the 2008 presidential election, Maryland gave 63 percent of its two-party vote to Democratic nominee Barack Obama, reflecting the Democrats two-to-one advantage over the GOP. Polls taken in March 2010 gave O'Malley between a 6-point and 7-point lead over Ehrlich, which is roughly the same as the victory margin O'Malley had over Ehrlich in 2006.[2] As a result of the nation's stalled economy, voters nationwide were venting their anger at government and establishment politicians. Encouraged by this political mood,

Ehrlich entered the race, leading political prognosticators to categorize it as "leaning Democratic."[3] Although not as helpful as a "toss-up" rating, this helped Ehrlich raise money and get free media coverage.

The Candidates

The 2010 Maryland governor's race was typical of many political rematches in that the incumbent and his predecessor squeezed out all other competitors. O'Malley ran against light opposition in the Democratic primary and spent most of the period prior to Maryland's September 14 primary day campaigning against Ehrlich. On the Republican side, several candidates openly discussed the possibility of running, but all of the serious competitors said they would step aside if Ehrlich entered the race—and all of them did. Businessman Brian Murphy challenged Ehrlich, and he would have remained largely unknown if not for his endorsement by former Republican vice-presidential candidate Sarah Palin.

The lack of serious challengers is not surprising. Most experienced politicians recognize that there is substantial risk involved in challenging a highly visible and popular primary or general-election opponent. As expected, on a low-turnout primary day, both O'Malley and Ehrlich coasted to comfortable wins: With 86 percent of the vote, O'Malley dispatched of J. P. Cusick and Ralph Jaffe; Ehrlich beat back Murphy's bid, taking 76 percent of the vote.[4] The audacity of Murphy's attempt to steal the nomination from Ehrlich did, however, manage to ruffle the former governor's feathers a bit. Interviewed live on radio by conservative talk show host Ron Smith, Ehrlich bristled at the idea of embracing Murphy and his supporters.

The Democratic Nominee

In many ways, O'Malley has the perfect profile for a Maryland gubernatorial candidate. Raised in the cities of Rockville and Bethesda in Montgomery County, he graduated college from the nearby Catholic University in Washington, D.C. and got his law degree from the University of Maryland Law School; he can claim deep roots in the voter-rich Baltimore-Washington corridor.[5] His early experiences as a volunteer in Iowa in Gary Hart's 1984 presidential campaign, and as state field director for then congresswoman Barbara Mikulski's successful 1986 campaign for the U. S. Senate, helped him develop valuable political skills and contacts. He expanded on these assets while serving as a legislative fellow for Mikulski, through his marriage to Catherine Curran, daughter of former state attorney general Joe Curran, and as assistant state's attorney for Baltimore City.[6]

In 1990, O'Malley made his first run for elective office, losing the Democratic primary for a seat in the Maryland state senate by a mere 44 votes. The following year he was elected to the Baltimore City Council, where he served for eight years. In 1999, he ran successfully for mayor of Baltimore. During his two terms as mayor he established a reputation as crime fighter, which raised his visibility both across the state and nation. He was named "The Best Young Mayor in the Country" in 2002 by *Esquire* magazine, and one of America's "Top 5 Big City Mayors" in 2005 by *Time* magazine. In that same year, *Business Week* designated him one of the five "New Faces" in the Democratic Party.[7]

O'Malley's performance as mayor and visibility on the national political stage, combined with his boyish good looks and the stylish image, which he had cultivated as the lead singer in a Celtic rock band, made him a very strong candidate for governor. In 2006, he defeated Ehrlich by a 6.5 percent margin.

The Republican Nominee
Ehrlich's ability to clear the Republican primary field of all serious contenders in 2010 reflected the conventional wisdom in the state the he was not merely the GOP's best hope, but its only hope. The golden boy of Maryland Republican politics, Ehrlich was raised in the working-class town of Arbutus in southwest Baltimore County. A talented athlete whose father sold cars for a living, as a teenager, Ehrlich was spotted playing pickup football by legendary political operative Nick Schloeder, and was given a scholarship to the prestigious Gilman School. His Gilman years paved the way to a Princeton degree and then law school at Wake Forest University. In 1986, the 29-year-old lawyer with a working-class pedigree and an Ivy League education won the first of two terms as a state delegate. After eight years in the Maryland General Assembly, in 1994 Ehrlich won the first of four terms as the congressman from Maryland's Second District—a seat made available when longtime incumbent Helen Delich Bentley opted to run for governor.

Representing a working-class, white ethnic district that included much of the eastern half of Baltimore County and portions of Harford

County, Ehrlich positioned himself as a socially moderate Republican in the tradition of Theodore McKeldin and Spiro Agnew, the state's two previous Republican governors. In 2002, his victory over incumbent Lt. Governor Kathleen Kennedy Townsend, daughter of Democratic icon Robert Kennedy, brought national attention to him and his running mate, Michael Steele, who became the first African American elected to statewide office in the state. The election provided the long-dormant Maryland Republican Party an infusion of new blood. Initially, Ehrlich waffled about whether to try to regain office. In March, with the political environment looking good for Republicans, he finally entered the race, but his hesitancy cost him valuable time to campaign and raise money. With a thin bench to choose from and Steele indisposed as Republican National Committee chairman, he chose as his running mate Mary Kane, who had served as secretary of state during his first administration and was married state GOP chairman John Kane.[8]

The General Election Campaign

The general election was a scandal-free, substantive debate between two candidates already familiar to the vast majority of state voters. Because Ehrlich is a social moderate on many issues, cultural arguments were superseded by the debate over the two candidates' economic visions for the state. As both O'Malley's challenger and immediate predecessor, Ehrlich attempted to paint the Democrat as a tax-happy, anti-business liberal who increased the state's debt and reduced its economic competitiveness. O'Malley responded by reminding voters of the sales, property, and flush taxes Ehrlich approved during his tenure, even as he touted himself as a governor who made tough budgetary cuts while still finding ways to fund education and other public priorities.

Once the primaries were over, the nominees battled to define the state's past and its future. With funds provided by the Republican Governors Association, Ehrlich mocked O'Malley's "Moving Maryland Forward" campaign theme with a television ad claiming the Democrats had "moved Maryland backward" during his term. When O'Malley expressed his support for the so-called Purple Line extension of the Washington Metrorail system in Montgomery County and a new Red Line metro expansion in Baltimore, Ehrlich called the projects unaffordable. When Ehrlich promised tax breaks for Maryland veterans, O'Malley decried them as another "budget busting" tax giveaway. Both candidates were operating with the political constraints of reduced tax receipts and fiscal worries fueled by the state's $1.6 billion budget gap. The only difference was which priorities each candidate deemed essential, and which too expensive.[9] Both candidates had the wherewithal to campaign vigorously, with O'Malley spending $11.2 million and Ehrlich spending $7.3 million as of two weeks before Election Day.

The Outcome

What made the O'Malley-Ehrlich rematch so interesting is how the 2010 political environment differed from the previous two gubernatorial cycles. In 2002, Ehrlich defeated a weak opponent in a generally strong Republican cycle to win an open seat; four years later, as the incumbent, he lost to O'Malley, a strong challenger running with a strong Democratic tailwind. For the rematch, O'Malley was the incumbent seeking reelection in a very difficult Democratic year, which made the contest closer than it otherwise might be for an incumbent Democrat running in one of the bluest states in America.

In the end, the partisan tilt in Maryland was more than sufficient for O'Malley to hold off the state's most prominent and competitive Republican in an otherwise tough year for Democrats, in Maryland and nationally. O'Malley won, 55.8 percent to 42.3 percent—a 13.5 point victory that more than doubled his 6.5 point margin over Ehrlich four years earlier. Democrats also managed net gain of two Senate seats and seven in the House of Delegates. (The one bright spot for state Republicans was Andy Harris's defeat of rookie Democratic congressman Frank Kratovil). O'Malley racked up huge margins in Baltimore City, Montgomery, and Prince Georges counties, as expected, plus Howard and Charles counties, while keeping Ehrlich's margins in the remaining Baltimore suburbs and the rural portions of the state sufficiently low enough to give the Democratic incumbent a surprisingly strong reelection victory. On election night, O'Malley said, "We're going to have a lot of tough days still ahead of us, but we are coming back."[10]

Ehrlich's candidacy in 2010 met two of the five conditions necessary for a Republican gubernatorial victory in Maryland: An attractive candidate in possession of strong campaign skills and an anxious electorate—though one that was not nearly as hostile as voters in other parts of the country. Lacking was a strong rationale for his candidacy, a weak Democratic opponent, and a Democratic Party tainted by scandal or divided by a salient deep-seated issue. Ehrlich's late start to the campaign did not help, nor did O'Malley's significant campaign war chest, or the fact that the well-educated and highly unionized state was buffered better than most against the economic downturn. The 2010 election delivered no new electoral headlines in the Old Line State, as the Democratic Party and its politically formidable incumbent governor held steady.

Endnotes

[1] en.wikipedia.org/wiki/Maryland, retrieved April 1, 2010.

[2] John Wagner, "Robert Ehrlich Says He'll Make Another Run for Maryland Governor," *Washington Post*, March 31, 2010, p. A1.

[3] Aaron C. Davis, "Analyst: Maryland Governor's Race 'Competitive'," voices.washingtonpost.com/annapolis/2010/04/analyst_maryland_governors_rac.html.

[4] Matthew Hay Brown, "Primary turnout hits historic low," *Baltimore Sun*, September 15, 2010, weblogs.baltimoresun.com/news/local/politics/2010/09/primary_turnout_hits_historic.html.

[5] www.governor.maryland.gov/biography.asp, retrieved April 29, 2010.

[6] en.wikipedia.org/wiki/Martin_O%27Malley, retrieved April 29, 2010.

[7] Ibid.

[8] Liam Farrell, "Ehrlich chooses Kane as running mate," *The (Annapolis) Capital*, July 1, 2010, www.hometownannapolis.com/news/top/2010/07/0135/Ehrlich-chooses-Kane-as-running-mate.html?ne=1.

[9] Julie Bykowicz, "O'Malley 'moving Maryland backward,' RGA claims," *Baltimore Sun*, September 21, 2010, weblogs.baltimoresun.com/news/local/politics/2010/09/omalley_moving_maryland_backwa.html; Annie Linsky, "Ehrlich promises tax break to vets," *Baltimore Sun*, August 24, 2010, weblogs.baltimoresun.com/news/local/politics/2010/08/ehrlich_promises

_more_money_to.html; Matthew Hay Brown, "O'Malley supports Purple Line, dodges on gas tax," *Baltimore Sun*, August 10, 2010, weblogs.baltimoresun .com/news/local/politics/2010/08/omalley_purple_line_gas_tax.html.

[10]Scott Calvert, Julie Bykowicz, and Gus Sentementes, "O'Malley wins second term as governor," *Baltimore Sun*, November 3, 2010.

Chapter 18

Breaking the Wave: The Massachusetts Gubernatorial Race of 2010

by Dr. Agnes Bain

Professor of Government at Suffolk University

In early September 2010, in an op-ed piece for the *Metro*—the free broadside available at every train station and commuter rail stop—Governor Deval Patrick of Massachusetts wrote: "My opponents in this race are good people, but we have fundamentally different values and a fundamentally different approach to building a stronger Commonwealth."[1]

The governor was wrong. Voters in Massachusetts did not see the 2010 gubernatorial race as a choice between or among different values. His unfavorable ratings improved, but remained high up to the eve of the election. The voters were largely unhappy with the politics of Beacon Hill. Still, Deval Patrick and the Democrats in Massachusetts managed to buck the nationwide wave of Republican victories in a race that came down to issues of temperament, likeability, and the best ground game in the history of the state.

How did Deval Patrick, the man who was elected with nearly 54 percent of the vote in a three-way race in 2006, come to be in this predicament as the campaign of 2010 unfolded? He had been elected on a message of hope and change, and to the chant of "Together we can!" Many would argue that his 2006 campaign had been an incubator for Barack Obama's successful presidential run in 2008. Patrick was a political unknown who upset establishment Democrats. He went from the Chicago housing projects to a Massachusetts prep school, and then went to Harvard and Harvard Law. Patrick's career began as a civil rights lawyer, first at the National Association for the Advancement of Colored People (NAACP), and then in the Clinton administration before moving to work as general counsel to various corporations.

Patrick won the 2006 election handily. He took the oath of office in January 2007 as the first African American governor in Massachusetts history, and only the second African American governor in the country since Reconstruction.

Some might say that the Patrick administration quickly hit the iceberg known as the "Great Recession." Critics might counter that Patrick, in governing, steered the ship of the Commonwealth through icy seas with all the acumen of the captain of the *Titanic*. The budget deficits kept growing and Patrick continued to cut spending, thus angering both his opposition and his base.

By August 2008, a poll found that 49 percent of respondents said that Massachusetts was headed in the wrong direction. While Patrick's approval rating remained high (51 percent), 40 percent of respondents thought that he was a worse governor than expected and 32 percent were undecided.[2]

Thus, the way was open for credible challengers. The Republican nominee would be Charlie Baker, who declared his candidacy in July 2009. Baker was a Harvard graduate and political insider who claimed outsider status. He was a cabinet member of the Republican Weld-Cellucci administrations, first as undersecretary for health, then as secretary of health and human services, and finally as secretary of administration and finance, from 1994 to 1998. Baker left public service in 1998 to become CEO of Harvard Vanguard Medical Associates and quickly moved to become CEO of its parent company, Harvard Pilgrim Health Care. He is largely credited for turning around this failing HMO and making it into one of the top-rated health plans in the country.[3]

In September 2009, State Treasurer Timothy Cahill, who had endorsed Patrick for governor in 2006, left the Democratic Party to mount a campaign for governor as an independent. Cahill probably correctly calculated that, even though Patrick was generally unpopular, he could not be beaten for the Democratic nomination. While Massachusetts is often seen as a one-party state, the fact is that only 35 percent of voters are registered Democrats and 12 percent are Republicans. A solid 51 percent are independent/unenrolled.[4] Cahill set out to mine that large group of independents as well as disaffected Democrats to create a viable candidacy.

Tim Cahill is a product of local schools and experiences. Cahill graduated from Boston University with a degree in political science, and he held elected office as a city councilor and a county treasurer before running successfully for state treasurer in 2002, reelected in 2006.[5]

In January 2010, the solid-blue state of Massachusetts did the unthinkable and elected a Republican, Scott Brown, to fill the Senate seat left vacant by the death of Ted Kennedy. Brown, a little-known state senator, overcame state attorney general, Martha Coakley, who was considered the front-runner for most of the race and at one point enjoyed a 30-point lead in the polls. Brown's meteoric rise and victory was a "wakeup call" for a complacent Massachusetts Democratic Party. The numbers suggest that it may have been, in part, a referendum on Patrick.

In a poll taken in February 2010, shortly after the Brown victory, Patrick had a 50 percent unfavorable rating, with only a 38 percent favorable, reversing the earlier poll. However, Cahill and Baker both had visibility problems. 14 percent said they had never heard of Cahill and 35 percent said they had never heard of Baker.

What was worse for Patrick was that 60 percent of voters said that it was time to give someone else a chance. When asked if Patrick was a weak leader or the victim of a bad economy, 68 percent said he was a weak leader while only 22 percent blamed the economy. But in spite of all that, amazingly, when asked who they would vote for in a four-way race between Patrick, Baker, Cahill, and Jill Stein (Green Rainbow Party), Patrick topped the ballot with 33 percent.[6]

Republicans correctly believed that the governor was vulnerable. But as the polls showed, he could win if the opposition was fragmented. So, the first strategy was to eliminate Tim Cahill as a viable competitor, clearing the way for a Baker victory.

Meanwhile, there was activity on the ground. Patrick's campaign went into full swing and the governor was suddenly stumping around the state. Baker set out to rebrand his campaign. In mid-May he rolled out the slogan, "Had enough?" on his website, in an attempt to tap into the anti-incumbent mood. He reported that the slogan crystallized after months of talking to voters across Massachusetts.[7]

The Summer of 2010

By early June, Cahill was trying to stay relevant while Baker had launched an ad of his own seeking to increase name recognition.[8] The *Boston Globe*, which tends to be the more liberal of the two major newspapers, carried stories that featured Patrick and Baker but gave Cahill less ink.

Patrick, for his part, stayed on message. When attacked by Baker and Cahill for raising taxes, Patrick responded, "Both Charlie and Tim are right: It's their money; it's the taxpayer's money. We understand that. But it's also their overcrowded school, and their broken roads and bridges and their broken neighborhoods and broken neighbors. And it's time for us to take responsibility for that, too."[9]

Patrick also addressed the labor unions, which had thus far failed to endorse him. In a Labor Day speech he said, "Some of you are so mad about our disagreements that you will support someone else or sit out the race entirely. But we have shown that we do not, and will not, take you for granted. And I think you better be careful, respectfully, not to take us for granted, either."[10]

By early September, Patrick was still holding a slim lead over Baker in various polls.[11]

The View from the Campaigns

From a series of interviews conducted between late July and early September we are able to get a sense of the campaign from the perspective of the three principal contenders. Interviews were conducted with Sydney Asbury, campaign manager for Deval Patrick, on July 30, 2010; Tim Cahill, candidate for governor on September 8, 2010; and Amy Goodrich, communications director for Charlie Baker on September 14, 2010.

When asked if they were hoping that people would vote *for* Baker or *against* Patrick and Cahill, Goodrich responded that the "Had

Enough?" slogan came from people out on the trail reacting to bad choices made over the past four years. They saw voter anger and resentment. "Polls show most people don't believe that Patrick deserves a second term. Our job is to show that Baker is the only alternative."

The Cahill campaign was asked if they were sticking with less spending, lower taxes, and more jobs, and how that differentiated them from Baker. Cahill responded that the theme was the need for independent leadership—to break free from two parties. He was promoting smaller government for small business and middle-class voters. He argued that this theme differentiated him from Baker, saying, "My story shows that I am different than Baker."

All three campaigns claimed to organize by ward and precinct in a retail style, but that they were also counting on a more wholesale strategy. Asbury described building a grassroots infrastructure from 2006 to the next level by finding committed people to serve as messengers. They wanted 10 regional offices with field staff to organize 21,700 messengers who would each talk to 50 people they know and ID them as Patrick voters, and have personal conversations with them. Asbury noted that besides the grassroots network she had described, they were running a retail campaign. "[The governor] feeds off people's energy and is very effective."

Goodrich said that the Baker campaign was identifying captains by Senate district. Also, they uniquely used an online action center that connected all the field operations. "Baker is reaching beyond the GOP base and inviting independents and Democrats [to town hall meetings]," Goodrich noted. "A lot are showing up."

Goodrich described their media strategy in two parts. Part 1 had been "Get to know Charlie." He clearly needed to be introduced. She claimed that it "took longer than expected," and that Baker was not leading in the polls for this reason. Part 2 depended on attacks, and responses to those attacks. "We can do better" was their Part 2 slogan. "Our strategy is to target everyone who is unhappy," Goodrich said.

To Cahill, independents were, of course, vital. He said, "I'm the legitimate choice they have never had before." He believed that message would resonate with independents.

All three campaigns had clearly paid attention to the Scott Brown phenomenon and the anti-incumbent mood in general. Asbury said that Scott Brown had taught them a tactical lesson—the unenrolled are critical—and Democrats need to show up. Brown had campaigned differently—more retail—which, she said, was Coakley's mistake. The anti-incumbent mood is real, but she claimed not to see it so much on the ground in Massachusetts. Goodrich said that Brown's election was significant, but that all other Republicans cannot depend on that. Brown is personable. Not all candidates are. Brown was a wakeup call for Democrats, and mobilized Republicans. "People are paying attention, feel that their vote matters." In answering this question, Cahill waxed philosophically, "It would be good for Baker if I wasn't here, but I am. We will both benefit from the anti-Beacon Hill mood but all of us have been on the inside. It is hard to figure out how to win this race. It is a chess game. I spend time thinking hard about how it all plays out. I am going after any and all voters."

Fall 2010

The first televised gubernatorial debate was held on September 7, 2010.[12] In the debate, Baker claimed that the race was about jobs, taxes, and spending, and he continued to drive the point that the state needed tax, fiscal, and regulatory policy to create a predictable economic environment. Cahill said that he wanted tax cuts to make the state more competitive. Patrick reiterated his theme that the campaign was about different choices and different values and that he wanted to invest in health care, education, and job creation to "finish what we started."

On September 8, reacting to the candidates' performance in the first televised debate, the *Boston Globe* struck at Baker: "He's annoyed when anyone asks him a question, annoyed as he explains how the governor has never done anything right, annoyed that he has to submit himself to this unbecoming process known as a gubernatorial campaign."[13]

By early September, Baker and Cahill were both running positive ads. Patrick had still not hit the airwaves but, on September 14, the day of the primary election, the pro-Patrick forces struck. An outside 527 group calling itself Bay State Future, which is affiliated with the Democratic Governors Association (DGA), began running anti-Baker ads. The ads focused on Baker's role in the Boston Central Artery/Tunnel Project, or "Big Dig," claiming that he was the "chief architect" of the financing scheme that cost the taxpayers billions of dollars.[14]

In the second gubernatorial debate, held on September 21, 2010,[15] Baker reiterated his message, lumping Patrick and Cahill together: "If you think they are doing OK then vote for them, if not then vote for me." Cahill struck out at Baker, accusing him of lying about his record. Ultimately, both candidates ended up yelling at each other. Patrick seemed to remain above the fray, arguing that the role of government was to help people and not "kick them to the curb." He ended by saying that he governs with "optimism and energy."[16]

The Cahill campaign was running into serious trouble. First, his chief strategist resigned, and his reputation had been made working on Republican campaigns. The very next day, Cahill's campaign manager also resigned. Both men dismissed Cahill as a spoiler and urged him to quit the race. Cahill responded by saying that he would stay in the race and that this development was "a speed bump, not an accident."[17]

On October 1, 2010, a tropical storm hit Massachusetts with high winds and driving rain. That same day a tsunami hit the Cahill campaign. His running mate, Paul Loscocco, dropped out of the race and defected to the Baker camp, loudly and publically endorsing the Republican candidate. Loscocco appeared at a news conference with Charlie Baker barely two hours after he had given Cahill the bad news, and said, "It is clear to me that Charlie Baker and Richard Tisei have the best chance of defeating Governor Patrick and taking Massachusetts in a new direction. . . . I cannot and will not let my ego get in the way of doing what's right for Massachusetts." Cahill's reaction was combative. He said, "I am not a quitter. I've never quit on anything I've done. As for not having a lieutenant governor, I don't plan to die and we can save money on that useless job."

Interestingly, Cahill was now an angry candidate sitting on $2 million, but he did not mount an attack campaign against Baker in the weeks after this debacle. He had said that he would not go negative, and he was true to his word.

On October 14, 2010, a new Suffolk University poll showed Patrick leading by 7 points, 46 percent to 39 percent over Baker. Cahill was clinging stubbornly to 10 percent, and only 4 percent were still undecided. Patrick led by 11 percent among women and older voters. Still, his approval rating was only 45 percent, and 48 percent of likely voters said that someone else should have a chance to be governor. Most respondents, 80 percent, had heard of the Cahill campaign issues and Baker's role in them. Moreover, 53 percent of those questioned expected Patrick to be reelected, while only 31 percent expected Baker to win. The poll's margin of error was 4.4 percent.[18]

The Patrick lead was evolving in spite of a barrage of negative ads by Baker and the Republican Governors Association (RGA) in the final weeks of the campaign. His "dirty work" was done by Bay State Future (a newly formed 527), and by the Massachusetts Teacher's Association, which ran a couple of ads critical of Baker on behalf of Patrick.

It seemed, however, that Charlie Baker's strategy of funneling voter unhappiness was beginning to wear thin. At one point Patrick quipped, "If I walked on water, Charlie Baker's response would be, 'See, I told you Patrick can't swim.'"[19]

Patrick and the Massachusetts Democratic Party were making good on their strategy to beat the Republicans with a ground war that would reverse the tide of GOP voter enthusiasm. They travelled throughout the state, led by the governor himself. Not only did Charlie Baker have a suburban strategy, he rarely campaigned west of Worcester, which is actually in the middle of the state. The Patrick campaign worked the western part of the state hard, in conjunction with their plan to win the state's 10 largest cities.[20]

The Final Days

The last Suffolk University poll was released on October 28, 2010. Pollster David Paleologos again gave Patrick a 7-point lead, 46 percent to 39 percent, with Cahill at 9 percent. This was true in spite of the fact that 50 percent of the respondents still thought that Massachusetts was heading in the wrong direction, and 49 percent felt that it was time to give someone else a chance to be governor. Patrick's favorable/unfavorable ratings were now dead even at 44 percent each. On the question of who had the best temperament to be governor, Patrick again topped Baker, 46 percent to 22 percent.[21]

They were right. The final votes were as follows: Patrick 48.8 percent, Baker 41.7 percent, and Cahill 8.0 percent. Cahill did better than any other independent candidate in the state's history but could not get out of the single digits. In his acceptance speech, Patrick claimed, "We had a plan, we worked hard, and we stuck with Massachusetts—and tonight, the people of Massachusetts have stuck with us."[22] That night, Patrick overcame a Republican tide that swept nearly all of the rest of the country. Patrick claims that he will not seek another term; that this was his last campaign for governor. In spite of all the election night noise, Patrick himself put the best punctuation mark on his election a few days before the final vote. In an interview he said, "You are surrounded by people, advisers, telling you what to turn yourself into. If you don't know who you are all the way into your core, I'm not sure this is worth it."[23]

Endnotes

[1]*Metro*, September 2, 2010.

[2]Suffolk University Political Research Center, www.suffolk.edu/research /1450.html.

[3]*Boston Globe*, September 12, 2010.

[4]Massachusetts Election Division, Office of the Secretary of State, www.sec .state.ma.us/ele/

[5]www.timforgovernor.com/.

[6]Suffolk University Political Research Center, www.suffolk.edu/research /1450.html.

[7]Michael Levenson, "Baker slogan tries to tap into voters' discontent," *Boston Globe*, May 18, 2010, A1 and A9.

[8]Noah Bierman, "Baker ad seeks name recognition," *Boston Globe*, June 15, 2010, B1 and B4.

[9]Michael Levenson, "Rivals battle over taxes, health: Patrick, Cahill and Baker trade accusations in feisty appearances on State House steps," *Boston Globe*, August 12, 2010, B1 and B15.

[10]Pater Schworm, "Patrick seeks to cement union ties: But warns he's not 'governor of labor'" *Boston Globe*, September 7, 2010, B1 and B4.

[11]Frank Phillips, "Election season goes into top gear: 3 gubernatorial rivals, legislative hopefuls run hard," *Boston Globe*, September 6, 2010, A1 and A6.

[12]Broadcast on WBZ-TV with moderator John Keller.

[13]Brian McGrory, *Boston Globe*, B1

[14]Noah Bierman, "Setting the stage for November: Challengers put Patrick on defensive in radio debate," *Boston Globe*, September 15, 2010, A1 and A14.

[15]Moderated by John King of CNN.

[16]Brian C. Mooney, "Feuding challengers miss an opportunity," *Boston Globe*, September 22, 2010, A1 and A7.

[17]Stephanie Ebbert, "Cahill vows he will stay in race: Campaign manager is latest to resign," *Boston Globe*, September 25, 2010, B1 and B3.

[18]Suffolk University Political Research Center, www.suffolk.edu/research /1450.html.

[19]*Boston Globe*, October 27, 2010, A1 and A13

[20]Noah Bierman and Michael Levenson, "Candidates picking their spots: In final push, Patrick, Baker focus on core constituencies," *Boston Globe*, October 29, 2010, A1 and A10.

[21]Suffolk University Political Research Center, www.suffolk.edu/research /1450.html.

[22]Lisa Wangness, "Tonight the people of Massachusetts have stuck with us," *Boston Globe*, November 3, 2010, A9.

[23]Brian McGrory, "Learning curve," *Boston Globe*, October 27, 2010, B1.

Chapter 19

The Republican Revival in Michigan

by Dr. Michael W. Traugott

Professor of Communication Studies and Research Professor at the Center for Political Studies at the University of Michigan

The Republican Party had unprecedented success in the 2010 general election in Michigan, sweeping contests all across the ballot. They were led by Richard (Rick) Snyder, a first-time candidate, who won an open contest for governor when Democratic incumbent Jennifer Granholm could not run because of term limits. Given the condition of the state's economy, high unemployment, and her low approval ratings, she would not have had much luck against Snyder, anyway. But she cast a big shadow over the race as her lieutenant governor, John Cherry, an early favorite to succeed her, ultimately decided not to run.

Snyder invested a lot of personal resources in his campaign, and he started early in competition with a large Republican field in order to secure the nomination. As a result, to appreciate the dynamics of the contest, the gubernatorial election has to be viewed in three phases: (1) the pre-primary period, (2) the primary contests, and (3) the general election. Rick Snyder had to defeat four primary opponents to secure the nomination, while his ultimate opponent, Lansing mayor Virg Bernero, had just one: the Speaker of the House. Snyder's extended effort and his personal contributions of almost $6 million dollars gave him distinct advantages in the fall campaign that the Democrats could not overcome, especially given the national forces at work in the electorate.

The Background to the Campaign

The manufacturing-based economy in Michigan has historically out-performed the United States in good times and underperformed it in bad times. This is due to the relative strength or weakness of its auto industry. In the 1990s, unemployment in Michigan was lower than in most of the rest of the United States, but in 2002, just as Jennifer Granholm was elected, it passed the national figure by 3 percentage points. When the 2008 recession set in, unemployment in Michigan reached 14.5 percent in June 2009, compared to 9.7 percent nation-ally. Governor Granholm's approval rating stood at 49 percent in fall of 2006 when she stood for reelection, but it had declined to 27 per-cent in April 2010, compared to 44 percent for Barack Obama. Given the dissatisfaction with the Democratic governor, together with the slide in Obama's approval rating (which typically occurs in the first two years of a presidential first term), Republican prospects in Michigan were looking up.

Granholm won reelection in 2006 by defeating a conservative Republican businessman from the west side of the state, Richard DeVos, who had self-funded his campaign with resources from a sub-stantial family-owned business. In 2010, another Republican busi-nessman, Rick Snyder, decided to contest the Republican primary. He was from Ann Arbor, in the southeastern part of the state, and his financial resources came from his background in accounting and ven-ture capital investments in Gateway and other businesses. He was also pro-choice, uncommon for Michigan Republicans since the peri-od when William Milliken was governor in the 1970s.

Early in 2010, two significant events occurred. First, on January 5, Lt. Gov. John Cherry dropped out of the race because of funding problems and a lack of support due to his close association with Granholm. Then, on February 7, Rick Snyder bought a 60-second television ad during the Super Bowl to introduce himself to Michigan citizens as "one tough nerd." The ad featured both Republican and Democratic "career politicians" who had failed the state, while high-lighting Snyder's Michigan roots and three academic degrees from the University of Michigan. He paid for the ad himself, signaling his willingness to use his own funds to support his campaign. It initiated his strategy to build name recognition, run as an outsider with busi-ness management skills, and attract Democrats and independents to his coalition, based upon those qualities. At this stage, there were seven other Republicans interested in the nomination. One failed to qualify for the ballot, and two others (including the secretary of state) withdrew early. In his primary run, Snyder faced Peter Hoekstra, a U.S. representative; the attorney general, Mike Cox; the Oakland County sheriff, Mike Bouchard; and a state senator, Tom George.

On the Democratic side, there were originally eight candidates interested in the contest, but five of them had dropped out by the beginning of March. The two leading candidates were Virg Bernero, the mayor of Lansing, and Andy Dillon, the Michigan House Speaker. Alma Wheeler Smith, a state representative, stayed in until May, and then it became a two-man race.

The Primary Contests

Polling began in 2009, and it showed that Snyder was invisible in the field until after the Super Bowl ad; but in March he became the third-choice candidate among likely Republican primary voters behind Cox and Hoekstra. His strategy for the primary was to have the socially conservative candidates divide that portion of the core Republican vote, primarily on the west side of the state, while he would attract some crossover Democrats to participate in the Republican primary in the rest of the state. Just before the primary date, Snyder ran an ad containing an endorsement from Bill Ford, chairman of Ford Motor Company, the one Michigan automaker that did not ask for bailout funds from the federal government. In the final published pre-primary poll, he had pulled slightly ahead of Cox and Hoekstra, although all candidates had a level of support that was statistically indistinguishable. Cox was endorsed by Michigan Right to Life and the Michigan Chamber of Congress, and Hoekstra's congressional district was in the western part of the state. The last pre-primary poll showed that Cox and Hoekstra were dividing the votes of abortion opponents.

Snyder had turned down public financing of his primary campaign in lieu of providing his own support. Records filed with the state show that he raised $5.9 million through the primary—almost all of it his own money— and only about 40 percent of what DeVos had spent to win the nomination in 2006. This included expenditures of $2.4 million on television advertising, invested in the period from the Super

Bowl to the end of March, three weeks in May before Memorial Day, and then for the five weeks leading up to the primary. Hoekstra and Cox received less than $700,000 each in public funds to match the funding they raised through their campaign committees. On August 3, Snyder won the Republican primary with 36.4 percent of slightly more than one million votes cast, almost 10 percentage points more than Hoekstra and 13 percentage points more than Cox. His average cost per vote (contributions/personal vote) was $21.21, far less than the $36.86 that DeVos spent on his primary victory in 2006.

Across the summer, the pre-primary polling showed Bernero and Dillon in a tight race, with Bernero pulling slightly ahead in the last poll conducted before the election. Bernero reported raising $112,000 for the primary, while Dillon reported raising nothing. The Genesee County Democratic Committee raised and spent more than $2 million dollars on ads supporting Bernero and attacking Dillon; two groups (Advance Michigan Now and Northern Michigan Education Fund) raised and spent almost $1 million dollars in support of Dillon. Major unions supported Bernero and opposed Dillon because he favored a review of fringe benefit plans for state employees. On August 3, Bernero won the primary with 58.6 percent of the vote and at a cost of $3.72 per vote. Dillon received 41.4 percent of the vote at a cost of $8.42 per vote.

The General Election Campaign

After the pairing for the general election campaign was known, news organizations began to organize their coverage. As usual, that involved sponsoring polls to include in their Labor Day campaign kick-off stories. The structural issue was that Snyder had spent almost $6 million in six months on an advertising campaign designed to build name recognition in order to defeat a set of opponents, while Bernero had raised no money, although unions and issue groups had spent some money on his behalf in a negative campaign against his main opponent in the last few weeks before the primary. As a result, the early polling reflected this disparity in name recognition and image. Two polls conducted right after the primary showed Snyder with leads of 19 and 27 percentage points, and most of the subsequent coverage of the general election was framed by the perspective that

Snyder might have an insurmountable lead and could spend whatever amount he needed to maintain it, while Bernero faced a difficult challenge to catch up. No poll conducted in the period from Labor Day to just before Election Day showed Bernero closer than 13 percentage points, and the two final preelection polls conducted for Michigan news organizations showed Snyder with an 18 percentage point lead in the week before the election.

One way that Bernero might have been able to engage Snyder and present the contrast in their positions was to appear on the same stage in debates. Following the standard strategy of front-runners and distant challengers, Snyder wanted to limit their joint appearances while Bernero wanted to hold as many debates as possible. In mid-August, it was reported that Bernero had accepted an invitation to appear in three debates, the first on September 21. But in early September, Bernero offered Snyder a proposal for eight debates. Snyder made an offer of three debates, but Bernero refused. After a long period of stalemated negotiations, the two candidates' management teams agreed to a single debate held on a public television station on Sunday evening, October 10. The timing and venue of the broadcast assured that the live audience would be small, and the date assured the Snyder team that there would be time to recover from any potential slipups. The debate was uneventful and produced limited press coverage; polls conducted within a week of the debate did not show any shift in support for either candidate.

By the end of the campaign, Snyder had raised and spent slightly more than $8 million dollars while Bernero had raised $1.1 million, including matching state funds. Each campaign was supported by the same level of advertising in the general election campaign, and each distributed it in the same way across each of the state's media markets with almost half of the money spent in the Detroit area, including the suburbs. None of this moved the electorate very much. About $5.4 million was spent on behalf of Snyder, including $3.6 million from the Republican Governors Association. Bernero was supported by about $5 million dollars in advertising expenditures, including $3.7 million by the Democratic State Central Committee.

On Election Day, Snyder led a Republican ticket that swept through the state. The Republicans won every statewide office and recaptured two Democratic seats in the U.S. House of Representatives.

The state legislature went from divided control to solid Republican control. Snyder won almost every one of the 81 counties in Michigan, although he lost his historically Democratic home county by a narrow margin. He defeated Bernero by almost 600,000 votes statewide (58 percent to 40 percent), even as he lost the Democratic stronghold of Wayne County by 100,000 votes.

In the end, Rick Snyder was the right candidate for the times. He was an amateur with no previous political experience, rather than an incumbent career politician. He was an experienced business manager running in a state where the budget was in serious trouble and the two parties were at odds in the state legislature. Just as important, he was a Republican running in an off-year where anti-incumbent and anti-Obama sentiment was very strong. While there was relatively little Tea Party movement activity in Michigan, Snyder was able to harness these feelings in Michigan and ride them to a landslide victory. Now we wait to see how this will translate to political leadership in Lansing.

Chapter 20

Bellwether Backdrop for Blunt's Blowout: The Missouri Senate Race

by Jo Mannies

Senior Political Reporter at the
St. Louis Beacon

For a Missouri U.S. Senate contest initially billed as a titanic neck-and-neck battle between two of the state's best-known family dynasties, the race between Republican Roy Blunt and Democrat Robin Carnahan took a surprising turn. Blunt won in a blowout.

The southwest Missouri congressman's victory margin of almost 14 percentage points was one of the largest in recent state history, exceeding the predictions of political pundits and all but one of the final public polls.[1] Blunt's stronger-than-expected showing came largely from his success in racking up huge pluralities in Republican rural Missouri, where he captured about two-thirds of the vote. A Democrat running statewide needs to keep down the Republican rural advantage to the mid-50s, percentage-wise.

At the same time, Blunt held down—or eliminated, in some cases—Carnahan's perceived advantage in the big-city suburbs around Kansas City and St. Louis. In recent elections, these areas have trended Democratic. As a result, her strong ending in the two cities' urban cores did not matter.

How did Blunt do it? He succeeded, in part, by making his contest a referendum on the national issues—rising budget deficits, health care changes and continued high unemployment—that had created angst and anger among many voters.

Both candidates echoed national themes in their attacks for months. Blunt, a 14-year congressman, was blasted as a Washington insider too close to banks and lobbyists. Carnahan, Missouri's secretary of state, was painted as a classic Democratic liberal in lockstep with an unpopular president.

Blunt's lopsided win swiftly prompted debate among experts over whether it signaled a permanent shift in Missouri's political allegiance. David Robertson, a political science professor at the University of Missouri-St. Louis, contended that Blunt's sizable victory was evidence of Missouri's continued conservative shift, particularly when coupled with the state's 2008 election results. Missouri voters had slightly favored Republican John McCain, who carried the state by under 4,000 votes over Democrat Barack Obama.

That result broke one of the best bellwether records in the country. Until 2008, Missouri voters had sided with the national presidential winner in all but one election since 1904.

"Missouri is no longer a certain indicator of national trends," Robertson said, "because its voters have become slightly more conservative and Republican than the nation as a whole." But Ken Warren, a political science professor at St. Louis University and a pollster, argued that the 2010 U.S. Senate results actually bolster Missouri's bellwether image. Blunt's strong finish was indicative of the national Republican tsunami, he said.

In 2006, during the national midterm election, Warren noted that Missouri voters had swung the other way. Voters narrowly sided with the Democratic U.S. Senate nominee, Claire McCaskill, in her successful ouster of Republican incumbent Jim Talent. McCaskill's win had been part of a national Democratic wave.

Warren declared that the 2010 results further underscore that "Missouri voters are highly susceptible" to the national political winds.

National Mood and Themes Overpower Family Ties

By the 2008 election, Robin Carnahan was already considered Missouri's strongest Democratic contender in the upcoming battle for the Senate seat of retiring Republican Christopher "Kit" Bond, a former governor who had held the Senate post for 24 years.

Carnahan, 49, is the only daughter of the late governor Mel Carnahan and former U.S. senator Jean Carnahan (D-MO). Jean

Carnahan had served two years in the U.S. Senate when she was appointed governor, following her husband's posthumous election in 2000, defeating Republican incumbent John Ashcroft. The late governor and his eldest son, Randy, had died in a plane crash three weeks before the election. Robin Carnahan's grandfather, A. S. J. Carnahan, served in Congress for 14 years in the 1940s and 1950s.

Robin Carnahan had been a key behind-the-scenes tactician in a successful 1999 effort to block a ballot initiative to allow most adult Missourians to carry concealed weapons. But the public first took notice when she delivered an emotional eulogy at her father's televised memorial service.

In 2004, during a strong pro-Republican election year in Missouri, Robin Carnahan still won her first bid for secretary of state—knocking off the most prominent Republican woman in the legislature at the time, the state House Speaker, Catherine Hanaway, of suburban St. Louis. During her first term, Carnahan attracted generally favorable headlines for her professional performance. She also got married and in 2006 was diagnosed with breast cancer, which was successfully treated with surgery and chemotherapy.

In 2008, Carnahan was the state's biggest vote-getter on the ballot, by either party, as she handily won reelection to a second term. So it was no surprise when, on February 3, 2009, Carnahan formally announced her candidacy via a video posted on YouTube and her new campaign website. She promised to focus on fiscal accountability, and "rebuilding the economy so it works for everyone."[2]

Blunt, meanwhile, had openly acknowledged as late as early 2009 that his chances of winning did not look good, given the national mood at the time and the euphoria over Obama's election and inauguration. Still, he went ahead and formally launched his candidacy on February 19, 2009 with a series of events around the state. His first announcement event was in Carnahan's own backyard of St. Louis, with a gathering at Harris-Stowe State College, a predominantly black institution.

Such a kickoff was in line with Blunt's political past as one willing to buck the tide. Blunt, 60, is a former teacher and college president. He grew up as the son of a dairy farmer who later served in the legislature. Blunt got his own start in politics in 1973, when Governor Bond (the Republican he hoped to succeed in the U.S. Senate), named him to fill a vacant spot as Greene County clerk. Blunt held that post until 1984 when he was elected Missouri's secretary of state.

In 1992, Blunt was in his second term when he bucked state Republican leaders to run for governor. Blunt was challenging the state attorney general, William L. Webster, the politically connected favorite. Blunt narrowly lost in the primary after running a series of negative TV ads that portrayed Webster as corrupt. Webster ended up in prison. By 1996, Blunt had healed any party rifts enough to win election to the U.S. House. Blunt's easy manner, staunch conservation, and meticulous attention to political detail helped him swiftly move up the ranks to become House majority whip by 2003, working closely with the House majority leader, Tom DeLay of Texas.

Blunt also attracted attention as he became one of the House's top fundraisers, taking in more than $22 million while serving in the House. But DeLay's legal and ethical troubles caused perception problems for Blunt. By 2009, Blunt no longer held a House leadership post.

That backdrop was among the reasons some prominent Missouri Republicans—led by retired U.S. senator John C. Danforth—were publicly arguing in early 2009 that Blunt was not their party's best option for the 2010 election.

In May 2009, Danforth conducted a swift tour around the state, including a stop at the state capitol in Jefferson City, to promote the prospects of a political unknown he considered more suitable: Tom Schweich, a St. Louis lawyer and law professor who had just held several State Department posts in the Bush administration. Schweich also had worked with Danforth during the former senator's tenure as U.S. ambassador to the United Nations, and as leader of a government inquiry into the 1993 Branch Davidian siege in Waco, Texas.

But Danforth, Schweich, and their allies dropped their insurgency within a month and endorsed Blunt at a high-profile June 2009 Republican unity dinner in St. Louis. Republicans privately credited Lt. Gov. Peter Kinder, the top Republican in the state capital, with persuading Schweich to run for state auditor instead.

Political Winds Shift in Favor of Blunt

While the GOP was coalescing behind Blunt, Carnahan spent 2009 holding public events highlighting her successes as secretary of state. Her campaign website displayed photos of Carnahan running her family's rural Missouri cattle farm and holding an online contest to choose a name for a new foal. The winning moniker: Moxie.

In the eyes of some, it was Blunt who displayed moxie as he sought to persuade Carnahan—then leading in the polls[3]—to engage in early debates. She declined, saying such events would be unseemly before candidate-filing officially got underway in February 2010. By then, the political mood—nationally and in Missouri—had shifted. In January 2010, polls began showing Blunt in the lead. That is where he remained.[4]

Carnahan unsuccessfully sought to take back the momentum with a new campaign theme that centered on her promise to fight the "bull" in Washington. Both candidates and their parties also set up special websites for particularly harsh attacks on their rivals. One of the state Democratic Party's most active sites targeting Blunt was called theveryworstofwashington.com, and one of the state Republican Party's attack sites was rubberstamprobin.com.

Blunt tackled potential trouble in the spring and summer when many Tea Party groups around the state embraced his best-known primary challenger, state senator Chuck Purgason (R-Caulfield). Still, Blunt dispatched all nine of his GOP rivals in the August 3 primary by collecting 71 percent of the statewide vote. Blunt then swiftly courted Tea Party support and ignited thunderous applause when he unexpectedly took the stage at a huge "9/12" Tea Party rally in St. Louis on the grounds of the Gateway Arch.

Carnahan had trouble attracting similar enthusiasm within Democratic ranks, even though she had no serious Democratic primary challenger. She found herself having to explain to those in her own party why she agreed with Blunt, not Obama, when it came to retaining all the Bush-era tax cuts, including those for the wealthy.

In the fall, there were few public forums for Blunt and Carnahan to air their differences and potentially change their contest's dynamics. The day after their mutual primary victories, Blunt had called for a series of public debates. But, comfortably in the lead, he soon played down that idea and eventually agreed to two debates in October. Only one was televised.

Blunt campaign chairwoman, Ann Wagner, says the pivotal points in the campaign came earlier. The first, she says, was President

Barack Obama's appearance at a July 8, 2010 fundraiser for Carnahan in Kansas City. Video footage from that event, especially Obama's praise of Carnahan, became a mainstay of anti-Carnahan attack ads throughout that fall.

The second key event, said Wagner, was when the White House opted to make a public a list of the major beneficiaries of federal stimulus aid for alternative energy projects. One of the largest went to Carnahan's younger brother.

Blunt's most successful line of attack dealt with over $107 million in federal tax breaks in the stimulus program that went to a mid-Missouri wind farm co-owned by Carnahan's younger brother, Tom Carnahan. Although federal officials said that Robin Carnahan had no role in the aid, the matter showed up repeatedly in TV attack ads. Most of those ads did not come from Blunt. They were produced by several outside groups, notably the U.S. Chamber of Commerce and two new organizations—American Crossroads and Crossroads GPS—cofounded by former Bush aide Karl Rove. Combined, the independent groups have acknowledged spending more than $8 million attacking Carnahan in TV ads, fliers, and automated phone calls.

That barrage overwhelmed the anti-Blunt ads aired in Missouri by the Democratic Senatorial Campaign Committee (DSCC) and several allied outside groups, including Commonsense Ten, Votevets.org and the League of Conservation Voters. One DSCC spot highlighted the lobbyist career of Blunt's wife. During the final weeks, the state AFL-CIO and other labor groups also spent money on fliers and get-out-the-vote drives on Carnahan's behalf. But by then, even she was acknowledging that Blunt had the edge.

All the outside spending rivaled that spent by Blunt and Carnahan. Their latest campaign reports, filed in mid-October, showed that Blunt had raised $10.9 million, while Carnahan had collected $9.6 million. He still had $2.3 million to spend during the final couple of weeks, while she had less than $900,000 for her final push.

Still, Blunt found himself at the center of an unwanted controversy just two weeks before the election. The state Democratic Party released documents that it said showed that Blunt's family, 20 years earlier, had improperly hired an illegal worker from Nicaragua. The documents included a letter that Blunt had written on official state letterhead while he was secretary of state, seeking federal help for the woman's bid to seek asylum in the United States. Blunt said the woman had been a church acquaintance of his wife at the time, and denied that the woman had worked for his family. The flap prompted a couple of tense encounters between Blunt and reporters during the final days of his campaign, but otherwise failed to resonate with the public or voters.

Since his huge victory on November 2, all of the political attention in Missouri has centered on what Blunt's success means for the state and the Republican Party in 2012. Put simply, the state Republican Party is ecstatic. Blunt's coattails helped sweep Schweich into the state auditor's job and contributed to historic GOP gains in the state legislature amidst the red tide that swept most of the nation.

Endnotes

[1] www.RealClearPolitics.com, which calculated Blunt's preelection edge at 10.4 percentage points based on an average of all final public polls.

[2] www.robincarnahan.com.

[3] www.RealClearPolitics.com, citing PPP, Jan. 10–11 and Nov. 13–15, 2009; Wilson Research, March 7–9, 2009; Democracy Corps, April 28–30, 2009; Momentum Analysis, Sept. 15–19, 2009; Rasmussen Reports, Dec. 15, 2009.

[4] www.RealClearPolitics.com, Rasmussen Reports, Jan. 19, 2010; PPP, March 27–28, 2010.

Chapter 21

A Tale of Two Reids: Nevada's Senate and Governor Races of 2010

by Jon Ralston

Political Columnist at the Las Vegas Sun; *and Host of*
Face to Face with Jon Ralston

As 2010 began in Nevada, two Reids were destined to be on the ballot—Senate Majority Leader Harry Reid, seeking a fifth term, and Clark County Commission chairman, Rory Reid, seeking the governorship.

Most knowledgeable observers thought this was less of a dawning dynasty than a murder-suicide pact. Reid the Elder, who was manifestly unpopular, would kill Reid the Younger, who was largely unknown and would be burdened with his father's negatives, and then the majority leader would expire from many, many self-inflicted wounds.

Why did one lose and the other win? This is a story of a father and son, of one Reid who came prepared for anything and the other, unprepared for everything.

How Harry Reid Survived the Wave

In 1998, Sen. Harry Reid had a political near-death experience. Running for a third term, he nearly lost—by 428 votes—to Rep. John Ensign, an ambitious soldier in the Gingrich Revolution class of '94. Reid was determined never to be caught by surprise again and he vowed to have the best campaign team money could buy when next he had a competitive race. Reid coasted in 2004 after another congressman, Jim Gibbons, opted out of the race to pursue a bid for governor the next cycle. But from the moment he took over the next Congress for ousted minority leader Tom Daschle, Reid knew the Republicans would come after him in 2010. So he slowly began assembling a team to fortify himself. He knew his limitations as a candidate—bereft of charisma, Reid is the consummate inside player and disdains the public part of his role. He brought in an operative from Missouri named Rebecca Lambe, who had developed a reputation as a master of field operations for major candidates there. Reid knew he had to rebuild the party infrastructure and turn the state from red to blue.

Serendipity intervened in late 2007, as he took advantage of an opportunity for Nevada to become an early presidential caucus state. Reid knew this would generate interest among the faithful and help to register voters. It did, and more than 117,000 Democrats came out to the caucuses. Democrats had a 100,000-voter edge by the election, and a Democratic wave—led by Barack Obama—washed over the state. Reid had accomplished the first step of his plan, erecting a voter registration bulwark against whatever the Republicans might throw at him.

Reid's support in Nevada was never robust—he usually won one of 17 counties (Clark County, which includes Las Vegas). It slowly began to atrophy after he became Senate majority leader, as the Obama agenda became increasingly unpopular. By the middle of 2009, national pundits were calling him very vulnerable, especially if Rep. Dean Heller, a young congressman in the Ensign mold, challenged him, even though Reid had raised a large sum for his reelection.

On June 16, 2009, the world changed for the Republican Party in Nevada. Nevada's other senator, Ensign (he won an open seat in 2000), who had been considered presidential timber and was planning a trip to Iowa, announced in a Las Vegas news conference that he had had an extramarital affair. The state GOP now had two crippled leaders—Gov. Jim Gibbons, who had become a national laughingstock because of his personal and professional behavior, and Ensign, who, having demanded that President Clinton resign during the Lewinsky scandal, some speculated might have to resign, as sordid details of his own affair unfolded.

Meanwhile, the Reid money machine was cranking. As *Roll Call* reporter John McArdle wrote on July 15, "Sen. Harry Reid (D) raised $3.25 million between April 1 and June 30 and ended the second quarter with $7.33 million in cash on hand 16 months from the 2010 election." As MSNBC's *First Read* daily email posited that same day, "Folks, that is a lot of money for a Senate race at this point in the cycle—especially for someone without an opponent right now. (As Reid's people note, the haul and cash on hand is MUCH bigger than Daschle and McConnell had at a similar point in the cycle)."

Nevada's unemployment rate was already soaring. Foreclosures were crippling the economy. Reid knew he needed a reported $25 million as a prophylactic against the GOP assault to come.

But no major candidate had announced yet. A former anchorwoman and state senator named Sue Lowden, now running a gaming company and chairing the Republican Party, was thought to be interested. A former assemblywoman with a far-right following named Sharron Angle had announced she was considering a bid, as were a few lesser-known folks, including John Chachas, a member of a prominent rural Nevada family who had lived in New York City for 20 years and made millions on Wall Street.

As summer waned, the dominoes began to fall. On August 7, Danny Tarkanian, son of the legendary University of Nevada "Runnin' Rebels" basketball coach, suddenly announced he would take on Reid. Tarkanian had just won a libel lawsuit arising from a failed state senate bid. Four days later, Heller announced he would run for reelection, citing the Ensign announcement as part of his reason for not challenging Reid.

Just so no one would forget her, Sue Lowden released the results of a new survey. "In a hypothetical ballot test head-to-head matchup, Reid secures just 42 percent of the vote versus Sue Lowden as a GOP challenger, who earns 48 percent at this time. Lowden's lead over Reid grows larger after basic biographies of the two candidates are shared," the pollster's memo said.

On August 23, the *Las Vegas Review-Journal*, which would engage in an 18-month crusade to knock off Reid, released a Mason-Dixon poll under the headline, "Reid Faces Uphill Battle." Tarkanian was up, 48 to 39; Lowden, 45 to 40. The family name also was helping Tarkanian, who led Lowden 33 to 14 in the GOP primary matchup. Sharron Angle was not even tested.

Reid was in trouble. A poll by the liberal *Daily Kos* website on September 4 showed him with a 52 percent unfavorable rating. The Reid campaign knew the challenge ahead and was busy hiring researchers, field personnel, and others to assemble a formidable staff as the majority leader continued to raise funds toward that $25 million goal.

By early September, ambitious Republicans were smelling blood. A former state senator from Carson City, Mark Amodei, announced he was in. Angle had raised only $100,000, but in a September 23 appearance on my statewide broadcast television show, *Face to Face*, she said that if she could just survive the primary, the outside money would come rolling in. "The person who comes out of this primary will have millions as well [as Reid]," she said, presciently.

Lowden waited until October 1, when the third quarter reporting period was past, to announce her bid. She was already deemed the candidate with the best chance to beat Reid despite Tarkanian's name recognition.

Reid soon began a warm and fuzzy "Let me introduce myself" television campaign, which he could afford to do, although it did nothing for his woeful approval rating. In contrast, on October 20, a former aide was quoted in *Politico* as saying Reid would "vaporize" anyone the Republicans nominated—a reminder of Reid's ruthless, Machiavellian reputation.

By year's end, not much had changed. Reid was up to $15 million in his war chest, but he was spending some of it on his ineffective ad campaign.

By March, Reid had no fewer than 23 opponents in all, including a dozen Republicans and a Las Vegas businessman named Scott Ashjian, who had formed the Tea Party of Nevada. Ashjian was pilloried by Tea Party activists and GOP stalwarts as a stalking horse for Reid, but it quickly became clear that he despised the senator, and was in it because he craved the attention. Would he be a factor in siphoning votes from the GOP nominee? With a "none of these candidates" option on the ballot, every vote thrown there, or for one of the minor party contenders, could help Reid.

The Nevada Republican Party, crushed by the lack of leadership and its two scandalized leaders, was doing little to help. The Democrats still had a 60,000-voter edge in the state and raised 10 times as much as the GOP in 2009, reports showed.

Another Mason-Dixon poll taken in April showed Lowden, who began an early TV campaign, was running away from the field. Angle was languishing at 5 percent. The primary was only two months away.

Three days before that poll was released, however, the seminal event of the primary had taken place, although no one in the media knew about it yet. Lowden, during an appearance in the rural town of Mesquite, not far from Las Vegas, had raised the idea of bartering for health care. A state Democratic Party tracker–and the party was a wholly absorbed subsidiary of the Reid campaign—had capture the moment on video and it was soon on national blogs. Eric Kleefeld of *Talking Points Memo* posted it on April 12. Many expected Lowden to immediately clarify that she meant "haggle" or "bargain." Instead, she went on a Reno-based television program, *Nevada Newsmakers*, on April 20 and talked about how Americans should "change the system . . . our grandparents would take a chicken to the doctor."

The Reid campaign, which feared a Lowden candidacy the most, seized on the comment and made sure the world knew about it. Soon, it was viral. Lowden became the object of national ridicule. "The Chicken Lady" was born; her candidacy began to die.

The trajectory was swift. The national Tea Party Express, on Tax Day, endorsed Angle and began raising money for her. Soon, the anti-tax Club for Growth, which had backed Angle against Heller for Congress in 2006, ponied up, too. Angle had money for television ads, and, combined with her base, she seemed to have the upper hand. Tarkanian, flailing about for an opening, began to harshly attack Lowden and indicated she could not win a general election.

By April 30, Patriot Majority, a third-party group run by a former Reid press secretary, began pounding Lowden on television. The Reid folks once thought the best they could do was batter Lowden before she won. However, it soon became clear that she might actually lose the primary, and, as she made shaky television appearances, what appeared so promising on paper was now in reality disintegrating.

By late May, Angle had a slight lead in the polls, and by primary night on June 8, her momentum was even greater than anyone imagined. She won in a landslide, with 40 percent of the vote to Lowden's 26 percent and Tarkanian's 23 percent.

The Reid campaign was ready. What happened next was a textbook case of defining your opponent before she can define herself. Before the GOP nominee was done celebrating her victory on June 8, the Reid campaign had two anti-Angle websites ready to go. Soon afterward, the majority leader released ads portraying Angle as "extreme" because of claims made on *Face to Face* that she wanted to "phase out" Social Security and Medicare, in addition to her statement before a small group that it is "not my job to create jobs."

Angle, who had run most of her campaigns out of her Reno living room, had no idea what hit her. The National Republican Senatorial Committee tried to put a cocoon around her—they had hoped Lowden would be the nominee—and tried to restrict Angle's appearances to friendly media. But, as *Politico*'s Ben Smith put it on Twitter three days after the primary: "Reminds me of 1st days of Palin candidacy. Bottomless well, apparently unprepared campaign." Meanwhile, the ever-ready Reid campaign was already working all the "angles" (pardon the pun). They had ads on Hispanic television. They had catalogued everything Angle had ever said publicly. They had non-stop advertising spots running.

A day after Angle won, a Rasmussen Reports poll showed her up 11 on Reid; by July 13, Rasmussen had it as a dead heat—46 to 43—where it would remain until November. The Angle campaign was thoroughly unprepared for the barrage, lacking the skills or wherewithal to respond while beset by internal bickering.

The conventional wisdom that Reid was dead had changed. The sense that he had been blessed with the one nominee who could lose to an incumbent with a 50 percent unfavorable rating began to take hold.

The next few months featured the roll-out of a remarkable series of Angle statements—some captured by Reid trackers, others simply because she talked to friendly and mainstream media. They included:

- As first reported by *Washington Post* liberal blogger Greg Sargent, Angle had told Seattle conservative radio talk-show host Lars Larson in January 2010: "If this Congress keeps going the way it is, people are really looking toward those Second Amendment remedies and saying my goodness what can we do to turn this country around? I'll tell you the first thing we need to do is take Harry Reid out."
- In another interview with a conservative talk-show host, Reno's Bill Manders, she had this exchange:

  MANDERS: *Is there any reason at all for an abortion?*
  ANGLE: *Not in my book.*
  MANDERS: *So, in other words, rape and incest would not be something?*

ANGLE: *You know, I'm a Christian and I believe that God has a plan and a purpose for each one of our lives and that he can intercede in all kinds of situations and we need to have a little faith in many things.*

- In early July, she responded to a question by Las Vegas conservative radio host Alan Stock about what she would do if a father had raped his daughter and she had become pregnant: "I think that two wrongs don't make a right. And I have been in the situation of counseling young girls, not 13 but 15, who have had very at-risk, difficult pregnancies. And my counsel was to look for some alternatives, which they did. And they found that they had made what was really a lemon situation into lemonade."
- On August 1, she told Fox's Carl Cameron that she wanted to be make the media her friend. "We wanted them to ask the questions we want to answer so that they report the news the way we want it reported."
- On August 4, I reported in the *Las Vegas Sun* on a tape of an interview she did with the Tru News network earlier that year, in which she said, "What's happening [in America] . . . is a violation of the first commandment," and added that entitlements "make government our God."
- On October 1, during an appearance in Mesquite, the town that caused Lowden's downfall in the primary, the local newspaper reported that Angle was asked about "Muslims taking over the U.S." Her answer was stunning: "We're talking about a militant terrorist situation, which I believe isn't a widespread thing, but it is enough that we need to address, and we have been addressing it," Angle said. "Dearborn, Michigan, and Frankford, Texas are on American soil, and under constitutional law. Not Sharia law. And I don't know how that happened in the United States. It seems to me there is something fundamentally wrong with allowing a foreign system of law to even take hold in any municipality or government situation in our United States." In fact, there had been a skirmish in Dearborn involving some Christians and Muslims, but Sharia law had not been implemented. And Frankford, Texas, no longer existed. As there was no truth in her outlandish claims, Angle would later explain that she had "read that somewhere."

With that kind of ammunition, she would have been declared dead many times except for one thing: Reid's negatives were so high that he could never get that far ahead. Angle stayed close with the help of American Crossroads, a Karl Rove-inspired group, which ran a series of "Really, Harry?" ads that tried to refocus the race on the economy.

Every poll showed the race was a dead heat, except for one outlier: a poll done for the Retail Association of Nevada by well-known national pollster, Glen Bolger. The survey, released on September 24, showed Reid ahead by 5 points, 45 to 40. That mirrored Reid's internal polls—they consistently showed the senator ahead from September onward.

By mid-October, the national media believed the race was a tossup. After the only debate, on October 14, in which Reid looked shaky and old at times while Angle held her own, the media started to say Angle had the edge.

Public polls seemed to confirm this—three in one week showed Angle leading 49 to 45—CNN/Time, Rasmussen, and Mason-Dixon. But they all had flawed samples, and Reid's internals showed him holding to a 4- or 5-point lead.

Days before the debate, Angle shocked the nation by revealing she had raised $14 million in the quarter, believed to be the third-largest quarterly haul in U.S. Senate race history behind Scott Brown and Rick Lazio. Tea Party fever across the nation had filled her coffers. (Angle would eventually report raising $21 million for the race, just a million less than Reid, and would be buoyed by $10 million in outside spending versus $6 million for Reid, as reported in the *Washington Post* a week after the balloting.) But what Angle did not reveal was that most of the $14 million was gone, spent on direct mail advertising to raise the funds, and ads on illegal immigration to keep pace with Reid.

The senator never lost the upper hand on television in the final weeks, even though he made a few gaffes of his own—suggesting no Hispanics should ever be Republicans and telling MSNBC's Ed Schultz on October 21, "People have been hurting and I understand that. And it doesn't give them comfort or solace for me to tell them, you know, but for me, we'd be in a worldwide depression. They want to know what I've done for them."

Unbeknownst to Angle's campaign, even though its internals showed her leading, and crushing Reid among independents, the die had been cast long before. The Reid campaign put its foot on her throat the night she won the primary and had not lightened the pressure. There were regular endorsements from prominent Republicans that depicted Angle as "extreme" and "dangerous." The Reid press operation was relentless, pushing Angle's missteps with every outlet, save for the *Review-Journal*, which stayed dedicated to beating Reid and whose pollster said the weekend before the election, " I think the odds are pretty good that Angle's going to win."

She did not. Buoyed by a strong showing in early voting, a two-week period before Election Day, Reid built up a huge bank of votes. There was no GOP wave here. Thanks to a base energized by two presidential visits and a couple by Bill Clinton, Reid held on to that lead on Election Day. The majority leader surprised everyone by getting to 50 percent and winning by nearly 6 points. Two alternative choices that were expected to be factors—"none of these candidates," and Nevada Tea Party candidate Scott Ashjian—were not factors. Combined, they received less than 3 percent of the vote. The choice between the lesser of two evils was apparently a clear one for half of Nevada's electorate, which gave Reid a much larger margin of victory than his near-death experience in 1998 with John Ensign.

The Sins of the Father: The Governor's Race

In mid-2001, Rory Reid told his dad, Sen. Harry Reid, that he was thinking of running for an open seat on the Clark County Commission, the most powerful local government body in Nevada, with dominion over the moneyed Las Vegas Strip and many regional functions. Reid the Elder urged Reid the Younger not to run, telling him local government was a political boneyard—that no one ascended from that bog to the heights of statewide office. Too many enemies made on a weekly basis. Wait for another opening, Harry urged Rory.

Rory Reid did not listen to his father. He ran in 2002, was reelected in 2006, and decided to run for the governorship in 2008. He had just come off helming Hillary Clinton's presidential bid in Nevada, and she had won the caucus in the state. Reid, though, might have competition—Assembly Speaker Barbara Buckley, one of the smartest, toughest lawmakers Carson City had seen, was musing about a bid, too.

In a maneuver that would have made his father proud, Rory Reid released a poll halfway through the year, reported in my *RalstonFlash.com* newsletter, that showed him crushing Buckley in a primary, 51 to 20. He also was well ahead (49 to 32) of the controversial governor, Jim Gibbons, who had been enmeshed in tawdry scandals and had been adjudged singularly ineffective by observers. Gibbons, whose negatives sometimes soared as high as 60 percent in some polls, was seen by some as potentially viable in a GOP primary, but carrion in a general election. The Republican vultures were circling. Candidates who coveted the post and party insiders who feared the loss of the governorship soon began to surface. By late fall, North Las Vegas mayor, Mike Montandon, a long shot, and a recently deposed state senator, Joe Heck, a longer shot, were musing about the race, showing how weak the incumbent was. Ever the solipsistic trial balloonist, Las Vegas mayor Oscar Goodman dropped hints he might be interested too. The martini-swilling Democrat was notorious for floating his name but never following through for higher office, preferring his political career stirred not shaken.

On January 10, 2010, Reid's campaign manager, David Cohen, wrote a memo that began, "Two weeks into the New Year, I can see our path to victory clearly. . . ." He went on to argue that Reid's favorable media coverage, bulging war chest, and top-notch staff gave him a decided advantage.

Reid spent the next six months quietly raising money while Buckley, prohibited from fundraising during the biennial legislative session, could only sit on the campaign sidelines. Reid was trying to create an air of inevitability by midsummer as the session ended, including an announcement by gaming giant MGM Mirage that it would support the county commissioner who oversaw its Strip interests. Reid serially rolled out union endorsements and let out the word he would have $3 million in the bank soon.

Even if Buckley relented, Reid might have a large problem. Rumbles began to surface in March that Brian Sandoval, a former legislator and attorney general, was thinking of leaving his perch as a federal judge to run for governor. Sandoval was said to be bored with the job. His friend, Pete Ernaut, a prominent GOP consultant, had chatted with him about running. Ironically, Sandoval had been recommended in late 2004 by Harry Reid, which was widely seen as a move to keep the telegenic Hispanic out of Reid the Elder's political way. Now he was threatening the son if he resigned and sought the governorship.

In July, the Republican Governors Association (RGA) quietly conducted a poll to gauge Sandoval's viability against Gibbons and Reid. The RGA folks, knowing Gibbons probably could not win, were looking for an alternative and liked what they saw.

On August 15, Sandoval announced he was leaving the bench. He said no more, but he didn't have to. He was in the governor's race a month later. Even before Sandoval made it official, though, the first poll, released in the *Las Vegas Review-Journal* on August 21, showed the ex-judge as the front-runner over the damaged incumbent. He led Gibbons, 33 to 17. (Montandon would never be a factor, and Heck would drop out to run for Congress.) In a three-way primary matchup, Goodman led with 34 percent, followed by Buckley at 25 percent, and Rued at 13 percent. In a two-way matchup, Reid trailed Buckley, 43 to 22. Sandoval beat all comers—Goodman by 7, Buckley by 8, and Reid by 17.

The outlook was extraordinarily bleak for Reid because his negatives were soaring, despite the millions in his war chest. His high unfavorable rating had less to do with his performance on the County Commission and more with his toxic last name—even though no one really knew him. His father's 50 percent negative rating was raining down on the son, whose negatives were not much below that.

Inside the Reid campaign, he and his advisers continued to believe Buckley would not run and that Sandoval would be damaged after a primary with Gibbons and Montandon, and that the incumbent had an outside chance to win in a GOP-only contest.

Buckley did recede on September 11, 2009, citing family concerns. She had long wanted to spend more time with her son after being term-limited out of the legislature. Initial polls, including one taken for the *Review-Journal* and released November 5, showed Reid down 15 points to Sandoval. How could he change that without changing his last name? It would turn out that he could not.

The trajectory of the race was relatively predictable from the time Sandoval entered in September. He never trailed in the polls and essentially played a front-runner's strategy—few debates, no positions beyond "no new taxes" and parry every attack in the primary and the general election.

A winter special session to make budget cuts allowed Gibbons to look gubernatorial. But the impact was evanescent. By the Ides of March, Goodman's familiar Hamlet act was over and he announced what most insiders already knew—he would not run, as a Democrat or an independent.

Reid continued to put out policy treatises that generally were either ignored or criticized for not having funding sources. He became known as the "man with the plans," but he had no clear plan to defeat Sandoval. Reid's numbers did not move, even though his pollster, John Anzalone, continued to show him closer than public surveys.

Sandoval just stuck to his anti-tax message. In one only-in-Nevada moment at the end of March, Sandoval was interviewed on the radio by his opponent's ex-wife, Dawn Gibbons. He made his stance on taxes even more unequivocal:

> GIBBONS: "Is there any situation in which you would consider raising taxes?"
>
> SANDOVAL: (With nary a second's hesitation) "No."

A Democratic front group run by Reid's former campaign manager began airing ads to try to damage Sandoval in the primary, assailing him and his role as attorney general in acting on behalf of the governor to pass the budget in 2003. He was portrayed as a hypocrite for being a conduit for a tax increase that session. The ads had little impact. On June 2, as expected, Sandoval crushed the damaged incumbent, 55 to 27. The general election, such as it was, was on.

It soon became clear that Reid was hoping people would forget who his father was. His website did not have his last name, his campaign paraphernalia read "Rory 2010" and the national media picked up on it after his first ad: "Harry Reid's son leaves last name out of first campaign ad."

By trying to draw attention away from his greatest liability, Reid the Younger had drawn even more attention to it. Meanwhile, Sandoval eschewed most interviews and forums as Reid kept releasing plans and getting no traction. Mason-Dixon polls published in the *Review-Journal* consistently and immutably showed him trailing badly: July 17, 47–36; August 14, 52–36; September 11, 52–36; October 15, 53–34; and October 30, 54–38.

There were three debates, but none produced any momentum for Reid. He tried a last-ditch ad campaign, portraying Sandoval as in the pocket of banking lobbyists, who Reid argued persuaded him to leave the federal bench to serve their interests. But the connections were tenuous, and while Democrats began to coalesce behind the nominee as the election approached, Reid still trailed by double digits.

Sandoval also had to weather a tempest in late July over his support for Arizona's controversial illegal immigration law—a position he had taken in the primary. It became more of an issue when a news director for a Spanish-language television station alleged Sandoval had claimed his children "don't look Hispanic" during an interview. There was no video of the comment, but that did not stop the Reid campaign from stirring up the controversy in the Hispanic community. (Sandoval would go on to lose the Hispanic vote by a wide margin, according to exit polls.)

It also did not help Reid that so much of the state's political oxygen was sucked away by the U.S. Senate race, or that his father's strategy of getting people to hold their noses and vote for him could not help his son: Many such voters surely would have a one-Reid limit.

The money also appeared not to matter. By virtue of his relationship with the Clintons and his perch on the Clark County Commission, which has jurisdiction over the Las Vegas Strip, Reid eventually would raise $2 million more than Sandoval—$6.3 million to $4.2 million. However, when you are running against an unblemished foe with low negatives and yours are over 40 percent, you cannot squander the summer with feel-good ads.

Sure enough, on November 2, Sandoval won by 11 points, 53 to 42, becoming the state's first Hispanic governor and an incipient national figure. Eleven months after Cohen's "path to victory" memo, in the same year that his father had made a miraculous recovery, the son's ill-fated bid had ended disastrously.

Chapter 22

New Hampshire: The Swing State Swings Right

by Dr. Dante Scala

Associate Professor of Political Science
at the University of New Hampshire

In February 2009, after a brief flirtation with joining President Obama's cabinet, New Hampshire's Republican senior senator, Judd Gregg, announced that he would not seek a fourth term in the U. S. Senate. Gregg's retirement appeared to be one more sign of the emerging dominance of the Democratic Party in the Granite State. After decades of also-ran status, the Democrats had become the majority party, controlling the governor's office, both houses of the state legislature, and three out of four seats in its congressional delegation. The sole prize left for the Democrats was Gregg's seat. To some observers, his retirement was an implicit admission of how difficult it was going to be for the Republicans to hold that seat.

Waiting in the wings to snatch this last prize was Paul Hodes, the two-term congressman from the Second District, bordering Vermont. Hodes had gained office three years earlier, upending six-term GOP incumbent Charlie Bass in the Democratic wave of 2006; he won reelection easily in 2008. Although the congressman was a relative unknown compared to prominent Democrats, such as Governor John Lynch and Senator Jeanne Shaheen, his bid for higher office certainly appeared viable. In February 2009, even a generic Democrat looked more than capable of winning a Senate race in a state turning blue.

A year and a half later, Hodes's campaign was a ship run aground, helpless to move as the tide went out—and to the right. New Hampshire, true to its bellwether status, had soured on the perform- ance of Obama and the Democratic-controlled Congress, just as the nation had. In February 2009, Obama had the approval of two-thirds of New Hampshire voters, according to a poll conducted by the University of New Hampshire Survey Center; a year and a half later, the president's approval rating had slumped to just 46 percent. Although New Hampshire had weathered the recession better than most, Granite State voters were still wary of the future and unhappily focused on the cost of federal bailouts, health care reform, and the 2009 stimulus package. For years, Democrats had been warmly received by New Hampshire independents increasingly hostile to George W. Bush. But in 2010, Yankee attitudes had turned icy toward the new party in power, and Hodes struggled to find traction. In sum, a race that origi- nally appeared to be a strong pickup opportunity for the Democrats had fallen far down the list of seats likely to change hands, and Hodes wait- ed in vain for the Democratic Senatorial Campaign Committee to make significant advertising buys on his behalf.

Republican Primary

While Hodes ran unopposed within his party, several Republicans made a bid for the GOP nomination. Foremost among them was state attorney general, Kelly Ayotte, who had been reappointed to the post by Governor Lynch after her original tenure under Lynch's predeces- sor, Republican Craig Benson. Ayotte enjoyed high name recognition within the state, thanks in part to her prosecution of two prominent murder cases while in the attorney general's office, one of which resulted in the death sentence for the murderer of a police officer. She also took a challenge to the state's parental notification law to the U. S. Supreme Court, though the outcome was eventually rendered moot by the law's repeal.

Upon her entrance into the race, Ayotte became the anointed front-runner, complete with the support of Senator Gregg and the national Republican establishment. However, Ayotte did not deter others from entering the race, such as Ovide Lamontagne, a favorite of social conservatives, who had last run for statewide office in 1996.

Another potentially formidable obstacle to Ayotte emerged when Bill Binnie, a wealthy businessman, announced that he would self-fund his bid for the Senate. Binnie was a newcomer to New Hampshire politics, but in some ways was a throwback to traditional Yankee Republican values: frugally conservative on economic issues, but moderate on issues such as abortion. (Another self-funder, Jim Bender, also joined the race.) Ayotte now faced the challenge of defeating both a candidate to her left in the primary *and* a candidate to her right.

Binnie set out to build his name recognition early in 2010, running ads on WMUR-TV, the only New Hampshire station that broadcasts statewide. His message: In a time of severe economic distress, New Hampshire needed to send a proven job-creator to the Senate. Meanwhile, Ayotte felt the pressures of her front-runner status and the challenges of being an establishment candidate in a decidedly antiestablishment year within the GOP. New Hampshire media focused on less-praiseworthy aspects of her tenure as attorney general. On her watch, for instance, a mortgage brokerage ran a Ponzi scheme that cost investors more than $30 million. At public hearings, Ayotte said that the matter had never reached her desk, but a report from the state legislature assigned part of the blame to her office for failing to act. Waiting in the wings, Paul Hodes briefly ran ads during the summer, highlighting Ayotte's denials of responsibility. By mid-summer, Binnie appeared ready to make the race for the nomination a two-person contest.

Then the roof fell in on the novice candidate. A socially conservative advocacy group, Cornerstone Action, began to run ads declaring that Binnie was "shockingly liberal." The candidate fired back, complaining to the Federal Election Commission (FEC) that the Ayotte campaign had coordinated illegally with Cornerstone. Then the *New Hampshire Union Leader*, an influential voice among New Hampshire conservatives, ran a news story claiming that Binnie's company had moved jobs to Mexico. Binnie responded with a full-page ad in the *Union Leader* denying the story; the publisher of the paper described the candidate as "a bully with a big bag of money." Finally, Binnie squared off against Ayotte herself, and the two engaged in a vigorous exchange of negative ads as the primary neared.

As is often the case in multicandidate primaries, negative ads lead voters to look for candidates staying positive. For New Hampshire

Republicans, Ovide Lamontagne was such a sunny alternative. During the primary season, Ayotte had received an endorsement from Sarah Palin as well as a national pro-life group; but Lamontagne benefited from a late *Union Leader* endorsement, as well as vocal support from conservative talk-radio host Laura Ingraham. As Binnie staggered toward the finish line, Lamontagne surged into second place despite his paltry fundraising and paid media. On Election Day, Ayotte's support appeared solid, but the conservative insurgent was the only candidate with momentum. That night, Lamontagne ran up an early lead based on returns from the Greater Manchester area. As the evening wore on, Ayotte slowly chipped away at her rival's margin, then took the lead for good in the wee hours of the morning. The choice of the GOP establishment had held on—barely. She finished with 38 percent of the vote, and a 1,659-vote margin of victory.

General Election

Kelly Ayotte had walked a tightrope for a year during the battle for the nomination of her party. The day she emerged as the GOP nominee, her path to the Senate widened considerably. Advocates for her Democratic opponent, Paul Hodes, had hoped that Ayotte moved too far to the right during the primary, making a general-election appeal that much more difficult. A Palin-endorsed candidate, they speculated, would not fare well among a socially moderate electorate. In this optimistic scenario, Granite State voters finally might turn to the Democrat, as they had done in 2006 and 2008.

It quickly became apparent, however, that it was Hodes who appeared to be lacking as the seven-week general campaign began. The Democrat had trailed Ayotte in the polls since 2009, and the first post-primary surveys confirmed that the Republicans' internal contest had done nothing to change this. Post-primary surveys indicated a significant lead for Ayotte; the well-respected University of New Hampshire Survey Center put the margin in double digits. According to the survey center, the hard-fought primary had energized the GOP base, rather than dividing and demoralizing it. In comparison, Hodes was still having trouble rallying Democratic adherents to his cause a year and a half after his campaign had begun. To the Democrats' dismay, independent voters seemed quite comfortable with Ayotte and her brand of conservatism; they had been breaking from the Democrat for more than a year and showed no signs of reconsidering their decision.

Hodes was stuck in a hole and he did not appear to have the resources to climb out. The Democrat had raised slightly more money than his Republican opponent ($4.7 million, to Ayotte's $4.4 million), but also had burned through far more of his funds. Hodes only had approximately $250,000 on hand for the homestretch while Ayotte had $1 million to spend, according to October campaign finance reports. To make matters worse, Ayotte enjoyed significant backing from outside groups (such as Karl Rove's 527, American Crossroads), while Hodes's supporters were scarce. Republican-allied groups spent nearly $900,000 opposing Hodes, while the Democrat's allies spent some $60,000 opposing Ayotte. The Democratic Senatorial Campaign Committee, faced with defending incumbents around the country, had scarce resources to devote to a contest that appeared out of reach. As a result, Hodes found himself double-teamed both by his opponent and by an allied group when he aired his advertisements on television.

Finally, Hodes found himself on the wrong side of the issues that mattered most to New Hampshire voters in this election cycle. Granite State voters' preference for socially moderate, fiscally conservative policies had been at odds with the actions of the national Republicans during the Bush era. The first two years of the Obama presidency, however, made these centrist voters question the fiscal prudence of the Democrats as well. The passage of the federal stimulus act, as well as health care reform, left congressional Democrats on the defensive nationwide in the 2010 cycle. For Hodes, a Democratic congressman trying to become a senator, this was an especially uncomfortable position.

The Democrat tried to persuade voters that he, too, was a fiscal conservative, touting his opposition to the bailout of Wall Street financial institutions. "Unlike those who believe 'fiscal conservative' means simply starve government and do away with government," Hodes said in an interview with the *New Hampshire Union Leader*, "I think it means being fiscally responsible about finding places to cut, finding places to hold the line and at the same time making sure we're doing what we need to do to shore up a very fragile recovery and help businesses create jobs for the future. You've got to walk and chew

gum, and that means rebuilding the middle class on a firm foundation." He said, "And that means clean energy, education, health care
and infrastructure investment to keep our country productive."
Hodes also supported the extension of the Bush tax cuts for those
making less than $200,000 a year, while accusing Ayotte of fiscal irre-
sponsibility for supporting the extension of tax cuts for the wealthy.

Ayotte, as a member of the "out" party, framed the race as a referendum on the performance of the ruling party in Washington. In one
advertisement, Ayotte is standing at the intersection of two paths in the
woods. "America's future can go down two different paths," she says,
Paul Hodes's way, a path "of more spending, higher taxes and more government control over our lives." Then her alternative, "We can change
direction and go forward with core principles. Don't spend more money
than we have. Small businesses create jobs better than the government
does. And taxes are too high already. That's the path I'm taking."

New Hampshire voters followed Ayotte down her path, and
never looked back. The Republican's second election night, unlike
her primary victory, was quickly concluded and almost devoid of sus-
pense. The Republican finished the night with 60 percent of the vote
and held Hodes to just under 37 percent. While incumbent
Democratic governor John Lynch won a historic fourth term, it was
Ayotte's victory that set the tone up and down the ticket. The New
Hampshire GOP, which seemed on the verge of becoming the state's
minority party after consecutive losses in 2006 and 2008, swept both
House seats and regained control of both houses of the state legislature by wide margins. Nearly two years earlier, Judd Gregg had
seemed in danger of ceding his seat to a Democrat. Instead, it was the
senior senator's favored candidate—another Republican from his
hometown of Nashua—who was headed to Washington to take his
place. Ayotte was set to join Democrat Jeanne Shaheen to make the
fourth all-female state delegation to the U.S. Senate.

Chapter 23

New York: A Protest Opportunity Squandered

by Dr. Jeffrey M. Stonecash

Maxwell Professor of Political Science
at Syracuse University

New York's 2010 gubernatorial election, despite the recent dominance of voting by Democrats in the state, provided an opportunity for the protest sweeping the nation to play a significant role.[1] The election, however, provided an example of the limits of protest candidates. A candidate from business won an upset victory in the Republican primary, but his prospects declined as his history, impulsive behavior, and inappropriate comments tarnished his image.

The Context

New York, with the highest state and local taxes in the nation, has experienced an ongoing frustration that a protest candidate could have exploited. The population of the state has not grown much in recent decades and there are regular arguments that the state is not sympathetic to business.[2] The enactment of the state's budget has consistently been very late,[3] and critics of the legislature argue that it is dysfunctional and incapable of responding to statewide public policy problems.[4] The prior four years of gubernatorial behavior had further undermined public confidence in political figures. Eliot Spitzer, the former attorney general of New York, was elected in 2006 with a promise to "clean up" the existing state political process. Then, in 2008, he was forced to admit he patronized prostitutes and illegally moved money between accounts to hide his payments. Later that year, he resigned and was replaced by his lieutenant governor, David Paterson, who became the first black governor of New York. Paterson's image was soon tarnished by admissions that he and his wife had each had affairs and that he had used cocaine. In 2009, stories emerged that his aide was allegedly involved in a domestic violence incident, and Paterson had personally called the victim the night before she was to testify. These stories damaged his prospects, and he withdrew from the race for 2010. The image of state government in 2010 was not at all positive. There was potential for a protest candidate to take advantage of the situation.

The Candidates

Into this context stepped two candidates endorsed by the major parties. Andrew Cuomo, the son of former governor Mario Cuomo, quickly emerged as the Democratic candidate. He ran his father's campaigns in the 1980s and then became assistant secretary of housing in 1993 and secretary of housing in 1997 under Bill Clinton. He returned to New York in 2001, and in 2002 he challenged Carl McCall, then the comptroller of the state, for the Democratic gubernatorial nomination. This challenge angered many blacks and liberals because McCall was the first black in the state to be nominated as a gubernatorial candidate. Cuomo eventually withdrew late in the race, but still spent several years patching up relations with the minority community. After he was elected as attorney general in 2006, he built a reputation similar to that of Eliot Spitzer's— someone willing to take on corporations.

The Republican nomination process did not go as smoothly. The party designated Rick Lazio as their nominee in a June state convention. He was a member of the House of Representatives in the 1990s and had run against Hillary Clinton in 2000 for the U.S. Senate seat, but stumbled after appearing to try to physically intimidate her during some debates. Despite Lazio having the party designation, Carl Paladino was able to secure enough votes in the convention to force a primary in September. Paladino stunned New York Republicans by beating Lazio by a 2-to-1 margin in the primary.[5] Paladino presented a clear choice to New Yorkers. He indicated his complete disgust with the continually drawn-out budget process in Albany, and the levels of taxes and spending in the state. Early on his image was dominated by his declaration that he would go to Albany and clean it up with a baseball bat.

The Partisan Context

The initial difficulty Paladino faced was partisanship. Over time there has been a clear shift in voter support away from the Republican Party. In New York, a registering voter has the option to "enroll" in a party. An individual might choose to enroll to indicate attachment to a party or to be eligible to vote in the party's primary. Figure 23.1 presents total party enrollment within the state since 1950.[6] The most significant change within the state has been the steady erosion of the Republican Party's percentage of registrants.

Figure 23.1—Total Party Enrollment Trends in New York State, 1950–2010

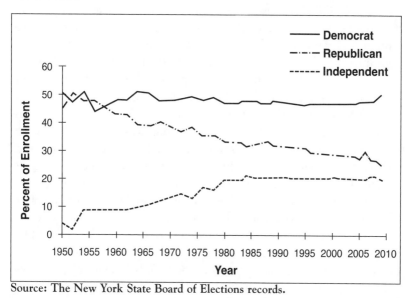

Source: The New York State Board of Elections records.

The decline in enrollment in the Republican Party, however, has not produced an increase in Democratic enrollment. The percentage enrolling as Democrats has remained at just under 50 percent for over 60 years. The Republican decline has resulted in a steady increase in the percentage declining to enroll in a party.[7] However, while voters have become uneasy about the Republican Party, they have not embraced the Democratic Party. This lack of movement to the Democratic Party has been exploited by some Republican gubernatorial candidates, such as George Pataki, who was elected governor in 1994, 1998, and 2002. The combination of national voter anger at Democrats, frustration with the New York political process, and numerous independents could have provided a base for a candidate like Carl Paladino.

The Campaign

The New York gubernatorial campaign began in earnest after the September primary. Andrew Cuomo had good ratings in the electorate, with his favorable–unfavorable ratings in the summer at roughly 55 percent favorable to 25 percent unfavorable, depending on the poll. Paladino was largely unknown in the beginning. A poll on June 22 (Quinnipiac College) indicated that his ratings were 10 percent favorable and 10 percent unfavorable. A September 1 poll (Quinnipiac) showed that he was at 16–13. He was relatively unknown and had an opportunity to present himself as an outsider who would change the political process in Albany. In a poll of likely voters (Quinnipiac) distributed on September 23, his favorable–unfavorable ratings were 36–31 and the matchup was 49 percent Cuomo to 43 percent Paladino. The results received considerable attention and indicated that there was the possibility of a real race.

Paladino squandered that opportunity in short order. The press soon discovered that Paladino had a 10-year-old daughter from a prior affair and that his wife knew about it. He then had an encounter in which he physically threatened a news reporter because he did not like his questions. He followed that with a presentation to a conservative Jewish group where he bashed gays, citing their behavior in gay parades and stating that no one should let their children see such events. Overall, he demonstrated that he was volatile and had a short fuse.

The result was a dramatic change of his ratings within a short period of time. As figure 23.2 indicates, all of those without an opinion of Paladino quickly moved to having an unfavorable view of him.[8] As an inexperienced candidate who did not exercise verbal restraint, he self-destructed in the campaign. Cuomo's ratings remained largely unchanged during this time.

Figure 23.2—Paladino Ratings in 2010

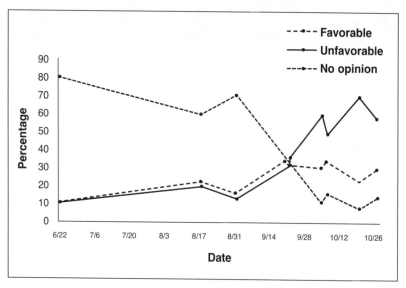

Source: Siena College and Quinnipiac College polls.

The Election

The impact on the candidates' images was that more voters trusted Cuomo than Paladino. In the exit polls (posted on CNN's website), 50 percent said Cuomo was honest and trustworthy and 47 percent said he was not. In contrast, 23 percent saw Paladino as honest and trustworthy and 75 percent did not. Paladino was still able to win his own party (27 percent of New York voters), conservatives (30 percent of voters) and those positive about the Tea Party movement (36 percent of voters), but he could not gain much support beyond that.

Table 23.1 shows voter choices by party, ideology, and opinion of the Tea Party movement.[9] Cuomo was able to win Democrats, liberals, and those opposed to the Tea Party by large margins. He won moderates and those neutral about the Tea Party movement by large margins and he also won independents.

Table 23.1—Gubernatorial Choice from Exit Polls

	Governor Choice	
	Cuomo	Paladino
Party ID		
Democrat (46%)	92	6
Independent (27%)	50	41
Republican (27%)	20	76
Ideology		
Liberal (29%)	88	7
Moderate (41%)	71	24
Conservative (30%)	23	74
Opinion of Tea Party		
Support (36%)	28	68
Neutral (27%)	67	29
Oppose (27%)	89	4

Source: CNN exit polls.

Paladino began the gubernatorial campaign as a candidate who might have capitalized on the frustration with the state political process and the economy. As an inexperienced candidate he appeared unprepared to act in the public eye. His behavior and comments during the campaign created a negative image among voters and he was never able to capitalize on the political climate that prevailed in 2010. The result was that the political context of the state—the dominant Democratic Party enrollment—played out again and Cuomo won the race with 61.5 percent to Paladino's 34 percent.

Endnotes

[1]David Halbfinger, "After New York Losses, Head of State G.O.P. Is Under Fire, *New York Times*, November 3, 2010, www.nytimes.com/2010/11/04/nyregion/04nyrepubs.html?scp=2&sq=Edward%20Cox&st=cse.

[2]Stephanie Lundquist and Amy Widestrom, "The Economy, Taxes, and Policy Constraints in New York," in Robert F. Pecorella and Jeffrey M. Stonecash, *Governing New York*, Fifth Edition, (Albany: SUNY Press, 2006), 249-260.

[3]Jeffrey M. Stonecash, "The Legislature, Parties, and Resolving Conflict," in Robert F. Pecorella and Jeffrey M. Stonecash, *Governing New York*, Fifth Edition, (Albany: SUNY Press, 2006), 165-192.

[4]See: The Brennan Center for Justice report: *The New York State Legislative Process: An Evaluation and Blueprint* for Reform, at www.brennancenter.org/content/section/category/ny_reform/.

[5]David Halbfinger, "Paladino Rout of Lazio Jolts New York G.O.P.," *New York Times*, September 14, 2010, *www.nytimes.com/2010/09/15/nyregion/15webnygov.html*.

[6]The percentage of individuals choosing independent in the 1950s understates the existence of independents (non-enrolled) since most counties did not provide the option of "non-enrolled" until the late 1950s. Data are taken from the New York State Board of Elections records.

[7]This is occurring across the Northeast. See Howard L. Reiter and Jeffrey M. Stonecash, *Counter Realignment: Political Change in the Northeast* (New York: Cambridge University Press, 2011).

[8]Data taken from polls published by Siena College and Quinnipiac College from June through late October.

[9]Data are taken from the CNN exit polls: www.cnn.com/ELECTION/2010/results/polls/#NYG00p1.

Chapter 24

The 2010 Ohio Midterms: Senate and Governor

by Jonathan Riskind
Washington Bureau Chief of the Columbus Dispatch

and Joe Hallett
Senior Editor of the Columbus Dispatch

Overview

The races for governor and United States Senate in Ohio were ready-made twofers for both political parties. Republicans viewed the Democratic governor, Ted Strickland, and his lieutenant governor, Lee Fisher, the Democratic Senate nominee, as a twosome who could be blamed for Ohio's loss of roughly 400,000 jobs, and the unemployment rate that hovered above 10 percent. Democrats viewed former U.S. representatives John Kasich (the GOP gubernatorial nominee) and Rob Portman (the Senate candidate), as a twofer who worked to protect Wall Street and Washington interests while everyday Ohioans struggled amidst the state's decade-long recession.

In the crosshairs of Ohio's blame-someone election stood President Barack Obama, who made a dozen visits to the state since carrying it by 4.6 percentage points in 2008. Making a final bid to save Strickland—by then, the underfunded Fisher was a lost cause—Obama appeared with them on Halloween at Cleveland State University. The 14,000-seat arena was about half full. It was a harbinger. Two days later, Fisher got crushed and Strickland became the first Ohio governor in 36 years to fail to win a second term.

On election night, Ohio GOP Chairman Kevin DeWine carried a broom on stage at a downtown Columbus hotel and was cheered by the faithful delirious about their party's sweep. "Today," DeWine crowed, "we kicked down Obama's firewall."

And so, in 2012, the political world will gather once again in must-win Ohio to see if the wall has been rebuilt.

Governor—By Joe Hallett

More than an hour into the morning of November 3, and minutes after doing yet another live interview on Fox News (his former employer), John Kasich bounded onto the ballroom stage at the Columbus Renaissance Hotel with his beautiful wife, Karen, and their twin 10-year-old daughters. He jabbed the sky with both fists. "Guess what, I'm going to be governor of Ohio!" Kasich shouted, figuratively pinching himself to make sure it was true.

The son of a mailman from McKees Rocks, Pennsylvania, Kasich was elected 69th governor of the nation's seventh-largest state by dint of his knack for picking the right moment at the right time. He had been in Congress in 1994 to abet the Gingrich revolution, was House budget chairman when Bill Clinton signed the first balanced budget since a man walked on the moon, and was popular enough among Republicans to mount a credible but short-lived run for president in 2000 before bowing out to endorse George W. Bush.

After eight years as an on-air personality for Fox News, and Columbus-based managing director for Lehman Brothers, Kasich, 58, had become rich and was itching for a return to the public sector. He truly believed that the time he had spent pitching deals to CEOs and arranging finances for small businesses gave him the know-how to restore jobs to Ohio's chronically ailing economy.

On June 1, 2009, in front of a cheering crowd in the Columbus suburb of Westerville, his adopted hometown, Kasich launched his campaign, positing it as "a movement to save Ohio." Although unknown to most Ohioans, Kasich once again had picked the right moment at the right time. He promised a "new way," even though his prescription to cure what ailed Ohio—lower taxes, less government spending, a smaller bureaucracy, and fewer business regulations—was right out of the national Republican playbook.

It is hard to know whether Kasich's message resonated with voters. He won only 49 percent of the vote, the first winning gubernatorial candidate since 1978 to fail to get at least 50 percent. What is knowable is that Ohioans were ready for something—and someone—different, even though they may have personally liked their amiable governor, Ted Strickland, a former 12-year congressman and Methodist minister.

"I think it was a vote for change; I don't think it was a vote for Kasich," Aaron Pickrell, Strickland's campaign manager, told the *Columbus Dispatch* a day after the election. The GOP's DeWine, in an interview with the newspaper on the same day, acknowledged that Kasich's victory and the party's sweep of all five statewide executive offices resulted from a populace angst-ridden about economic security.

"I'm smart enough to realize, and I'm drilling into our winners, that they did not win because people came running back to our party because they love it," DeWine said. "They were partly frustrated and disgusted with what's going on in Washington and Columbus, so they were looking for an alternative."

It was Strickland's misfortune to be the incumbent at the wrong time. For him, the election-year political climate could hardly have been worse. Along with staggering job losses, the state's rising poverty indicators were nothing short of brutal. Going into 2010, one in 10 Ohioans were receiving food stamps, nearly one in five received Medicaid benefits, Medicaid paid for one in three births in the state, and 42 percent of Ohio schoolchildren were on the federal free or reduced-price lunch program.

Such dire statistics compounded for Strickland in Ohio the anger—and fear—that boiled through the electorate nationwide. Just four years after he had won 72 of 88 counties to end 16 consecutive years of GOP gubernatorial control with a 24 percentage-point win, Strickland went into his reelection wearing a bull's eye. Voters were locked and loaded, looking for someone to blame.

Although Strickland rightly protested that he could not be held responsible for the national recession, Kasich had begun hammering him for losing jobs long before his candidacy announcement. At a dozen or so county GOP rubber-chicken dinners leading to the May 4 Ohio primary, Kasich reminded his already ginned-up base that Strickland had failed to keep the seminal promise of his 2006 campaign—to turn Ohio around—and that the nice-guy governor seemed helpless to stop the job-hemorrhaging.

From a makeshift dais ringed with hay bales at a barn in Westerville, Kasich officially kicked off his candidacy by saying of Strickland: "If you have a house on the river and the flood's coming, he's going to show up Saturday morning with a box of doughnuts and a pot of coffee, you'll sing *Kumbaya* and hold hands and watch your house float down the river."

The irony of Kasich's attack is that Strickland's response to the recession was, in part, to follow the GOP manual. He cut the state's income and property taxes, reduced state government by 5,000 jobs, froze university tuition rates for two years, and initiated a successful effort to attract jobs in the emerging green energy sector.

Down-and-out Ohioans, however, were in no mood to believe that good things were actually happening. Although both Strickland and Kasich were unopposed in their respective primary elections, the May 4 results yielded an ominous sign for Strickland: his 620,963 vote take was fifth best, topped by four other Republicans led by Kasich with 735,790 votes. Admitting an "enthusiasm gap" favoring Republicans and with his own poll numbers in the gutter, Strickland determined that his only option was to pull Kasich into it, and then step over him to win on November 2.

Kasich's résumé made that task easier. Kasich, who boasted that he was architect of balancing the federal budget in 1997 while in Congress, had spent the last eight years as one of about 700 managing directors of Lehman Brothers, the Wall Street giant whose collapse on September 15, 2008 is oft-cited as precipitating the financial meltdown. Heading into 2010, the avarice of Wall Street was a part of the octane mixture that fueled voters' anger, and Strickland was determined to exploit it.

Kasich was, relatively speaking, a small fry at Lehman, but Strickland sought to portray him as a Wall Street powerbroker and the veritable right hand of Dick Fuld, Lehman's disgraced chairman. On primary Election Day, May 4, Strickland went on the attack. He aired a TV ad that blamed Kasich for supporting trade deals while in Congress that lost jobs for Ohio "and then Congressman Kasich moved to Wall Street and made millions working for Lehman Brothers."

On May 12, eight days after launching the ad, Strickland went to Ohio Democratic Party headquarters to deliver his first major campaign speech, proffering a continuing theme that Kasich's "Wall Street values" ran counter to Ohioans' "Main Street values."

"When Lehman Brothers plummeted into the largest bankruptcy in the history of the United States, Congressman Kasich and the top people at Lehman Brothers put out their hands and kept getting paid," Strickland told cheering Democrats. "And while he was taking home a massive salary and bonus, living on the fruits of bankruptcy, people who saved all their lives for retirement took home the rind."

Aided by similar attacks, including TV ads from labor unions and the Democratic Governors Association (DGA), Strickland relentlessly pounded Kasich for having Wall Street values. He was hoping to define an opponent that most Ohioans still did not know. The Kasich campaign denied that the attacks were hurting, but belied that argument when, in his first campaign ad in mid-July, Kasich spoke into the camera and personally rebuffed the Lehman Brothers attacks.

Strickland, Kasich said in the ad, "can't campaign on his record, so he and his friends try to tear me down. Here's the truth: I didn't run Lehman Brothers. I was one of 700 managing directors. I worked in a two-man office in Columbus." Kasich quickly pivoted to a series of positive ads focusing on his commitment to get Ohio working again. Meanwhile, the Republican Governors Association (RGA) was on the air throughout the summer with a series of TV ads featuring average Ohioans uttering the same walk-off line: "Strickland didn't get the jobs done." In all, the RGA said after the election that it had spent nearly $12 million to help Kasich in Ohio.

Such was the story throughout the campaign: Kasich blaming Strickland for Ohio's job losses and Strickland portraying Kasich as a creature of Wall Street. With six weeks to go, a race that numerous polls had shown Kasich leading comfortably suddenly had tightened up. A September 26 poll sponsored by Ohio's eight largest newspapers showed Strickland had closed Kasich's lead to just 4 points.

Neither candidate lacked money, combining to spend more than $35 million while untold millions poured in from allied party and independent groups. Democrats complained that Fox News had become a Kasich campaign surrogate. Kasich had made 60 appearances on Fox, including 18 on *Hannity*, hosted by his close friend Sean Hannity, and 17 on *The O'Reilly Factor* since March 2008, when Kasich announced his interest in running for governor. During a number of Kasich's appearances on the shows, his campaign's web address was streamed and viewers were invited to contribute to his campaign. Moreover,

Rupert Murdoch, head of News Corp., Fox's parent company, contributed $1 million to the Republican Governors Association because, he said, of his "friendship with John Kasich."

Strickland was not lacking high-level surrogate support, either. Obama, Biden, and former president Bill Clinton raised money and rallied supporters for Strickland on multiple occasions. They girded against the crucial battleground state slipping from Democratic control heading into 2012.

By the weekend before the election, Strickland's unrelenting attacks against Kasich had drawn the race into a virtual tie—Kasich up 2 points in the Dispatch Poll (conducted by the *Columbus Dispatch* newspaper), and 1 point in the Quinnipiac University Poll. That was exactly where Strickland and the Democrats wanted it to be. For two years, they had been building a get-out-the-vote (GOTV) machine that would put them on top in a close election, they believed.

Strickland and other statewide candidates had ceded their ground operations to the Ohio Democratic Party. It was the base of the GOTV operation and receptacle for millions of dollars that had poured in from national Democratic organizations, Obama's political operation, state party donors, and more than a dozen "party building" trips to other states that Strickland had taken. The resources made the Ohio Democratic Party the largest state party organization in the country, boasting more than 300 paid field workers across the state. By Election Day, the party said it had made millions of phone calls to voters and knocked on thousands of doors.

The $20-million Democratic effort fell short. The enthusiasm gap that Strickland and party officials had claimed would be more than offset by their GOTV machine held steady; less than 48 percent of registered voters cast ballots, the worst participation in a statewide election since 2002. Strickland was doomed by voter falloff in the state's big six urban counties from the governor's race four years earlier. In fact, the 10 counties that had the largest decline in total votes from 2006 accounted for 57 percent of Ohio's registered Democrats. Strickland won 47 percent of the vote statewide, no better than where polls had put his approval rating all year.

"Had this been any other election, we would have rolled," Ohio Democratic Party Chairman Chris Redfern told *The Dispatch.* "This was a national tide that swept Democrats out of office. I don't know what else we could have done."

Kasich's prize for winning: An $8 billion deficit in his first two-year state budget. He had vowed during the campaign not to raise taxes—indeed, he promised to cut them—leaving painful reductions in state services and programs as his primary option for dealing with the budget. Two years hence, Redfern predicted, Kasich would be rendered unpopular by his budget decisions. And Obama? Well, Obama had nowhere to go but up after the 2010 election.

"This election is just a snapshot in time," Redfern said, looking ahead to 2012. "Tomorrow, it will be different."

Senate—By Jonathan Riskind

On the Friday before the November 2 election, U.S. Senate candidate Lee Fisher aired a defiant TV ad, a spot that the Ohio Democrat readily admitted on-camera few voters would ever see. The spot contained Fisher's basic message, his argument that Republican rival Rob Portman was too cozy with Wall Street interests and tied to the Bush administration policies that Fisher contended led to the Great Recession of 2008. The spot also contained a dash of humor, laced with a dose of bitterness.

"Pay very close attention to this ad because you're not going to see it too many times. My campaign doesn't have millions of dollars to run lots of ads. No scary black-and-white pictures and creepy music here," Fisher said into the camera, before launching into his anti-Portman message.

Then he ended the spot with, "I'm Lee Fisher. I approve this message, and yes, we barely paid for it. But I'm sure proud that Wall Street and the Washington lobbyists didn't."

A few days later, Portman easily defeated Fisher, winning more than 56 percent of the vote to Fisher's 39 percent. Portman, the former GOP congressman from Cincinnati and Bush administration trade representative and budget director, had enjoyed a double-digit lead in the polls for weeks, and blasted his own message across the Ohio airwaves with the aid of a campaign chest that topped $14.5 million by October 13. By contrast, Fisher took in just over $6 million, and was forced to spend much of that on a contested primary against Secretary of State Jennifer Brunner. That battle alienated many Democratic Party progressives from Fisher's general election campaign and may have helped keep Fisher from ever throwing his campaign against Portman out of first gear.

Portman aired about a dozen ads, and aired them far and wide and often, all across the state. Until his limited-run, final Friday poke at Portman, Fisher had aired just one general election spot. Fisher's futility was demonstrated when he scraped together enough campaign cash to air one last spot before the Ohio State University–University of Minnesota football game on the Saturday night before the election. It apparently aired just once, and only in Columbus and perhaps a few other markets. Its take-away? Portman was not to be trusted because he graduated from the law school of Ohio State's archrival, the University of Michigan.

Portman had the money and resources to pound away at his argument that Fisher was a failed "jobs czar," a reference to the post of Ohio director of development that Fisher also assumed when he became lieutenant governor in 2007. He remained in the development post until he launched his Senate bid in 2009.

Fisher and Gov. Ted Strickland were responsible for roughly 400,000 lost Ohio jobs during their time in office, Portman said. He claimed that the economic policies he advocated, which included keeping all of the 2001 and 2003 tax cuts plus granting additional tax breaks, such as a one-year payroll tax suspension, would lead to job growth.

What Portman did not mention was that Ohio had been hemorrhaging jobs since 2000, with the total figure approaching 600,000 lost by fall of 2010. Among those in a position of power during much of that time frame was Portman—who was an influential member of the GOP House majority until he left Congress in 2005 to become Bush's trade representative and then budget director. Portman left Washington in 2007 to return to private law practice in Cincinnati before he launched his Senate run.

Fisher's campaign problems were not limited to money, of course. He burned through senior campaign staff at a rapid pace, but more importantly, he was running for Senate in a terrible climate for Democrats. Two years after Barack Obama swept into the White House and Democrats increased their House and Senate majorities, the economy could not seem to be shaken out of its doldrums. The unemployment rate was high—with Ohio's exceeding 10 percent—and voters were focusing their anger on Democrats.

For all of Fisher's attempts to link Portman to the Bush administration, and the voter anger directed at George W. Bush in the past, it just was not a message many voters seemed to buy in 2010. They wanted to know, now, what had happened to the "change" they thought they were buying in 2008.

Meanwhile, the national Democratic Party seemed to accept pretty early on that it was not going to win the Ohio seat being vacated by two-term GOP senator, George V. Voinovich. Winning the Ohio seat, while it would have been a nice pickup, was not one of the main concerns of a party trying to safeguard its 10-seat majority and preparing to stave off the embarrassment of Senate Majority Leader Harry Reid of Nevada possibly going down to defeat at the hands of a Tea Party candidate.

While national Democratic and liberal group money was spent elsewhere, conservative groups were happy to jump into the fray in Ohio to pump up Portman's chances even more. Groups like the U.S. Chamber of Commerce and American Crossroads aired hundreds of thousands of dollars worth of pro-Portman or anti-Fisher ads—though they soon shifted most of their money to other races given Portman's mushrooming lead.

In addition, while Fisher defeated Brunner in the May 4 Ohio primary by a handy 11-point margin, it was easy to spot plenty of signs pointing to Fisher's ultimate demise at the hands of Portman in the November general election.

Fisher was the candidate anointed by Gov. Strickland and the Democratic Party establishment in the Buckeye State to run for the Senate. Meanwhile, the GOP establishment had chosen favorite son Portman to run on its side of the Senate race ticket.

A Cleveland-area car dealer, Tom Ganley, threatened to make a self-funded, Tea Party-inspired primary run at the establishment conservative Portman.

In November 2009, it appeared that Ganley was making good on his threat when he aired a TV spot touting his ability to create jobs. It looked like Portman, who by the end of 2009 already had $6 million in his campaign chest, would have to spend significant time and money on the primary campaign trail to ensure his place on the general election ballot.

Ganley dropped from the Senate race by mid-February, choosing instead to spend his time and money pursuing a U.S. House seat, challenging Betty Sutton, the Democratic representative in the northeast Ohio Thirteenth District..

Fisher did not get so lucky. Secretary of State Brunner made good on her vow to stay in the Democratic Senate primary until Election Day on May 4. Not much separated Fisher and Brunner on the issues.

Brunner waged an underfunded but extremely aggressive campaign against Fisher, going after liberal Democrats and female voters and criticizing the party establishment for allegedly trying to shut her out of the process. Brunner careened around the state in a 1991 school bus she called *The Courage Express*, which she bought on eBay for $2,050. She placed the word "courage" above her logo: World War II-era feminist icon "Rosie the Riveter."

Finance reports showed her with only about $79,000 on hand for the final weeks of the campaign, compared to Fisher's $1.8 million. Polls showed Brunner remaining in striking distance as late as March, with a Quinnipiac University poll showing that 40 percent of Democratic voters remained undecided.

Finally, a few days before the election, a Quinnipiac poll showed Fisher with a 17-point lead. The actual result on May 4 was an 11-point margin for Fisher—but he spent most of his campaign funds to beat Brunner. An angry Brunner refused to endorse Fisher after the primary, which further divided a Democratic base that seemed to lack the energy and enthusiasm of GOP loyalists.

It was a general election that promised a clear choice between candidates for Ohio voters.

Unlike the Fisher–Brunner primary, where there were no major differences on issues, there were plenty of disagreements between Fisher and Portman over issues. Fisher backed Democrats' health care bill, while Portman agreed with Republicans who wanted to repeal the new law. Portman wanted to extend all of the 2001 and 2003 Bush tax cuts. Fisher agreed with Obama's call to allow the tax cuts for households earning $250,000 and more to expire, although Fisher strayed a bit and midway through the fall proposed allowing a one-year extension of tax cuts for those making up to $1 million.

It was a mainstream conservative Republican versus a mainstream liberal Democrat in a swing state that went for Obama in

2008, but was suffering from economic woes even more than the nation as a whole.

Fisher wanted to press the case that going back to GOP rule would halt progress being made by Democrats on all fronts—and to paint former Bush aide Portman as part of the past problems. Portman wanted to portray Fisher as the failed "job czar" that voters should hold responsible for state job losses during the recession, and also use as a proxy for any dissatisfaction with Obama and his policies. (The term "job czar" was a jab at Fisher's role as Ohio director of development when he took office as lieutenant governor in 2007.)

But it was Portman who had the money to get his message out to the voters, a big advantage, especially in a year where the political climate was so tough for Fisher and fellow Democrats.

After the news that Portman had a huge money advantage after the second-quarter of 2010, about $8.8 million to about $1 million, Fisher may have regretted this line in a June 29 fundraising appeal: "Potential supporters will look at our next contribution report to measure our campaign's readiness and decide whether they want to step onto the field or sit on the sidelines this fall."

At age 59, Fisher's long career in Ohio politics—from the Ohio House and Senate to Ohio attorney general to gubernatorial nominee in 1998, and then finally lieutenant governor—was over with his Senate loss. A week after the election, he told supporters he would not likely run for public office again.

54-year-old Portman, on the other hand, seems headed not just for the Senate, but possibly for consideration for the national ticket in 2012 or 2016.

Chapter 25

Pennsylvania: An Open-Seat Governor's Race and a Senate Incumbent Loses

by Dr. G. Terry Madonna

*Director of the Center for Politics and Public Affairs; and
Professor of Public Affairs at Franklin and Marshall College*

With Governor Ed Rendell term limited, the 2010 Pennsylvania governor's race featured contested primaries in both major parties. The ubiquitous and outspoken Rendell remained, however, very much a part of the debate. His eight-year tenure, complete with large increases in education and economic development spending, together with his ritualistic recommendations for a variety of tax increases, framed much of the campaign debate. By 2010, the recession and the governor's call for increased spending and taxes pushed his popularity to the lowest levels of his governorship.[1] The governor studiously avoided any public involvement in his party's primary campaign, although he tacitly supported one of the Democratic candidates, and several of his major campaign finance operatives made sure that the candidate raised the money necessary to earn the Democratic nomination. Two overriding themes dominated the Democratic primary: The large state deficit and the need to stabilize the state's budget were the major issues of contention, followed by the broad issue of government reform—mostly focused on ethics practices, campaign finance regulations, and legislative transformation. In 2009, the legislature and the governor wrangled for 101 days beyond the June 30 constitutional budget deadline before adopting a $28.2 billion budget that closed a $3.2 billion deficit, but required no new taxes. The budget was balanced by using monies from the state's "rainy day fund," the MCare retention account, several billions in federal stimulus monies, and reductions in some state programs. The state budget situation was ominous again in 2010, with the state facing a $1.6 billion deficit. The state also had to deal with the loss of federal stimulus monies and the possibility of a $53 billion pension debt. Similar to 2009, the legislature and the governor divided over the size of the budget and taxes needed to sustain it. But with legislative elections looming in the fall amidst an anti-incumbent mood among the electorate, the governor and the legislature worked out a compromise budget with a modest .6 percent increase in new spending and no new taxes or tax hikes. Against the backdrop of the compromise, however, was the general understanding that the next governor would inherit a structural deficit in the neighborhood of $5 billion.

The Democratic Primary

Despite the declining popularity of Rendell and the horrendous long-term state fiscal picture, a strong field of four Democrats sought their party's nomination: Allegheny County executive, Dan Onorato; state auditor general, Jack Wagner; Montgomery County commissioner, Joe Hoeffel; and state senator, Anthony Williams. At the beginning of the campaign, the perceived front-runner was the Allegheny County executive, Dan Onorato, the candidate tacitly supported by Rendell and who benefitted from the governor's prodigious fundraising team. Additionally, for two years Onorato had worked Democratic power brokers and party leaders for their support. Onorato's case for the nomination lay in what he claimed was his success in rejuvenating the economy of the Greater Pittsburgh area; first in saving his county from bankruptcy and later in economic development and job creation.

Auditor General Wagner, whose office had conducted high-profile audits of state government departments and agencies, relied on his reputation as a fiscal watchdog; he was relentless in arguing for a smaller and reformed state legislature. He also piled up a series of endorsements by 40 of 67 county party organizations, individual party leaders, and local union leaders. A former president of Pittsburgh City Council and state senator, Wagner had been elected twice to his statewide post—his reelection totals in 2008 exceeded President Obama's 10-point victory in the state.[2]

The third candidate, Joe Hoeffel, was one of three Montgomery County commissioners. He endeavored to carve out a niche as the liberal candidate, repeatedly emphasizing his support for abortion, gay rights, and gun control. He attempted to rally Democratic liberals in the Philadelphia suburbs and the Lehigh Valley. Moreover, his advocacy for a graduated state income tax solidified his standing as the liberal in the field. His promotion of liberal causes earned him the endorsements of several women's organizations. A perennial candidate, his name had appeared on ballots 17 times since 1974. Importantly, he had served in the state legislature and Congress, and had unsuccessfully challenged Senator Arlen Specter in 2004.

The final candidate, and a late entrant into the race, state senator Anthony Williams, announced his candidacy in February 2010, months after the other candidates. Williams, a social liberal, billed himself as a different kind of candidate. He contended he was a business-friendly Democrat whose support for the adoption of school choice legislation—permitting parents to use vouchers to send their children to schools of their choosing—made him unique among the Democratic candidates. Williams believed his strong Philadelphia base and the endorsements of important city politicians, including Mayor Michael Nutter and Congressman Bob Brady, who was also the City Democratic Committee chairman, would be decisive.[3]

The candidates differed somewhat in ideology, style, and emphasis. However, they generally reached broad agreement on the state's fiscal plight, a general willingness to contain spending, and a desire to oppose raising the state's income or sales tax. Onorato and Wagner had long been pro-life on abortion—though as the primary progressed they moderated their positions somewhat to appeal to some liberals in the Democratic electorate—and both expressed opposition to stiffer gun control legislation. Hoeffel did emphasize the need to double the spending on infrastructure, however. As they traversed the state, they engaged in a mostly civil campaign—highlighted by some 30 debates and forums. In fact, the first of the relatively few negative commercials did not appear until the very tail end of the May 18 primary campaign.

Public opinion polls had the election close as late as six weeks before the primary, though the candidates remained largely unknown to Democratic voters. The April 7 Quinnipiac University Poll had Onorato, the best known of the Democratic candidates, leading his closest rival, Jack Wagner, by 7 points, but 64 percent of likely Democratic voters did not know enough about Onorato to have an opinion about his candidacy.

Onorato eventually secured the nomination handily, in substantial part because of his superior fundraising—$9 million by the end of April—and a targeted media message about jobs and economic development. His media blitz, which began a month before the primary, proved decisive; he spent $6.7 million on television commercials. The commercials improved his name recognition and on the eve of the balloting, he led the field by 25 points in the RealClearPolitics average of the polls. The only other candidate to raise sufficient resources to run a statewide media campaign was Williams; he raised $6 million during the primary, about 90 percent of which came from a small group of tuition voucher supporters. But his commercials, largely portraying him as a candidate who would "think out of the box," proved ineffective. Pete DeCoursey, Capitolwire bureau chief, estimated that Onorato spent thirty dollars on television advertisements for each twenty-three dollars spent by Williams, compared to one dollar for Hoeffel.[4]

Onorato won decisively in the primary. He earned 45 percent of the slightly more than one million votes cast. His closest competitor, Wagner, trailed with 24 percent while Williams and Hoeffel managed 18 and 13 percent, respectively. Onorato's impressive victory was amplified by his sweep of 62 of 67 counties. He romped almost everywhere, defeating Wagner in their home Allegheny County by a 53 to 37 percent margin. Williams won Philadelphia and Hoeffel won Montgomery County, but Onorato carried Bucks, Chester, and Delaware, denying the southeastern candidates a victory in the voter-rich Philadelphia suburbs. Onorato immediately became the consensus candidate of the party. The relative lack of acrimony in the primary allowed the nominee to move ahead swiftly in full general election mode without much fence mending.

Corbett an Easy Primary Victor

Early in the gubernatorial campaign, the Republican primary appeared likely to be a high-profile, competitive contest, but one that ultimately turned into an easy victory for the state's attorney general,

Tom Corbett. At the outset of the campaign, the field included Pat Meehan, a former U.S. attorney from Eastern Pennsylvania who had successfully prosecuted a number of public corruption cases against Philadelphia politicians, and Jim Gerlach, a congressman representing the Sixth Congressional District. In the end, both withdrew, leaving Corbett to face Sam Rohrer, a little-known conservative state representative from Berks County. Rohrer did have the support of some Tea Party and 9/12 organizations in the state, but with virtually no financing, Corbett's organizational and financial resources overwhelmed Rohrer's campaign. Rohrer was hampered in part because of his votes in 2001 for a controversial pension boost for lawmakers and other elected state officials and employees, and an even more controversial 2005 pay hike for state legislators and other state officials.

Corbett's electoral advantages were substantial. He was endorsed by the state Republican Party and had amassed a sizable war chest. His résumé included a stint as a prosecutor in Allegheny County, and as U.S. attorney in the Western District of Pennsylvania. He was appointed attorney general of Pennsylvania in the aftermath of the 1995 mail fraud conviction of state attorney general Ernie Preate. In 2004, Corbett won election to his own term, and was reelected in 2008 by 380,000 votes—out-polling John McCain in the state by 360,000 votes. In 2008, he had to swim against the strong Democratic tide that produced a 10-point Obama victory in the state; he amazingly carried 15 of the state's 19 congressional districts.

Perhaps the most important element in propelling his gubernatorial candidacy was his indictment of 25 state lawmakers, past lawmakers, and legislative staffers for a variety of public corruption charges stemming from the use of state resources for campaigns purposes. These prosecutions, the largest number by an attorney general in state history, gave Corbett a significant electoral advantage. These prosecutions were not without controversy, however. Some Democratic leaders and several gubernatorial candidates criticized Corbett—calling the prosecutions selective and political, while demanding that he resign his position because his candidacy for governor was inconsistent with his role as a neutral prosecutor. The call for the attorney general to relinquish his post while he continued his gubernatorial candidacy would dog Corbett throughout the campaign, notably in July, when the *Philadelphia Inquirer* joined the critics urging him to step down.

During the course of the primary campaign, Corbett noticeably tacked to the conservative side of ideological spectrum by (a) signing a no-tax-hike pledge, (b) joining 13 other state attorneys general in a federal law suit challenging the constitutionality of the comprehensive health care reform bill passed by Congress in March 2010, (c) arguing for spending and program cuts in the state budget, and (d) railing at federal spending, calling it "an addiction" during a campaign stop in Western Pennsylvania. Additionally, his campaign appearances were replete with calls for tuition vouchers, a ban on public sector strikes, the privatization of the state-owned liquor stores, and a part-time legislature.[5]

The primary election results were a foregone conclusion. Rohrer was overwhelmed at the polls. Corbett won 69 percent of the vote, while Rohrer's 31 percent represented only 269,893 votes out of almost 860, 000 cast in the primary. Consistent with the one-sided nature of the contest, Corbett captured 65 counties, Rohrer but two—his own Berks and neighboring Lancaster. Despite some pleas by Tea Party activists to run a third-party candidate, and the failure of his defeated opponent to endorse him, Corbett moved forward out of the Republican primary with a united party behind him, including many Tea Party adherents.

The Big Battle Looms

The primary was no sooner over than the general election campaign began. The nominees began a sprint to the November election. They traversed the state doing not just multiple events a week, but multiple events almost daily. Much of the campaigning was routine and produced little fanfare until Corbett ignited a political controversy in early July. On July 9, while campaigning in Elizabethtown, the attorney general told public radio reporter Scott Detrow that there were plenty of jobs available, but that extending unemployment benefits kept recipients from accepting jobs until the benefits had expired. Corbett then proceeded to say that some construction company operators had told him that workers were refusing to return to their old positions until the benefits ran out. Democrats immediately accused him of being insensitive to the plight of the jobless, portraying him as out of touch with the problems of hardworking Pennsylvanians.

Immediately, Onorato began a seven-day tour of six cities, asserting that his opponent was "insulting hardworking people." The dust-up was widely reported in the state print and electronic media, and the blogosphere erupted for weeks. Some newspapers editorialized against his statement. Initially, the Corbett campaign was unresponsive—it took several days until Corbett finally apologized, explaining that he was referring only to some—not all—unemployed workers and that his comments were poorly worded. He also gave a qualified endorsement to the temporary extensions of unemployment benefits then before Congress; his qualification was based on paying for the benefit extension out of the unspent federal stimulus monies.[6]

At the start of the general election campaign, Corbett maintained a solid 8- to 10-point lead in the public polls, and Onorato began the fall campaign a clear underdog. Corbett maintained that lead, and not a single public poll throughout the campaign reported Onorato leading. Onorato also faced the daunting task of attempting to follow an unpopular Democratic governor. Ed Rendell's job performance had dropped to the mid-30s during much of the year, and the governor's constant call to raise taxes to balance the state's budget was decidedly unpopular. Corbett, sensing the importance of the issue, used his personal appearances and TV ads in an attempt to tie Onorato to Rendell. He also regularly argued that Onorato exaggerated his claims that he created jobs, reduced unemployment, and enhanced the business climate in Allegheny County. Corbett also made people aware that Onorato instituted a large tax on liquor and backtracked on a pledge to lower property taxes. In turn, Onorato portrayed the attorney general as unprepared to govern the state, lacking the expertise and executive experience to handle the governorship. He also hit Corbett on the unemployment misstep and argued that he switched positions by considering raising fees and unemployment contributions—thereby violating his tax pledge.[7]

Despite the wrangling on qualification, the issues differences between the candidates remained somewhat small on the most important issues to voters—taxes and the fiscal situation of the state. Both candidates promised not to raise sales, income, or other direct taxes, and they agreed to reduce and eliminate various business taxes in the state. Because of the fiscal plight of the state, both candidates pledged fiscal restraint and promised budget and program cuts. They agreed on the value of early childhood education, supported the death penalty, committed themselves to legislative reform, opposed gay marriage and the legalization of medical marijuana, and supported a limited constitutional convention. They disagreed on a few issues, however: the taxing of natural gas from the Marcellus Shale formation; the national health care law; changes to the state law that allowed the use of deadly force outside of the home and required gun owners to report lost or stolen guns; and certain adoptions to the state's abortion law. But unlike most past gubernatorial elections, social and cultural issues were relatively unimportant in the outcome of the election.

The three gubernatorial debates produced no headline or game-changing moments. As the candidates crisscrossed the state throughout the fall, Corbett stuck to a front-runner approach. He appeared at mostly controlled events, limited press availabilities, and largely talked in generalities. Still, he made it clear that deep cuts would occur, including a 10 percent reduction in the funding of state agencies. For his part, Onorato stressed his executive experience and job creation credentials while attempting to portray Corbett's lack of executive appearance as a liability.

The ad wars began in late summer and both candidates had more than sufficient resources to flood the airwaves with commercials. Corbett spent $24 million and Onorato $20 million during the course of the entire campaign, but Onorato's more expensive primary $10 million to only $4 million spent by Corbett left him in the final weeks of the campaign at a disadvantage. In the waning two weeks of the race, Corbett had a $10 million to $3.7 million advantage with on-hand cash, giving him a much stronger media presence as the election came to a close.[8]

The Final Results

Corbett had maintained a substantial lead in the polls throughout the fall, at times extending into double digits, except for one brief period toward the end of the campaign when the race tightened. The outcome was neither unexpected nor controversial. The attorney general easily defeated his opponent by 9 percent: 54 percent to 46 percent, or by about 350,000 votes. Corbett's victory was impressive; he won 63 of 67 counties, losing only three counties in the

Southeast—Philadelphia, Montgomery, Delaware—and Lackawanna in the Northeast. Onorato did not win a single county west of the Susquehanna River. And for bragging rights, Corbett narrowly edged out Onorato in Allegheny, their home county. Corbett's victory was even more impressive when considering how well he did among a range of demographics. He won males 59 to 41 percent, white voters 61 to 39 percent, those 65 and older 63 to 37 percent, all income groups earning over $30,000 per year, and all education levels from high school graduates through postgraduate studies.[9]

Conclusion

In the end, Corbett's advantages were just too overwhelming. Just as important, he ran against a candidate who never found a break-through moment, who did not find an issue that moved voters either for him or against his opponent, and who could not shake the unpopularity of his predecessor. Pennsylvania's vaunted tradition of changing political control of the governorship every eight years since 1954 continues without interruption.

THE U.S. SENATE RACE
Specter Changes his Party

On April 28, 2009, Senator Arlen Specter stunned Pennsylvanians and his U.S. Senate colleagues by abruptly announcing he was changing political parties. He began his public career in 1964 as a top staff lawyer on the Warren Commission, investigating the assassination of John F. Kennedy. While in service on the commission he helped frame the single-bullet theory that argued a single shooter assassinated Kennedy. Specter returned to his law practice in Philadelphia and was elected district attorney in 1965, switching his party affiliation to Republican. He was reelected in 1969 and defeated in 1973. His taste for public office was merely wetted by his foray into local politics; he ran for senator in 1976 and governor in 1978, but could not survive the primaries. In 1980, the indefatigable Specter ran for the U.S. Senate a second time and eked out a narrow primary victory. Then, aided by Reagan's first presidential election victory, he defeated his Democratic opponent by 2 percentage points.

His Senate career has had a noticeable tendency towards independence and moderation but more often he supported his own party's initiatives. He voted for the Reagan and Bush tax cuts, the Iraq War, tough crime fighting measures, and he supported his presidents' nominees to the Supreme Court, with one major exception. The one exception, his strong and effective opposition to Robert Bork in 1987, was condemned by conservatives. Reversing course in 1991, he provided the impetus for the confirmation of Clarence Thomas with his forceful interrogation of Thomas detractor Anita Hill. However, his patronizing treatment of Hill sparked outrage in the state among feminist groups and Democrats, resulting in the closest general election of his Senate career—his narrow 1992 defeat of women's rights activist, Lynn Yeakel. Specter's second political scare came when he narrowly survived his 2004 primary, defeating Pat Toomey by a scant 17,000 votes out of more than a million. And Toomey was back in 2010.

Specter's vote for the $782.2 billion stimulus package in February 2009, as only one of three Republican members of Congress to do so, created a firestorm among Pennsylvania Republicans. The furor among Republicans did not abate after March 24, when he announced his opposition to the Employee Free Choice Act, despite having been one of its original cosponsors. For several weeks prior to April 28, he publicly denied he would switch parties, though he held out "an abstract possibility" he might run as an independent. Specter was also encouraged to jump parties by leading Democrats—Rendell, Vice President Joe Biden, and Senator Bob Casey. Ultimately, his party switch was motivated almost solely by the haunting fear than he would be denied renomination. Serious health problems—including bouts with a brain tumor and Hodgkin's lymphoma—and his advanced age, 79, emerged as potential difficulties for the incumbent.[10]

The Republican contest had two candidates before Specter announced his party change. The first to announce was Johnston resident, Peg Luksik. She had sought the governorship three times, once as a Republican and twice as a third-party candidate. Mostly known for her opposition to abortion, she expressed vehement opposition to Specter's support of the stimulus package. She would provide minimal opposition to Toomey's candidacy, who declared on April 17. Toomey had served three terms in Congress representing the Lehigh Valley Fifteenth Congressional District before he challenged Specter in the 2004 Republican primary. After his graduation from Harvard, he became a Wall Street trader, working first for Chemical Bank in 1984, and then joining Morgan, Grenfell & Co. in 1986. Throughout his Wall Street career he engaged in interest and currency swaps and sold derivatives, an aspect of his career that would later become a staple of his general election opponent's campaign. In 1991, he moved to Allentown, Pennsylvania where he opened Rookies, a sports bar, before his successful congressional candidacy in 1998. Following his defeat by Specter in 2004, he became president of the Club for Growth, a pro-business, low-tax, free market organization. Though pro-life on abortion, he spent his congressional career and his time with the Club for Growth arguing for low tax policies and limited government regulation.

Specter's greatest concern was his opponent. Some public polls that matched Toomey against Specter had the former Lehigh Valley congressman leading, and Toomey came into the contest swinging. He rapped the Senator for "increased government spending ... in favor of the unprecedented Wall Street spending, and 'massive stimulus spending.'" [11]

Sestak Emerges

Even before Specter's party switch, the Democratic primary was unsettled. After briefly considering a run for the seat, Chris Matthews, host of MSNBC's *Hardball with Chris Matthews*, opted to renew his cable television contract. Additionally, state representative Josh Shapiro and Joe Torsella, chair of the State Board of Education and a close friend of Rendell's, had considered running, but neither joined the contest. That left only Joe Sestak, the Seventh District congressman, as the other Democrat to file for the Senate seat. In 2006, the ambitious Sestak had defeated Republican incumbent Curt Weldon, 56 to 44 percent, in the district located mostly in Delaware County, a close suburb of Philadelphia. A 31-year veteran of the U.S. Navy, Sestak achieved the rank of admiral before a questionable 2005 naval reassignment. His credentials also included service in the Clinton White House as director for defense policy on the National Security Council. After the terrorist attacks on September 11, he became the first director of the Naval

Operations Group. Between his various naval assignments he earned an MPA and a Ph. D. from Harvard University.

For most of his short congressional tenure, Sestak can best be described as moderate in his voting proclivities. His *National Journal* voting rating before 2009 showed Sestak as a centrist—with liberal scores before the Obama presidency mostly in the 60 percent range and conservative ones in the 30 percent range. However, he has shown himself to be a consistent advocate of Obama's ambitious agenda: He supported the stimulus bill, cap and trade, health care, the auto manufacturing bailout, the financial regulatory overhaul, the Afghanistan troop surge, a comprehensive immigration proposal, and the Employee Free Choice Act.

Sestak had emerged as the likely nominee before Specter's party switch. Sestak had been recruited by Senator Robert Menendez, chair of the Democratic Senatorial Campaign Committee (DSCC). But everything changed on that fateful April day. Almost immediately, the Democratic establishment rallied behind Specter, who received the endorsement of President Obama, Vice President Biden, Rendell, and Casey. Specter easily obtained the endorsement of the Democratic State Party and most of the county party organizations joined the Specter campaign.

However, Sestak was undaunted by the coalescing of Democratic leaders and many of the state's most powerful unions around Specter. He had visited all 67 counties in the state before his formal announcement, and he made it clear that he would not shrink from the contest. For much of the campaign, Sestak was the underdog. His attacks on Specter focused on two fundamental points: The senator was not really a Democrat, based on his record of voting for Republican polices, and his party switch was about nothing more than the senator's political survival. As the primary progressed, Sestak became more the populist by inveighing against the Washington establishment, arguing that Washington was broken, while curiously not mentioning the fact that his party controlled the presidency and Congress. He also began articulating policies promoting the growth of small business and the middle class—which became the hallmark of his campaign rhetoric.

In February, a question by a Philadelphia television host ignited a debate that would last for months. During an interview on *Voice of Reason*, a Comcast cable show hosted by Larry Kane, Sestak admitted he had been offered a high-ranking position the previous July by the Obama administration, if he would withdraw from the Senate race. State and national Republican leaders called for a congressional inquiry and an investigation by a special prosecutor appointed by the attorney general, suggesting that a federal law might have been violated. Sestak refused to provide substantive details, but the controversy continued to swirl around his campaign.[12] Specter maintained a substantial lead over the lesser-known Sestak for much of the primary campaign, despite very weak performance polling numbers himself. Only about one-quarter of the state's voters indicated that Specter deserved reelection. Among registered Democrats, he consistently held a double-digit lead among Democratic voters—a lead he maintained until Sestak began his television advertisements a month before the primary.

By the May primary, the senator was only viewed favorably by 41 percent of the state's voters, with 47 percent holding an unfavorable view of him. More problematic was that a low number of voters gave him a positive job performance—only 5 percent said he was doing an "excellent" job, while 29 percent said he was doing a "poor job." His overall performance was rated 32 percent positive, 62 percent negative.[13]

The campaign was joined in April, when the major points of contention between the two candidates were aired in television commercials. Specter unleashed an ad on April 21 asserting that Sestak had been relieved of his naval command for a "poor command climate," a charge the congressman's campaign strongly refuted, in part by Sestak's former superior, Admiral Vernon Clark. Clark said that he had given Sestak the charge to propose naval cutbacks, which drew the ire of naval brass. The second charge dealt with missed congressional votes. By Specter's count, Sestak missed 127 of them in 2009, which the congressman did not deny. Sestak countered with the point that he had missed the votes because he had chosen to visit all of the state's 67 counties and to remain by his dying father's side.[14]

But it was Sestak's commercials that provided the biggest boost to his campaign. His campaign unleashed a media blitz during the last four weeks of the campaign, spending $1 million a week on television ads. Without doubt, the most effective and devastating commercial began airing 12 days before the election. It linked Specter to former president Bush and Sarah Palin, and used Specter's own words—that he had switched parties to get reelected.

A Stunning Defeat

The results of the primary stunned Pennsylvanians. Some were shocked that Specter lost, but even more so because of the overwhelming nature of Sestak's victory. The 8-point victory, 54 percent to 46 percent, was impressive, but more surprising because he carried 64 of 67 counties, leaving Specter with victories in his home base of Philadelphia, Lackawanna, and Dauphin counties. The defeated senator did not carry a single county west of the Susquehanna River; he also lost the four suburban Philadelphia counties and the Democratic ones in the Southwest, including Allegheny (Pittsburgh), the second-largest Democratic county in the state.

In the end, Specter was defeated by a confluence of factors. The paltry 22 percent of Democrats that voted consisted primarily of very partisan, loyal Democrats who refused to accept Specter's party change. The moderate Specter was also trapped in the growing polarization that gripped the state. His five terms additionally weighed him down in an increasingly anti-incumbent environment. Finally, his age and health problems contrasted unfavorably to his younger and more vigorous opponent. The latter point became more conspicuous when, during the annual Democratic Jefferson-Jackson Dinner in Allegheny County on May 12, he not once, but twice, thanked the Republican committee folks there for their support.[15]

The Fall Campaign

Toomey and Sestak had appeared at two pre-primary forums and had struck a note of congeniality; they had pledged a campaign of ideas and collegiality. Any notion that the campaign would be devoid of rancor did not last long. The fall campaign, replete with millions spent on television commercials, soon turned into a brutal ad war that played out the national themes. The campaign became a referendum on two narratives. Toomey and his supporters relentlessly attacked Sestak for his "liberalism," meaning his support for the Obama agenda, its spending, and the government regulation that accompanied it.

Toomey reiterated these themes repeatedly and seldom wandered off message—always with the premise that Sestak's congressional votes had hurt economic growth, wreaked havoc on free enterprise, and threatened the long-term viability of the economy. Sestak, in turn, went after Toomey's Wall Street connections, his past activities selling derivatives, his support for changes in Social Security, and the year he spent in Hong Kong working for a Chinese businessman. The lesson for voters was that Toomey supported the interests of Wall Street over the middle class, and that his past congressional votes on trade measures gave evidence that he had deserted American workers in favor of shipping jobs overseas. The ad wars—about $22 million spent on behalf of Toomey and $16 million for Sestak—that accompanied these arguments flooded the airwaves in record spending by third-party interests, party committees, and the candidates. [16]

An estimated $50 million was spent in the Senate race, with Toomey having a $6 million advantage. According to the Center for Responsive Politics, $25 million poured into the race by the party committees and third-party interests, $13.5 million on behalf of Sestak and $12.2 million for Toomey.[17]

The Tight Finish

Sestak surged in the polls by mid-October. Toomey had held a consistent lead outside of the margins of the public polls but Sestak's effective ads, continuing the assault on Toomey's past private-sector employment and congressional record caused the race to narrow. By mid-October the contest became a nail-biter and only several points separated the two. Throughout the year, public polls showed an enthusiasm gap that worked in the Republican Party's favor. Democratic voters indicated they were much less likely to vote, by 8 to 12 points.

Democrats realized their only prospect for victory was to encourage turnout in their main urban stronghold, Philadelphia. Leading national Democrats made repeated visits to the state, headlined by President Obama, Vice President Biden, and former president Clinton. Additionally, the Democratic Party and the unions put millions into get-out-the-vote efforts. But in the end, the national wave was too much to overcome. Sestak fell just short of victory.

The Vote

Toomey eked out a narrow, hard-earned 51 percent to 49 percent triumph, accompanied by a 60-county sweep. Not surprisingly, he lost Philadelphia, Allegheny, and Sestak's home county, Delaware. But he did win two suburban counties, Bucks and Chester, and his old congressional district in the Lehigh Valley. As expected from the results of the preelection polls, Toomey won male voters 56 percent to 44 percent, whites 57 percent to 43 percent, seniors 59 percent to 41 percent, those earning more than $50,000 55 percent to 45 percent, Republicans 92 percent to 8 percent, and importantly, independent voters 55 percent to 45 percent. Sestak easily won female voters 54 percent 46 percent, blacks 93 percent to 7 percent, young voters 61 to 39 percent, those earning less than $50,000 55 percent to 45 percent, and Democrats 90 percent to 10 percent.[18]

Pat Toomey joins Democrat Bob Casey in the Senate, but Toomey is not likely to join Casey in many important votes in the 112th Congress. Casey has been a firm supporter of President Obama's agenda, but Toomey has pledged to be cooperative and seek compromise. Only time will reveal the full implication of the Toomey victory for both the state and the nation.

Endnotes

[1]The May 2010, Franklin & Marshall College Poll found Governor Rendell's popularity at 41% favorable and 47% unfavorable.

[2]Pete DeCoursey, Capitolwire.com, May 16, 2010.

[3]James O'Toole, *Pittsburgh-Post Gazette*, April, 29, 2010.

[4]The final Muhlenberg tracking poll completed on May 15 gave Onorato a 24-point lead over closest opponent Williams, Capitolwire.com, May 16, 2010.

[5]Pete DeCoursey, Capitolwire.com, March 8, 2010.

[6]Amy Worden and Angela Couloumbis, "Pennsylvania gubernatorial candidate Corbett dogged by jobless comments," *Philadelphia Inquirer*, July 20, 2010; Chris Brennan, "Onorato using his jab Ripping Corbett for comments on joblessness," *Philadelphia Daily News*, July 15, 2010; Peter Jackson, "Onorato favors work search mandate for Pa jobless," Associated Press, July 14, 2010.

[7]Complete polling results in the governor's race can be found at www.real clearpolitics.com.

[8]Laura Olson, Capitolwire, September 22, 2010, December, 3, 2010; Associated Press, Harrisburg Bureau, December 3, 2010.

[9]Complete election results are available from the Pennsylvania Department of State and the Pennsylvania exit poll at abcnews.go.com/politics/2010 _elections/pennsylvania?ep=gov_pa.

[10]Josh Drobnyk, Los Angeles Times, March 19, 2009; Laura Vecsey, Harrisburg Patriot News, March 24, 2009.

[11]Mike Faher, Tribune Democrat, March 19, 2009; Pete DeCoursey, Capitolwire, April 17, 2009.

[12]Eric Boehm, Pennsylvania Independent, May 20, 2010.

[13]Pre-primary polling results can be found in the May 2010, Franklin & Marshall College Poll at politics.fandm.edu and the results of the public polls are contained on the RealClearPolitics website.

[14]Marc Levy, "Specter undone by missteps, long history in GOP," Associated Press, Harrisburg Bureau, May 23, 2010.

[15]Jonathan Martin, Politico, May 12, 2010.

[16]Thomas Fitzgerald, "Toomey appears ahead, Sestak not far back," Philadelphia Inquirer, November 1, 2010.

[17]Thomas Fitzgerald, Jeff Gammage, and Mari Schaefer, "Toomey Beats Sestak," Philadelphia Inquirer, November, 3, 2010; Marc Levy, "Pa. Senate race becomes big draw for outside money," Associated Press, Harrisburg Bureau October, 29, 2010.

[18]abcnews.go.com/politics/2010_elections/Pennsylvania?ep=sen_pa.

Chapter 26

2010 Rhode Island Governor's Race

by Steve Peoples

National Political Reporter for Roll Call;
Formerly, Political Reporter for the Providence Journal

In a year of historic gains for the GOP, Rhode Island voters wrote a different story for the history books in 2010. It was a man who had abandoned the Republican Party—a candidate widely considered the most liberal in a four-way gubernatorial contest, a former U.S. senator who believes Sarah Palin is a "cocky whacko," and an early supporter of President Obama—who claimed the Ocean State's top elected post on November 2.

In doing so, Governor-elect Lincoln D. Chafee will become the first independent to occupy the governor's office in state history. And he will hold the unwelcome distinction of having done so with the lowest level of support on record.

Though he was well known, well liked, and well financed, Chafee won with just 36.1 percent of the vote in a contest in which less than half of registered voters participated. The secretary of state's office confirmed that the previous record low for a successful gubernatorial candidate had been set more than 135 years earlier.

Ultimately, there is little doubt that Chafee benefited from the dynamics of an unusual and crowded field coupled with the implosion of Democrat Frank T. Caprio. In a year dominated by conservatives across the nation, the liberal Chafee also showed remarkable resilience, surviving repeated and well-funded attacks from the right and left, a late charge from Republican John Robitaille, the abrupt resignation of his campaign manager, and a plan to raise taxes curiously released the day he declared his candidacy.

Rhode Island's 2010 gubernatorial contest may also be remembered as the race of the scion. The fate of these men could have been determined more by their fathers than by their own merits, or the quality of the races they ran.

Both Chafee and Caprio hail from families whose names carry considerable weight in a state where who you know matters almost as much as who you are.

Caprio is the son of a municipal court judge who is also a local television star and leader of the board that controls the state's public college and university system. Allegations that Caprio's father used that influence to secure jobs for friends surfaced a month before Election Day. It was soon thereafter that Caprio made a decision that will long haunt Rhode Island politics. Facing news that President Obama would not endorse him, Caprio told the president to take his endorsement and "shove it."

Governor-elect Chafee is the son of an Ocean State political legend. The Republican John H. Chafee represented Rhode Island in the U.S. Senate for nearly 23 years, having previously won two terms as governor.

The younger Chafee followed his father to the U.S. Senate, having been elevated from Warwick mayor to U.S. senator after his father's untimely death in 1999. Just four years ago, Rhode Island ousted the popular Republican from his Senate seat in favor of a Democrat. The upset reflected the political climate at the time and the growing outrage toward President Bush and the GOP.

It was a very different political climate in 2010 that allowed the son to again follow the father into history, this time as Rhode Island's 74th governor. It was not an easy road.

The Campaigns Start

Chafee unofficially launched his campaign in a crumbling brick building dotted with donated office furniture in an industrial corner of Pawtucket. Visitors were warned of unusual odors, and the tiny staff was largely volunteers.

Such was the spring of 2010 for an independent gubernatorial candidate who struggled to raise money in a state mired in recession. Rhode Island's unemployment rate was among the worst in the nation, peaking at 13.4 percent in January. While it was no secret that he had access to a personal fortune, it was also no secret that Chafee was loathe to dip into his family's pocket to fund his political ambitions.

The political landscape was far from settled that spring. While the Tea Party movement forced battles among Republicans elsewhere, the showdown in the Rhode Island governor's race was within the Democratic Party, where two heavyweights—Caprio and Attorney General Patrick Lynch—were in the midst of a bitter primary. Moderate Party founder Kenneth Block had secured his fledgling party's nomination, but it was largely assumed he was simply after the 5 percent needed to keep the Moderates on the ballot in 2012.

Even in the spring, months before Lynch would drop out, many believed that Caprio was the man to beat. In an election year where the economy was the number one issue, here was a business-friendly Democrat who majored in economics at Harvard and spent nearly four years guarding the state's finances as the general treasurer.

A few miles from Chafee's dilapidated headquarters, a young and excited Caprio staff buzzed about in a modern office in the heart of the capital city's bustling Federal Hill neighborhood. Months before his opponents, Caprio's fundraising machine was clicking on all cylinders. He reported $1.6 million in his campaign account at the end of March. Chafee had less than $400,000 at that time, though he would ultimately depend heavily from his family fortune, loaning his campaign $1.6 million by the end of the contest. The Republican Robitaille, a top communications aide for the term-limited Governor Donald Carcieri, reported just $87,000.

While he nearly played spoiler in November, Robitaille was largely considered an afterthought for much of the campaign—not because of his party affiliation, but because he simply was not a strong candidate. If known at all to Rhode Island voters, it was for his brief role as an aide to an unpopular governor. Robitaille would depend on public financing since he had little personal wealth to jump-start a candidacy that surprised even Carcieri. He had failed in his only previous run for office: a 2008 bid for state representative.

In many ways, Robitaille was the only true conservative—fiscally and socially—in a cycle that offered such candidates across the country a favorable outlook. Caprio positioned himself as a conservative Democrat, pledging to cut pension benefits to the displeasure of the state's powerful public employee unions. Chafee's fiscal policy was by far the most liberal. He suggested only minor pension changes and favored plans to raise sales taxes, evidenced by the endorsement of the massive teachers union, the National Education Association.

But the national climate, and the state's electoral history, offered the Republican some hope.

While Rhode Island is universally recognized as being deep blue, the GOP has occupied the governor's office for 16 of the last 20 years. With strong Portuguese and Italian populations, the state is among the most Catholic in the nation and therefore relatively moderate on social issues. The most popular voter registration designation is not Democratic.

Nearly 49 percent of 700,000 registered voters were not formally affiliated with any party, according to data reported by the secretary of state's office in August; 41 percent were Democrats, and just 10 percent were Republicans.

"There has never been a better opportunity for the Republican Party," Robitaille told supporters on the July night he won his party's endorsement. Perhaps that is why Caprio wanted Robitaille out of the race.

The Final Months

It was the second Thursday in September when the news broke.

Caprio had visited the Republican National Committee's Washington headquarters in the early spring. While the reason was never clear—opponents suggested it was to discuss switching parties, while the Democrat insisted it was simply to meet with a staffer with Rhode Island roots—Caprio knew the numbers did not add up.

"You didn't have to be Nostradamus to figure this out," state Republican Party chairman Giovanni Cicione reflected after the election. "Linc had the good sense to run to the left. That left a three-way race with two candidates running on the same message. How could that work?"

Cicione continued, "I think [Caprio] had a chance if he ran as a Republican, which is why he was down there talking to the RNC in February. We all knew that he could be governor if he ran as a Republican."

Later that same Thursday, Robitaille added to the drama. He told the *Providence Journal* that a Caprio intermediary had offered him "anything, anything you want to get out of this race." Robitaille reported that several "former movers-and-shakers on the political landscape" had approached him, on Caprio's behalf, in the previous five to six weeks. He also confirmed a face-to-face meeting with Caprio roughly three weeks earlier, in which the Democrat gently encouraged him to step aside.

Chafee, whose party allegiance had long been a topic of conversation, was largely silent as he watched the squabbling. The former Republican senator had walked away from the GOP three years earlier, quietly changing his voter registration status after losing a 2006 Senate reelection bid. After adopting the independent label, he was among the first prominent Rhode Islanders to back a long-shot presidential candidate named Barack Obama.

Even though he was known for veering from the script, Chafee avoided major missteps in the campaign's final months. Voters slowly warmed to his plan to help close chronic budget gaps with a 1 percent tax on exempt items such as groceries, and the "Trust Chafee" movement took hold.

He sidestepped a potential disaster in mid-October, when campaign manager J. R. Pagliarini acknowledged receiving unemployment benefits while on the Chafee payroll. Pagliarini resigned as soon as the news broke. Voters were quickly reminded of allegations that Caprio's father had used his influence in the state's higher education system to arrange jobs for friends. Pagliarini said that the elder Caprio had even offered him a job.

While Caprio's internal numbers suggested trouble earlier, he was statistically tied or ahead in every public poll from the beginning of August through mid-October. That changed on October 21. A Rasmussen Reports poll showed Chafee leading by 7 points. Two more polls released in subsequent days suggested similar, or larger margins.

Things were unraveling quickly. With the election less than two weeks away, it may have been too late to right the ship. But the Caprio campaign saw an opportunity when President Obama came to town.

The Last Push

Air Force One touched down in Rhode Island eight days before the election. A story on the front page of the state's largest newspaper that day proclaimed that the president would not endorse anyone in Rhode Island's governor's race. He was in town simply to raise money for First Congressional District Democratic candidate David Cicilline and the Democratic Congressional Campaign Committee.

Obama had stumped for gubernatorial candidates elsewhere, but he would not help Caprio directly. White House spokesman Bill Burton offered this explanation: "As it relates to the local politics, out of respect for his friend, Lincoln Chafee, the President decided not to get involved in this race."

Thus, Caprio was speaking to a local talk-radio host on the morning of Obama's arrival when he fired a shot that will long be remembered. "He can take his endorsement and really shove it as far as I'm concerned," Caprio said on the live broadcast.

Later in the day, he dismissed the advice of Democratic representative Patrick Kennedy and repeated the remark for the television cameras at the Warwick Mall. The angry comment went national and dominated the local news cycle for days.

There is little doubt that it was a calculated political move by a candidate who was already slipping in the polls. He may have had few other options. Caprio painted himself as a conservative, but chose not to switch parties. He could not convince the Republican Robitaille to leave the race. So, he did something he hoped would bring Republicans to him. He fired an on-air insult at a Democratic president who had won the Ocean State by 21 points in the 2008 election and enjoyed a 56 percent approval rating into late October. Ironically, as angry conservatives lashed out at the president across the country, Rhode Island will be remembered for the fiery comments of a lifelong Democrat. It would prove to be the death blow in a campaign that was already slipping.

"He basically told more members of the Democratic base to go with Chafee. I think if you're a minority in Rhode Island, he told you to run to Chafee," said Gene Ulm, a partner with the national Republican consulting firm Public Opinion Strategies. "Also, he stepped over the line. I think he was fine in saying, 'Look, I'm the independent man.' But he said 'shove it' once on the radio and then re-taped it again for the cameras."

Polling supports Ulm's analysis. Three days after the insult, 36 percent of respondents said they were less likely to vote for Caprio because of the remark, according to an NBC 10-Quest Research survey. Just 7 percent said they were more likely to vote for Caprio. By election night, the outcome was already a foregone conclusion.

Having been a force in virtually every public poll for the entire cycle, Caprio finished a distant third, earning just 23 percent of the vote. Robitaille shocked local observers by making it a contest, falling just 9,000 votes short with almost 34 percent. The Moderate Block earned a meaningful 6 percent, having polled significantly lower for much of the cycle.

That left Chafee to claim Rhode Island's top elected post with just 36 percent of the vote, the lowest level on record. In doing so, the soft-spoken, career politician rode a wave of his own making to the governor's office, becoming perhaps the most successful liberal in a 2010 cycle dominated by conservatives.

"Rhode Island is making history tonight," a smiling Chafee told jubilant supporters in his victory speech. "This is a special place we live in."

Chapter 27

South Carolina's Governor's Race

by John O'Connor
Political Columnist at The State *Newspaper*

The results in South Carolina's 2010 gubernatorial race followed past patterns—a long-shot candidate defeats well-established favorites—but Nikki Haley's capture of the governor's mansion was anything but typical.

Haley, a Republican state representative from Lexington County, had little money, a small, inexperienced campaign staff, and a daunting primary field. She also had to contend with the political fallout of South Carolina governor Mark Sanford's June 2009 admission of an extramarital affair, which cost her a potent fundraiser and political ally, and gave opponents the opportunity to connect her with Sanford, her tarnished political mentor.

But Haley was a talented, disciplined candidate who benefitted from a network of Tea Party activists who were influencing the national and South Carolina debates. Haley got an early endorsement from Jenny Sanford, who was the state's first lady at the time, and a well-timed second bump from former Alaska governor Sarah Palin. Trey Walker, campaign manager for Attorney General Henry McMaster, said their polling showed exactly when McMaster, the one-time front-runner for the Republican nomination for governor, was passed by Haley: May 18.

The poll tracked a three-week period in May, during which Haley's support jumped 20 percentage points, moving her to first place from fourth. Haley never looked back—despite unproven allegations of adultery—on her way to the Republican nomination in the four-way primary between Haley, McMaster, U.S. representative Gresham Barrett, and Lt. Gov. Andre Bauer. "That's when we knew there wasn't anything we could do," Walker said. "We were two ships passing in the night." Haley's win continued a Palmetto State habit of choosing newcomers over experience.

The Playing Field

Sanford, limited to two terms in office, was expected to be a dominant influence on the 2010 race to succeed him. Sanford had run for governor promising to root out the "good ol' boys" who controlled much of South Carolina's state government through the legislature. He fostered a contentious relationship with lawmakers—best evidenced when he brought two piglets into the State House in 2004 to protest a pork-laden state budget.

Sanford's tearful admission of an extramarital affair fundamentally changed the race, as a governor who enjoyed 70 and 80 percent approval ratings dipped well below 50 percent.

No other politician in the state had Sanford's fundraising clout; he was sitting on more than $1.5 million in his campaign fund. But after Sanford admitted to an extramarital affair following an exposed five-day tryst in Argentina, Haley could not afford to associate with the man who had helped persuade her to run for chief executive.

Haley had the advantage of support from the Tea Party, whose activists got behind her early on to support her bill requiring legislative roll call votes.

On the Democratic side, five candidates entered the race before state senator Vincent Sheheen's fundraising muscle and experienced campaign team squeezed out two candidates, including a high-powered Columbia lobbyist. Sheheen had the appearance of the nominee early in the primary.

The Republicans

The Republican primary featured two candidates, Attorney General Henry McMaster and Lt. Governor Andre Bauer, who had won statewide races and were well known to voters. Two other candidates,

U.S. representative Gresham Barrett and state representative Nikki Haley, were less known, but Barrett could tap his D.C. contacts, while Haley could tap some of Sanford's supporters.

As with past South Carolina elections—and coupled with an unusual year of voter unrest across the country—the newcomers had the advantage. In 2002, little-known Sanford defeated the attorney general and lieutenant governor to take the Republican nomination. In 2004, Jim DeMint surprised many by besting former governor David Beasley for the U.S. Senate nomination.

Walker, McMaster's campaign manager, said they had viewed the GOP race as a Cold War standoff between superpowers McMaster and Barrett, misreading the political insurgency that Haley had tapped into.

Tim Pearson, Haley's campaign manager, said they believed they could win the primary if they were outspent 2 to 1, but worried if opponents banked a larger margin. Haley struggled to raise money throughout the primary with just over $800,000—the least of any Republican candidate. Barrett, by contrast, spent more than $2.4 million. Barrett still raised more money than Haley during the two weeks prior to the runoff.

None of it mattered. With natural political skills, well-timed endorsements, and a caustic series of accusations that galvanized her support, Haley did not need the money or professional political network of her opponents to win the primary.

How Haley Won

Even though Haley was a candidate with undeniable charisma and political skills, it still took a confluence of endorsements, adulterous accusations, and one racial slur to cement her overwhelming GOP primary victory.

After losing Sanford as an ally and fundraiser, Haley's campaign found it far more difficult to raise money than they expected. Occasionally, Haley's campaign manager, Tim Pearson, said that events barely yielded enough money to pay for the gas to get there. However, they gave the little-known Haley a chance to meet voters face to face. "It had been clear in smaller audiences. She had a good message," one-time rival McMaster said. "The candidate herself was the key."

She needed a little help from her friends as well, with the first assist arriving in a November endorsement from the first lady, Jenny Sanford. Pearson said the campaign had only raised $147,000 the previous quarter and even the campaign doubted her viability. "The Charleston money crowd, who had no dog in the fight, started to come our way," Pearson said.

Haley got an assist from ReformSC, a third-party group founded to advertise Sanford's government reform agenda. The group—tapping money mostly raised from Sanford donors—spent $400,000 on statewide television ads featuring Haley at an April State House Tea Party rally.

Haley was gaining some steam, but Sarah Palin took her national. The Haley campaign was in Charleston, preparing for campaign stops with Jenny Sanford, when Todd Palin called. Palin said his wife, the former GOP vice-presidential nominee, would be in Charlotte the next day for a National Rifle Association (NRA) meeting. She wanted to come to South Carolina to endorse Haley. The Haley campaign, and friends such as RedState.com's Erick Erickson, had been trying for months to land a Palin endorsement.

"It came at such an important time when people wanted to see credibility," Haley said, "When they saw the momentum but wanted to feel more." Even so, the true audience was the national and local media, bumping Haley to near-universal name recognition.

Prior to the Palin rally, Walker said the McMaster campaign's media monitoring showed that McMaster was getting about 100 mentions a month on television news—the most of any campaign. The week of the Palin announcement, he said, Haley jumped to about 300 mentions on television news.

Haley was already dominating media coverage when political blogger Will Folks posted a story on his website—just 15 days from the primary—claiming an "inappropriate physical relationship" with Haley, the married mother of two. The bombshell shut down the Haley campaign for more than a week, as Folks released late-night phone records and text messages trying to prove his claim, and Haley denied an affair. Rival campaigns were ignored. They risked a political minefield if they did weigh in on the story.

A week later, Folks's claim was followed by two more thunderbolts. First, Columbia lobbyist and Bauer advisor Larry Marchant claimed a one-night stand with Haley at a 2008 Utah school choice conference. Then, the Thursday before the election, state senator Jake Knotts called Haley—and President Barack Obama— "ragheads" on an Internet political show.

Knotts, who resembles the Boss Hogg character on the popular 1980s TV show, *The Dukes of Hazzard*, was the perfect foil to crystallize Haley's stump speech pitch—she was the candidate that the Columbia "good ol' boys" feared.

Barrett's campaign manager, Luke Byars, said their polling showed Haley's numbers falling, but rose again after Knotts's comments. Haley nearly won the primary outright, giving Barrett no chance to chase her down in the runoff two weeks later.

"None of it would have mattered if she wasn't as good a candidate as she is," Pearson said, adding what Haley's opponents also admitted: They could not build any momentum. "If any of [her opponents] had taken off, this wouldn't have happened."

The Democrats

The Democrats entered the cycle holding just one of nine statewide elected offices—Superintendent of Education Jim Rex—and seeking their first gubernatorial win since 1998. Most expected Rex would run, as well as one state lawmaker from a group of young friends— who turned out to be Camden state senator Vincent Sheheen. Charleston state senator Robert Ford also entered the race early, the only black candidate, pushing a left-field mix of expanded gambling and vouchers for private school tuition, all while accusing the Democratic establishment of blackballing him with donors.

Sheheen acted the front-runner early, aggressively raising money on his way to a $1.7 million primary haul. Columbia lobbyist Dwight Drake entered the race, but none of the candidates could raise the money to compete with Sheheen. Dick Harpootlian, the former South Carolina Democratic Party chairman, said of Rex's spring fundraising reports, "It made it clear to me he couldn't compete. I told Vincent, 'You got it.'"

How Sheheen Won

Sheheen won because he started early, tirelessly raised money, and squeezed out the field as he assumed the look of the nominee.

Sheheen spent the majority of his war chest on media. But he also spent it at the right time, keeping his powder dry until the last few weeks before the primary, despite pressure from some of his backers to spend money in the spring, in hopes of raising his name recognition. State Superintendent of Education Jim Rex ran just one ad mere days before the primary. It was too late to make an impression.

"Even though Rex had statewide name ID, Ford almost beat him," said Lachlan McIntosh, a Democratic political consultant who worked for Mullins McLeod, a Democratic candidate who had dropped out of the race in February. "You've got to communicate with voters. There's no way around it."

When Columbia attorney and lobbyist Drake entered the race in August, he was prepared for the humbling task of shuffling, hat in hand, to the party's moneyed faithful, asking for cash. "He'd already shored up much of the support [of Democratic Party stalwarts] before the rest of us even got out there," Drake said, "Many in the party thought nobody else was running."

The General Election

Haley entered the general election a budding national superstar, garnering two appearances on the cover of *Newsweek* before winning the governor's mansion. Early post-primary polls showed Haley with a double-digit lead.

On July 20, Sheheen released 10 years of income tax records at the media's request, later releasing legislative emails and computer hard drives. When she did release tax records, the documents showed the self-proclaimed accountant and small businessperson had routinely missed filing deadlines and accrued more than $4,400 in fines.

Her tax records also showed that Haley and her husband were in deep financial trouble in 2006, spending half the household income to pay interest on their mortgage. News reports showed Haley was hired for a fundraising job created for her at a public hospital—which was seeking state approval for heart surgery center—and was paid a higher salary than others in similar jobs. Records showed Haley sought donations from payday lending firms she once regulated as chair of a House subcommittee, and was paid $35,000 severance after she was asked to take a leave of absence by the hospital.

Sheheen's campaign was trying to build the narrative that Haley could not be trusted, hammering her hypocrisies in television ads. A small group of Republican activists emerged at the end of September questioning Haley, dredging up the adultery allegations from the primary, and pressing her on her delinquent tax payments, employment, and other unanswered questions.

All of those efforts had an impact—Haley's 51 to 47 margin of victory was the smallest of any statewide Republican candidate—but voters said they were more concerned about other issues: national health care, deficits, and illegal immigration. Haley tied Sheheen to Washington Democrats, particularly after Sheheen said he supported portions of the health care reform law that required coverage of adult children and preexisting conditions.

"She was the beneficiary of events totally beyond her control," said Dick Harpootlian, arguing that Sheheen would have won in a normal year. "They were voting against things that had nothing to do with improving the quality of life in South Carolina."

But Haley's campaign noted that she was the first to correctly recognize the electorate's mood. "She was a better candidate," Pearson said, "and her message was more in line with the voters of the state."

Chapter 28

Texas Governor's Race

by Jay Root

*Political Reporter at the
Associated Press*

With an anti-incumbent mood brewing in the country and the most popular Republican in Texas plotting to oust him, longtime GOP governor Rick Perry was not exactly a safe bet for reelection in the early run-up to the 2010 governor's race.

After all, Texas voters always had a tendency to punish governors who tried to stay in office too long. When the state had two-year terms, no governor ever won more than three in a row. Even after four-year terms were introduced in the 1970s, voters kept throwing out the incumbents. It was not until 1998, when Republican governor George W. Bush was at the height of his popularity, that Texans offered their top state elected official a chance to serve eight consecutive years as governor. As it turned out, Bush left office voluntarily after getting elected president in 2000.

No one paying attention to Texas politics, even back then, doubted the drive and ambition of the man who succeeded Bush. Perry was a handsome farm boy from West Texas who had switched parties in 1989. He was one of only three Republicans to win statewide office in Texas the following year, when conservative Democrats still dominated the Lone Star State. He served eight years as agriculture commissioner and had been lieutenant governor for just two when opportunity struck in December 2000, when and he was called on to fill the remainder of Bush's term.

By 2008, Perry was in his second term and had shattered all the longevity records, becoming the longest-serving governor ever and naming more officials to state boards and commissions than any other—including six of the nine sitting Texas Supreme Court justices. Still, the idea that Perry would run for—and eventually win—an unprecedented third four-year term in office was not taken seriously in the pre-staging phase of the approaching midterm election. It's not that Perry had ever ruled it out. Most observers figured he just wanted to make sure the jockeying to replace him would not undermine his authority as governor.

"The talk that he might do it started soon after he won [his second term] in 2006," wrote *Texas Monthly* chief pundit Paul Burka, in a March 2008 article. "Most folks wrote it off then as an effort to spike the idea that he was a lame duck."

By then, popular U.S. senator Kay Bailey Hutchison had already begun to flirt with the idea of running for governor, telling reporters in late 2007 that her decision would not depend on whether Perry would try to reach for a jaw-dropping 14 years at the helm of the second-largest U.S. state. Burka, echoing the widespread conventional wisdom of the day, predicted in *Texas Monthly* that Hutchison would beat Perry 60 to 40 if she faced him in the GOP primary.

There was every reason to believe that might happen. Perry had won the 2006 five-way governor's race with only 39 percent of the vote, and Hutchison had won three terms to the Senate with more than 60 percent each time. Simply put, she was the state's top vote-getter.

But on Thursday, April 18, 2008, Perry put to rest any notion that historic precedent or a potentially nasty primary battle with Hutchison would scare him off. He unexpectedly blurted out his intention to seek a third term during an impromptu chat with reporters at a Republican Governors Association meeting near Dallas. It sent shockwaves throughout the corridors of the Texas capitol.

"There's a lot of wet diapers in Austin right now," political commentator Ross Ramsey told the *Fort Worth Star-Telegram* after Perry's comments hit the news.

After Hutchison made it official in December 2008, the Perry campaign's rapid response set the tone for the bitter days ahead. In a December 4 email message to the Associated Press, Perry spokesman Mark Miner coined a dubious nickname designed to highlight

Hutchison's controversial vote in favor of the $700 billion Wall Street bailout. It would be used again and again in the campaign against Kay Bailey Hutchison. "Kay 'Bailout' has been talking about running for governor and passing legislation for years and neither has ever happened," Miner said

The game was on. To the horror of Republican donors and lobbyists of all stripes, who hate uncertainty above all else, a rare GOP family feud had finally spilled out into the open.

Hutchison represented the blue-blood, country club Republican set that had dominated the internal GOP machinery before the rise of religious conservatives. However, she had not faced a tough election fight in years.

Perry came from the social conservative wing of the party and was an acolyte of former U.S. senator Phil Gramm, the former Texas A&M economist whose embrace of Ronald Reagan and famous defection from the Democratic Party in 1983 had made him a hero in the conservative movement. Perry was also battle-tested, having survived razor-thin contests and tens of millions of dollars in negative advertising thrown at him in nasty statewide election contests. Still, Perry had never faced a serious primary battle, and he seemed to be on the ropes as 2009 began. A volatile legislative session had just gotten underway, and a February Public Policy Polling survey showed Hutchison leading Perry by an eye-popping 56 percent to 31 percent (*Fort Worth Star Telegram*, Feb. 25, 2009).

A turning point came in April, when followers of the nascent Tea Party movement held rallies around Texas and the nation to mark the dreaded national tax-filing deadline. *Time* magazine said that Perry, dressed in jeans and a baseball cap, was "one of the few major politicians to appear at the tea parties across the country." At one of them, Perry even suggested that Texans might get so fed up with federal involvement that they could rise up and secede from the Union.

"If Washington continues to thumb their nose at the American people, you know, who knows what may come out of that," Perry said, according to the Associated Press. The remarks touched off a national media feeding frenzy, and made Texas the butt of talk-radio jokes, but Perry had struck a chord with his conservative base.

In a gleeful May 2009 memo to key conservative supporters—a document that was quickly leaked to the news media—Perry consultant Dave Carney expressed the widely held view within the campaign that support for Hutchison was based on a weak foundation that already had begun to crack. A poll cited in Carney's memo showed the race had become a statistical dead heat "all without us firing a single shot."

Despite spending a quarter century in state elective office, Perry had begun to position himself as an outsider, a states' rights conservative who would keep the evil influences of Washington out of Texas. His opponent was turning out to be the perfect foil: a 16-year Senate veteran who had seemingly carried enough pork through Congress to risk trichinosis. While it may have helped in past elections to be known for bringing home the bacon, it was radioactive in 2010.

Hutchison unsuccessfully tried to downplay her vulnerabilities, such as her pro-choice views and previous support for embryonic stem cell research. After a five-day, 19-city tour in August, Hutchison threw everything she could at Perry, portraying him as corrupt and arrogant, while reminding voters about past Perry controversies over transportation projects and the governor's failed attempt to mandate an HPV vaccine for teenage girls. She also got high-profile endorsements from former president George H. W. Bush, former vice president Dick Cheney and former Bush White House adviser Karen Hughes. But try as she might, Hutchison could not peel away Perry's support among conservatives, and he kept improving his standing among the party's rank and file.

While Republicans were drawing all the political money and attention, Democrats, predictably, struggled for relevancy. The first real candidate to emerge was Tom Schieffer, a former legislator and brother of CBS newsman Bob Schieffer. But Schieffer had close business and political ties to George W. Bush, under whom he had served as ambassador to Japan and Australia. Schieffer had so much trouble shoring up his Democratic credentials and raising money that his candidacy did not last more than a few months.

The impact of the emerging Perry–Hutchison duel stretched into the Democratic race when Hutchison, in November 2009, publicly changed her mind about resigning her Senate seat before the March 2 primary. Wealthy Houston mayor Bill White, who had already declared his intention to run for Hutchison's seat once she vacated it, had long denied any interest in switching to the governor's race. However, her constant wavering and indecision shuffled the deck.

Just as Schieffer's candidacy collapsed, White jumped into the race and became the instant, prohibitive front-runner. Defeat-weary Texas Democrats saw White as their best chance to capture the governor's mansion since Ann Richards, the last Democrat to live there.

White still had to face multimillionaire Farouk Shami, maker of the popular Chi flat iron, but the Houston businessman never had a chance. A political novice, Shami spoke with a heavy Palestinian accent, seemed to know next to nothing about state government, and repeatedly uttered a string of cringe-inducing statements, including his famous remark during one televised debate that "a day without Mexicans is like a day without sunshine." Only deep pockets and a large TV advertising presence kept Shami from being written off as a joke. On Election Day, White trounced Shami 76 to 13.

On the Republican side, consultant Carney's description of Hutchison's support being "a mile wide and an inch deep" had come true. Out on the campaign trail, Rick Perry became the voice of the little guy, the Texas country boy who had no use for federal bureaucrats and political insiders. He made "stimulus" sound like a dirty word.

It was striking how much supporters at Perry's rallies sounded like the TV commercials bashing a seemingly out-of-touch Senator Hutchison, who was elected to statewide office 16 years ago, just like Perry. "I think she's been gone from Texas too long," said retired teacher Larry Thompson, who went to see Perry speak at the Day Break Coffee Shop in Lubbock. "She says one thing when she's here in Texas and another thing when she's up in Washington" [author interview]. By the time they were done with her, Hutchison was struggling to explain that she was, in fact, from Texas—a La Marque native who can trace her ancestors to the Texas Revolution.

Hope also began to fade among Hutchison supporters that the third Republican candidate in the race, Debra Medina, would force the race into a runoff. After Medina suggested that the 9/11 terrorist attacks might have been the work of U.S. government conspirators, her candidacy began to fade. On election night, Perry won with 51 percent of the vote, compared with 30 percent for Hutchison and almost 19 percent for Medina. Perry got barely more than the 50 percent he needed to avoid a runoff, but only a year earlier, polls had shown he was trailing Hutchison by 20 points. In other words, Perry had engineered a 40-point-or-greater swing.

In the general election contest, Perry immediately and predictably labeled White "Liberal Bill," and associated him with an unpopular President Barack Obama. Rather than pivot to the center, Perry stuck with his anti-Washington tirade, and it was the perfect year for it. As he had done in the primary, Perry also played up the economy in Texas, which has weathered the recession better than many other states. White seemed to take Hutchison's shotgun-style approach: He played up Perry's deep ties to lobbyists and donors, highlighted the state's high dropout rate, dredged up the HPV controversy, and blamed the governor for the looming, multibillion-dollar state budget shortfall. Perry's core message could fit on a postage stamp. White could not seem to settle on one.

"You tell me what White's message is because nobody knows it," said Chuck McDonald, lobbyist and former spokesman for the late Democratic governor Ann Richards. "You say Rick Perry, the voters says jobs. You say Bill White and the voter says mayor of Houston, which is where he started" [author interview].

As autumn approached, Perry was feeling so confident that he declined to debate his Democratic opponent, refused to meet with newspaper editorial boards and, directing his populist ire at Washington and Barack Obama, hardly even mentioned White's name on the campaign trail.

As November 2 drew near, the two candidates engaged in an increasingly negative TV ad war and swapped accusations that the other was corrupt. Perry also got slammed in several late-breaking investigative stories that raised questions about donors' influence on him, and he predictably lost every major newspaper editorial.

It is worth noting that White was the first Democratic gubernatorial candidate since Ann Richards to win more than 40 percent of the vote. But with a strong Republican headwind blowing against him in an already red state, he never even came close to knocking Perry off his game. With his 55 to 42 victory over Bill White, Rick Perry preserved an uninterrupted winning streak that began in the Texas House in 1984, and 26 years later, allowed him to claim the title of the longest-serving governor in the United States.

Notes

Notes

Notes

Notes

Notes

Notes

Notes

Notes

Notes

Notes

Notes

Notes